ANTHROPOLOGIZING
SRI LANKA

ANTHROPOLOGIZING SRI LANKA

■

A Eurocentric Misadventure

SUSANTHA GOONATILAKE

Indiana University Press
Bloomington and Indianapolis

This book is a publication of
Indiana University Press
601 North Morton Street
Bloomington, IN 47404-3797 USA

http://iupress.indiana.edu

Telephone orders 800-842-6796
Fax orders 812-855-7931
Orders by e-mail iuporder@indiana.edu

The paper used in this publication meets the minimum requirements of American National Standard for Information Sciences—Permanence of Paper for Printed Library Materials, ANSI Z39.48-1984.

Manufactured in the United States of America

Library of Congress Cataloging-in-Publication Data

Goonatilake, Susantha.
Anthropologizing Sri Lanka : a eurocentric misadventure / Susantha Goonatilake.
p. cm.
Includes bibliographical references and index.
ISBN 0-253-33999-5 (cloth : alk. paper) — ISBN 0-253-21437-8 (pbk. : alk. paper)
1. Ethnology—Sri Lanka. 2. Sri Lanka—Civilization. 3. Orientalism. 4. Eurocentrism. I. Title.

GN635.S72 G66 2001
305.8'0095493—dc21

00-053538

1 2 3 4 5 06 05 04 03 02 01

This book is dedicated to the Buddhist monks of Sri Lanka—for 2,300 years searchers for truth "for the benefit of the many."

CONTENTS

■

PART III

FINDING THE SINHALESE THROUGH SORCERY

PART IV

SINHALESE FRATRICIDE

PART V

THE SOCIOLOGY OF

THE ANTHROPOLOGIST TRIBE

INTRODUCTION

■

Anthropology and oriental studies were two formal means of Euro-American culture to observe other cultures. Anthropology was classically used to study non literate cultures. At the time of decolonization, this was looked at suspiciously by the cultures subject to anthropology's gaze. Oriental studies, used to examine non-European civilizations, had an ideological mode, best described by Edward Said's term *Orientalism.*

Recently Sri Lanka, primarily her Sinhalese Buddhist population, has emerged as an important subject of anthropologists. Taking into account her size and population, Sri Lanka probably has the highest density of anthropology studies in the whole of Asia. Further, much more important for studies on Sri Lanka—especially at the present time of instability in the country—is the fact that in the last two decades, western scholarship on the country has been dominated by anthropology. And in contrast to the period before, these anthropology studies have overshadowed works of economists, political scientists, geographers, and sociologists.

But Sri Lanka has, for well over two thousand years, been a civilization with a developed city culture, and with a literati conversant with, and formal discussions on, issues of life and philosophy. These Sri Lankan literati discussed the human condition, especially of human behavior, and developed a formidable and comprehensive literature on psychology. In this, the Sinhalese formal concerns had commonalities of aims with anthropology.

During this period of 2,300 years, Sri Lanka was not an isolated island. European classical writers called it "mediatrix"—the halfway house in the trade routes connecting the then civilized worlds of the Mediterranean, South Asia, and East Asia. At her shores, the representatives of the literate peoples of the world met as traders. Sri Lanka and her inhabitants are referred to, and described in the earliest Greek and Latin literature, as they are in the earliest Chinese literature, as well as in the classical South Asian literature of Sanskrit and Pali and later, in vernacular languages. Sinhalese themselves traveled far and wide. By the early Christian era, there are records in Latin and in Chinese of Sinhalese ambassadors to Rome as well as to China. And in turn, the earliest literature read and written in Sri Lanka in Sinhala, Pali, and occasionally Sanskrit finds descriptions of distant lands, their people and ideas. One of the oldest encounters of ideas with the then civilized West which Sinhalese knew at least from the pre-Christian era was the records of lengthy philosophical discussions between the Buddhist monk Nagasena and the Greek King Menander, who ruled a small state in Northwest India—a remnant of Alexander's incursion into India. So just as other nations viewed Sri Lanka, her literati viewed the world from her strategic location.

This book is about how recent anthropologists have viewed this complex civilizational entity called Sri Lanka. It examines this literature taking as examples the four most prolific authors who attempt to make a more or less *total* sense of the country. It explores how they capture the social reality of Sri Lanka. It is a journey into the facts that are narrated, the methodology used, and the conclusions arrived at by these writers. This, then, is an exercise in the sociology of anthropology.

I organize my narrative on how Sri Lankan reality is depicted by taking the larger view of a long historical encounter between Sri Lanka and the West. As I could not do justice to all the anthropology on the country, I chose those who had been the most prolific. They are Richard Gombrich, Gananath Obeysekera, Bruce Kapferer and S. J. Tambiah. Two (Obeysekera and Tambiah) are ex–Sri Lankans who have worked for the last thirty years, in fact virtually their whole adult life, in Europe and America practicing this Eurocentric art. The two others are Britishers (Gombrich and Kapferer) working in Britain and Australia. The universities they cover include key intellectual centers in the West: Oxford (Gombrich), Cambridge (Obeysekere), Princeton (Obeysekere), Harvard (Tambiah), and London (Kapferer).

The book is divided into five parts. In the first part I contextualize the anthropology of Sri Lanka. I show how for nearly two and a half millennia Sri Lanka has figured in the Western imagination, culminating in the present anthropological take on the country. I record also the growth of anthropology as a discipline culminating in the far-reaching critique in the 1970s at the very time anthropological studies on Sri Lanka was taking hold. But anthropology itself was a part of an intellectual package that since the 17th century had accompanied changes in European civilization. I compare the knowledge and belief systems that accompanied the growth of anthropology in Europe with the knowledge and belief systems in Sri Lanka. This latter composite view of the world from Sri Lanka had similarities as well as differences with the knowledge systems before the growth of post-17th-century European knowledge as well as after it. Aspects of Sri Lanka's formalized view on human behavior, Buddhist psychology, have recently percolated into the West. This has muddied the classical relationship of Sri Lanka as the Other of anthropology's formal human behavior theorizing. The Other's (Sinhalese) formal psychology is now helping observe the observer's (Westerner's) mind. This partial change of roles is accompanied by a larger shift as the center of gravity of the world—economic and cultural—increasingly shifts to Asia. These, then, are the major contextual factors that I explore in Part I.

The next part considers two of our four authors, Gombrich and Obeysekere, in four chapters. In the first chapter it examines the study by Gombrich of village Buddhism, and in the next three chapters their thesis of "Protestant Buddhism" and its subsequent transformation. These chapters go into the details of Gombrich and Obeysekere's methodology and the contextual knowledge the authors have of both Protestantism as well as of Sinhalese Buddhist practice and precept.

The three chapters in Part III examine the three books by Kapferer on Sri Lanka. Instead of looking at Sri Lankan culture through Buddhism as a key window or as an important component, Kapferer examines Sinhalese society through practices of exorcism and sorcery, which are indulged in by a lower-class minority. His aim is to see Sinhalese society through the world view of the latter to define what he says is *the* Sinhalese society and culture. In his second book Kapferer extrapolates these views to the society at large through Louis Dumont's theories of hierarchy. This theory of *Homo hierarchus* was generated by Dumont for India, but Dumont specifically excluded Sri Lanka from it. Kapferer tries to explain Sri Lanka's ethnic tragedy by applying Dumont's theory. I examine the various constructions of Kapferer as to how they fit both the facts and the norms of scientific theory. As Kapferer consciously changes his methodology in the four editions of his three books, I trace Kapferer and his changing methodology through our different contextual factors.

Part IV constitutes two chapters which examine the three books by Tambiah on Sri Lanka's ethnic problems. One chapter contains material I first used in a long review done jointly with my wife on Tambiah's second book, published in the University of London journal *South Asia Review.* Tambiah's adherence to both fact and acceptable method is examined in this section.

The first four parts reveal that the anthropology of the four authors is seriously flawed with respect to basic facts on the ground, the methodology used, and the conclusions arrived at. This post-colonial anthropology appears worse than anything colonial anthropology wrought, and, in fact, worse than the colonial writings of the 19th and early 20th centuries on Sri Lanka. One of the worst sets of distortions in the second book by Tambiah resulted in a public debate in Sri Lanka, very possibly the widest debate any anthropology text ever had created among its subject matter. It led to a Sri Lankan human rights lawyer whose views were distorted by Tambiah writing to the offending anthropologist and his department, University (Harvard) and the Ethics Committee of the American Anthropological Association. This was published also in the Sri Lanka press, and extracts are reproduced in the book.

The last part, Part V, examines in three chapters why this gross distortion and flexibility of ground fact has occurred. It is an excursion into the sociology of anthropology of Sri Lanka. This section describes the views the different authors have of each other and the chain of academic and popular citations that is let loose by their writing. It identifies also the peers and key informants for this anthropology. This is an identifiable group of Sri Lankans who fill in the contextual details of the complex reality that is Sri Lanka. It is this set of institutions and individuals working largely outside the university structure and public domain that acts as a social cognitive matrix that filters the local reality for the visiting anthropologists. The re-emergence of a virulent colonial anthropology in Sri Lanka is examined in this last part from the perspective of particular social structures in Sri Lanka that generate and legitimize knowledge.

PART I

■

THE GLOBAL AND CIVILIZATIONAL CONTEXT

CHAPTER 1

■

Contextualizing the Anthropology of Sri Lanka

This book examines, through some representative major texts, anthropology's description of Sri Lankan reality. This examination is of a particular social epistemology that struggles to grasp the complex reality that is Sri Lankan society. It takes into account the context within which Sri Lankan anthropology functions. Its context is that of a world where both the observer and the observed, anthropology and its Other—Sri Lanka—are changing. The anthropology of Sri Lanka is therefore a civilizational encounter between the West and its Other, Sri Lanka. We therefore must locate both anthropology and Sri Lanka amidst major historical and geopolitical shifts.

One of these changes of an "epochal" kind is an ongoing shift of the economic and political axis of the world toward Asia and away from "Euro-America"—the heartland of anthropology. Both Sri Lanka and anthropology are caught up in this change.

The broad cognitive apparatus of the West, which provides the background from which anthropology operates and views its Other, is also changing. These cognitive shifts within the West are also due to inflows of cultural elements from Asia, including some from Sri Lanka. Among the major canvases on which this cognitive context is played out are changing views in the fields of religion, philosophy, and science, areas that have an influence on anthropology.

To take this large canvas into account, our first chapter will therefore explore the following: (1) the ongoing shift to Asia, which necessitates a contextual discussion; (2) the location of Sri Lanka historically in the cross-currents of an East–West civilizational encounter—one becoming an Other for the other; (3) the growth of anthropology and other colonial-era comparative sciences; (4) the different modes of apprehending the world through philosophy, religion, and science in the Sri Lankan and Western contexts, which provide the broader epistemological background to anthropology; (5) the role of religion, namely, Christianity and Buddhism, and the major cognitive challenges made to them by the Scientific Revolution; (6) the acceptance of Sinhalese Buddhist psychology as a cognitive apparatus for human behavior in today's West; and (7) the state of the discipline of anthropology at the time our anthropologists began their foray into Sri Lanka.

These seven topics will provide the prior backdrop to our foray into the anthropology of Sri Lanka as a civilizational encounter.

(1) THE CHANGING GEOPOLITICAL AND CULTURAL AXIS OF THE WORLD

Anthropology emerged as a formal discipline only during the last century, although its roots go back to the voyages of discovery that brought new human groups—as well as new plants and animals—to the Western imagination. Its emergence occurred at a time of European dominance and expansion, and it became a major intellectual Western lens for categorizing and understanding non-Europeans.

Anthropology's present, however, must be viewed in the midst of a diminution of European hegemony. This diminution began nearly forty years ago, at the time of the decolonization of the world, and led to a rethinking of anthropology. Present changes include a pervasive globalization and a shift of the centers of gravity of the world away from their Eurocentric moorings. In this second shift, the center of growth and development in the world is moving away to the non-European parts of the world, most significantly to Asia, implying a massive tilt of the civilizational axis of the world.

Due to these geotectonic movements, no island, least of all Sri Lanka, can be viewed as isolated. And no discipline, least of all a colonially derived one such as anthropology, can remain an intellectual island of isolated concepts.

This broad axial shift is illustrated in the cultural sphere, where one is seeing a partial lifting of the hegemonic European cultural blanket of the last three centuries. Signs already exist. Thus, the best novelists in the largest carrier of "global" culture, English, are today those of Asia. The Philippines are the capital of the cartoon film world. Designers from Hong Kong and Japan set clothing fashions. These shifts are harbingers of greater cognitive shifts to come. Invariably the shift to Asia will consequently ease, and in fact necessitate, changes in many fields, including anthropology. There will be changes in the cross-traffic of nodal ideas as well as in what constitutes anthropology's "Other."

The global demographics of the science (natural and social science) communities are today changing dramatically. Already there are more people with a natural science training in developing countries such as India and China than there are in many developed countries. At the moment, there are deficiencies in this non-Western scientific community in terms of its productivity and creativity because of a variety of sociological factors. But these gaps are being overcome. To take just one natural science subject, one can point to the emergence in less than ten years of India as a software-developing superpower. Further, research institutes and universities in Western countries are being increasingly manned by migrants from Asia. The key names in future discoveries should increasingly reflect this multiple ethnic mix. What is true of resource-intensive natural sciences could become more true of the social sciences, where academic costs—without the need for laboratories and other expensive equipment—are much less. As the social and natural science enterprise takes hold tightly across the globalized world, there is no doubt that, purely due to demographics, the future practitioners are increasingly going to come from outside the Western world. But the shift to Asia will entail greater changes in the social sciences than just those changes caused by a demographic shift.

The social sciences arose after the Enlightenment and were partially ideological adjuncts to the rise of Europe as a hegemonizing civilizational entity. Anthropology, Sinology, and Indology, which all saw non-Europeans as backward, reflected this Eurocentrism. The two grand theorists in sociology, Marx and Weber, both saw Asia as backward and static, as illustrated by Marx's residual category, the Asiatic mode of production, and Weber's rise of capitalism through Protestantism. Yet, recently, the world's economic dynamos have been today's "Asiatic modes of production." This economic rise of Asia makes nonsense of the received wisdom of Marx, Weber, and possibly much of the existing social sciences, and requires an urgent rethinking.

"Modernism" (together with the social sciences) was in many ways the ultimate intellectual culmination of the Enlightenment and the European project. The demise of modernism and the emergence of postmodernism in Euro-America could also be seen as a reflection of the exhaustion of the Enlightenment project on the terms and agendas set by itself, and so the need for new non-Eurocentric agendas.

As the macro relations between the Other and the Observer in anthropology are now changing amidst these global tectonic shifts, one has to unearth, in a comparative perspective, the epistemological givens of both anthropology and its Other. These are the epistemological groundings of cross-cultural intellectual history, philosophy, science, belief, and knowledge, which the Eurocentric anthropologist unconsciously takes for granted when he views from his vantage point his Other. Let us begin by taking a long-range and cross-cultural perspective of his Other, namely, Sri Lanka.

(2) SRI LANKA AND THE WEST: CROSS-CIVILIZATIONAL TRAFFIC

Europe's knowledge and perception of the East and Sri Lanka predate by millennia anthropology's beginnings in the 19th century. There were exchanges between the East and West of knowledge and perception of each other from early times. These exchanges structured European views of the "Other" of Europe. From very early times Sri Lanka was at the crossroads of this global East-West traffic in perceptions. Let me deliberately take a detour to those early times.

It was only after the war of the Greeks with the Persian Empire that the East entered in a major way into the Western psyche. The constructed division into an Orient and an Occident was born then, together with the concept of Europe. In this constructed East, Persia occupied an intermediary position between Greece and South Asia—"India." Scylax and Ctesias, two Greeks employed by the Persians, wrote standard descriptions of the India of pre-Alexandrian times—as it were, the first anthropology of South Asia. They wrote of fantastic and bizarre creatures of South Asia, descriptions that crept into the later European constructions of India. These included bizarre beings who were dog-headed, had blanket-type ears, or were one-footed. Recent commentators, however, have noted that these descriptions are clearly translations from Sanskrit mythology (Halbfass 1988 p. 10).

But apart from this fanciful anthropology, there was another more matter-of-fact tradition of East-West encounter that is just as old. Thus Herodotus, the major Greek historian, wrote that the Persian Emperor Darius I (521–480 B.C.) would frequently call on Greeks and Indians for advice and discussion. Herodotus also records that in the Persian war (484–425 B.C.), Persians recruited Indian soldiers (Chowdhury 1988 p. 67). Xerxes led an expedition against Greece using, among others, Indian troops. Herodotus described a medical discussion at the court of King Susa between Indians and Greeks (Jaggi 1973 p. 207). Later, Aristoxenes (320–300 B.C.) mentions a philosophical dialogue between an Indian philosopher and Socrates (Chowdhury 1988 p. 67). There are many more examples of such realistic, matter-of-fact intellectual encounters with South Asia, which I have recorded elsewhere (Goonatilake, Susantha, 1998).

Aristotle (384–322 B.C.), in his book on the world, *De Mundo*, mentions Sri Lanka (Weerasinghe 1995 pp. 1–2). Another Western description of Sri Lanka is given by Onesicritus of Astipalacia, who accompanied Alexander the Great on his eastern campaign (326–323 B.C.). Strabo quotes Onesicritus to indicate that he knew the size of the island, the length of travel from there to the Indus region, and the type of ships used by the ancient Sinhalese. Megasthenes (321–297 B.C.), the ambassador of Seluccus Nicator who visited the Mauryan court of Chandragupta in the 3rd century B.C., also recorded the size, location, nature, settlements, and products of the island. These two authors referred to the country as Taprobane, a corruption of the Sanskrit Tamraparni (Pali, Tambapanni), one of the ancient names for the Island (Guruge 1993 pp. 12–13).

Sri Lanka is depicted most prominently and in relative detail in the earliest Greek map, that of Ptolemy (2nd century A.D.); in fact appearing as large as the Indian mainland. The places in this realistic map have been correlated with descriptions in ancient Sinhalese historical chronicles and epigraphy. Bjorn Axelson and Michael Jones have noted that the cognitive distortion in the map was probably due to a socially derived "mental map," which reflected the relative importance of Sri Lanka in the Mediterranean mind at the time (1987 pp. 447–464).

The Roman historian Pliny (77 A.D.) describes the Sinhalese king's sending four ambassadors to Rome. Basing his account on the envoys' description, Pliny gives an almost idealized picture of the country's political, judicial, administrative, and democratic systems (Guruge 1993 p. 13). The envoys, Pliny also mentions, gave information about Sri Lanka's trade relations with China (Seres). In fact, the leader of the Sinhalese delegation mentioned that his father had been to China several times (Weerasinghe 1995 p. 23). This would indicate that in this one 1st-century household, namely, that of the leader of the Sinhala delegation, there was simultaneously knowledge of both Rome and China, the biggest non–South Asian civilizational entities at the time. And because travel to China and Rome would necessarily have taken father and son through other countries, this single household also had personal knowledge of several lands in between. This indicates that the personal geographical knowledge of this one family exceeded that of any other household until the voyage of Magellan, fifteen hundred years later.

In the Sinhalese intellectual tradition, the Greek presence also looms large in the popular *Questions of Milinda (Menander)*. These are the records of religious and philosophical dialogues between the Buddhist monk Nagasena and the Indo-Greek ruler Menander. Extensive Roman coins found in Sri Lanka also testify to these Mediterranean contacts. Sinhalese historical chronicles record the presence of Greeks in the early Christian centuries in its capital city, Anuradhapura (5th century B.C.–10th century A.D.). A Nestorian cross, circa the 4th century A.D., has been found in its ancient capital. Cosmas Indicopleustes (6th century A.D.) describes Sri Lanka as the "mediatrix" of the trade between the East and West (Guruge 1993 p. 13). He says, "as its position is central, the Island is a great resort of ships from all parts of India, and from Persia and Ethiopia. In like manner, it dispatches many of its own ships to foreign ports. And from . . . China . . . it receives its silks . . . and other products, and these it passes again to the outer ports" (Weerasinghe 1995 p. 35).

But the Mediterranean was not the only region caught in the cognitive cross-traffic through ancient Sri Lanka. Sinhalese chronicles show that by the early Christian centuries the Sinhalese were aware not only of the regions of South Asia and the classical West but also of China and Southeast Asia.

Chinese records mention several journeys of Sinhalese to China. In 429 A.D., three Sinhala Buddhist nuns went to China. In 431 A.D., the Sinhala monk Sanghavarman reached China. In 456 A.D., five Sinhala monks were sent to China by the Sinhala king. The Chinese Buddhist traveler Fa Hsien came to Sri Lanka in the 5th century. I-tsing (635–712) recorded several other Chinese monks visiting Sri Lanka. The traffic between Sinhala and China was thus intense. Reflecting this, the ancient Chinese author Li Chao recorded that among the vessels calling on Chinese ports, "the ships from the Lion Kingdom (Sinhala—Sri Lanka) were the largest, with stairways for loading and unloading which are several tens of feet in height" (Weerasinghe 1995 p. 35).

Branches of Sri Lankan temples have been found in Java and India, and Sri Lankan arts are found all over Southeast Asia, in Burma, Thailand, Cambodia, Laos, Java, and the Celebes (de Silva, K. M., 1981 p. 55). Scholar-monks from these territories visited Sri Lanka to learn, and Sinhalese monks in turn went to these countries and had a strong intellectual impact, as, for example, in Burma, Thailand, Cambodia, and Laos.

During the second Christian millennium, contacts with the West continued. Thus Marco Polo came to Sri Lanka in the 13th century, and the Arab traveler Ibn Batuta in the 14th century. Connections with Persia are recorded, as are connections with Byzantium, North Africa, and the Arab countries. These were followed by other Arab and European travelers down to the period of the voyages of discovery, as recorded in several European and Arabic travelogues.

The Sinhalese-language literature of the last millennium mentions dozens of countries, their inhabitants, and their languages, indicating the geographical knowledge of these countries available in Sri Lanka. Many of these countries referred to are today parts of India, Pakistan, and Bangladesh. But there are several countries outside the region that indicate the breadth of Sri Lankans' geographical knowledge.

Thus *Pujavaliya* (13th century) refers to forty-four countries, the *Dambadeni Asna* (14th century) lists sixty countries, and *Rajavaliya* (17th century) lists forty-three countries, including Germany, Borneo, China, Naples, Portugal, Spain, Italy, and Greece (Weerasinghe 1995 pp. 9–12). Apart from these texts, literature from the previous millennium continued to be read. So the geographical knowledge contained therein, especially of the Mediterranean, should be added to the information in the more recent texts.

The Sinhalese Buddhists studied in contemporary anthropology are, however, only a part of the totality of Buddhist travelers. By the middle of the first millennium A.D., Buddhist pilgrims had covered virtually the whole of Asia. But there are other tantalizing possibilities that suggest the reach of these Buddhists. Thus, according to some American archaeological research, Buddhist pilgrims from China went as far as the Americas. In the opposite direction, Buddhist artifacts have been found as far away as Rome, in ancient London, and under the earliest church in Sweden (Christophersen 1988; Nakamura 1973 pp. 254–257).

Even leaving out the still not fully substantiated areas, ancient Buddhists collectively had a geographic perspective as large as that of Europe immediately after the voyages of discovery, and definitely much larger than the European view in the Middle Ages. And if we recall that it was the voyages of discovery that made Europe discover its "Other" and began the intellectual enterprise that gave rise to anthropology, we realize that these Buddhist visitors would also have internalized many observations of the people of the countries they visited.

How far were Sri Lankan Buddhists influenced by this cross-traffic of their Buddhist brethren? Sri Lanka was, as we have seen, at the crossroads of international travel at the time. Its own monks and nuns traveled widely. Many of these travelers stayed away for months and years, ample time to exchange information and views on other countries with their fellow monks, nuns, and merchants. So it is not unreasonable to expect that the wide collective geographical knowledge of other Buddhists would have seeped into the knowledge base of the Sinhalese.

(3) ANTHROPOLOGY AND OTHER COLONIAL COMPARATIVE SCIENCES

Anthropology arose out of the colonial period with the urge to classify and understand non-Europeans whom the colonizers encountered—a process parallel to the efforts to classify exotic plants and animals found after the voyages of discovery.

Particular mention should be made of the Portuguese Garcia d'Orta, whose descriptions of South Asian medicinal plants had a profound influence on his contemporary scientific world (Boxer 1963; Lach 1977 p. 434). The process reached its culmination with Linnaeus in the 18th century (Boxer 1963 pp. 509–518). Both Garcia d'Orta and Linnaeus had South Asian and Sri Lankan connections.

But just as there was an interest in classifying plants and animals in post-Renaissance Europe, a prior interest in classification of plants and animals had existed in the subcontinent. Standard Ayurvedic texts like *Caraka* and *Susruta,* which were also used in Sri Lanka, described a much larger number of plants than had been captured by the pre–voyages of discovery European imagination. But let us return to other classification tendencies during the early European encounter in both the South Asian mainland and Sri Lanka.

Thus, a half-century after d'Orta, the Indian emperor Jehangir was also involved in a naturalist exercise, as Rahman has documented (Alvi and Rahman 1989). Rahman's thesis is that Jehangir (1605–1627) exhibited the same qualities of collection and comparison found in post-Renaissance Europe, and hence his work was not very different from the beginnings of modern botany. Jehangir's penchant for collection was found farther south, in Sri Lanka, in the case of Emperor Jehangir's near contemporary Rajasinghe, who "collected" exotic humans.

Gombrich recalls that King Rajasinha II (1635–1687) "collected" European prisoners. The number of specimens in this human zoo he mentions was very large, about a thousand such prisoners in the course of the king's lifetime (Gombrich 1991 pp. 30–31). They were kept in comfort and honor in various villages. We know about this "interest in anthropology" of Rajasinghe only from a Eurocentric bias, through the writings of an Englishman, Robert Knox, one of the prisoners. He wrote a book on his stay in the country. Knox was insightful, but hardly a man with a broad intellect. As Gombrich recalls, he misunderstood Buddhism (1991 pp. 30–31). Only Knox's version of this civilizational encounter has yet surfaced. The story from the other side could possibly exist, in as yet undiscovered Sinhalese records. This is not a fanciful notion, because, as Malalgoda has pointed out, there is a rich collection of Sinhalese manuscripts in monastic libraries scattered all over the country but not yet accessed by anthropologists (Malalgoda 1976 p. 5).

What motivated King Rajasinghe could not have been cruelty, because he provided his "collection" with comfort and treated them with honor. A strong element must have been curiosity and perhaps a desire for embellishment in the manner of the bourgeois and aristocratic houses in 17th- and 18th-century Europe that were embellished with African servants. What drove the king's curiosity would not have been very different from that which drove Europeans to collect plants and animals from the different areas of the world after the voyages of discovery. Rajasinghe's collection could undoubtedly have been inspired by the same collecting and classifying impulse. In that sense he was perhaps partially a true anthropologist, albeit of a mildly cruel kind, keeping the prisoners in gilded cages. He himself would not have seen this in a bad moral light, because he probably approached the prisoners with the same paternalistic mindset with which he approached his own citizens.

Sri Lanka had a continuous exposure to a large melange of exotic foreigners as well as a long intellectual tradition of discussing human behavior. But it did not develop a separate discipline of human behavior titled anthropology. It broadly stuck to Buddhism's explanation of human behavior at both the individual and the social level. This approach may not have yielded a formal social science (which, one should add, some anthropologists, including Kapferer, disclaim for their art), but the Buddhist heritage in Sri Lanka contains elements of science, psychology, and philosophy which have been taken seriously in some quarters in Western psychology, philosophy, and science. We will now explore this Sri Lankan intellectual tradition, because it has implications for our later discussions.

(4) THE OBSERVER'S AND THE OTHER'S INTELLECTUAL CONSTRUCTS: "RELIGION," "PHILOSOPHY," AND "SCIENCE"

The intellectual gaze of Europe on its Other through anthropology was an accompaniment to major changes in European civilization's means of apprehending the world. Before the onset of European modernity, Europe's formal eyes had used philosophy and religion. Through the centuries, this was gradually replaced for most purposes by science, although philosophy and religion continued to have a role, albeit a diminished one. Among contemporary Sinhalese Buddhists, religion and philosophy, as well as the science of Europe, shape their ideas, often as underlying unconscious factors.

But "religion," "philosophy," and "science" have different connotations from a Sinhalese Buddhist perspective and a Eurocentric one. These themes need to be explored in a cross-civilizational perspective, sketching also how the Buddhist contribution, especially that of the Sinhalese, has interacted in the European intellectual world.

The English word "religion" has a heavy set of connotations, carried over from Judeo-Christian roots. This same word, "religion," is also carried over by many sociologists and anthropologists, as well as by popular usage, to describe South Asian belief systems. But South Asian belief systems differ widely from Judeo-Christian systems. Some groups, such as the Charvaks, were out-and-out materialists. Some systems, including Buddhism, could in contemporary parlance be considered to have some characteristics of atheism. As a central feature, all South Asian belief systems possess a heavy overlay of philosophy. Some people, such as the Jains, found mathematics an important ally, in fact mathematizing some of their belief systems and developing important mathematical findings on the way (Goonatilake, Susantha, 1998 pp. 27, 60). The Buddhists, on the other hand, made important psychological observations.

Over the last few decades, several serious studies have emerged that lay bare from an East-West comparative frame many Eastern philosophical positions that accompany Eastern "religions." University departments have been devoted exclusively to this area of study, and journals such as *Philosophy East and West* are exclusively devoted to the topic. Generally speaking, South Asia, in the formulation of Moore, has an "almost infinite variety of philosophical concepts, methods, and attitudes. . . . There are many differing approaches to reality . . . [and] . . . to truth" (quoted in Bishop 1975 p. 3).

But modern philosophy in the West arose with the unraveling of the Middle Ages through the Renaissance, the Scientific Revolution, and the Enlightenment. All these events of the last few centuries changed Western thinking. There have been many studies in the tradition of East-West comparative philosophy indicating that although Buddhist and modern Western approaches may not necessarily agree on the answers to key questions, they sometimes address broadly similar problems.

Let us take Hume, who was a father figure in this post–Scientific Revolution philosophy. He influenced the political and social thought enterprise of the Enlightenment by creating a climate of ideas that challenged the status quo. Several commentators, such as Whitehead, Moorthy, and de la Vallée Poussin (Jacobson 1969 pp. 17–38), have pointed to the surprising and detailed similarities between some of the thoughts of David Hume and those of the Buddha, especially in relation to the idea of the self.

Jacobson observed that in both these philosophical viewpoints, separated by more than two thousand years, "there is no thinker but the thoughts, no perceiver but the perceptions, no craver but the cravings. . . . The similarity. . . . is striking" (1969 p. 18). Jacobson has explored further similarities, and has put them into perspective with respect to the European intellectual climate at Hume's time. Jacobson pointed out that the years from 1600 to 1769 were the period during which "the Orient contributed most to Western thought" (1969 p. 18). Jacobson rejects the notion of an independent discovery of ideas by Hume and holds the view that Hume was influenced by the ideas from China pouring into Europe at the time. And as part of that transfer from China came Buddhist ideas (1969 p. 26).

In the Enlightenment, the Sinhalese also featured partly in the imagination of Voltaire and Diderot. Voltaire spread the view that (Western) religion was derived from what the Indians had believed in the distant past. Voltaire was also of the view that India had prior claims in secular learning and worldly culture (Halbfass 1988 pp. 57–59). Voltaire, in *Zadig*, refers to Nabussan, the king of Sri Lanka (Serendib), who is pictured as one of the best rulers of Asia, being of an amiable disposition and liked by everybody. The story by Voltaire paints the Sinhalese king as a nontyrannical, indulgent ruler, kind to his subjects (Dewaraja 1989).

In the 18th century, Diderot and the Encyclopedists had the then farfetched dream of capturing all the then existing knowledge. In the third edition of his *Encyclopedia* (1781), Diderot looked at Sri Lanka positively. He made the observation that according to Sinhalese law the king himself could be executed for violation of the law (Dewaraja 1989). This was possibly somewhat of an over-reading of the non-divine nature of the Sinhalese king, especially the obligation of the king to his subjects exemplified by the Dasa Raja Dharma. Yet the story indicates the positive image of the country in the early years of modern Europe.

More recently, studies by comparative philosophers have indicated considerable overlap between key Western philosophers and Buddhism. These Western philosophers include Hegel, Schopenhauer, and Nietzsche (described in detail in Goonatilake, Susantha, 1998). In the case of American philosophers, Dale observed that there were South Asian influences, including Buddhism, on William James, Charles A. Moore, Santayana,

Emerson, and Irving Babbitt, influences that helped enlarge the debate on philosophy in America, for example, in epistemology, in psychology, and on ideas of the self (Riepe 1967 pp. 124–137). William James had ideas of the self "which could have been written by a Buddhist." Buddhism's process approach likewise has influenced or found parallels in Western philosophers such as Charles S. Peirce, John Dewey, William James, Alfred North Whitehead, and Charles Hartshorne (Jacobson 1988 p. ix). Price has seen significant parallels between Buddhism and early-20th-century thought (1955 p. 229).

The *Questions of King Milinda* (*Menander*) is one of the most popular Buddhist texts in Sri Lanka, and Price says of this text that it "might almost have been written in Cambridge in the 1920s" (1995 p. 229). Hanna has seen parallels and similarities with Buddhism in the phenomenology of Husserl and Heidegger (1993 pp. 41–57). Heidegger is quoted as saying, "If I understand [Buddhist ideas] correctly, this is what I have been trying to say in all of my writings" (Smith 1965 p. xii).

One of the most seminal philosophical figures in this century, because his ideas deeply influenced Einstein and the latter's theory of relativity, was Ernst Mach. Mach's philosophy was very sympathetic to Buddhism, because like Mach, Buddhism denied a permanent self. There were, thus, possible indirect backdoor influences of Buddhist ideas on Einstein through philosophical ideas associated with both Hume (another key influence on Einstein) and Mach. These were two of the few philosophers whom Einstein read between 1902 and 1904, immediately before his paper on special relativity. Einstein studied Hume's book *The Treatise on Human Nature,* which had strong echoes of Buddhism (Miller 1987 p. 39). Einstein gave Mach credit for significant influences on his own thinking, in the development of both special relativity and general relativity (Graves 1971).

Mach himself had an attraction to Indian literature and science, including Indian mathematics. Some of his friends, such as Paul Carus and Theodor Beer, were Buddhists. Mach also contributed to Paul Carus's journals *The Open Court* and *The Monist* (Jackson 1968 pp. 74–75). Mach's first direct appreciation of a Buddhist philosophical orientation, especially with relation to the relativity of the observer (central to Einstein's theories), was revealed when he wrote, in his *Analyse der Empfindungen* ("Analysis of Sensations"),

> But to ask that the observer should imagine himself as standing upon the sun instead of upon the earth, is a mere trifle in comparison with the demand that he should consider the Ego to be nothing at all, and should re-

solve it into a transitory connection of changing elements. (Blackburn 1972 pp. 287–288)

Buddhism's central thesis denies a permanent Ego and considers both the observing Ego and the observed world as transitory. Incidentally, it is significant that Mach's *Analyse der Emfindungen* was translated into Sinhalese soon after it appeared; in fact, Sinhalese was the first language into which it was translated from the German original (Blackburn 1972 pp. 288–289).

The other scientific revolution of the 20th century—quantum physics— also resonated with Buddhist epistemology. The best way to illustrate this is to quote Robert Oppenheimer, the head of the Manhattan Project in the 1940s, which gave the world the atomic bomb. Commenting on the peculiar nature of quantum physics, Oppenheimer wrote: "If we ask, for instance, whether the position of the electron remains the same, we must say 'no'; if we ask whether the electron's position changes with time, we must say 'no'; if we ask whether the electron is at rest we must say 'no'; if we ask whether it is in motion, we must say 'no.' The Buddha has given such answers when interrogated as to the conditions of a man's self after his death, but they are not familiar answers for the tradition of seventeenth and eighteenth century science" (1954).

To illustrate the continuing uses of Buddhism in philosophy and science, one can give the example of Varela and his co-authors in a well-reviewed book, *The Embodied Mind*. These authors used insights from Buddhist philosophy and mental practices to solve some pressing natural science problems (Varela et al. 1993). Varela and his co-authors apply the concept of mind and body in Buddhist theory and meditative practice to several problems in cognitive psychology, evolutionary theory, linguistics, neuroscience, artificial intelligence, and immunology.

The above examples are only an indication of the fact that, as the West unfolded its philosophy in the last few centuries, many areas of similarity between Buddhist and Western positions were revealed. I have gone out of the way in the above descriptions to indicate from Western sources that Buddhism in its core is nearer to the Western category of philosophy and is at least partially a more observational approach than the revelatory religions of the Judeo-Christian traditions. I have also shown that these Buddhist philosophical and observational positions at times bear directly on issues of science.

What appears from the above listing of East-West comparative considerations, therefore, is that a facile East-West comparison between "science" and "philosophy," on the one hand, and "religion," on the other, has many pitfalls. There are much larger elements of both the philosophic and the scientific in South Asian belief systems, some of these elements in fact having deeper resonances with the scientific endeavor in the West than did Christianity. But this does not mean that Buddhists were "more scientific" than Europeans. What these contextual factors raise are wider questions concerning the nature of science, the nature of philosophy in East and West, and the nature of belief systems such as the revelatory Judeo-Christian religions and the non-revelatory South Asian ones. These facts will become important in our later discussions on the anthropology of Sinhalese Buddhists.

Generally speaking, Western religions are revealed systems, presumed to be revealed by a higher power, "God." Buddhism is, at least partly, experiential and experimental, built on individual perceptions and experiences, not necessarily on another's unverified word of his experience. In Buddhism this sense of personal experience and verification is central to its theory. But practice, let me hasten to add, does not always follow theory (or, more accurately, does not follow the popular ideology of what a "correct" and "scientific" theory should be).

(5) THE SCIENTIFIC REVOLUTION: CHRISTIANITY AND BUDDHISM

Comparisons between Christianity and Buddhism will occur in the later discussions of our anthropologists of Sri Lanka. Therefore it is necessary also to put in more detailed perspective here the contrast between revealed Christianity and at least partly philosophical and experiential Buddhism. This is best seen in Christianity's encounter with science.

The development of science from the 17th to the late 19th century was a profound encounter with Christianity, almost always with Christianity trying to impede science's progress. A discussion of the nature of what is meant by "religion" when one considers Christianity and Buddhism would be incomplete without examining this encounter between science and Christianity from a historical perspective, and then comparing it with Buddhism.

The scientific methodology implies a set of skeptical procedures that yield verifiable results. But all Indian belief systems, including Buddhism, were interested in valid and correct knowledge. The proper means to knowledge are described in many Buddhist texts. These emphasized skepticism, observation, and reason. Thus, in the well-known *Kalama Sutta,* the Buddha asserted explicitly:

Do not put faith in traditions even though they have been accepted for long generations and in many countries. Do not believe a thing because many repeat it. Do not accept a thing on the authority of one or another of the Sages of old, nor on the ground that a statement is found in the books. Never believe anything because probability is in its favor. Do not believe in that which you have yourselves imagined, thinking that a god has inspired it. Believe nothing merely on the authority of your teachers or of the priests. After examination, believe that which you have tested for yourselves and found reasonable. (Quoted in Jacobson 1988 p. 17)

The effects of the Scientific Revolution rocked the Western social system and Christian-impregnated culture in many important ways. In the Christian rendering, "God" had in a short time created man (and woman as an afterthought) in "His" image, as well as man's abode, the Earth. This miracle took only a few days and occurred only in the very recent past. This was, to be exact, in 4004 B.C., according to the detailed calculations of the 17th-century Bishop Usher. God's creation, man—in fact sculpted in God's image—had primacy over all the other creatures because God had specifically created them for him, including his mate, woman, out of man's rib. The earth itself was specially privileged because it was the abode of God's special creation, man. The heavens therefore had to circle around Earth, man's abode, and time itself began only a short time ago, with this "Creation."

Copernicus challenged this central position of man's abode; Darwin was to challenge the special position of man in the living kingdom, and the narrow concept of time was challenged by subjects such as geology. In addition, the views of Freud and his followers challenged some of the handed-down orthodoxy regarding the nature of the psyche and the mind.

Yet, in Sri Lanka or anywhere else in South Asia, as I have pointed out elsewhere (Goonatilake, Susantha, 1984, 1993, 1998), these discoveries of science would not have had the negative impact they caused in Europe. None of the South Asian traditions, unlike the Judeo-Christian one, specially privileges man or his abode. In addition, in all South Asian traditions, fundamental horizons such as those of time and space are much wider, more imaginative, and more sophisticated. In the nonphilosophical, more popular traditions, humans are only one of a variety of beings, animate or "ethereal"; a human may be reborn as one of these creatures, and, in the reverse direction, one of these beings may be reborn as a human. Humans in this mythical scheme are related to all other animals.

Further, in all South Asian belief systems, large time spans occur, comparable with those found in modern astronomy. South Asian perspectives also hold that the earth is only one world among many abodes of sentient beings. To fully appreciate the extent of this width of vision, one should mention that in the Buddhist tradition there are three world systems, minor, middling, and major. A minor world system has hundreds of thousands of suns and earths and "higher worlds." The middling world system is a hundred thousand times as great, and the major system one hundred thousand times still greater (Jayatillake, K. N.,1980 pp. 1–12). These three systems, one should note, are not to be equated with modern astronomy. But they indicate, in contrast to similar imaginative constructs in the pre-modern Western traditions, that there was a much broader vision.

Time in the South Asian traditions has a very different place from its place in the Judeo-Christian tradition: "The universe is very old, its evolution and decline are cyclic, repeated ad infinitum" (*Encyclopedia of Buddhism* 1979 Vol. V), the longest such cycle being 311,040,000 million years long (Basham 1953 p. 320). The Christian perspective, with the creation of life only a few thousand years ago, pales in comparison with these infinitely broader horizons. So does the European idea of one single abode for creatures—apart from hell and heaven—in comparison with the innumerable universes of the South Asian mythical schemes. So a theory which denied the exclusiveness of man's abode, such as Copernicus's heliocentric system, would not have created the controversy in South Asia that it did in Europe. It could well have been accepted easily. Neither would Darwin's theory of evolution have had the effect it did in Europe. Wilberforce, a Protestant bishop, campaigned most vehemently against the evolutionary theories of Darwin in the 19th century (a campaign, one should note, that has not died down, as witness today's demand among American Christian fundamentalists for the teaching of creationism together with evolution in schools).

Most South Asian schemes also include evolutionary cosmogonies. Thus, Buddhists have evolutionary schemes that start with the remote past and extend to the distant future, with very large time spans. Ninian Smart characterizes the Buddhist evolutionary scheme *parinama* as meaning "that nature is a unitary entity which evolves in varying forms, including minds" (1964). An interconnectedness of all life-forms is a central element of South Asian belief systems. Higher animals are taken to be sentient beings, differing from humans only in degree. With such belief systems, the Darwinian evolutionary scheme would not have caused the cataclysmic earthquake in South Asia that it did in Christian Europe.

The emergence of the Scientific Revolution and its social counterpart, the Enlightenment, was fueled by philosophers such as Hume, who influenced the European *Zeitgeist.* Hume made the church's teachings on faith unacceptable, which resulted in a climate of irreverence. These ideas of Hume went together with his ideas on the "self," which, as we have noted, parallel those of Buddhism, with Jacobson even claiming that these ideas were borrowed from Buddhism (1969 p. 26).

The emergence of the Scientific Revolution had another philosophical counterpart, in fact required it in a God-suffused culture. This was Descartes' invention of the dichotomy of the mind and the body. This dichotomy allowed God to exist but shielded the scientific domain of inquiry from direct theological influence. Descartes' dichotomy is now breaking down in science, leading to a different view of the subject-object, mind-body relationship in several disciplines. Buddhism does not include this dichotomy.

The other cataclysmic challenges to the European psyche were the new insights into the human condition produced by Freud and his followers. Freud is now considered unscientific and a sort of folk psychologist, but some of his broad ideas, such as the existence of a subconscious, still remain current. Freud's importance, however, lay not in the validity of his theories but in the shock he gave to the European collective psyche, as well as the core idea that one can indeed think of mental phenomena objectively and analytically.

Yet South Asian theories, in contrast to those of pre-20th-century Europe, dealt with the human condition, mind, and personality on a much larger analytical canvas. All the South Asian schemes, including Buddhism, were observational, depending partly on "meditation." There were beliefs accepting the unconscious, and some branches of Buddhism, such as *Tantra,* evoked sexuality. The psychology of Buddhism was more varied, richer, and more sophisticated than simpleminded Christian dogma. The theories of a Freud or a Jung could easily have found a place, though perhaps not a prominent one, in this broad spectrum of intellectual positions.

The worldview of scientific man went through another sea change in the 20th century with the arrival of the perspectives of relativity and quantum physics. These diminished still further the acceptability of the uniqueness of a single observational platform. But by the 20th century, Christian orthodoxy had lost its earlier hold, and so this new physics was less debated in the Western religious public sphere. One could again note that South Asian cosmogonies would not have had difficulties in adjusting to the new physics.

Mach's remarks on observational platforms in Buddhism implied that Buddhism, because it denies a permanent self from which to view the world, was even more radical than the theories of Einstein. (Let me hasten to add that this congeniality of world views does not by any means imply that Buddhists had a prior inkling of Einstein's theories of relativity.) Key changes were also brought about by quantum physics, which presented contradictory views on the nature of the very small and the interconnectedness of phenomena. Space does not permit further elaboration on this here, except to mention that some of these views introduced by the new physics have, as I have noted earlier, their resonances in the multiple logics and the interconnectedness of phenomena that occur in Buddhism (as well as other South Asian discourses) (see Chapter 9, "Digging Deeper: Exploiting Philosophy for Science," in Goonatilake, Susantha, 1998, for details).

It is clear from the discussions in this section that the key figures (Copernicus, Darwin, Freud) that freed Western man from religious orthodoxy and created a scientific spirit in him would have challenged the philosophical orthodoxy of Buddhism only mildly, if at all. This does not imply that Buddhists were more scientific than Europeans. It only raises wider questions concerning the social context of science, the relationship between history and science, and what constitutes science. These questions also touch on the social sciences, often implicitly, as unconscious philosophical assumptions are made.

(6) TAKING "SINHALESE PSYCHOLOGY" SERIOUSLY

One intellectual field that has considerable import for anthropology and the study of human behavior in general is psychology. Recently, several Buddhist conclusions on mental processes, especially of the Sinhalese variety, have been taken literally and seriously by Western scientific personnel. Increasingly within the last twenty years, these Buddhist discussions, including texts that originated in Sri Lanka, or are widely used in the country, have been corroborated as Western psychologists and physicians have taken the observations literally and tested them in laboratory and medical milieus (representative of this literature are Kabat-Zinn et al. 1992; Walsh 1988; Sweet and Johnson 1990; de Silva, Padmal, 1984; Goleman 1981; Bograt 1991; and Donaldson 1992). Let us explore this further.

One of the earliest Western scientific descriptions of the Sinhalese psychology tradition based on firsthand exposure to the nature of meditation found in Sri Lanka was given by the academic psychologist Jack Huber in his book *Through an Eastern Window*, written on the basis of his encounter with meditation in Burma in the mid-1960s. (The Burmese meditation tradition is identical with the Sinhalese one, being derived from the latter.)

After this exposure to meditation, Huber records, "something had happened to me" (1967). In describing the nature of meditation he quickly refutes popular Western misconceptions of the word "meditation." He points out that the word usually has a religious connotation, but as he experienced it, it was not an occult, mystical, or "spiritual" phenomenon. It was "not religious in any of the usual senses of the word" (p. 108). Elsewhere, I have recorded in some detail how Buddhist descriptions of meditation and behavior have been taken in their literal meaning by down-to-earth Western medical personnel and shown to have nonmystical, even measurable correlates with the physical body and mind—correlates that these experimenters found to agree with descriptions in the Buddhist texts (Goonatilake, Susantha, 1998). I will briefly recall these findings.

Thus, Daniel Brown and his colleagues read the standard literature on mindful meditation in the Sinhalese tradition and observed that in these texts there were often references to increases in perception in the act of meditation. They decided to take these descriptions literally and studied them using the Rorschach test and the tachistoscope (Walsh 1992 pp. 32–38). They noted that, indeed, as the texts said, there were important changes in information processing and perceptual sensitivity in mindful meditators. Their detailed results were in agreement with the Sinhalese Theravada literature that stated that *Vipassana* helps one focus the mind and reduces intrusive associations, images, and thoughts.

An advanced group they called the "insight group" had begun to experience the classical stages of *Vipassana*—insight—as described in the texts. These advanced meditators exhibited a rich variety of associations. Whereas the average subject would give only one or two associations, these advanced meditators would give ten or more associations, and if asked, they could continue giving further associations. Also, in normal subjects, tests repeated days after the original test elicited many of the subjects' earlier responses. But, in the case of the advanced meditators, primarily fresh responses were produced.

A fourth group studied by the experimenters and relevant to one of our anthropologists studied in this book—Gombrich's discussion of the allegedly "mystical" nature of Enlightenment, *Nirvana*—was the group described in the classical Theravada literature as having reached the first stage in the four steps to "Enlightenment." This group exhibited several differences among its members. Some saw the images shown to them as mere emanations of their own minds. Others could be aware, from moment to moment as they responded to the images shown, of the processes by which their stream of consciousness began to be organized as forms and images.

The last group studied was the group whose members had developed meditation techniques to the highest level. These are those who, in the Theravada tradition, would be considered in the final two steps to Enlightenment. The responses of these advanced meditators to the Rorschach blot were both strikingly similar to and strikingly different from normal results. As one unique manifestation of their development, the meditators now perceived the images seen, as well as the ink blot itself, as the mind's projections. In comparison, non-meditators accepted without question the physical reality of the ink blot, although some of them later understood that they themselves would be projecting images onto the blot.

The advanced meditators had yet another unique response; the experimenters could not find among them evidence of the normal psychological conflicts that are found as an everyday aspect of the human condition. This result is a corroboration, yet again, of the classical literature, which says that psychological suffering can be eradicated in the final stages of meditation.

These differing effects of meditation were also seen in the results of tests of perceptual sensitivity. Meditators improved their visual sensitivity, and this persisted even after meditation was stopped. A heightened ability for discrimination was also seen in meditators when they were in deep meditation, but not afterward. These studies indicated that advanced meditators could detect perceptual events that are below the threshold of non-meditators. The authors concluded that the results literally confirmed the descriptions given in the classical literature on meditation (Walsh 1992 pp. 32–38). The most comprehensive compilation of this classical literature is the *Visuddhimagga*, written in 5th-century Sri Lanka. The results obtained by the studies indicate that Sinhalese forays into descriptions of the human condition are not mystical or "spiritual" in the Western sense, and have much to offer the modern psychological and human sciences. They also have had uses for modern psychotherapy. Let me briefly refer to a sample of the Western literature on these modern use possibilities.

It has been noted that the Theravada tradition uses meditation to change perception and cognition as well as for personal development (de Silva, Padmal, 1985, 1990). Herbert Benson, the well-known Harvard psychologist, in his *Maximum Mind*, charted experimentally the effect of various meditation techniques, and showed, on the basis of standard psychological tests, higher levels of cognitive growth after meditation (1987 p. 7). Buddhist psychology in this sense has become a tool of scientific study, a bridge between human experience and cognitive science (Varela et al. 1993 pp. 31–33). Others have shown that cognitive changes associated with "mindfulness" in *Vipassana* meditators results in the "deautomatization" of consciousness. This results in a mode of perceptual organization that is radically different from the normal one, a process of "cutting away false cognitive certainties." It results in new perceptual activities, hitherto blocked or ignored, a new clarity in apprehending the world (Bograt 1991).

Buddhist meditation-derived techniques have successfully treated diseases such as generalized anxiety disorder, phobias, and panic disorder brought about by false cognition. These treatments have also entered standard medical texts (see Beck and Emery 1985). A review of these Buddhist-derived techniques in a major journal notes that through meditation-derived techniques one can bring about cognitive shifts that can be used for observing and changing behavior and limiting destructive cognitive patterns. Such techniques can help deeply reorient a variety of the attributes of an individual, including the sense of well-being, purpose in life, emotional attitudes, and sense of identity (Bograt 1991). This is only a brief sample of the Buddhist psychology that has crept into post-1970s Western psychology. I have described these, in detail, elsewhere (Chapter 8, "A Search for New Psychologies," in *Toward a Global Science: Mining Civilizational Knowledge,* 1998). Hundreds of research reports on the topic have been published. Almost every week, one researcher has noted, one sees reports in this burgeoning new field (Moyers 1993). The output in this general genre is many times more than the amount published on most psychotherapies. Only behavior modification and biofeedback probably generate more studies. The published research covers a wide variety of topics and includes physiological, psychological, and chemical factors (Walsh 1992 p. 32).

(7) WHAT IS DELIVERED TO THE ANTHROPOLOGISTS FROM THE EUROPEAN HERITAGE

At the time of decolonization, anthropology went through deep upheavals as its captive subject matter, "natives" around the world, shed their colonial masters. A long debate on the nature of the subject ensued in the 1960s, giving rise to an attempt to decolonize the subject. This decolonization exercise was paralleled, and partly fueled, by other intellectual developments in Europe and America, the home ground of anthropology. "Natives" were also getting restless on the home turf of Europe and America. For example, American youth and blacks were involved in various forms of uprisings. Approaches derived from a revolutionary creed that was designed to overthrow the Western order, namely, Marxism, were also now entering the debate. It is against this background that we must explore the worldview that was delivered to our anthropologists by their subjects as they embarked upon their respective forays into Sri Lanka from the early 1970s onward.

Anthropology, which was originally the study of social groups in the countries that would become the Third World, was now being debated as colonial empires collapsed in the post–World War II period. A changing relationship with the traditional hunting-ground of anthropologists, namely, the colonies, consequently emerged. These discussions in the 1960s pointed to the relationship between colonialism and anthropology and attempted to show that anthropology largely presented an ideologically biased viewpoint on non-European countries.

Thus Hooker, in a paper titled "The Anthropologists' Frontier: The Last Phase of African Exploitation," related the changing position of anthropologists to the dismantling of colonialism. Originally, according to Hooker, the subject had grown as the handmaiden of colonial governments, although anthropologists sometimes found themselves in sympathy with the interests of Africans. However, because of the stigma of the colonial connection, Africans remained suspicious of the discipline (1963).

Maquet showed how, although the anthropologist was generally concerned with the "primitive aspects" he studied, he was nevertheless engaged in developing ideas that were ideologically useful to colonial exploitation. To Maquet, the anthropologist was a representative of the middle classes of the dominant white colonial presence, that is, that stratum which was completely involved with the colonial system. Maquet predicted that with the dissolution of the colonial relationship, anthropology would actually dissolve, and a more objective body of theory divided between history and sociology would emerge (Maquet 1964).

Peter Worsley also prophesied the end of anthropology. He too was concerned with describing the collapse of the colonial relationship and the beginnings of a universal society in the Third World that would challenge the assumptions under which anthropology grew (Worsley 1966). Two years earlier, the then leading French anthropologist, Claude Lévi-Strauss (1966), had also affirmed the general suspicion that anthropology aroused as a result of the colonial relationship. He recognized the Third World's hostility to the subject as but a natural reaction to a body of knowledge that legitimized the colonial relationship. He felt that for anthropology to be viewed as legitimate by the Third World, it should undergo a process of change, dissociating itself from the colonial system, so that "by allowing itself to perish another [could] be born again in a new guise." Onwuachi and Wolfe (1966) also agreed with the general opinion about the colonial relationship and were of the view that anthropology, if it did have a future in Africa, would have one only after genuine and careful reorganization (Lévi-Strauss 1966).

In 1968, three significant papers in the Social Responsibility Symposium of *Current Anthropology* voiced concern abut the ethical position of the subject, as well as its value assumptions. Berremen (1968) was concerned about the use of research material by groups such as the CIA and the U.S. armed forces against the people who were studied. Gjessing also traced the general relationship of the subject with Western colonialism and found that the subject grew in response to demands made by imperialism, and that its subject matter was ideologically useful in justifying colonial domination (1968). Gjessing, like Maquet earlier, emphasized the Western middle-class orientation of the subject and questioned the idea of its scientific neutrality. Of the three papers in this symposium, Kathleen Gough's "New Proposals for Anthropologists" was perhaps the most influential. She found anthropology to be simply "a child of Western imperialism" whose function was to interpret the non-Western world within the value system of capitalist society. She noted that within the subject, problems arising from confrontations with Western domination had not been properly covered in the literature (Gough 1968).

Anderson, placing himself again within this general trend, traced how anthropology grew, playing a dual role of advisor and ideologist to the imperial system (1968). Banaji in his "Crisis of Anthropology" attempted to trace the problems of anthropology after the period of decolonization. The emergence of economic changes and revolutionary movements within the Third World, he observed, had made the traditional anthropological approach, subject matter, and field observations less relevant to theoretical considerations. Because of its growth from imperialism, the discipline, he suggested, finds it impossible to adjust itself to an antiimperial world. Banaji suggested a change in anthropological stands toward one of exposing the imperial system and taking political action on behalf of the "primitive groups" still surviving (1970).

Some of the criticisms in the 1960s and 1970s also pointed out basic fallacies in key anthropological concepts such as the "tribe" and the role of kinship. Thus, talking from an African perspective, Mafege pointed out that the "tribe," a key word in the anthropologist's vocabulary, often does not exist in the indigenous African situation. He indicated that the word and the ideology of tribalism had been *created* by anthropologists and colonial authorities. He further highlighted the ideological base for the use of the concept of a tribe, that it helped sustain the power of the then European ruling classes and the new African elite (1971).

In a significant study that went to the root of the ideology of anthropology, Finnegan subjected available evidence on "primitive" societies to re-examination with respect to the popularly held notion of kinship being dominant in these societies and the common association between kinship and ascription. Her conclusion was that popular assumptions about the "primitive" had led to these beliefs, and that in actuality there was no automatic correlation between kinship and ascription. She concluded that the assumptions that a primitive society is dominated by kinship and that kinship necessarily involves rigidity and ascription give a most misleading picture of actual, complex situations. Kinship is used in such a community more as an ideology of expected behavior, and in this sense serves the purpose of a myth. These myths serve an ideological purpose much the same as "democracy," "socialism," etc. do for the modern Western world (Finnegan 1971 p. 173).

Magubane pointed out the use of anthropological categories to misinterpret African reality by the use of a concept such as "Westernization" or "modernization" within an urban situation. In the urban situation, the African was expected to conform to the cultural standards of the European presence, such as those relating to dress, education, occupation, etc. To the anthropologist, the African might be human only to the extent that he conformed to a set of status indices showing the absorption of the values of this dominant culture (Magubane 1971).

Asad found that anthropology was rooted "in an unequal power encounter between the West and the Third World." He stated that this encounter gave the West access to cultural and historical information about the societies it dominated and also generated a certain form of universal understanding that tended to reinforce the inequalities in capacity between European and non-European worlds (1973). Adding to the same perspective, Goddard pointed out that the principal concern of anthropology was the problem of social order in a colonial context. Anthropologists took the colonial situation for granted, often capitalizing on it and sometimes actively supporting it, and failed to perceive the overall fabric of domination in which the subject matter of their study lived (1969).

By the 1970s, these criticisms were having their effect on the main thrust of anthropological inquiry, and conventional colonial anthropology was becoming defensive. Leclere acknowledged that imperialism had given birth to an ideological discipline and that anthropology, reflecting as it did colonial attitudes, was being rejected in the 1970s by both Third World intellectuals and Western radicals. He suggested a new anthropology related to the spirit of the Enlightenment which would give room to the universal and liberalizing sciences (1972).

Recognizing the need for the decolonization of the subject, Stavenhagen (1971) suggested decolonizing the applied social sciences and bringing forth new approaches from the viewpoint of the oppressed in the Third World, thereby changing the content and form of the discipline. A Black American anthropologist, Jones (1970), a member of the oppressed culture in a metropolitan country, suggested a "native anthropology." He pointed out that a Third World anthropologist studying in the metropolitan countries also brings a distorted perspective to the field. Further, theories and concepts in anthropology were being formulated from the point of view of Western ideology, Western needs, and Western lifestyles. He suggested the growth of anthropology from what he calls a native perspective, that is, from a perspective that would admittedly be biased in favor of the native anthropologist's own social group, just as the earlier anthropologist was biased in the opposite direction.

The restructuring of the subject as suggested by different writers had still not succeeded by the 1970s. Andre Gunder Frank, who equated anthropology with ideology and applied anthropology with politics, pointed out that in certain contexts the criticism of anthropology had still not been sufficiently understood, that the piper still called the tune, and that "so called indigenous neo-colonial anthropology" still needed to be decolonized (Frank 1976).

By the late 1970s, many of these criticisms were having some impact on the perceptions of anthropology. New journals had internalized some of these criticisms (for example, *Critique of Anthropology* and *Economy and Society*). There was also some convergence between the critique in anthropology and a similar critique in development theory and sociology. Yet in contrast to sociology, the impact of the critique of anthropology had not yet taken sufficient root by the late 1970s. Thus the World Congress of Anthropology held in December 1978 in New Delhi could be contrasted strongly with the World Congress of Sociology held in July 1978 in Stockholm (both of which congresses I attended). Whereas the papers presented at the sociology conference reflected the impact of the new criticism, the majority of papers presented at the anthropology conference, especially those by South Asian authors, reflected classical views.

CONCLUSION

The seven broad areas discussed above provide the general contextual background within which our anthropologists began their foray into Sri Lanka in the 1970s. In this chapter we have looked at the shift of the world axis to Asia; the geopolitics of knowledge arising from Sri Lanka's position at the global crossroads for over two millennia; the emergence of anthropology as a colonial science; the differences between religion, philosophy, and science in the Sinhalese and Western contexts; the Scientific Revolution and its implications for Buddhism and Christianity; the encroachment into Western academia of aspects of Buddhist psychology as a legitimate exploration of behavior; and the state of anthropology as our four authors began their journey.

These factors encompass the richness of the cross-cultural context that surrounds any serious description of the anthropology of Sri Lanka. Sri Lanka, we therefore must recognize at the beginning, is not the isolated primitive village, the classical hunting-ground of anthropologists. It is a rich civilizational entity with a long political and intellectual history which has been at the crossroad of major civilizations for well more than two thousand years. So our description of the different anthropologists' descriptions of Sri Lanka must by necessity take this rich context into account. Let me begin with Gombrich and Obeyesekere.

PART II

■

PROTESTANTISM
AND TRANSFERENCE
IN SRI LANKA

CHAPTER 2

■

Changing Precepts and Practices of a Culture

Our foray into the work of Gombrich and Obeyesekere begins with Gombrich's *Buddhist Precept and Practice* (hereafter abbreviated to Gombrich 1991 in the citations) and then goes on to their *Buddhism Transformed* (hereafter abbreviated to GombObey 1988). Since our focus is only on those anthropological studies which analyze Sinhalese Buddhist society as a whole, we will ignore Obeyesekere's earlier work, *Land Tenure in Village Ceylon: A Sociological and Historical Study* (1967), on a specific aspect of Sinhalese society. We also ignore his later works, such as *Medusa's Hair: An Essay on Personal Symbols and Religious Experience* (1981), for similar reasons. *Buddhist Precept and Practice*, because it attempts to make an assessment of Sinhala Buddhist society as a whole through a single field study, is, therefore, a good starting point for us.

THE METHODOLOGY OF GOMBRICH

Gombrich is trained as a philologist, but in this study he moves to the territory of the social sciences. His fieldwork lasted a year. His mission is to see the distinction between what people say they believe and what they say they do, and what they in actuality believe and do; the latter he calls religious behavior (1991 p. 5).

Gombrich sketches briefly the approach to and methodology of his study of religious change. He indicates that religion can be studied by many professionals, including theologians, historians, sociologists, anthropologists, and psychologists. The latter, for example could, in turn, vary from social psychologists to behaviorists to psychoanalysts (1991 pp. 1–3). Gombrich, however, believes such academic boundaries are artificial. He also wishes to approach his study in a Popperian mold, that is, with a hypothesis that later can be disproved, which the philosopher of science Karl Popper says is the hallmark of good science (Gombrich 1991 p. 4).

The Sinhalese scholar monk Walpola Rahula is praised as one who helped Gombrich by answering many questions (Gombrich 1991 pp. x, ix). Rahula's *What the Buddha Taught* is given fulsome praise as combining "authenticity of indigenous tradition with scholarship matured at universities both East and West" (p. 85), while Rahula's *History of Buddhism in Ceylon* is described as outstanding and invaluable, a work that could be consulted by all serious students of Buddhism (p. 31).

Gombrich bases his study on an area ten to twenty miles from Kandy. He stayed there for one year and did about thirty-six interviews. At first he wanted the book to consist of only the interview material together with the accompanying descriptive notes. But that would have been unintelligible to an outside audience. He notes that explaining the assumptions on which the questions to the monks were based would itself have required much extra space. So he has formulated the book to deal only with certain intellectual issues raised in his study. He has also ignored such areas as politics for the same reasons of brevity. He emphasizes that his is not a book on religion in a Sinhalese village but a study of traditional Buddhism (1991 p. 43).

Let me now draw out his salient points. I do not limit myself to his ethnographic observations, the reportage meant for a Eurocentric, non–Sri Lankan audience; but just as he does, I draw out largely intellectual issues.

THE ESSENCE OF GOMBRICH'S STUDY

Gombrich first delineates the precepts and doctrines of Buddhism. He notes that the Buddha said that one should not take any doctrine on trust; rather, one should accept it only after examining it (1991 p. 9). He further says that *Nirvana*—the end goal of Buddhists—is a "mystical" release from normal states of consciousness. He defines *dukka*—the first Buddhist truth of the world—as suffering. Yet he mentions that individuals do not want an extinction of sensation (p. 19). He is surprised that a belief system which has as a central tenet what he calls "the world is sorrow" can, under the right circumstances, attach great spiritual value to joy (p. 295).

Moving on to practice in Sri Lanka, Gombrich reveals a fair familiarity with the historical outlines of Sinhalese Buddhism. He says that the great Sinhalese historical document, the *Mahavamsa*, begun in the 6th century, is a written chronicle of varying but sometimes "considerable excellence." As contemporary confirmation, Gombrich finds that many festivals as described in the *Mahavamsa* differ very little from what is practiced today (1991 p. 53). He describes the vicissitudes that Buddhist practice has gone through, requiring regular reforms under different patrons. Illustrating this regular need for reform, Gombrich recalls the *Mahavamsa*'s words that before Parakramabahu instituted his reforms, the situation was such that "in the villages belonging to the Sangha [the monastic order] the good morals of monks consisted only in their supporting their wives and children" (p. 38, quoting *Mahavamsa* LXXVIII, 3–4). The most recent reforms under royal patronage were, Gombrich notes, in the 18th century (p. 41).

Gombrich operates within a Eurocentric framework, which occasionally comes to the surface in the questions he asks and the statements he makes. Thus, he says that as the Buddha is dead, the problem is raised in the Western mind (meaning his own) "about places filled and functions performed by the Christian God" (1991 p. 168). Yet in his non-interpretive ethnographic sections, he describes the daily practice of Buddhism in the village in generally accurate terms. Gombrich mentions that Buddhism accepted as given the world of the time, as long as it did not go against key Buddhist fundamentals. The given cognitive map of the world was taken for granted. Within it, the Buddha had seen the truth (pp. 84–85).

One approach to practice that comes as a novelty to Gombrich—who is of the Jewish faith—is that the average lay person is no more concerned with denying or accepting the existence of a new supernatural being than the average Westerner would be with accepting or denying the existence of a new nuclear particle. Such matters are taken as normal aspects of life. So a Buddhist who believes in gods can be excused of incorrect doctrine (Gombrich 1991 p. 55). Further, belief in gods and the supernatural, Gombrich notes, was not an extraneous addition to the traditional belief system. Such beliefs had always been there. So it would not be unnatural for a Buddhist to accept the existence of the Christian God, in addition to other gods of the indigenous variety. Buddhists only consider gods to be a type of supermen who can grant favors, but who are themselves subject to the same general moral laws as humans (pp. 57–58).

Gombrich describes these supernatural beings—*pretas, gods,* and *demons*—as derived from and subsumed into Buddhism. That is, they are looked at through the worldview of Buddhism (1991 pp. 190–194). But these entities do not exist as permanent fixtures; they change through history. Thus, gods have changed in importance over time. Natha, one of the powerful gods in earlier centuries, has now been almost forgotten (Gombrich 1991 p. 208).

But these beliefs in the supernatural also exist in the Sinhalese village within a framework of disbelief.

In Gombrich's village, there was much skepticism about *bali* ceremonies, which evoke the supernatural, and their efficacy. Some people believed that this alleged "efficacy" was all in the mind. A person described by Gombrich as the "perfect man in the street" said bluntly that he did not go for all this *yaksha* (demon) stuff (1991 p. 247). There was also skepticism about the usefulness of gods. One of Gombrich's respondents mentioned that he went to Kataragama—the place of pilgrimage of a popular god—for fun, *vinodeta*. He attacked the priests at Kataragama as dealers in lies and drinkers of alcohol (p. 249).

Gombrich notes that this skepticism is not limited to the contemporary Sinhalese. He recalls Robert Knox, the 18th-century English prisoner of King Rajasinghe, who upon his escape wrote *An Historical Relation of the Island of Ceylon*. In the Sinhalese heartland, untainted by the European inroads on the coast, Knox observed Sinhalese attitudes to beliefs. Knox wrote:

> There are few or none zealous in their worship, or have any great matter of esteem for their Gods. [But] they seldom busy themselves in the matters of their Religion, until they come to be sick or very aged. They debar none that will come to see the Ceremonies of their worship, and if a stranger should dislike their way, reprove or mock at them for their Ignorance and Folly, they would acknowledge the same, and laugh at the superstitions of their own Devotion, but withal tell you that they are constrained to do what they do, to keep themselves safe from the malice and mischiefs that the evil spirits would otherwise do them, with which they say, their Country swarm. (1911 p. 132)

And if the gods do not deliver, Knox adds,

> I have often heard them say, Give him no Sacrifice, but shit in his Mouth, what a God is He? So slight an estimation have they of their Idol-Gods. (p. 132)

Gombrich observes that although at times people would go beyond the call of reason, no one would admit to going beyond the rational. This, Gombrich notes, is the opposite of Christianity, which specifically commends going beyond reason (1991 p. 308). Yet the Sinhalese, Gombrich claims, have no equivalent to laws of nature. He says that according to the Sinhalese there is an operative factor called *svabhavaya*, its "own essence" (pp. 169–170). Gombrich explains this as "things work according to the way they are."

Monks, Gombrich observes, do not subscribe to exorcism and other non-Buddhist practices that are sometimes indulged in by lay Buddhists.

A monk in a law court is a far commoner sight than one in a *devale*, a shrine for a god (1991 p. 178). Even practices that to an outsider appear to be Buddhist rituals are not what they seem. Gombrich describes the painting of eyes on an image of the Buddha, and he brings great inter-pretative import to it, saying that after the eyes are added, the statue becomes some sort of god (pp. 162–163). But, on the other hand, monks interviewed by Gombrich said that no offerings, or flowers, or any reci-tations of verses had any intrinsic value. What mattered was not these outer forms but the thoughts behind them (p. 138).

Gombrich also describes what he considers to be elements of recent practice. He says that there are two types of Buddhism today: modern Buddhism, taken largely from Western (translated) sources, and tradi-tional Buddhism (1991 pp. 64–65). He also finds that the prevalent view—that Buddhism is not a religion but a practice and a way of life—is a modern invention (pp. 74–76). One would expect the believers in this so-called "Western" Buddhism to be members of the English-speaking upper layers of society. Yet Gombrich also observes that the upper and middle classes believe in astrology and in auspicious practices. He also finds that those who believe more strongly in Buddhism believe less in astrology (pp. 173–174).

He gives the name of a standard book, Narada's *The Buddha and His Teaching*, as a guide to Buddhism. But he says that he will not refer to this book, since he is interested in finding out what a particular group believe in. He will use information given directly by the villagers and monks themselves (1991 p. 67). A book Gombrich often refers to is a Sinhalese book, *Bauddha Adihilla*, which gives a summary of Buddhist practices. This gives the regularly used prayers, as well as excerpts from medieval Sinhalese texts, including particular forms of worship to be performed at centers of pilgrimage around the country (Gombrich 1991 p. 383). Pil-grimages are a common Buddhist practice. There have been important places of pilgrimage from time immemorial. These include the place of the Buddha's footprint, Sri Pada, the center of pilgrimage *par excellence*. There are also the sixteen places, *solos mahasthana*, which the Buddha is said to have visited and which have been centers of pilgrimage from the Anuradhapura period (3rd century B.C.–12th century A.D.) (Gombrich 1991 pp. 128–129).

Gombrich finds that education and learning is an important Sinhalese Buddhist value. He finds that the study of *Abhidhamma* is considered the highest level of attainment before Enlightenment (1991 p. 310). He finds that meditation is the most highly esteemed form of human activity. He also finds it a "passive" activity (p. 309). He finds that the virtues valued most in Sinhala Buddhist society are *santa danta,* being polite in the fullest sense, and *karunawe*—kindness, compassion. He finds the generosity of the Sinhalese borders to Western eyes incredible. He finds monks kind, hospitable, and worldly (pp. 311, 379).

Gombrich also takes up some issues for detailed treatment. He devotes one chapter to the problem of total responsibility for one's own actions that is a central feature of Buddhism. He also explores the fact that even people who subscribe to the no soul (*anatma*) theory believe that they will survive death. He presents his own explanations on the nature of "soul" and "no-soul" (1991 pp. 86–88). A central finding of Gombrich's studies is that the differences between Buddhist practice and principle were as great in the *Mahavamsa* period as they are today. Gombrich asserts that Rahula incorrectly identifies the aberrant practices as popular Buddhism (pp. 372–373).

This is a summary description of Buddhist "theory and practice" as Gombrich found it in his study of a village in the central highlands of Sri Lanka close to the last Sinhalese capital of Kandy. Gombrich and Obeyesekere then explore the transformation of Buddhism in their jointly written book, *Buddhism Transformed: Religious Change in Sri Lanka* (1988). The canvas here is large, namely, the totality of Sinhalese Buddhist practice and its transformation.

But this transformation is not just the transformation of the theory and practices that Gombrich studied in his village. It is of a larger scope: the transformation of an *earlier* transformation that had allegedly occurred among Sinhalese Buddhists.

THE FIRST TRANSFORMATION:
THE PROTESTANT BUDDHISM THESIS

This first transformation is what Obeyesekere had earlier described as "Protestant Buddhism," an alleged change in Sinhalese Buddhism that occurred in the late 19th and early 20th centuries. Let me first describe Obeyesekere's thesis of Protestant Buddhism and then its transformation, as the authors describe it. Obeyesekere first introduced the term "Protestant Buddhism" in an article published in 1970. Malalgoda accepted and used it in his work, which was on the movement's origins and covered the period 1750–1900 (cited in Gombrich 1991 pp. 372–373). But Malalgoda took the story only up to Protestant Buddhism's greatest figure, Anagarika Dharmapala, the Sinhalese founder of international

Buddhism. Obeyesekere, on the other hand, described in relative detail the life and thought of Dharmapala.

Gombrich and Obeyesekere note that the appellation "Protestant Buddhism" was also taken up by other members of the scholarly community (GombObey 1988 pp. 6–7). In the usage of Obeyesekere, Protestant Buddhism has a double meaning. It originated as a protest against the British and against Protestantism, but incorporated "salient characteristics" of the latter. Protestant Buddhism, allegedly following Protestantism, undercut the importance of the monk—the religious professional—by making it the responsibility of every Buddhist to care for the welfare of Buddhism as well as to strive for "salvation" (GombObey 1988 p. 7). The Buddhist individual, like the Protestant, now pursues his own goals (pp. 215–216).

Gombrich and Obeyesekere label the Sri Lankan Anglophone middle classes "an *haute bourgeois*" (1988 p. 211). Colombo, these authors say, is the home both of this bourgeoisie and of the proletariat who are alien to the traditional two-thousand-year-old agrarian society (p. ix). For nearly a century, Obeyesekere claims, Protestant Buddhism was limited to a large number of the Sinhala- and English-educated living in Colombo, Galle, and Kandy, as well as to an emerging middle class of Sinhala-educated minor government officials living in rural areas. Protestant Buddhism, Gombrich and Obeyesekere claim, has now spread and has a hegemonic hold over the rest of the nation (p. 7). The focus of their book is the vicissitudes of this Protestant Buddhism as it has changed in recent decades.

As examples of this supposed Protestant Buddhism, the authors give the following. The reformist monk Mohottivate Gunananda founded the "Society for the Propagation of Buddhism" in 1862, in imitation of the "Society for the Propagation of the Gospel," and "on a press originally imported by the Missionary Society began to print replies to Christian propaganda" (GombObey 1988 p. 203). The authors quote from Olcott, the American who was associated with the Buddhist Renaissance, to the effect that unlike other monks the polemical monk Gunananda looked people straight in the eye instead of dropping his eye as other monks did (p. 219). As examples of Protestant Christianization, the authors see the imitation of Christian organizations in "The Young Men's Buddhist Association," formed by an ex-Catholic, and "The All Ceylon Buddhist Congress" (p. 234). As further examples of emulation of Protestantism, they cite the use of songs at Vesak (the main event in the Buddhist calendar) modeled on Christmas carols, the sending of greeting cards at Vesak, and the establishment of Buddhist schools emulating the Christian ones (p. 205). The Buddhist flag itself, the authors add, was invented by Olcott (p. 204).

The reach of Protestantism among the Sinhalese was seen in the guidance given on secular life. Anagarika Dharmapala brought out a popular pamphlet, "The Daily Code for the Laity." It was first published in 1898 and had gone through nineteen printings by 1958. The book gave detailed rules for how to conduct oneself. A total of two hundred rules governed, among other matters, how to eat food, chew betel, wear clean clothes, use the lavatory, walk on the road, behave in public places, behave in public transport, and behave in front of the Sangha, as well as rules on how women and children should conduct themselves (GombObey 1988 p. 214). Gombrich and Obeyesekere also mention that during this period, as in other colonies around the world, Victorian sexual mores were adopted by the Sinhalese (p. 256).

Another feature of Protestant Buddhism was the individual's own seeking of the ultimate goal of Buddhism. The authors compare this to the Protestant Reformation, in which "the priest and the saint as essential links between men and God" are rejected (GombObey 1988 p. 215). They quote from Dharmapala's diary the following entry as illustrating this sense of individual search: "Oh, the bliss of solitude . . . by Dhyana [meditation]" (p. 216).

Gombrich and Obeyesekere claim that other features of Protestant Buddhism included the abandonment of Buddhism's "traditional" eirenic treatment of other religions for a more polemical stance, and the development of a fundamentalist approach to Buddhism. Nineteenth- and 20th-century Sinhala Buddhists also claimed that the difference between Buddhism and Christianity was the difference between a philosophy and a religion (GombObey 1988 pp. 221–222). Buddhism was now not a religion but a philosophy (p. 218). Further, the authors note that there were few scriptures available in Sinhala, as contrasted with those in Pali (a language that was to Theravada Buddhism what Latin was to Catholicism). They claim, therefore, that Protestant Buddhism was "a Protestantism without a Bible" (p. 208). These developments also led to a dependence on English-language-based concepts among Sinhalese Buddhists (p. 208).

The authors admit that in the past, too, there had been similar tendencies. But instead of simply accepting these tendencies in context, the authors attempt to provide explanations for them. They say that such tendencies exist because Buddhism is considered to require periodic "purifications" (GombObey 1988 p. 208). The authors state that reform movements in the Sangha, such as movements to expel the bad monks and encourage the good, had always come from within the Sangha, and not from the laity, the latter acting only as the executant (p. 225).

After the arrival of Protestant Buddhism, Theravada also looked down on Mahayana. This, according to Gombrich and Obeyesekere, is a recent innovation guided by remarks made by Rhys Davids, the translator of Pali texts into English, who equated Lamaism with "popery." The authors think this looking down on the Mahayana is also related to the Protestant belief that Catholicism is a mass of ritual and superstition. They say that such analogies have contributed to the prevailing anti-Mahayana prejudice (1988 p. 220).

The practice of monks' officiating at and blessing all types of undertakings is mentioned as influenced by Christianity (GombObey 1988 p. 228). The authors claim that "the validation of lay work to advance social welfare in general and Buddhist causes in particular" is another imitation of Christianity (p. 232). They find direct Christian influences in the creation of "chaplaincies" in hospitals and military establishments. They mention that in the same vein, a monk had now become the president of a nurses' union (p. 227). Among other alleged "Christian influences," they mention the chanting of *Pirit* on the national radio every morning. They say that in this way "Buddhism is purveyed to the layman, brought to him in his own home, instead of having to seek out the monk" (p. 228).

Gombrich and Obeyesekere mention the "Protestant" reformist Dharmapala's statements condemning the rise of drunkenness among the Sinhalese and the ignorance of Ceylon Buddhists as the utterings of a "man full of painful ambivalences" (1988p. 213). They assume Protestant anti-clericalism in Dharmapala's statement that "The Bhikkhus in Ceylon are indolent and ignorant of the *Paramatthha Dhamma* [Ultimate Truth], and they keep up their position by a smattering of Pali grammar and Sanskrit prosody" (quoted in GombObey 1988 p. 226). They assert that Dharmapala became the Luther of Sinhala Buddhism (p. 378).

Theravada Buddhism as practiced in Sri Lanka, Thailand, Burma, Laos, and Cambodia, the authors claim, has as a central institutional feature the distinction between monks and laity (GombObey 1988 pp. 4–5). Traditional Buddhism, the authors say, rests on the recognition of two separate sets of values, those of life in the world and those of the higher life of leaving the world. Protestantism does not have this division, and the Protestant orientation has now intruded into Sinhala Buddhist life (p. 273). This stage halfway between the religious and the lay world is central to the authors' "Protestant" theory. Anagarika, the role taken by Dharmapala, was such a person—halfway between the clergy and laity, and so between salvation and the everyday world (p. xi). As an example of the halfway stage between monk and layman, the authors mention Dharmapala's wearing of white clothes (p. 216). The authors claim that through the creation of the interstitial role between monks and laity, the ground was prepared for monks to become involved with the world. They claim that monks "can now pattern themselves after a Protestant clergyman" (p. 227).

Dharmapala had mentioned that he acquired the meaning for his role in renouncing the world and working for humanity from three sources. They were the life of Bodhisat Sumedho, Edwin Arnold's poem on the Buddha, *The Light of Asia,* and Blavatsky's writings (GombObey 1988 p. 217). To Gombrich and Obeyesekere, it is the ghost of Protestantism, through its impact on Theosophy, that is the background influence for many of the changes (p. 217).

Dharmapala traveled widely, for example, in Burma, India, Thailand, America, Japan, and several countries in Europe. He thus became the "founder of international Buddhism" (GombObey 1988 p. 206). But Anagarika (Dharmapala) also attacked Indian merchants, Muslims, and Tamils as economic exploiters of the Sinhalese (GombObey 1988 p. 213). Later, Olcott and Anagarika began drifting apart, Anagarika refusing to accept the teachings of Theosophy as part of Buddhism. An important instance of nontheoretical disagreement was Olcott's demeaning of the Sinhala palladium, the Buddha's tooth relic, calling it an animal bone (GombObey 1988 p. 206).

Gombrich and Obeyesekere say that the vast majority of Protestant Buddhists today do not go the whole ascetic way, renouncing family life. They wear white clothes in their everyday worldly business, "even" become vegetarians, or at least give up beef, and take alcohol "only for medicinal purposes" (1988 p. 233). They give an example of a Protestant Buddhist, a university lecturer named Kodikarnaracci, who preaches against taking alcohol and who states that eating meat and smoking are not good for the breath (p. 236). Part of the Protestantization through blurring of the distinction between monk and layman is achieved through the practice of meditation. The authors wonder how meditation could be so routinized as to end up on the Sri Lankan school curriculum (p. 236).

The authors state that their 1988 book on what they claim are transformations in Buddhism is in no way exhaustive and that they have uncovered only a fraction of what is going on, suggesting that more work should be done in Sri Lanka and other Theravada countries (GombObey 1988 p. xiii). They also mention that their narrative is full of details and colorful facts, and they state that theories may date, but not documents

(p. xi). The fieldwork for this book was carried out in the 1970s together with that for Obeyesekere's *Medusa's Hair*. The jointly written book, the authors say, was written sporadically. The book specifically states that it ignores two key events, namely, the 1983 riots and the 1987 "Peace Accord," brought about by Indian forces—implying, of course, that the book was completed after these events (p. x).

Gombrich and Obeyesekere go on to describe how "Protestant Buddhism" is being transformed.

"BUDDHISM TRANSFORMED"—AGAIN

First the authors give a fair interpretation of Buddhist doctrine, including its theory of no self (GombObey 1988 p. 15). Buddhism, they say, "considers the mind to be the instrument of salvation" (p. 16). And the authors mention that the aim of Buddhism is to see the world with dispassionate lucidity, and that even at its least sophisticated level, Sinhala Buddhism has been informed by these values (p. 27). Learning and literacy are considered high values in Buddhist society. Male literacy in Sri Lanka in the early 19th century, the authors note, quoting the German sociologist Heinz Bechert, was as high as that in then fast-industrializing Britain (p. 207).

Gombrich and Obeyesekere delineate two aspects of the Sinhalese Buddhist belief system. One deals with "salvation" according to Buddhism, and the other with spirit religion, the irrational (1988 p. xi). Although Buddhism proper gives no authority for the irrational, the supernatural, and the worship of gods and the propitiation of demons, Sinhala Buddhism has always included such actions and beliefs (p. 3). The authors aim to document and explain contemporary change in both these spheres—Buddhism and the spirit religion.

Gombrich had earlier described, in his *Precept and Practice,* the Buddhism actually found in the 1960s in a village setting. What the two authors now document are recent changes in Protestant Buddhism. Protestant Buddhism influences "urban" Buddhists, a group which the authors tell us is not necessarily defined by physically living in a town or a village. "Urban" Buddhists' beliefs are to be distinguished from the beliefs of traditional Buddhist peasants (pp. 4–5). The authors describe the emergence of cult groups of the spirit religion as symptomatic of the changes in Protestant Buddhism. Thereby they hope "to build up a picture of the sea change that has overtaken the mass of Sinhala society" (p. 67).

Most of the changes of concern to the authors began to become visible in the 1940s but became widespread in the 1960s and 1970s. These changes spread from Colombo to the periphery of the country (GombObey 1988 p. 6). The changes the authors see in many Sinhala Buddhist societal settings have led to the emergence of what they term a "post-Protestant" society, which is disoriented and which has a new religious culture. Just as Buddhism changed in the hands of the new middle class to become Protestant Buddhism, the spirit religion has been changing its character in the hands of the urban poor. Although Obeyesekere and Gombrich describe these two changes as separate phenomena, they maintain that they do so only for convenience of description. They state that the two phenomena are complementary and that they intermingle (p. 9).

The values of the urban poor, the authors assert, are different from those of the bourgeoisie, and also from traditional village Buddhism. The ethos of the Sinhalese bourgeoisie is related to Victorian Protestantism. The ethos of the urban poor, on the other hand, is related to the emotional religiosity of Hinduism—*Bhakti*—and is contrasted to the puritanism of the bourgeoisie. The Buddhism of this bourgeoisie has been profoundly influenced by Protestantism, Orientalism, and Theosophy; the spirit cults of the urban poor, on the other hand, have been influenced by *Bhakti* (GombObey 1988 p. 11).

The authors describe the changes in these two realms of belief by resorting to Max Weber. They describe Weber's use of the term "rationality" as having two senses. Weber uses "rationality" in a strong sense, the use of abstract concepts to define the image of the world, as well as in a second, instrumental sense, the reaching of defined practical ends by precise calculation of means. Dharmapala, the authors say, saw Buddhism, in contrast to Christianity, as rational. He also exhibited an instrumental rationality. Initially, claim the authors, Protestant Buddhists followed Weberian rationality in economic life. So Protestant Buddhism was rational in both of Weber's senses (GombObey 1988 p. 104).

The authors find that this Weberian rationality is not characteristic of the recently evolved Sinhala religion. They say there is confusion among the lower strata who have not fully become Protestant Buddhists. They still live in a partly traditional cosmology, and they are incompletely indoctrinated into the new world because of the presence of only a few textbooks in Sinhala. The traditional cosmology does not help them cope with the changing world. Especially in times of want and scarcity, their inner world cannot make sense of the outer world. A solution available earlier in such circumstances, the authors claim, was to withdraw from the world and meditate (GombObey 1988 p. 14).

They say that meditation "sets out" to see the world but was available traditionally only to monks. In the modern day, Sinhalese are trying to reconcile the ordered reality of everyday social life with radical Buddhist meditation. The authors call this a re-mystification of the world. This, they claim, is a reconciliation that in Buddhist doctrinal terms is "theoretically impossible" (GombObey 1988 p. 15).

Another re-mystification mode they identify is the increase in the love of a god through ecstatic practices (GombObey 1988 p. 15). The contemporary Sinhala scene, claim the authors, is characterized by the widespread acceptance of possession as something positive (p. 36). In many of their case studies, a guardian deity manifests itself by possessing the believer. This is in spite of the fact that possession itself is considered an illness by Buddhists. There are also stringent Buddhist strictures against possession on holy days. Such practices do not fit into Buddhist concepts of self-control and awareness (p. 28). What Buddhism inculcates is the very opposite of ecstasy, "a serene joy, a tranquility" (p. 29). In discussing trance phenomena, Gombrich and Obeyesekere also mention that modern meditators, too, sometimes experience what can be described as a trance (p. 27).

As symptomatic of the changes, the authors describe a phenomenon, the *Bodhi Puja,* which was popular in the 1970s and 1980s and which since then has largely vanished from the scene. This was a type of collective worship partly modeled on earlier practices. The authors give a reasonably commonsensical view of this worship form and its spread. It is a patchy description, similar to others indulged in throughout the book, but no theorizing is introduced. At one point, however, the authors try to say that this type of worship could have come from Protestantism because the best-known monk associated with this worship form was born in the town of Panadura. They point out that the town of Panadura was the center of the famous debate between Christians and Buddhists in the 19th century, and also that there are churches, Christian schools, and a powerful Christian elite in the town (GombObey 1988 p. 386).

In correspondence with the general changes that the authors describe through their examples, they mention that the pantheon of Sinhala Buddhists has also changed in terms of deities' relative importance. The god Kataragama has eclipsed the god Vishnu. Kataragama is now rising to become a Bodhisatva like Vishnu. The deities Kali and Suniyam are likewise being transformed (GombObey 1988 p. 33). Further, other deities and objects of veneration have also appeared.

One of the rising places of worship that Gombrich and Obeyesekere document is the shrine of the god Kataragama. The people quoted by the authors say that they go to Kataragama for "joy," signified by the Sinhala word *vinoda* (GombObey 1988 pp. 191–192). The authors, however, reject this explanation.

The authors mention that the dance performed today at Kataragama is more often than not the Portuguese-derived *baila*. They mention that there is today an erotic aspect to the dancing, with, say, middle-class matrons swinging their "reluctant buttocks to the swinging music." Their conclusion is clear: this eroticism is specific to the changes at Kataragama (GombObey 1988 p. 193). Among the reasons for the development of the erotic *kavadi* dance, the authors cite the growth of sexual frustration among youth. This sexual frustration, they say, is increasing because young men and women today postpone marriage until they find suitable jobs (p. 199).

The authors are surprised when the chief fire walker disapproves of the lack of self-control and the emotional display in fire walking (Gomb-Obey 1988 p. 413). They see a deeper meaning in these changes. They state that ethical changes in society are "anticipated and worked out" at the Kataragama shrine (p. 415) and, more significantly, that the priests of Kataragama are "theoreticians whose views seem to anticipate changes in the religion of the Sinhalas" (p. 417).

Gombrich and Obeyesekere mention that the Kali goddess is also propitiated "all over" urban Sri Lanka. But they add in the following sentence that the Kali shrines attract only a few individuals and are very small (GombObey 1988 p. 141). The curious example of a lady in a canteen who was possessed by the goddess Bhadra Kali is described. This Buddhist lady dabbled in the spirit world and was later converted to Christianity. She charged for her services, and her acquaintances became jealous because of the increased income this brought her. As a result, she claimed, she was subject to sorcery. To counteract it, she tried various means, including a Roman Catholic priest who practiced exorcism; she then tried astrology, and finally Pentecostalism. In this Christian fundamentalist sect she found her ultimate spiritual home, and her whole family converted to Christianity; she maintained that Jesus had spoken to her through the voice of Kali (p. 56).

One of the new objects of veneration that the authors observe in Sri Lanka is the Indian holy man Sai Baba. The devotion some Buddhists have for Sai Baba is explained by the authors as due to the breakdown of traditional authority. Sai Baba provides "a refuge from a harsh and unintelligible reality," promoting an "overpowering intimacy between the worshiper and his god" (GombObey 1988 p. 53). The authors describe a devotee of Sai Baba who has strayed from true Buddhism and believes, in addition to the Buddha, in other personages exemplified by pictures at his home of the Virgin Mary, Jesus, Ramakrishna, and a village guardian god. The Buddha images are kept at a lower level, signifying, according to the authors, a lowering of the status of the Buddha (p. 54).

As symptomatic of the changes, Gombrich and Obeyesekere describe new roles "deviant" from tradition, as, for example, females taking on the roles of priests—*kapuralas* (1988 p. 47). The authors give examples of changes in names as signifying the changes in roles in the new religious dispensation. *Maniyo,* which they define as a very formal name for "mother," has emerged to describe female priests, as has the word *sami* to describe a *kapurala* (p. 38).

The authors maintain that generally there is a flight to the occult, and give the impression that this is widespread. They offer as examples of this phenomenon the evidence of palmistry, astrology, and the occult in newspapers. They take as illustrative of the trend sensational headlines such as one claiming that a past prime minister has been reborn as a god (GombObey 1988 p. 59). They give an example of an occult practitioner who worships Mara. Many of his clients are Roman Catholics (p. 62). The authors state, when discussing a clairvoyant, that almost anything unusual is attributed to a supernatural cause. These unusual occurrences include a bus coming quickly, which is attributed to Kataragama (or Sai Baba) sending it. Similarly, a stranger is thought to be a deity in disguise. The world has become "de-rationalized" for these believers in the clairvoyant (p. 63).

Gombrich and Obeyesekere give the reason for new religious behavior as the general breakdown of the community and the traditional forms of social control and their replacement by possession. Spirit religion is changing, and with the breakdown of kin groups and other communities, cults provide surrogate communities. Demonic beings of the village are in the process being converted into divine beings of the city (GombObey 1988 p. xi). Cases of benign possession multiply, as opposed to the more traditional malign forms. Similar acts of reinterpretation, the authors claim, are responsible for the changes occurring at Kataragama (p. 39).

Gombrich and Obeyesekere point out that money from the worship of deities at the Bellanwila Buddhist temple is being used to build a large Buddha shrine, implying that this is somehow wrong (1988 p. 43). The authors, however, observe that Buddhist monks do not approve of the changes toward the occult. Two monks, when asked for their views, responded with telling answers: the older said it was only "entertainment" (*vinoda*); the younger, a school vice-principal, corrected his senior and said it was "folly" (*modakama*) (p. 63).

SOME "LEADERS" OF THE TRANSFORMATION

As examples of changes in Buddhist practice, Obeyesekere and Gombrich describe three selected Buddhist "leaders." One, a Mr. Perera, uses meditation in daily life (1988 p. 325). Another example of a Buddhist "leader" is a monk who has ordained himself (p. 325). The third leader, a Mr. Jayasuriya, teaches a quick, direct method of Enlightenment. The authors claim that his behavior is typical of sectarianism anywhere, especially in the modern world (p. 377).

The other person that the authors put into the category of a Protestant sect leader is Uttama Sadhu (GombObey 1988 p. 371). Other details are given by the authors of the eclectic search "for truth" by Uttama Sadhu and Jayasuriya. Obeyesekere and Gombrich consider that these two are making a move toward *Tantra* as opposed to *Bhakti* as well as pushing fundamentalism to its extremes (p. 376).

The authors also cite the case of Nissanka, who says that the Buddha is only one in a succession of saviors. They consider this another example of Protestant Buddhism (GombObey 1988 p. 377). They trace the small, eccentric sect (their words) of Jayasuriya through the Protestant Buddhist revolution to an uncertain future. They consider Dharmapala the Luther of Sinhala Buddhism, while Jayasuriya becomes analogous to one of the sectarian enthusiasts of the 17th century (p. 378). The authors observe that Jayasuriya's sect condemns all traditional hierarchies and structures of authority, and they detect egalitarianism in all the sect's activities (p. 380). This sect reminds the authors that extreme Protestantism has been the road to secularization (p. 381).

The authors describe the mixing up of categories by one of their "leaders." They attribute this to a mood in the society at large. As another example of this mood, they give the case of the hallucinatory inscriptions which the well-known archaeologist Paranawithana saw in his dotage. The archaeologist claimed to see micro, interlinear inscriptions, which nobody else could read (GombObey 1988 p. 349). The authors give, as examples of the collocation of topics in the Sinhala imagination, Tamil, astrology, and black magic. The monk-poet of the 15th century Totagamuwe Sri Rahula was proficient in all three, according to popular tradition (p. 49).

The authors' examples of those who have transformed Buddhism through possession include many who have traveled the world. For example, the Buddhist fire walker they study, Muthukuda Sami, had lived in India for four years studying Indian approaches to the occult. Subsequently he joined the British army and participated in the World War II battles in Egypt and Italy (GombObey 1988 p. 412). Another fire walker, Vijeratne Sami, tells the authors that there are two types of occult science, one Indian and the other Californian (p. 413). When one of the authors returned to Britain, he was contacted by a devotee of Mr. Jayasuriya, who was a graduate student in chemical engineering at a British university (p. 356).

Among the transformations of tradition referred to by the authors are false interpretations of Sri Lankan society in the past by Nandasena Ratnapala, falsehoods that are the basis of the Sarvodaya movement (GombObey 1988 p. 244). The authors point out that Sarvodaya has brazenly invented an idealized, simplified, past village life that never actually existed. The village as described has no vices or folly, a far cry from everyday life as described in both Sinhala historical writings and those of Buddhism. The authors again inject Protestantism into Sarvodaya's invented village life (p. 252).

As another example of the creation of a modern tradition, the authors give the example of Mapalagama Vipulasara Thero. The authors were drawn to this monk because he had officiated at the wedding of a young Danish artist (who had known the monk) to a Sinhalese woman. This monk had also previously constructed the wedding throne for a Sinhalese couple (GombObey 1988 pp. 266–267). The authors say that Vipulasara "claims to be a sculptor," which led to his patronage of the Danish artist who wanted a wedding ceremony (p. 266). The authors consider this event a significant example of the kinds of change taking place (p. 449).

There are many non-conformist monks who exist today, the authors note, in the context of the looseness of the structure. One illustration of such relative non-conformity is the growing by Vipulasara of a beard, actually stubble. The authors give an example of another monk, a vice-chancellor of a university, who grew stubble and had hair on his head to a degree unusual for monks. The authors say that Vipulasara's habit of moving quickly and energetically is in imitation of Mohottivatte Gunananda, who, the authors point out, was engaged primarily in debating Methodist and Baptist ministers and lay preachers. And as a final note on Christian influences, the authors say that Vipulasara's image is "close to the stereotype of the jolly Church of England vicar" (GombObey 1988 p. 266).

Gombrich and Obeyesekere offer as another example of the recent encroachment of the monastic order into lay activities the case of a monk, Nakulugamuve Sumana, who, having attended law school, wanted to practice law in the courts. This was refused by the Supreme Court, not by a bench of monks, on the grounds that he was not properly dressed. Several lay Buddhist organizations also objected to the monk's taking to the practice of law (GombObey 1988 p. 457).

The authors also make the observation that the spirit religion, instead of being restricted to Sri Lanka, is in fact the common heritage of the whole of the Asian subcontinent from Burma to Pakistan, from Nepal to Sri Lanka. They contrast this spirit religion with Indian classical religions such as Brahmanism, Buddhism, and Jainism. They argue that these religions inculcated self-control and decorum. Buddhism and Jainism, in particular, emphasized that salvation comes from complete mastery of the senses, emotions, and appetites. The authors say that spirit possession rituals are the very opposite of the self-control of the classical religions. They say the classical religions censored out possession and emotionalism; they were a civilizing influence on the rustics (GombObey 1988 p. 457).

Gombrich and Obeyesekere mention in the final part of their book that Sri Lankan sociologists have called for a non-Western sociology-anthropology (GombObey 1988 p. 456), but without mentioning any of these sociologists by name. The authors state that the Buddhist religion can indeed be analyzed in terms of the Indian intellectual tradition, more effectively than in Western terms. But they argue that just as they have used the Christian concept of Protestantism to analyze modern Buddhism, one can analyze the European Reformation through Indian religious concepts. The only difficulty, they claim, is that before this can be done, the non-Sanskrit reader has to be taught the Sanskrit religious vocabulary. So they use English translations of Sanskrit terms (p. 456).

The sections which I have summarized present the authors' descriptions of a village-based Buddhism relatively undisturbed by the external world; its alleged transformation through Protestantism; and its further transformation as this Protestant Buddhism itself changed. It is now necessary to see to what extent these three descriptions of Buddhism in Sri Lanka represent reality. This I will examine in three chapters. One, a relatively short chapter, will examine Gombrich's discussions on village Buddhism. The other two chapters will examine the two transformations. They are longer because they deal with context and civilizational transactions. The emphasis in all three chapters will not only be on empirical facts but also on methodological, epistemological, and civilizational issues.

CHAPTER 3

■

Precept and Practice of Buddhism

We should now examine Gombrich and Obeyesekere's findings, and see how they square with Sri Lankan actuality. Let us begin with Gombrich's study of precepts and practice.

WHAT GOMBRICH FINDS

Gombrich makes many commonsensical observations which are broadly true. But he trips up on several key issues.

Gombrich introduces many of his own Eurocentric interpretations of Buddhist theory into some of the most basic Buddhist principles. He thus says *dukkha*—the first truth of Buddhism—is suffering, noting, however, that believers do not wish for an extinction of sensation (1991 p.19). He is also surprised that this sorrowful belief system attaches such value (he calls it "spiritual value") to joy (1991 p. 295). He describes the end goal of Buddhism, *Nirvana*, as a "mystical" release from normal states of consciousness.

These are highly tendentious interpretations drawn from popular European misconceptions. The words "suffering" and "mystical" have Western connotations that Gombrich, especially as a linguist, could have been more careful about. Walpola Rahula, the scholar whom Gombrich praised so eloquently for his authoritative views on Buddhism, has pointed out that "suffering" is a false translation of *dukka*, which is "limited, . . . highly unsatisfactory, . . . superficial . . . and misleading" (Rahula 1978 p. 16). Rahula emphasizes that Buddhism is neither pessimistic nor optimistic but realistic. It is "quite opposed to the melancholic, sorrowful, penitent and gloomy." Rahula further points out that joy is indeed one of the seven aspects of Buddhist Enlightenment (p. 28).

Rahula, again, notes that Nirvana "is not produced like a mystic, spiritual, mental state" (1978 p. 40). It is often expressed in negative expressions like "extinction of thirst," "uncompound," "unconditioned," "absence of desire," "cessation," "blowing out," or "extinction" (p. 36). But Rahula points out that a negative word does not necessarily indicate a negative state, noting that the term for health, *arogoya*, literally means absence of ill health (p. 38).

Those Western scientists who have studied the major channel to *Nirvana* —"meditation"—have consistently emphasized meditation's matter-of-fact nature (see Chapter 2). Although Gombrich notes that Buddhists esteem meditation most highly, he himself does not explore it; nor does he consult the hundreds of Western psychological, medical, and other scientific sources of information on such explorations. His view of meditation itself, one of the most active of mental states, is, for a late-20th-century Westerner, decidedly quaint. He finds it "passive" (1991 p. 309).

Gombrich notes that knowledge of the *Abhidhamma*, the philosophical and psychological core of Buddhism, was considered to be a high achievement (1991 p. 310). But Gombrich himself does not try to examine the large amount of psychological material that this *Abhidhamma* material possesses, which would answer Gombrich's questions about *Nirvana* and meditation. If he had taken the Weberian injunction of *Verstehen* as a guide to the group being studied, he would have been curious to explore *Abhidhamma*, the group's own formal views on human behavior, psychology, and sociology, as, indeed, Western psychologists have done (see Chapter 2). In contrast to Gombrich, one should note parenthetically that Kapferer, one of the authors we will discuss in the next section, has literally taken the ideas of exorcists—Kapferer's subjects—as *his* lens through which to view Sri Lankan reality.

ACQUIRING BELIEFS

Gombrich correctly notes that the Buddha and the Buddhists took the given cognitive maps, where they did not go against key Buddhist fundamentals, and, within them, saw the truth (1991 pp. 84–85). So the average Sinhalese believes in gods and the supernatural, although these are not strictly called for in Buddhist theory. But even within this popular Buddhist tradition, there are several instances of questioning the givens, even of questioning general Buddhist assumptions such as rebirth. For example, the very popular 17th-century *Loweda Sangarawa* contains a well-known phrase, *paralowa athath nathath*, "whether or not there is an afterlife." Gombrich makes a gross simplification when he says that Sinhalese Buddhists have no equivalent to laws of nature (pp. 169–170). This is plainly untrue; Buddhists have sophisticated explanations of how the world-at-hand works, with theories of atomism, time, and logical processes.

Gombrich also says Sri Lankan middle-class Buddhists take their cues from "Western" Buddhist sources (1991 pp. 64–65). For a similar class reason, Gombrich ignores Narada's standard book, *The Buddha and His Teaching*, as a pointer to Buddhism (p. 67). But this attempt to erase what is presumed to be class-based Western Buddhism ignores the over-encompassing fact that all the Western translations of the 19th and 20th centuries were based on original Pali sources in Sri Lanka. Western translators of such Buddhist texts were helped and closely supervised by Sinhalese monks. The fact that today's Buddhists refer to Western-language Buddhist texts, therefore, does not mean that they are getting at "Western" sources, but rather that they are getting at the formal Sinhalese Buddhist heritage translated into English under direct Sinhalese guidance. Educated Sinhalese today have more familiarity with English than with Pali or medieval Sinhalese, and they naturally go to English translations.

If Gombrich implies that going to these formal sources is something un-Sinhalese, then he should remember that he himself has referred to the regular purifications of accretions throughout the centuries in Sinhalese Buddhist history. The search for a return to original sources, as well as the rigorous developments thereof, has been a constant theme throughout Sinhalese Buddhist history. In the same spirit, when the local monastic order had deteriorated, it was reintroduced from other countries. The most recent local purification attempts were the anti-*dusseela* (anti-impiety) campaigns in the 19th century, discussed in detail in Chapter 5.

Gombrich over-reads the addition of eyes to a Buddha image, saying that the statue becomes like a god when the eyes are painted (1991 pp. 162–163). But this is a common ceremony all over the Buddhist world. In this same tradition is the Japanese ceremony of painting Daruma (Bodhidharma) dolls' eyes. The anthropologist hunting for the exotic gives extra meaning when there is none. I have often wondered whether, in Christian practice, the drinking of the blood of Christ in the form of wine and eating his flesh in the form of bread is cannibalist in origin. But whatever its origin, I would not over-interpret these ceremonies as Gombrich attempts to interpret Buddhist ceremonies, and say that Christians evoke cannibalism in their minds.

Gombrich also uses the word "religion" in the Christian sense, essentially equating Buddhist "religion" with Christian "religion." One of Gombrich's central tenets (also a tenet of "Protestant Buddhism" theory) is the rejection as a modern invention of the idea that Buddhism is not a "religion" in the Western sense, but a practice and a way of life (1991 pp. 74–76). But there are *real* differences between Christianity and Buddhism vis-à-vis both modern science and philosophy, which I have drawn attention to in Chapter 2. These have to be examined and taken into account.

SOME METHODOLOGICAL ISSUES

There are also several key elements left out of Gombrich's narrative.

The class stratification of the society and its impact on religious beliefs are, except for one or two instances, left out by Gombrich. Left out are the entry of monks into political activities and their one-time pivotal role, especially in the 1950s and 1960s (Gombrich 1991 p. 43). This is a strange omission because it is one area where the monks' entry affected not only the precepts and practice of Buddhism but also those of the total framework of society. This is the area where Walpola Rahula, who is praised so wholeheartedly by Gombrich, was a pivotal figure (Gombrich 1991 pp. x, ix, 31, 85). The latter's most influential book, *Bhikkuge Urumaye* (The Heritage of the Bhikkhu), described the monks' involvement in socially oriented politics as an essential part of their historical practice.

Also left out of Gombrich's narrative is the impact on the people of contemporary education, of basically a modern Western syllabus, which has been the *major* socializing engine for nearly five generations in this highly literate society. The majority of Sri Lankans of the last half century or more have been to Western-type schools and have been exposed to contemporary thought, including science. Thus it is very possible that in Gombrich's area of study there are more people who study the elements of physics and chemistry than who study *sil*, the ten Buddhist precepts. So Western science has now become part of the belief system.

South Asian religions also cross subject matter with psychology. Gombrich mentions the importance of Buddhism to psychologists, implying that there are conceptual elements of use to psychology. He does not explore this further. Gombrich mentions, in the category of psychologies that could be used to study religion, social psychology, behaviorism, and psychoanalysis (1991 pp. 1–3). But he does not include humanistic psychology, which at the time the book was being published was coming into considerable prominence. The father figure in the field of humanistic psychology was the late A. H. Maslow, the theorist of self-actualization, and his last book identified his approach with Buddhist approaches (Maslow 1968 pp. 78, 110, 114, 119).

By the time Gombrich wrote his book, many works had been written

by contemporary Western psychologists, including his own British countryman R. D. Laing, on the usefulness of Buddhism to psychology. In fact,
Laing had been introduced to the world of Buddhism by Godwin Samararatne, the same person, we are informed by Gombrich in his *Buddhism
Transformed,* that Gombrich had turned to for help in his own Buddhist
studies. Now psychology, just like anthropology and sociology, attempts
to provide a formal window into human behavior. A truly local perspective, which is the stated aim of anthropology, should, or could, have used
Buddhist explanatory elements. With Gombrich's belief in the artificial-
ity of academic boundaries, he could well have reached out to these local
intellectual traditions (1991 p. 4). He did not.

Buddhism itself, in addition, has in its methodology several injunctions and procedures to find out what is true and untrue. These vary
from general charters for correct inquiry, such as *Ehi Passiko,* "Come and
see whether it is true," and the *Kalama Sutta,* the Buddhist Charter for
free inquiry, to detailed philosophical takes on epistemology. Some of
these injunctions in Buddhist observation and epistemology have been
favorably commented upon by comparative philosophers. There are also
many other methods of social observation in this Buddhist genre that
could fruitfully inform social scientists. These do not enter into the perspective of Gombrich.

Gombrich also evokes the falsification methodology of Popper as his
chosen approach (1991 p. 4). But the type of murky, rambling ethnography found in Gombrich's book, with hardly any core of theory that one
could put one's hands on, is hardly the type of material with which to
do a falsification exercise. The only theory that Gombrich seems to have
is that precept and practice do not agree in Sri Lanka, a truism in any
religious societal milieu. Gombrich's recourse to Popper seems to be
more of an academic embellishment than a methodological possibility.

Gombrich's study was limited by the small geographical area he studied, the time of one year he spent, and the (only) thirty-six interviews he
carried out (1991 p. 43). Out of this limited universe, he also deliberately
leaves out important areas such as the political, and then makes his story
implicitly reflect the whole country. This is too short a time and too re-
strictive a frame to encompass the nuances of a total civilization.

Gombrich's Eurocentricity makes him seek functions equivalent to
those of the Christian God in the Sinhalese Buddhist context. The mea-
suring rod is Christianity (1991 p. 168). But Gombrich's mission is the
difference between doctrine and practice (p. 5). Legitimizing his project, he also mentions in passing that Western Christians also believe
in ghosts, and that even now, some leading Christian denominations

perform exorcisms (p. 7). But his project has many presumptions built into it. Any religion would display major departures from its texts. This would be true of any Western country today that professes to follow Christianity, including countries such as Germany or Italy that have been formally ruled by Christian parties (there have never been Buddhist parties in power in Sri Lanka). The gap between the Christian precept of love and its practice was clear for Protestant Britain, Protestant Holland, and Catholic Portugal when they ruled parts of Sri Lanka, and for Germany during its Nazi period.

The obvious question that then needs to be asked is, why haven't there been studies similar to Gombrich's on his own Christian Britain? The answer is obvious. No one expects Britishers or Germans to go about with their Good Book in hand, checking every action they embark upon to see whether it tallies with the Bible's injunctions. So, Gombrich's study of precept and practice itself is in many ways meaningless; the practices of *all* religions and belief systems do not always match their precepts. Even if these factors are overlooked, no one would dream of studying British Christianity only by interviewing thirty-six individuals of British society taken from, say, one small Devon village. But, this is what Gombrich does for Sinhalese Buddhism. And so, Gombrich finds after his research that there have always been differences between Buddhist practice and principle, whether in the *Mahavamsa* period or today (1991 pp. 372–373). A whole book taken to come to an obvious conclusion. He also finds fault with Rahula for calling these aberrations popular Buddhism (pp. 372–373). A modern Western parallel would be to say that accretions to Christianity—most famously practiced by various American sects who perform their rituals on Sunday television—cannot be dismissed as popular Christianity.

The book, *Precept and Practice*, although it proves the obvious, contains, however, much ethnographic material that would be useful to the outsider. But it would not interest a Sri Lankan, to whom much of this ethnography would be familiar. It should be noted parenthetically that there are no such ethnographies of Western countries. For the West, there are travelogues, tourist brochures, and a constant flow of media and other information that connects to and describes a dynamic, changing social reality. But even as travelogue, there are limitations to the depth of Gombrich's study. Thus, Gombrich uses a Sinhalese book, *Bauddha Adihilla*, as a guide to Buddhist worship and practices. This book is used by modern Sinhalese, and so its content is understandable to all Sinhalese. But, puzzling in a person who was trained in South Asian linguistics and who has learned Sinhala, Gombrich requires the help of Dr. Kitsiri Malalgoda to properly understand its *contents* list. Malalgoda corrects Gombrich's translation of the contents list (Gombrich 1991 p. 383). If the list gave Gombrich such problems, one could only imagine what the full text did, as it described the precepts of Buddhist practice.

CHAPTER 4

■

Protestant Buddhism and Buddhism in Modern Protestantism

Gombrich and Obeyesekere's *Buddhism Transformed* describes two basic elements, the alleged arrival of "Protestant Buddhism" and its transformation. We have to examine the validity of both these theses, because the correctness of the second depends on the first being true.

INDIVIDUAL SEARCH

As a central element of Protestant Buddhism, the authors mention the individual's own pursuit of the ultimate goal, as in the Protestant Reformation, rejecting the priest as an essential link between man and God (GombObey 1988 p. 215).

Instead of being an external Protestant implant, however, the individual search is the very essence of Buddhism, emphasized in many Buddhist texts. Let me quote from the *Dhammapada*, the popular summary of key Buddhist teachings:

> Let the wise man make for himself an island which no flood overwhelms. (*Dhammapada* p. 87)

> If, as the disciple fares along, he meets no companion who is better or equal, let him firmly pursue his solitary career. Oneself is one's own protector, what other protector can there be? By oneself, indeed, is evil done, by oneself is one defiled. By oneself is evil left undone, by oneself, indeed, is one purified. Purity and impurity depend on oneself. No one purifies another. (*Dhammapada* 1988 p. 342)

> For the sake of others' welfare, however great, let not one neglect one's own welfare. Clearly perceiving one's own welfare, let one be intent on one's own goal. (*Dhammapada* p. 343)

> Make an island unto yourself. You yourselves should make the effort, the *Tathagatas* are only teachers. Far better is he who has tamed himself. (*Dhammapada* p. 547)

Control, therefore, your own self as a merchant controls a noble steed. (*Dhammapada* p. 598)

IRONY OF EIRENY

As for other facets of Protestant Buddhism, the authors see the giving up of what they allege was Sinhalese Buddhism's "traditional" *laissez-faire* attitude toward other beliefs and turning to polemics as a fundamentalist attitude toward Buddhism, Buddhism being considered a philosophy and not a religion, and using English-language concepts (GombObey 1988 p. 218).

These are again selective, misleading interpretations. We have already discussed in Chapter 2 the issue of differences between philosophy and religion which were real, not invented.

The apparent "eirenic" attitude toward other religions, it should be noted, existed together with a will to defend and spread Buddhism. The first Buddhist *missionary*, King Asoka, who introduced Buddhism to Sri Lanka in the 3rd century B.C., put it as follows in his edict no. 12:

> Whoever praises his own religion, due to excessive devotion, and condemns others with the thought "Let me glorify my own religion," only harms his own religion. One should listen to and respect the doctrines professed by others. (Translated by Dhammika 1997 p. 51)

The missionary techniques themselves had been established by the Buddha (whose words for his first five disciples were "Go forth among the people"). These tolerant missionaries debated and dialogued with others (a classic example for Sinhala Buddhism was the *Milinda Panha,* dialogues of a monk with a Greek king). An important Sinhalese debater, albeit from Mahayana, was Aryadeva (1st century A.D.), the principal disciple of Nagarjuna. He was such a heated debater that he was assassinated by his opponents.

Sri Lanka's defensive wars against South Indian invasions were also fought in terms of the protection of Buddhism. It was in the same spirit that with the collapse of the Sinhalese monarchy, monks attempted to get a Buddhist king from Siam. The scholar-monk Subhuti also wrote to a prince of Siam bemoaning colonial actions by the British in Burma, saying, "Although we have no King here [in Sri Lanka], we have always recognized the Kings of Burma and Siam as our Kings" (quoted in Guruge 1984 p. 83). And the historian Tennekoon Wimalananda has recorded the details of how a monk dragged down the British flag as it was raised in

1815 to signify the transfer of sovereignty to the British. Gombrich and Obeyesekere treat this well-documented fact only as *"tradition* [emphasis mine] has it that this monk dragged down the flag" (1988 p. 219). They throw doubt on this well-known fact in their eagerness to show that defense of one's own sovereignty, as well as the use of debate and dialogue and polemic, are themselves European imports via Christian Protestantism.

The authors, trying to show Protestant influence, mention that, unlike earlier monks, the reformist monk Gunananda did not drop his eyes in front of others but looked directly into their eyes (GombObey 1988 p. 219). But *ganinnanses,* the monks who existed before the 18th-century reforms, had families, and would surely have looked their children in the face, as well as others with whom they had a lay relationship. Further, monks had taken a leading part in anti-British movements and revolts as recently as a few decades before the arrival of the Theosophists. British governors also stated that monks carrying subversive messages from group to group were an incendiary force. Monks had earlier acted as ambassadors, lay advisors, and lawyers. One gets a very different picture from the one the authors try to paint. And most telling, Gunananda himself was involved in debates before the alleged introduction of the influence of Protestantism after the arrival of Olcott.

IMITATIVE PROTESTANTISM OR INTERNAL REFORM

A cornerstone of the "Protestant Buddhism" thesis is that the Buddhist revival was largely an externally driven one, brought about by the "Protestant" ideas of the Theosophists, especially of Olcott. But it was reports of the 19th-century debates between the Christians and the Buddhists, read by Olcott in New York, which eventually led to his arrival in Sri Lanka. And there had also been reforms in the 12th, 14th, and 18th centuries, all recalled by Gombrich in his earlier book (Gombrich 1991 p. 38, quoting *Mahavamsa* LXXVIII 3–4 and p. 41). Regular reforms were therefore a constant theme in Sinhalese Buddhist history.

The authors, to buttress the Protestant Buddhism thesis, say that the "Society for the Propagation of Buddhism," formed by Mohottivatte Gunananda, the key debater, was in imitation of the Christian "Society for the Propagation of the Gospel" (GombObey 1988 p. 203). The society's actual name, however, was *Sarvajna Sasanabhivrddhidayaka Dharma Samagama,* which directly translates as "Dharma Association Contributing to the Advancement of the Omniscient Sasana." The authors present a sim-

plistic over-reading of a translation. The translated name may have echoes of the English-language Christian organization, but not the Sinhala
original. The society was purely an internal development. The locally
grown Silvat Samagama of Velivita Saranankara of the early 18th century was formed for similar religious reform purposes (Malalgoda 1976
p. 220).

In contradiction to the "Protestant Buddhism" thesis, the conduct of
local Buddhists was being criticized long before Dharmapala began to do
so. A study by Tissa Kariyawasam (1973) documents these through the
Sinhalese literature of the time.

Thus, from 1864, there was intense criticism of prevailing Buddhist
practices. Reformists advocated that one should follow pristine Buddhism without worshiping statues and gods, revealing those very attitudes later attributed by the authors to alleged Protestant influences. In
1875, Gunananda had given Olcott the names of various learned Sinhalese monks who were later enrolled as members of the Theosophical Society in New York. Olcott, writing several years after the death of
Ambagahawatte Saranankara, the founder of the Ramanna Nikaya, noted
the latter's reform cry, saying he had "broken out in protest. . . . From the
start he made an impression, his sect grew strong . . . prospered and now
embraces a large body of zealous and able monks" (quoted in Malalgoda
1976 p. 167). This zeal and "Protestant" search was all homegrown, as
was readily admitted by the supposed harbinger of Protestant Buddhism
himself. This local search for pure Buddhism, for example in the widespread debate on pure (*seela*) and impure (*dusseela*) monks, continued
even after the arrival of Olcott.

HALFWAY HOUSES, MONKS, AND LAITY:
THE HERITAGE OF THE BHIKKHU IN LAY AFFAIRS

Gombrich and Obeyesekere claim that the "distinction between monks
and laity" is a central institutional feature in all Theravada Buddhist
countries (1988 pp. 4–5). They say that by creating a role between that of
the laity and that of the monks, Protestant Buddhism made monks "pattern themselves after a Protestant clergyman" and become involved with
the world (p. 227). Dharmapala was such a "halfway" person (p. xi).

But the idea of this "special role" does not tally either with history or
with experience.

Before the 18th-century reforms, monks—*ganinnanse*—had wives and
children and often tilled the land. And the wearing of white by Dharma-

pala, which is considered by the authors illustrative of his halfway status, is not unusual in Sri Lanka. Lay persons who practice *sil* on *poya* days, wear white, as do widows. In Cambodia and Thailand, there is a lay official called the *achar* who acts as a key intermediary between monks and laymen, and often has more knowledge of Buddhism than many monks. Another Southeast Asian "intermediate" example is the institution of *donchees*, female renunciates, some of whom live in the temple. The monks themselves, taken as a whole, function as an intermediary group in Thailand, Laos, and Cambodia because many males become monks as novices and give up the practice after a few months or years. And in key religious activities, the secular and the religious interpenetrate intimately with a festive air, dancing, and music. All this is very unlike the fictional separation that the authors have constructed.

The allegedly sharp division between monk and laity is a recent colonial construct, now perpetuated by our anthropologists.

As Edmund Perry points out in his foreword to a translated edition of Rahula's book, *Heritage of the Bhikkhu*, this subversion of the monk's role in the colonial era was due to a Christian "conspiracy to convert the Buddhist monk from public leader to disengaged recluse" (1976 p. xii). Perry continues, "The image of the Buddhist monk as a public leader engaging in social and political activities had been obscured, deliberately so, by Western colonialists and their accompanying Christian missionaries" (p. xii). Perry notes that a particular type of Christian monastic role was now imposed on the Buddhist monk. Through this imposition, the colonialists dispossessed the Bhikkhu of their influence on the population. As it is this same colonial tradition that our authors are continuing, it is useful to describe in some detail the actual historical role of monks as recalled in Rahula's book.

The Buddha himself was not isolated from society. He exhorted his disciples to wander from village to village instructing the people for their good and well-being (*Carata bhikkhave carikam bahujana hitaya bahujana sukhaya*). The Buddha also gave advice on how to lead a happy lay life.

In Sri Lanka, the expected role of monks split formally into two categories, one as town dweller interacting with the people, and the second as meditating recluse; these were later referred to respectively as *aranyavasi* (forest dweller) and *gramavasi* (village dweller) (Rahula 1976 pp. 25–28). As time passed, monks began to specialize in subjects such as languages, arts, prosody, poetics, science, history, and law, and wrote treatises on them. Monks taught all strata, from princes to peasants. Every Buddhist temple became a free school as well as a center of culture and communication. Sometimes, monks were given salaries (Rahula 1976 pp. 30–33).

Monks consequently played a leading role in national and cultural activities. According to the *Mahavamsa*, the nine-story Lovamahapasada (2nd century B.C.) was designed by monks, and the relic chamber of the Ruvanveli Seya was designed by Arahant Indagutta (Rahula 1976 p. 22). By the 5th century, Buddhist monks excelled in sculpting images of the Buddha, a celebrated Sinhalese sculptor Nanda Thera presenting the Chinese emperor with an exquisite image. Vihara paintings were also done by monks (Rahula 1976 p. 41).

Monks took a strong interest in national and political activities such as the selection and appointment of righteous kings (Rahula 1976 p. 22). A position equivalent to that of chief justice was held by a monk during the time of King Bhatiya (38–67 A.D.) (Rahula 1976 pp. 30–33). The Sangha negotiated a peace treaty between Viceroy Mahinda and King Sena II (851–885 A.D.). The Sangha prevented a civil war by settling a political quarrel during the time of King Udaya III (945–953 A.D.). Monks settled a political quarrel between Manabharana and King Gajabahu II (1137–1153 A.D.). King Parakramabahu (1236–1271 A.D.) took the advice of monks in deciding on his best successor. At the beginning of the 15th century, when there was fierce competition for the throne, the chief monk of the Vidagama Vihara adopted and educated a young son of Queen Sunethra, and had him crowned as Parakramabahu VI (1412–1467 A.D.). In 1760, when Governor Falk, the Dutch administrator of the maritime provinces, requested clarification on the Sinhala constitution, laws, and customs from the Sinhala government in Kandy, the query was answered not by ministers but by the *sangha sabha* headed by Velivita Saranankara. A monk from the district of Galle acted as a delegate to negotiate a trade pact between the Sinhala kingdom and the English (Rahula 1976 p. 51). Several rebellions were launched, in the face of British repression, to liberate the country in 1818, 1834, and 1848. They were all under the leadership of monks (Rahula 1976 p. 66).

Early on, the British had learned that monks sometimes became "lay" leaders and freedom fighters. Governor Maitland wrote, "The influence of the priest is very great, even greater in many instances than that of the *mudaliyars* [local administrators] themselves." A 19th-century report on temples said of Sinhalese monks, "Their *pansala* [temples] are the schools for village children, and the sons of even the superior headmen are very generally educated at them. They have also frequently, some knowledge of medicine, and when this is the case, they generally give the benefit of their advice gratuitously, which the *vedaralas* [lay physicians] seldom do" (quoted in Rahula 1976 p. 68).

Although he mentions the importance of Olcott, Rahula—unlike our authors—traces the latter's contributions only as part of a continuous narrative of similar contributions going back millennia—an important contribution, but nothing extraordinary in the long Sinhalese tradition. This historical continuity is also seen as Rahula relates more recent events in which monks, including Rahula himself, took the lead.

FAKE CHRISTIAN INFLUENCES

There are other important aspects of Sinhalese lay and monastic life which have been falsely ascribed by the authors to Christian influences. Gombrich and Obeyesekere thus claim that monks traditionally did no secular work before the coming of Protestantism (1988 p. xii). This, as we have seen, is not true. The authors see a direct Christian influence on "chaplaincies" in hospitals and military establishments (p. 227). The involvement of Buddhist monks and Buddhism with health has a long history, beginning with the Buddha himself and the building of hospitals all over India by Emperor Asoka. Ruins of several Buddhist hospitals are found in Sri Lanka. Medicine was practiced by monks; all the ancient medical works, such as the *Bhesajjamanjusa, Yogarnava,* and *Prayogarat-navaliya* were written by them.

Another activity that the authors say is due to the imitation of Christians is the pursuit by laymen of Buddhist causes and social welfare work (GombObey 1988 p. 232). But this again contradicts the well-documented history of social welfare policies which are integral to the Buddhist tradition. These include the establishment of hospitals, the setting up of wayside rest houses, and the building of irrigation works. These Buddhist welfare practices are found in the work of Asoka, the old Sinhala kings, and the Cambodian kings. The Buddha's phrase *Dasa Raja Dharma,* the "Ten Royal Qualities," referred to earlier, established the general parameters of these Buddhistic lay concerns.

Gombrich and Obeyesekere again claim a Christian hand when monks bless and officiate at different official gatherings including the blessing of military officials (1988 p. 228). This is again both historically and geographically untrue. Television news in Theravada Thailand and Cambodia daily depicts monks taking part in and blessing various types of lay occasions, including military ones. Such practices undoubtedly came from Sri Lanka.

The authors describe the chanting of *Pirit* in the morning on the national radio as due to Christian influence, claiming that in this way "Buddhism is purveyed to the layman, brought to him in his own home, instead of having to seek out the monk" (GombObey 1988 p. 228). But this has nothing to do with Christianity; it has all to do with the communication revolution, and such means of communication are used by all religions in the world.

As another case of Protestant influence, the authors give the example of a monk who wanted to practice law. This was objected to by lay Buddhist organizations (GombObey 1988 pp. 229–230). But this example of alleged Protestantism contains a contradiction. On the one hand, the monk could be engaged in Protestantization. But so also are those modern Buddhist lay organizations which, the authors claim, are modeled after Protestant templates, but which were objecting to the monk's practice of law. The question, then, is not who is more Buddhist but who is more Protestant, the monk who wanted to practice law or the lay organization which objected to it? But as we saw earlier, there is strong documentation of monks through the ages acting in the field of lay law, once, as we noted, with the Dutch.

CONSTRUCTING THE FLAG

In Gombrich and Obeyesekere's search for external roots for most elements of the Sri Lankan protest movement, they also argue that the Buddhist flag was invented by Olcott (1988 p. 204). This is completely wrong. The flag was conceived and made by locals. An authoritative description of how the flag was created is given in the *Buddhist Encyclopedia*, which cites several primary sources. There is also a monograph by Jothipala on the topic. Olcott in his own diary flatly denied that the flag was his idea. Olcott only suggested that the flag be shortened in accordance with international norms (Jothipala 1985 p. 12).

BUDDHIST AND CHRISTIAN FUNDAMENTALISM

Alleged "Buddhist Fundamentalism" occupies a central position in the thesis of Protestant Buddhism. Gombrich and Obeyesekere mention, in the same breath and with the same implied meaning, fundamentalism as it occurs in Christianity, Buddhism, and Islam, thus equating all these different "fundamentalisms" (1988 p. 448).

The authors treat Buddhist fundamentalism in terms of two different meanings, one reflecting its core and the other reflecting what is in the texts (GombObey 1988 p. 448). And when people disagree on the texts, the authors consider it as a dispute in fundamentalism (p. 456). If fundamentalism is used in its original meaning and not to mean a political force (both meanings being popular in Western usage—it is in the former sense that the authors use it), then one sees a big difference between the different religions.

The Judeo-Christian religions are, as we have seen in Chapter 2, revelatory religions. So going back to fundamentalism here is by definition going to the textual sources of what "God's messengers" said. The core of Buddhism is the observational practice of how the mind-body functions and the accompanying theory. So there is a major difference.

There were also in Buddhism periodic councils of monks to get rid of accretions to the doctrine that were considered untrue. At regular intervals there have been disputes within Sri Lanka about what constitutes true teaching, leading to many schisms. The removal of unnecessary accretions is thus not a modern invention that was guided by Protestant thought but a continuous Theravada Buddhist tradition.

These searches for the "original" truth were not just idle speculations reminiscent of Christian scholastic arguments on how many angels could dance on a pin. Buddhist orthodoxy directly attempted to relate itself (or at least partly legitimize itself) to what was observable and testable. The key fundamental texts in Sinhalese Buddhism, the 5th-century *Visuddhimagga* and the 12th-century *Abhidhammatthasangaha*, pertain to internal practice. These texts include sections on meditation, whose empirical validity does not rest on some mystical revealed fact or a message given by a god. Going back to sources in Sri Lanka involves, in essence, not checking scriptures against originals but checking practice against texts that document practice.

Grudgingly, Gombrich and Obeyesekere admit at one point that tendencies to get at the original core did exist in the Sinhalese past, but instead of considering them as matter-of-fact historical givens, the authors try to psychologize about them. The authors consider that Sinhalese Buddhism requires regular "purifications" (1988 p. 221). They thus give such acts a quasi-mystical role, something like a *potlatch*, a ritual offering to tradition.

The authors also search for divisions, such as the split between Mahayana and Theravada. Disingenuously, they claim that viewing Mahayana negatively is only a recent development, influenced by some remarks of Rhys Davids, who denigrated Lamaism as "popery." The authors link this negative attitude toward Mahayana to the Protestants' critique of Catholicism as ritualistic and superstitious, ignoring well-known ideological struggles between the two traditions (Goonatilake, Hema, 1974).

The authors also have it wrong when they imply that meditation should not be learned from a book, calling Dharmapala Protestant-influenced for doing that. They say that Dharmapala was "perhaps the first Buddhist to learn meditation from a book" (GombObey p. 237). This is untrue. The standard books on meditation were meant to be definitive guides; they are, therefore, a necessary addition to every temple library, and their study is compulsory for all monks. And in the West today, millions are learning meditation from books, many derived from the Pali originals.

"PHILOSOPHY" AND "RELIGION": EAST AND WEST

Gombrich and Obeyesekere look askance at 19th- and 20th-century Sinhala Buddhists who consider Buddhism and Christianity as respectively a philosophy and a religion (1988 pp. 221–222). Words such as "philosophy" and "religion" are, as we have seen in Chapter 2, European words with connotative baggage. There is now, as described in Chapter 2, an extensive literature in the West on the development of Buddhist philosophical traditions. By the 1980s, a large literature had grown up. Because Sri Lanka was an important intellectual home of Buddhism, this philosophical literature available on Sinhala Buddhism exceeds that available on its anthropology, but it is ignored by the authors.

In this same vein, the late Sri Lankan philosopher K. N. Jayatilleke attempted to see parallels between Buddhism and logical positivism in a University of London thesis, subsequently published as *Early Buddhist Theory of Knowledge* (1963). Jayatilleke, who had indulged in these respectable cross-philosophical searches—as several other Theravada scholars have done—later indulged in spurious projects, trying, for example, to show that rebirth could be "demonstrated." Gombrich and Obeyesekere jump on this and then laugh at the whole East-West comparison genre, sniggering at Jayatilleke's claim that some Buddhist philosophy includes aspects of Marxian and Freudian concepts. To the authors, the intellectual world emerges only from Europe. But Freud, Marx, and Buddhism have been compared by several more serious Western scholars for points of commonality, as well as differences (see Suzuki et al. 1960; Goleman 1981; Fromm 1967 p. 33).

If the philosophies of the East and West differed, as we saw in Chapter

2, so did their religions. All the Christian sects were based on revealed religious truth written down in authoritative texts. In South Asia, strong philosophical undertones concerning the nature of reality, whether the world is one or many, whether it is material or mental or both, are always intertwined with the "religious." The philosophical context exists as an *essential* explanatory factor in the religious scheme.

So there is a large difference in the connotations of the two words "religion" and "philosophy" in the two cultural realms—revealed Christianity and experiential Buddhism. There is also a difference between the two types of "religion" as to what are considered legitimate practices to be engaged in by informed persons, monks, or priests, and by the mass of the general population. So, equating "religion" and philosophy and dichotomizing science and religion is a much more complex exercise than it would appear from Gombrich and Obeyesekere's simplistic assumptions. Sir Edwin Arnold, the author of the *Light of Asia*, who became a champion of Buddhism, saw parallels between Buddhism and science, saying, "I have often said, and I shall say again and again, that between Buddhism and modern science there exists a close intellectual bond" (quoted in Guruge 1984 p. cxlvi).

BUDDHIST REVIVAL: RENAISSANCE OR IMITATION?

The key point in the whole Protestant Buddhism thesis is one of imitation of Christians. Examining this Protestant thesis closely then boils down to this primary question: Was the Buddhist revival simpleminded imitation or a self-confident creative act, reminiscent of the European Renaissance? (if one wants to use a Eurocentric metaphor).

The 19th-century Buddhist revival in British Sri Lanka (there had also been an 18th-century revival) was launched within a decade of the takeover of the island by Britain. With the removal of the Dutch, their religious restrictions on Buddhism also vanished. Consequently, under the first years of British rule, the number of Buddhist temples in the Sinhala districts increased significantly. According to records of the Church Missionary Society in Ceylon, within the first decade of British rule, the number of temples increased from between 200 and 300 to 1,200 (Balding 1922 p. 33). The Christian publication *Jubilee Memorials of the Wesleyan Mission South Ceylon 1814–1864*, published in 1864, also records that Buddhist opposition arose as Buddhist monks "were convinced that it was the intention of the missionaries to destroy Buddhism and place Christianity in its stead" (quoted in Guruge ed. 1965 p. xxx). One of the earliest signs of opposition was the publication as early as 1826 of parodies of Christian tracts (quoted in Guruge ed. 1965 p. xx).

Initially the monks were not interested in getting involved with debating Christians, considering, in their words, that "the British worshiped Christ and that the Sinhalese worshiped the Buddha." And that was the way, the Sinhalese Buddhists felt, that things should be. But after a series of provocations by the Christians, the worm finally turned. A series of direct debates between Buddhists and Christians now followed.

These debates with the Christians started as purely an internal Sri Lankan development, fed by outrage, as the Christians became more aggressive. A series of internal religious debates that had gone on earlier *among* the Buddhists themselves contributed to the combative mood. Before the debates with the Christians, Buddhists and monks were considered by the Christian missionaries as "vacant in countenance" and almost stupid. But in these debates Buddhists showed themselves to be alert, throwing out counter-questions to those posed by the Christians. The Buddhists initially rested their position on their own readings of the Bible. But as the controversies progressed, they got further ammunition from European writings themselves, such as those of the Free Thinkers. These European criticisms of Christianity were used to show that Christianity was under siege in its own homelands. In addition, the expressions of appreciation for Buddhism that were then beginning to appear in Europe were also mentioned (Malalgoda pp. 226–228). Reginald Copelston, the Bishop of Colombo, therefore complained at the time that "it is an error to suppose that Buddhism can be safely praised in England. All that comes out here and is made the most of" (quoted in Malalgoda p. 230).

An assertive Renaissance thrust is also seen in the caliber of the monastic scholars whose work preceded Olcott's arrival in the country. Letters written by many of the leading translators and writers of books on South Asia and Buddhism, such as Childers, Fausboell, Rhys Davids, Oldenberg, Rost, Muller, Minayeff, Hardy, Warren, Geiger, Lanman, Sir Edwin Arnold, and Paul Carus, brought together in a volume by Guruge, indicate the extent to which these writers were dependent for their work on these Sinhalese monks and their intellectual heritage (Guruge ed. 1984 pp. xiv, cxlii). Summarizing the nature of this debt, the great Danish Pali scholar Viggo Fausboell said in a letter:

> We, Europeans, must, of course, stand in need of such help as we are so far from the living fountains of Buddhism and so scantily furnished with materials. (Quoted in Guruge ed. 1984 p. xv)

The *selected* correspondence with these monks in Guruge's book comes to more than 450 pages, indicating the richness of this East-West exchange of scholarly views (Guruge ed. 1984 pp. xiv–xviii).

These monks displayed several of the characteristics of Renaissance men. Thus, Ven. Subhuti was, in the 1890s, one of the earliest in Sri Lanka to possess and use an electric torch, a wristwatch, an electric bell, and a phonograph. He also collected exotic plants, for example, from Denmark. He was interested in deciphering the Asokan Brahmi script. He located on a modern map of Asia for Childers, the author of a Pali dictionary, defunct ancient states such as Aparanta and Mahimsaka. His intellectual contacts covered the globe and ranged from Western Orientalists to Japanese and Thai royalty (Guruge ed. 1984 pp. 208–212). Subhuti had students from Burma, Cambodia, Thailand, and China. He was also fully immersed in the religious controversies of his time, offering his extensive knowledge of Buddhism to those who debated with the Christians (Guruge ed. 1984 pp. xxv–xxxviii, 13, 18, 126).

These monks subscribed to a very broad definition of learning. This included the study of the language and literature of Pali, Sanskrit, Sinhala, and Prakrit. The monks also studied *ayurveda,* the South Asian system of medicine, and other subjects such as architecture, statuary, and astrology—the last also implicitly including some aspects of astronomy. An important facet of their studies was the use of the comparative method. As accomplished scholars, they could compare—in literature, grammar, religion, philosophy, and history—theory with theory, text with text, and commentary with commentary. Many of the Western scholars who came into contact with them were amazed by their intellectual curiosity. As Guruge comments, where the Western scholars "expected religious conservatism and narrow mindedness, they were confronted with an amazing width of vision and an unbelievably refreshing liberality" (Guruge ed. 1984 pp. clxv–clxvii).

The monks also kept abreast of the progress of Western-based oriental studies, having books from Europe and America sent to them, including books on other Asian countries. They also helped European scholars establish contacts with scholars of other Asian countries, including, for example, Siam. They revised and corrected translations made by the Europeans, pointing out, where necessary, the translators' errors (Guruge ed. 1984 pp. 53, 57, 71, 67, 81). Polwatte Buddhadatta listed forty such scholar-monks, adding that there were more that he did not mention. So the intellectual base of the Buddhist Renaissance was large and predated the alleged "Protestant" influences (Guruge ed. 1984 p. lvii).

Other events show that the impulse for reform was largely internal.

Thus in 1864, a proposal was made for the establishment of a college of Buddhist studies to teach subjects such as Pali, Sinhalese, Sanskrit, and Buddhism together with other subjects such as history, logic, and medicine. Ten years later, in 1873, the college was established as the Vidyodaya Oriental College (Malalgoda 1976 pp. 239–240).

It was by reading a description of Migettuwatte's debates with the Christians that Olcott was sensitized to Sinhalese Buddhism. But Migettuwatte, although not a scholar-monk, was not uninformed of Western thought. He had referred to Isaac Newton in his debates (Abhayasundara 1990 p. 153). But this was not unusual. As Copper, the English editor of the debates, noted, "Some of the Buddhist priests are thoroughly versed in the works of modern scientists" (in Abhayasundara 1990 p. 155).

The Renaissance mood driven by the local cultural logic is seen in the initial relationship with our authors' "Protestants." When the journal of the Theosophists was established in 1879, Olcott invited Mohottivatte and Hikkaduwe to contribute to it. So Sinhalese in fact had begun reaching out to the world, using Olcott as a channel, before he reached Sri Lanka; this is the reverse of Theosophist influence on Buddhism (Malalgoda 1976 pp. 230, 242).

Olcott's correspondence from New York with Ven Piyaratana Tissa is very revealing about the power relationship that he established before he went to Sri Lanka. The relationship was that of student to guru, not of Protestant missionary to missionized. Olcott wrote,

> I pass among ignorant Western people as a thoroughly well informed man but in comparison with the learning possessed by my Brothers in the oriental priesthoods, I am as ignorant as the last of their neophytes. . . . To you and as you must we turn, and say: Fathers, brothers, the Western world is dying . . . come and help, rescue it. Come as missionaries, as teachers, as disputants, preachers. . . . Persuade a good, pure, learned, eloquent Buddhist to come here and preach, you will sweep the country before you. (Quoted in Guruge ed. 1984 pp. 338, 339)

Ven Piyaratana Tissa, to whom Olcott addressed this correspondence, had started the first modern Buddhist school—as distinct from temple schools—in 1869 in Dodanduwa (Guruge ed. 1984 p. 337). This predated by several decades the local schools that Olcott helped launch, and is to be seen as a direct precursor to these later ones. The Olcott-inspired schools were, therefore, but a continuation of local efforts.

Blavatsky and Olcott, one should also remember, saw the Theosophists as committed to spiritualism, a far cry from getting rid of superstition, the role that Obeyesekere assigns to them (Prothero 1996 p. 51). The influence of South Asian ideas on the Theosophists thus preceded their arrival in South Asia. The Theosophist Blavatsky's magnum opus, *Isis Unveiled* (1877), claimed to trace all modern Western knowledge to ancient Eastern sources (cited in Prothero 1996 p. 58). Instead of Buddhists changing their core values, it was, therefore, the Theosophists who changed theirs to fit in with what they assumed were South Asian values, even before they came to Sri Lanka. In their correspondence with South Asians while still in America, they discarded their earlier emphasis on spiritualism in favor of discrediting Christianity and promoting Asian religions in the West. Olcott's correspondence with Buddhist reformers in the East reveals this twin strategy of anti-Christian propaganda in the East and pro-Asian propaganda in the West. But the locals were very selective in their approach to Olcott. When Olcott wrote to Hikkaduve Sumangala that he planned to publish a series of English translations of Buddhist *Sutras*, the latter dissuaded him, saying that it was "a matter next to impossibility" to make a translation into English without losing the *Sutras'* "energy, sweetness and propriety" (Rev. Piyaratana Tissa Terunnanse to Olcott, in Guruge ed. 1984 pp. 339, 343).

When Olcott did arrive in Sri Lanka in 1880 and formally became a Buddhist, he had already been assigned a role by the locals, a role that he played. What the Sinhalese wanted was "support, sympathy and guidance" in their contest with the Christians. Olcott's assigned role was that of champion of the faith (Malalgoda 1976 p. 242). The general policy that Olcott now articulated, as Malalgoda points out, was but a continuation of what the locals had done through millennia (Malalgoda 1976 p. 245).

Olcott now said to the Sinhalese that the Buddhists should look at their greatest enemy, Christianity, which spent vast quantities of money to destroy Buddhism. He suggested forming societies similar to those of the Christians, to counteract them. Olcott suggested mobilizing the whole nation in the defense of Buddhism. But to the locals, this was a process that had been repeated several times over millennia in the country's history.

Olcott was taken into the local fold only after he became a Buddhist, and so a co-fighter for Buddhist causes. Olcott's intervention in Sri Lanka was allowed only within the limits set by the locals. Thus the Buddhist catechism written by Olcott was issued only after approval by a monk, a difficult, long-drawn-out process, as detailed by Olcott himself (see Guruge ed. 1984 pp. cxl, 350).

Olcott's freedom to interpret Buddhism had been frustrated on a number of other occasions by local monks and lay persons who stuck to their views. In 1885 some Buddhists wanted Olcott's *Buddhist Catechism* burned (Prothero 1996 p. 158). Olcott was carrying the weight of over two millennia of Buddhist text and practice in the country (Prothero 1996 p. 121). Malalgoda emphasizes that Theosophy itself developed in Sri Lanka "not so much as a new indigenous movement [but] as a *further stage of an older indigenous movement*" (1976 p. 246, emphasis mine). The Buddhist Theosophical Society (BTS) that Olcott founded had, in spite of its name, little to do with Theosophy. It was a Buddhist society plain and simple, used by the locals for their own Buddhist ends. A society more in keeping with the Theosophy of its founders, called the Lanka Theosophical Society, was ignored by the locals and was stillborn (Malalgoda 1976 pp. 246–247). The BTS continued the work done earlier by other Buddhist organizations but in an intensified form (Malalgoda 1976 pp. 247–255). Its key members were drawn from among people who had earlier been active in the Buddhist movement as leaders. But all the local Buddhists held very skeptical views on Theosophy as a belief system.

According to Olcott, only one monk in the whole of Sri Lanka believed in the existence of Mahatmas—one of the key tenets of Theosophy. Valigama Sumangala, a close associate of Olcott, categorically denied their existence. Olcott's other two key associates, Mohottivatte Gunananda (reading whose debates first led Olcott to come to Sri Lanka) and Anagarika Dharmapala (who was Olcott's most illustrious local associate), both became outspoken critics of Theosophy. Gunananda became the first Buddhist reformer to publicly censure Olcott, an attack which Olcott was to consider "a venomous attack on the Colombo Buddhist Theosophical Society and myself" (quoted in Prothero 1996 p. 123).

Dharmapala, dissatisfied with the intellectual content of Theosophy, wanted to remove the appellation "Theosophy" from the BTS. Hikkaduwe Sumangala wanted to resign from the Society. Olcott himself put it succinctly when he said, "Although Branches [of the BTS] which we organized in 1880 are still active . . . it is altogether within the lines of Buddhism. . . . When they [the Sinhalese] speak of themselves as Branches of our Society, it is always with this reservation" (quoted in Malalgoda 1976 p. 254).

The standard Eurocentric view in the 19th century, echoed by our authors now, was that until it was ignited by external stimuli from Olcott and others, there was no local Buddhist revival. Bishop Coppelston had dubbed the revival "external and artificial." But as Malalgoda states, "this was hardly an accurate description of events." It is precisely because Buddhists had been so active earlier that the Theosophists were so easily absorbed into the local movement (although Theosophy itself was not so absorbed). Olcott himself was to say that his group's impact was prepared by these prior activities (Malalgoda 1976 p. 256).

The inherent ideological tension between Buddhism and Theosophy was reflected in tensions between Dharmapala and Olcott, especially as the former worked hard to introduce Buddhism to India (Prothero 1996 p. 158). Soon a power struggle emerged between the two, which resulted in Olcott's resigning from the Maha Bodhi Society. Dharmapala then began making suggestions to Olcott that he should do more for Buddhism, including resigning from Theosophical activities and devoting all his time to Buddhism. And Dharmapala moved in 1898 to change the name of the Colombo Buddhist Theosophical Society to the Colombo Buddhist Society (Prothero 1996 pp. 159–172).

Soon the final breaks were to come. Dharmapala resigned, saying, "as a Buddhist, I sever my connection with the Pantheistic Theosophical Society." And Sumangala objected to seventeen instances of deviation from Buddhist views in the latest edition of Olcott's catechism. "Such an uncalled for attack on Buddhism," declared Sumangala as he resigned from the Theosophical Society, "we could expect only from an enemy of our religion" (quoted in Prothero 1996 p. 167). Worried that he would lose his contacts in the country, Olcott negotiated with Sumangala for a new edition of the catechism from which the offending elements were removed. But if Sumangala was reconciled with Olcott, Dharmapala was not to be mollified. "Although he [Olcott] became a Buddhist he does not seem to have grasped the fundamentals of Buddhism," Dharmapala declared (quoted in Prothero 1996 p. 172).

To summarize the Sinhalese experience with the Theosophist "Protestants" rather bluntly, the Sinhalese in their own Buddhist trajectory made use of these human tools in the Theosophical movement, found them both tactically useful and intellectually wanting, and were now charting their way on their own.

The outcome of the relationship with the Theosophists illustrates the real nature of the local revival, as one not of imitation but of filtration of what was essential as defined by locals. The examples given of alleged "Protestantism" are of an opportunistic use by locals of means, from whatever quarter they came. Earlier, these "tools" had come from India, Siam, and Burma. And these countries continued to provide "tools" and arenas of Buddhist discourse during this period too. In addition, "tools" for the 19th-century Renaissance came from Japan (Malalgoda 1976 p. 260).

Gombrich and Obeyesekere mention that only a few texts on Buddhism were available in Sinhala, the majority being in Pali. They therefore say that Protestant Buddhism was "a Protestantism without a Bible" (1988 p. 208) and find fault with the use of English translations. In the early period, a significant proportion of the literati knew Pali, whose place has now been taken, in part, by English; hence the importance of English translations from Pali.

When an ex-Catholic forms the All Ceylon Buddhist Congress, the authors see it as imitating Christian organizations such as the Young Men's Buddhist Association (GombObey 1988 p. 234). But these are superficial similarities. The Buddhist Theosophical Society, the major organization for agitation which was formed after the original American society, apart from a similar-sounding name, had a very different agenda and manner of functioning.

The authors claim that the *dayaka sabha*, the so-called donors' committees in the temples, were invigorated by the spread of Protestant ethics and the embourgeoisement of Sinhala society. But formal organizations had often sprung up to defend Buddhism, unconnected with Protestantism and the Theosophists, in Sri Lanka and in other Theravada countries. Thus, in Cambodia, there are also such formal temple bodies (pagoda committees) with a strong historical lineage. When almost all other institutions broke down in the aftermath of Pol Pot's rule, these lay groups performed a crucial part in rebuilding Cambodian village society (Collins 1998).

As other examples of presumed emulation of Christian practices, Gombrich and Obeyesekere mention the use of Christmas carol–type songs at Vesak, the use of greeting cards at Vesak, and the emulation of Christian schools by Buddhist schools (1988 p. 205). This again need not be considered emulation of Christianity in order to counter it, but can be explained much more parsimoniously by considering the acceptance of external innovations when demanded by the internal situation of the culture itself. Similar opportunistic acquisitions include the whole paraphernalia of Western science and technology.

DHARMAPALA:
RENAISSANCE FIGURE OR IMITATOR?

If the whole movement toward Buddhist revival was not an imitative act but one in keeping with past practice in Sinhalese history, then so was its leading exponent, Anagarika Dharmapala, hardly an imitative Protestant. We have already described his relationship with Olcott, the alleged harbinger of "Protestantism," and how Dharmapala (together with others) essentially went his own way. It is now necessary to sketch some other aspects of Dharmapala's character.

Dharmapala's reading and interests were very wide. No intellectual lightweight, he was well-read in the philosophical, scientific, and scholarly literature of both East and West. He was familiar with the history and the different thought systems of South Asia, the Arab countries, and the classical Greek tradition, as well as post-Renaissance Western philosophy. He knowledgeably discussed Western classical writers, such as Antiochus, Antiogonus, Aristotle, Democritus, Diogenes, Plato, Ptolemy, Pythagoras, and Socrates. He also spoke with facility on scientific figures such as Galileo, Einstein, Darwin, and Huxley, as well as on philosophers such as Machiavelli, Berkeley, Hume, Kant, Nietzsche, William James, Herbert Spencer, Spinoza, Schopenhauer, and Mill. He was especially enamored of Darwin, referring to him no fewer than fifteen times in his published writings (Guruge ed. 1965 pp. 19, 23, 102, 106, 107, 242, 299, 324, 325, 327, 405, 434, 435, 438, 653). His own philosophical position is seen in his view of Buddhism, which he said had no place for "metaphysics, logic, dialectics, loathsome ascetic habits, magic, bacchanalian revelry, priestly formulas, destructive rituals etc" (Guruge ed. 1965 p. 549).

His international friends and deepest beliefs were in keeping with this broad enlightened thrust. Among Dharmapala's friends was Sir Edwin Arnold, the author of *The Light of Asia,* who considered Dharmapala "my excellent friend." Among the Indian national leaders who befriended him were Sarat Chandra Das, Rajendra Prasad (who later became India's president), Rabindranath Tagore, and Mahatma Gandhi (Guruge ed. 1965 p. xlviii).

Dharmapala bemoaned the prevailing defeatist situation in India (Guruge ed. 1965 p. 399). He did not take only from the "Protestant" West. He took from wherever he saw fit. Thus, from Japan he took the use of lanterns in celebrating Vesak. He took from India the need to expand cottage industries. When it suited him, he quoted from British newspapers in his struggles.

He wanted the youth of the country to be educated broadly "to study politics, philosophy, history and industrial economics and to go to the root cause of our national decay" (quoted in Guruge ed. 1965 p. 517). He was critical of the existing education system that produced clerks in the country and wanted them "to migrate to Madras, Calcutta, Benares, Bombay, Lahore, Aligarh or Rangoon" for purposes of study, saying that in Ceylon one gets only a "bastard education" (quoted in Guruge ed. 1965 pp. 517–518).

For religious purposes, Dharmapala visited various places of religious interest overseas. But equally important, he visited other sites very much in tune with the industrial age. He toured the United States, visiting several industrial schools, and started an industrial school fund in San Francisco. He visited other industrial schools in London, Liverpool, Holland, Denmark, and Italy. Indicating his Asia-centric perspective, he started his first industrial school not in Sri Lanka but at Saranath, Benares, India (Guruge ed. 1965 p. xxxix).

To Dharmapala the models of development were America and Japan. He was a persistent and vociferous supporter of scientific and technological education (Guruge ed. 1965 p. lxxxii). He was critical of the lack of knowledge among locals. He attacked as drones those who went to England for pleasure without learning anything there (Guruge ed. 1965 p. 511). He said that "there is something about an alien rule, no matter how beneficial that stupefies" (Guruge ed. 1965 p. 694).

While Dharmapala was intensely hostile to British domination, he, like nationalists elsewhere, also criticized those performing the intermediary roles created by the colonial process. Dharmapala's criticism of the social role of Indian Borah merchants, Muslims, and Tamils as economic exploiters of the Sinhalese falls into this category of criticism of intermediaries. In comparative international perspective, these sentiments were not unusual during the colonial era. They were equivalent to similar nationalist criticism of Indian merchants by Burmese nationalists (the merchants were expelled after Burmese independence), criticism of the comprador bourgeoisie by the Chinese communists (the compradors were denounced as allies of British imperialists), criticism of Indian merchants by East African nationalists (the merchants were criticized for the reasons also mentioned by Dharmapala), or criticism of Chinese merchants by Indonesians (again for their intermediary role, exploiting the Indonesian peasantry). Thus, Dharmapala's criticism of intermediary groups was not a racial cry. In fact, in India he collaborated closely with Tamils.

As intellectual sources for Dharmapala, Gombrich and Obeyesekere mention the life of a renouncer, Bodhisat Sumedho, the poem *The Light of Asia,* and the work of Blavatsky (1988 p. 217). The use of these sources indicates Dharmapala's instrumental approach in dealing with his own concerns, choosing elements that could best help develop his own cultural world. Thus, although helped by Blavatsky, he opposed intensely the non-Buddhist aspects of Theosophy. But this actual selective Renaissance approach contrasts with the role assigned to Dharmapala by the authors, the role of imitation of Protestantism and Theosophy, a basic contradiction, because Theosophy in America went against Protestantism (GombObey 1988 p. 217).

Dharmapala's popular pamphlet, "The Daily Code for the Laity," giving 200 rules, should also not be seen as a Protestant import, as Gombrich and Obeyesekere imply (GombObey 1988 p. 214). These rules of Dharmapala did not appear out of the blue. There are similar detailed rules of conduct for monks on what to wear, how to talk, how to eat, how to chew food, and how to behave in public. These are the aspects that were formally transferred by Dharmapala to his book. There was always a horizontal percolation to the laity of these mundane rules for the monks, who lived among the people in a much more intimate relationship than did Christian priests. A good description of such percolation from the monastic realm to the lay realm is found in the emerging literature on the growth of Thai law from monks' law (Huxley 1996). The "Daily Code" of Dharmapala is therefore to be seen only as a formalization of such transfer processes. One can see very graphically this percolation of good Buddhist lay behavior even today in the everyday behavior of village Laotians, Thais, or Cambodians, all Theravadin Buddhists.

The authors' Eurocentric view again over-interprets Dharmapala's castigating of drunkenness among the Sinhalese, not as an important truth to be recognized by any reformer but as the expression of a "man full of painful ambivalences" (GombObey 1988 p. 213). The reformer, by the very nature of his mission, by definition has to be ambivalent toward those whom he is trying to reform—praising their good points while denigrating their negative aspects.

THE "CARRIERS" OF PROTESTANTISM

Blavatsky and Olcott, who allegedly brought Protestant rationalism to Sri Lanka, were themselves strong believers in the irrational and the mystical.

Blavatsky's biographers portray her as a true believer in the occult. A biography by Sylvia Cranston (1993), whose four earlier books had been on reincarnation, indicating her own New Age beliefs, documents this amply. Olcott likewise covered the spiritual and the occult beat, sometimes literally for New York newspapers (Cranston 1993 p. 124).

Blavatsky claimed to have obtained her occult knowledge from what she said were the Mahatmas, her Masters. Paul Johnson has written a book trying to elucidate the real sources of Blavatsky's Mahatmas (Johnson 1994). The central theme of Johnson's book, based largely on material from the Indian archives, is that the Masters of Blavatsky were not just a sheer invention of her imagination. They were based on a large group of men, and, on occasion, women, who helped Blavatsky throughout her life, collaborating with her and encouraging her. They included the founder of the Arya Samaj, Swami Dayananda Saraswati, Moorya, a leading member of the Punjab reform organization, and the then Maharaja of Kashmir. The Mahatmas' letters to Blavatsky were full of details about the Punjab and Kashmir (Johnson 1994 pp. 5–8). One such "Mahatma" included in Johnson's book is the Sinhalese scholar monk Sumangala. Blavatsky and Olcott had corresponded admiringly with the monk. Even before their arrival in Sri Lanka, he was made a member of the Theosophical Society's General Council and an honorary vice-president of the Theosophical Society. Olcott's later activities to encourage a worldwide Buddhist revival were planned in close collaboration with this monk and his colleagues (Johnson 1994 pp. 189–190).

The interaction of Theosophical thought with South Asia, it now appears from such recent work, perhaps subverted the West more than the West subverted South Asia's core beliefs. The authority of established churches, as Peter Washington, a recent biographer of Madame Blavatsky, points out, had already begun eroding in the 18th century and accelerated in the 19th century. Today this erosion has gone further, with a strong upsurge in Buddhist and Hindu beliefs among Western alternative groups and New Age followers. Some of these later changes are due to the reverberatory effects of Madame Blavatsky's heritage in the United States (Washington 1993 pp. 1–3), as well as to international Buddhism. In a Gallup poll taken in 1969, 20 percent of the U.S. population said that they believed in reincarnation. This percentage has since risen in the U.S., indicating the flow of South Asian ideas into the West since the time of the Theosophists (Cranston 1993 p. 504). Blavatsky's posthumous influence on the U.S. as a cultural conduit has been such that she has been called the mother of the New Age—the result of the post-1960s cultural revolution in America and the rest of the West (Cranston 1993 p. 524).

The leading Sri Lankan associate of the Theosophists, Dharmapala, was a delegate to the Parliament of World's Religions, which was planned as a celebration of Western civilization and its religions. Anagarika Dharmapala would attempt to turn it upside down. In his concluding speech at the opening ceremonies, he declared that the "Parliament was simply the reecho of a great consummation which the Indian Buddhists accomplished 24 centuries ago," meaning the Council of Asoka, the great Buddhist emperor of India (Fields 1992 p. 120).

A few days after the Parliament ended, Charles T. Strauss, a young businessman who was a student of comparative religion and philosophy from New York, pronounced the five Buddhist precepts at the end of a lecture by Anagarika Dharmapala. Strauss was evidently the first person to be admitted formally to the Buddhist faith on American soil (Fields 1992 p. 129). Reflecting the mood of the time, *The New York Journal* wrote: "It is no uncommon thing to hear a New Yorker say he is a Buddhist nowadays" (quoted in Fields 1992 p. 131).

Another significant event in the reverse flow of influence was the coming together of Soyen Shaku, a Zen monk (who had led a strict life for three years in Sri Lanka), and Dharmapala with the German émigré Dr. Paul Carus, the editor of the influential *Monist* and *Open Court*. All three shared the view that Buddhism "was more fitted than Christianity to heal the breach that had opened between science and religion, since it did not depend on miracles and faith" (Fields 1992 p. 128). Dharmapala returned to America in 1896 at the invitation of Paul Carus and lectured across America enthusing audiences all the way.

Close examination reveals that the effect of international Buddhism, and thus indirectly of Dharmapala and the Sinhalese Buddhist Renaissance, now reaches all the way back to the United States. Buddhism in America today has found many homes and many voices (Fields 1992). Several writers have drawn attention to its effect on American culture, including, for example, the effect on recent American poetry (Tonkinson 1995). The reform and protest movements associated with the 1950s Beat Generation and the 1960s counterculture included several threads that owed a debt to Buddhism. This international flow of Buddhist ideas (Inada and Jacobson eds. 1984) has had many effects, including material taught in medical and psychology faculties on the authors' own campuses. (I have given a summary of how some of these Buddhist influences have indirectly come into philosophy, psychology, and medicine in the U.S. in Chapter 2.) One could also say that the existence of the authors' own jobs is ultimately due to the creation of a climate conducive to Buddhist studies because of this inflow of Buddhism into the West, making it a legitimate area of interest and inquiry.

The fact that the Buddhist and Eastern enterprise has gone global, warts and all, including some of its more cultish aspects, is attested by many instances from Gombrich and Obeyesekere's book itself. The "leaders" whom the authors have studied are not those of the isolated anthropological village. One had studied Indian approaches to the occult in India for four years, then fought with the British army in Egypt and Italy in World War II (1988 p. 412). Another asserts the existence of two forms of occult science, one "Indian" and the other "Californian" (p. 413). By "Californian," the leader probably meant New Age, a cultural system deeply influenced by Buddhism. The New Age in turn now turns back and strikes Sri Lanka. Jayasuriya has, as a devotee, a graduate student in chemical engineering at a British university who contacts one of the authors in Britain (p. 356). The changing Protestant Sinhalese Buddhists seem to be everywhere, even in those disciplinary fields in the West which have more claims to science and rationality than anthropology does.

CONCLUSIONS

It was through Theosophical contacts in London that both Gandhi and Nehru became interested in India's own heritage (Cranston 1993 pp. 193–196). Gandhi told his biographer, Louis Fischer, that the "top Congressmen were Theosophists" (Fischer 1950 p. 437). But no one has suggested that the Indian independence movement and protest against British rule was due to a transfer of Protestant ideas through the Theosophists.

Obeyesekere had at an earlier stage used the concept of "Little Tradition" and "Great Tradition" to describe Sinhalese Buddhism (1963). This was another Eurocentric concept, which came into being after the previous hunting-grounds of anthropologists, such as the African region, were getting their independence, and other cultural entities, especially in Asia, were being recognized by anthropologists as civilizations. Gombrich and Obeyesekere now substitute another spurious "concept," namely, "Protestant Buddhism."

They put together two similar-sounding, conceptually unrelated words, "protest" and "Protestantism," and attempt to build their theory of Protestant Buddhism. It is like taking two other similar-sounding words, "deer" and "dear," and attempting to build a theory. Gombrich in his first book evoked the philosopher Popper's view of natural science theory, science as conjecture and refutation. In the case of "Protestant Buddhism," the empirical data, as well as the inherent contradiction within the term, calls for a complete refutation of this spurious "theory." No respectable natural scientist would even consider such a theory, let alone explore it.

Furthermore, Protestant Buddhism has denied locals their choice and converted them into imitative puppets, consigning them to the category of non-creativity to which colonial discourse had earlier relegated them.

CHAPTER 5

■

Protestant Buddhism "Transformed"

The alleged Protestant Buddhism that Gombrich and Obeyesekere described is, according to them, becoming "transformed" into a post-Protestant phase. The transformation is seen in class-based values. Let us first begin with the authors' class descriptions.

THE TRANSFORMATION OF THE *HAUTE BOURGEOISIE* AND OTHER CLASSES

The authors label the Sri Lankan Anglophone middle classes a high bourgeoisie, and from this description they partly derive the rest of their thesis (GombObey 1988 p. 208). Their label is far from the truth. This was a class closely tied economically and culturally to the colonial presence. Instead of being a "high" bourgeoisie, it was a dependent, imitative one, which was hostile to Buddhism and the local culture. The nature of this Anglophone South Asian class is illustrated by the well-known wish of McAuley, that "a class of persons, Indian in blood and color, but English in taste, in opinions, in morals, and in intellect" should be created (Edwardes 1967 p. 125). And for Sri Lanka, this dependent class is described by a British commentator, writing in 1843, as being "partial" to most things British (Bennet 1843 p. 48).

Consequently, the immediate inheritors of Sri Lankan independence in 1948 were themselves closely allied with, or were creations and benefactors of, the colonial presence. They, unlike their counterparts in neighboring India, had not seriously challenged the British, and they maintained after independence a continuity of perception with the colonialists (Singer 1964; Weerawardena 1960). As the American sociologist Marshall Singer noted in 1964, it is forgivable for a member of this elite "not to know who followed Rajasingha I to the Lion Throne of Lanka but it is down-right unthinkable for him not to know who signed the Magna Carta" (1964 p. 47).

Internal changes directly challenging this colonially derived elite arose from forces inspired by, among others, Dharmapala, and resulted in victory for these forces in the election of 1956. On every occasion in the election campaign of 1956, it was proclaimed that an English-educated dependent upper class ruled the country, leaving "the Sinhala educated as hewers of wood and drawers of water" (Weerawardena 1960 p.109). It was also argued that Christian missions had used their control over the education system to help build an imitative Westernized society.

Gombrich and Obeyesekere say that in the (post-1956) period they study, the values of the different classes changed. They claim that Buddhism changed in the hands of the new middle class, while "the spirit religion changed its character in the hands of the urban poor" (1988 p. 9). The authors assert that Sinhala Buddhist society today is therefore a disoriented post-Protestant society having a new religious culture.

The authors also say that Protestantism, Orientalism, and Theosophy influenced the Buddhism of the bourgeoisie, while *Bhakti* influenced the spirit cults among the poor (GombObey 1988 p. 11). The first part of the statement contradicts itself, especially when one takes the authors' contention that Theosophy was a channel for the introduction of Protestantism and rational ideas into Buddhism. Theosophy, an emotional and irrational orientation that embraced the occult, was vehemently opposed to the prevailing Protestantism in the U.S. As for the popularity of spirit cults among the poor, it could well be due to very instrumental economic factors, the lower classes being unable to afford a Western doctor to perform these rites, a theme to which we will return in greater detail in our study of Kapferer.

DANCING: RELIGIOUS AND WESTERN

Significant pointers to the changes that the authors claim have taken place are changes in the religious dances at Kataragama. But the "ecstatic dancing" which the authors refer to as emerging in religious dancing also exists in Western dancing. There are far more Western dancers in Sri Lanka, including *baila* dancers, than dancers at Kataragama. The authors, in fact, admit that the dance performed at Kataragama is quite often the *baila*, which has ecstatic features, but again they ignore commonsensical explanations in favor of their brand of exoticism (GombObey 1988 p. 193).

The period covered by the authors saw the spread of this "trance"-type *baila*. The *baila*, derived from the Portuguese, was earlier considered vulgar and was limited to a small section of the urban environment (largely the environs of Moratuwa town). A key official at Kataragama, the chief fire walker, objects to the lack of self-control and the emotional display in contemporary fire walking and dancing (GombObey 1988 p. 413). But through cassettes and urbanization, the *baila* has now spread widely. It is common today at many celebratory occasions, such as cricket matches and school and university outings—even in very rural areas.

Today's *baila* genre has also incorporated elements from traditional music, especially from music used at Kataragama, *kavadi* dancing, and local drumbeats. This is because *kavadi* and local drums have a fast beat and are amenable to dancing. *Kavadi*-derived tunes have also entered upper-class Westernized ballroom-type dancing, for example in Colombo hotels. Participants at these dances will look with humor at the statement immediately following Obeyesekere's comments on a middle-class ma-tron's reluctant buttocks swaying to the *baila*-type music of *kavadi* dance: "the erotic aspect of the main festival is then clear: the god is the lover, but his love life is with his mistress and not with his wife" (GombObey 1988 p. 194). One wonders who the lover is when such a matron dances to the same tune in a Colombo hotel.

Gombrich and Obeyesekere also say that this type of dancing at Kata-ragama is derived from *Tantra*. But hardly anybody in Sri Lanka has been exposed recently to the *Tantra* tradition. The emergence of *kavadi* dance with an erotic *baila* content is attributed by these two authors to the rise of sexual frustration among youth, who now postpone marriage (1988 p 199). But the same assumed sexual drives must then be pushing the spread of similar dancing in the Sri Lankan secular world.

ALCOHOL, VEGETARIANISM, AND SMOKING: EAST AND WEST

Another encroachment of Protestant Buddhism, the authors find, is the admonition against taking alcohol and the statement by a university lec-turer, Kodikarnaracci, that meat eating and smoking are not good for the breath (GombObey 1988 p. 236). Further, the authors' Protestant Bud-dhists wear white clothes for everyday work, and they "even" become vegetarians, or at least give up beef and take alcohol "only as medicine" (p. 233).

Wearing white is the norm for average Sinhalese, as it was for most South Asians, and has little to do with alleged Protestant Buddhism. Both the taking of alcohol and the taking of life are against basic Buddhist tenets and were rare in precolonial times. The spread of alcohol and meat eating is only a post–World War II phenomenon, and subscribing to vegetarianism and taking alcohol "only for medicine" are a part of the traditional culture, not of Protestant Buddhism. Meanwhile in middle-class Western abodes of the 1990s, it is normal, sometimes even socially required, to be vegetarian, to avoid beef and pork, and to consume alcohol only for the medicinal purpose of having one drink per day to avoid heart disease. Meditation, which Gombrich and Obeyesekere found incomprehensible as a part of the Sri Lankan school curriculum (1988 p. 236), has become so routinized in the U.S. that millions now practice this art.

THE JOLLY VICAR MONK

The authors mention that by allegedly officiating at the wedding of a Sinhalese girl and a Danish artist, the monk Mapalagama Vipulasara was creating a tradition, illustrative of Protestant Buddhism transforming itself (GombObey 1988 p. 449). One of the non-conformist activities the authors describe in Vipulasara is the growing of a beard. They mention that Vipulasara also moves quickly and energetically, imitating Mohottivatte Gunananda, who debated with Christians. And as the ultimate extension of these Christian values they mention that Vipulasara's appearance is close to the stereotype of a "jolly vicar" of the Church of England (p. 266). But these "observations" misread reality.

The question, based as it is on a loose organization, is how strongly "stereotypical" the Sangha has been through the ages. Many of the monks' disciplinary rules were created when particular acts came to be realized as undesirable, a matter of contingency regulating behavior, not applying a priori rules that would be self-evident from the core teaching. Especially in situations when monks are not under tight Vinaya control, they have been seen even in ancient times to go into aberrant behavior. Thus, before the 18th-century reforms, the then monks, *ganinnanses*, would have not been entirely clean shaven. They also had families (Malalgoda 1976 pp. 54, 57–59, 65). Such aberrations exist even now in remote areas. Thus, a well-known monk, Dimulagala Hamuduruwo, grew a beard. Incidentally, this monk was in the forefront in providing support for his flock, which was subject to ethnic cleansing by Tamil terrorists, until he himself was gunned down by the Tigers.

Gombrich and Obeyesekere say that Vipulasara had "claims to be a sculptor," which led to his patronage of the Danish artist who wanted a wedding ceremony (1988 p. 66). Now, in fact, Vipulasara not only has claims but is a well-known sculptor of Buddha statues, just as some of his ancient predecessors were. His works are found in key temples in several countries of the world.

But the incident that the authors "report" is seen in a different light when one asks the monk himself about it. In the authors' frenzy to ascribe everything Sri Lankan to a foreign source, they said Vipulasara was like an English vicar. When I visited him in 1997, Vipulasara had that same jolly, pleasant look, which, incidentally, he shares with many other monks. His room was cluttered with papers and documents. In the cupboards around his room were literally hundreds of items of Buddhist memorabilia given to him by dignitaries from all over the Buddhist world. On his table were a fax machine and four phones—one an international phone. In the adjoining room was the latest model computer. During the time I was in the room there was a steady stream of visitors, laity, and monks. The international phone rang and the fax machine whirred continuously. In the case of Ven. Vipulasara, his dealings were with people not only in the immediate Ratmalana town but also in the global village. For he and the other monks depicted in *Buddhism Transformed* are not English friars, nor, by any means, country yokels. They are today global players.

Ven. Vipulasara's story of the events leading to the wedding of the Danish artist is very revealing. The Dane, who had come to learn of the local culture from the monk, had met a Sinhalese girl and wanted to marry her. The monk advised him of the local customs. The venue agreed upon was a public hall on the temple premises, which the monk allowed to be used for lay purposes. The ceremony was conducted in the normal manner, with a lay person, not the monk, officiating. Thereafter, the couple went to the temple, which was nearby, to pay their respects to the monk, who chanted *Pirit*, the formal chant performed for anybody who comes for a blessing. This was the flow of events as it actually occurred, not the fictitious description given by the authors. The monk had *not* officiated at the wedding, as alleged in the book.

This wedding practice that Ven. Vipulasara allegedly engaged in, Gombrich and Obeyesekere say, finds reinforcement in the case of Sinhala Buddhist monks residing abroad. The followers of these monks in the West want a ritual in a Buddhist setting (GombObey 1988 p. 267). But these requests for alleged Buddhist weddings are not requests by Sinhalese, and are not, therefore, driven by Sinhala Buddhist values, whether Protestant or otherwise.

THE "TRANSFORMING" LEADERS

The different post-Protestant "leaders" presented by the authors form an important link in their arguments. Again, the "leaders" reveal a reality very different from the impression that the authors try to project.

One of their leaders, Mr. Perera, uses meditation in daily life. He says that it helps in leading the lay life efficiently. He also says that he can measure his progress by checking with the classic 5th-century manual the *Visuddhimagga*. The authors find this both strange and fundamentalist, with tendencies that "are more Protestant than any of the Protestant Buddhists [they] had encountered" (GombObey 1988 p. 317). But there are Western theories of managerial efficiency, derived from Maslow's theories of self-realization (McGregor 1957 pp. 23–30), which, as Maslow himself admitted, have parallels with Buddhism (Maslow 1968 p.114). And techniques derived from Buddhist meditation are used to increase sports efficiency. Western laboratories have checked for progress in meditation against the *Visuddhimagga,* as we noted in Chapter 2, and found that it correlates with different measurable states. The best-selling psychologist Daniel Goleman called the *Visuddhimagga* "A Map for Inner Space," using it as a title for one of his chapters (1988). But our authors see Protestant infiltration in this most central Buddhist practice, the act of meditation, whose central injunctions are not to speak emotionally from the heart. The authors, however, call meditation a "religion of the heart," which recalls the Protestant Christian appeal to the individual conscience (GombObey 1988 p. 320).

Another "leader," Mr. Jayasuriya, says that Siddhartha (the prince who later became the Buddha) removed mind from matter when the sun was high (GombObey 1988 p. 353). Such speculative explanations by isolated individuals are not rare, most notably, for example, in the U.S. But instead of viewing Mr. Jayasuriya's explanation in this light, the authors see the nonexistent influence of the Theosophists (p. 353).

Mr. Jayasuriya says he has experienced Enlightenment, using not only Buddhist techniques but also others, including the "power points," the seven *chakras* of the body. The authors label Jayasuriya's behavior as like that of a member of a Protestant sect. But Jayasuriya appears more as an imitator of the U.S. New Age. Books on the seven *chakras* can be found in many New Age–oriented bookshops in the West, but rarely in Sri Lanka. Indeed, our authors also refer to Jayasuriya's exposure to a New Age phenomenon, Transcendental Meditation, which he rejects. Further, Jayasuriya interacts with Western tourists, a probable channel for his New Age ideas.

Jayasuriya has a quick, direct approach to Enlightenment, and Gombrich and Obeyesekere claim that this is true of the modern world as well as sectarianism (1988 p. 377). Again the authors ignore the fact that the approach of Zen Buddhism is toward sudden Enlightenment. In the 1960s and 1970s, Zen was very popular among U.S. New Age groups. Again it is very possible that it was the New Age channel that influenced Jayasuriya.

The speculative Jayasuriya is also in touch with the writings of Lobsang Rampa, the author of *The Third Eye,* another New Age favorite. Jayasuriya's assistant is a Western-trained dental nurse. She receives a letter from a foreign monk stating that it would be best to burn all the books on Buddhism in his library—books written in twenty different languages—and that this would not make him sorry. Instead of just reading about *Nirvana,* he reasons, one should try to realize it. Gombrich and Obeyesekere claim that these views are in the Protestant tradition of "doing one's own thing" (1988 p. 356). The tension between books and the practice of searching for *Nirvana* is a very old one, the Sinhalese monastic order having split along these lines more than a millennium ago. This is not a Protestant or post-Protestant change.

The style of the authors is a not-so-subtle snigger at these three Buddhist "leaders" whom they have decided to study. In the U.S., Mr. Jayasuriya would not necessarily be discussed in the mocking way the authors talk about them. For example, when Jayasuriya claims that through his meditation he has reached Enlightenment, he may even be subjected to scientific examination, as we have seen in Chapter 2. Parts of the authors' present book was being written at a time when anthropology viewed even such experiences as drug-induced states taken as valid in their own "internal" right, as in the books by Carlos Castaneda on the exploits of the shaman Don Juan. The authors' framework is the West, but a selective West.

Further, some of the phenomena exhibited by the marginal Sri Lankan groups studied by the authors were gaining ground in the West at precisely the time this book was being written. Figures such as Maharishi Mahesh Yogi brought to the Western world a mixed bag of the scientifically provable (as attested in journals like *Scientific American* and *Science*) and the more spurious elements of their "philosophy." This general trend toward Easternization in some areas is seen in the 1990s writings of Deepak Chopra, the Western-trained Indian-born doctor practicing in the West. His books, which I do not consider scientific, have been on the non-fiction bestseller list for several months. Chopra's and the Maharishi's approaches match those of the "leaders" to some extent. Similar phenomena, however, have led to the transformation of a few alleged Protestant Buddhists in Sri Lanka, and of a much larger number of real Protestants in the United States.

Gombrich and Obeyesekere have also designated Uttama Sadhu as a Protestant (Buddhist) sect leader because he controls his order tightly, and his group includes formal admission, expulsion, and schism (1988 p. 371). But these qualities are not limited to Christian sects. The Buddhist monks' order always had formal entry criteria, expulsion procedures, and many, many schisms. Another alleged example of the "encroaching of Protestantism" is the statement by another leader, Nissanka, that the Buddha is just one of a set of saviors (p. 377). This, on the one hand, is the literal understanding of nonphilosophical Buddhism, which states that the present Buddha, Gautama Siddhartha, is only the last of a line of Buddhas that have already appeared.

Gombrich and Obeyesekere depict a small and eccentric (their words) sect's rejection of authority and traditional hierarchies as something strange, and remind themselves that extreme Protestantism was a path to secularization (GombObey 1988 pp. 380, 381). But the questioning of authority is very much a central feature of the Buddhist spirit, and there is no necessity for recourse to alleged imported influences to explain such a position. The authors are again wrong about their own countries of residence. It is extreme Protestant groups, especially in the U.S., that instead of embracing secularism have veered to anti-science positions, such as opposing the teaching of evolution, and are today in the vanguard of American reactionary politics and beliefs.

Godwin Samararatne is mentioned by the authors as the person who led them to the set of rather bizarre individuals they have studied. The question is, how were they chosen? An interview by the present author with Samararatne plainly reveals the authors' highly selective methodology (personal interview with Godwin Samararatne, 15 May 1997). Samararatne had been asked by Gombrich to provide some contacts with new cults. He threw out some names on the basis of the accident of his own knowledge, and not by any means as a representative sample. Samararatne himself does not take these groups as representative of Buddhist activities. There are at least 1,000 heads of temples, 30,000 monks, and tens of thousands of lay Buddhists who could well be considered more representative leaders. These more representative individuals, of course, live lives tangential to the type of phenomena and "leaders" documented by the authors.

MEDITATION, OTHER DEVIANCES, AND POSSESSION

Meditation and possession feature strongly in what our authors designate as post-Protestant Buddhism. But Gombrich and Obeyesekere bring highly tendentious attitudes to both phenomena.

They mention that both possession and meditation could be termed hypnomantic states or altered states of consciousness (GombObey 1988 p. 12). Elsewhere, they mention that meditation is a withdrawal from the world and a solution for troubled times (pp. 14–15). They also say that the attempt by lay persons to meditate is unheard of in Buddhist theory (pp. 14–15). The authors ignore the large number of studies that had appeared in the Western scientific literature on meditation by the time the book was being written, showing meditation to be very different from possession. Elsewhere the authors stated that the aim of *Vipassana* meditation is to see things clearly, but they do not seem to have internalized this observation (p. 26). If the two phenomena of possession and meditation are equal, as the authors claim, then the West, which has imported meditation practices, has been undergoing a religious transformation of the *Bhakti* kind—if we are to give the authors' explanation.

Further, Western studies show that Buddhist meditation, far from being a withdrawal from the world, helps one to be alert and aware of the world. And despite the author's allegation that it is impossible for laymen to meditate, in Theravada Buddhist Burma there is widespread use of meditation, as is amply documented in that gem of ethnography of non-Western psychology, *Through an Eastern Window* by Jack Huber (1967 p. 1). And Buddhist meditation is now, of course, widespread in the West.

Gombrich and Obeyesekere mention as unusual the fact that meditators have hallucinations at times, which the authors describe as "trance" —again making an equivalence with possession (1988 p. 27). But the classical Buddhist meditation literature acknowledge such hallucinations and describes how to deal with them.

The authors make another major error when they say that Buddhism takes the "mind" to be the instrument of salvation (p. 16). Here, they use the word "mind" in its Western connotation, assuming the mind-body split of a Cartesian worldview. Buddhism does not assume a mind-body dichotomy. Meditation, the means to one's goals—the author's "salvation"—assumes changes in both the "body" and the "mind."

Buddhism, the authors mention elsewhere, inculcates "a serene joy, a tranquility the very opposite of ecstasy" (p. 29). That is, they now imply that meditation is very different from possession. They also state that possession is frowned upon by Buddhist theory because it goes against Buddhist ideas of self-control and awareness, and that possession is considered an illness (p. 28). But for our anthropologists, this sickness represents Sinhalese Buddhist society, not the Buddhist mainstream. So the authors, generalizing from a few cases selected with an inbuilt bias, now conclude that possession is viewed positively in the contemporary Sinhalese Buddhist world (p. 36).

Gombrich and Obeyesekere mention females' becoming *kapuralas* as another form of deviant behavior (1988 p. 47). But gender and other roles in general have been changing in recent decades, taking "deviant forms." Thus, the traditional Ayurvedic families have seen their sons turn to other professions, such as Western medicine, or for that matter become Western anthropologists like Obeyesekere, whose father was an Ayurvedic physician (personal communication, senior faculty member, Sociology Department, Peradeniya University). Similarly a whole array of "deviant roles" in the traditional social structure, such as computer programmer, heart specialist, plastic surgeon, and biotechnologist, have come into being, challenging the traditional cultural structure. Most important, women have emerged as the key breadwinners in families, taking over the most central of traditional male roles. Women today are doctors, engineers, lawyers, and scientists—all traditional male roles. In fact, in this gender role change, Sri Lanka stands ahead of the U.S. So the fact that women are becoming *kapuralas* is probably due more to this general feminization of the job structure than to any transformation of alleged Protestant Buddhism.

THE BREAKDOWN OF COMMUNITY

Gombrich and Obeyesekere claim that the breakdown of community and its traditional social control has led to the practice of possession (1988 p. 39). The collapse of traditional authority and the desire to escape from harsh realities are also given as reasons for the growth in the numbers of Sai Baba's followers (p. 53). The problem with this omnibus explanation is that many other coping mechanisms exist to deal with the breakdown; the overwhelming bulk of the population is not resorting to possession. Further, Sri Lankan magicians regularly perform on the public stage the alleged miracles of Sai Baba purely to laugh at him, showing a spirit of utter disrespect. This disrespect is in keeping with Gombrich's own findings in his earlier case study, as well as with Knox's 18th-century descriptions of the disrespect that Sinhalese have for their gods.

The authors' ruminations are ex cathedra, unsubstantiated statements —at best informed guesses. Different and more reliable methodologies of theory construction from the facts themselves, such as those based on "grounded theory" (Glaser and Strauss 1967), could have provided more relevant explanations.

Thus, a study on the breakdown of formal authority and its values in an industrial setting in Sri Lanka, conducted by the present author in 1970 using the grounded theory approach of Glaser and Strauss, found that employees in the factory had differing frames of legitimate authority and corresponding values. These different frames were used by the employees opportunistically, that is, through an instrumental rationality, as a means to their own self-defined ends. Belief in God-men would be in many cases due to a similar instrumental rationality.

Gombrich and Obeyesekere mention as unusual the use by the Bellanwila temple of money from the worship of deities for the construction of Buddhist buildings (1988 p. 43). But such instrumental funding exists all over the world; for example, in the West, money gathered during the time of the robber barons and worker repression now feeds the purest intellectual concerns through organizations such as the Rockefeller and Carnegie Foundations. Further, many of those who come to Bellanwila do so for the purpose of passing modern exams, for instrumental needs in the Western cultural sphere. Such instrumentalism exists elsewhere in Asia, as when top Japanese corporations host Shinto ceremonies or when Chinese millionaires pray to Buddhist gods. To further complicate the anthropologically constructed world of the authors, one should note that the chief monk of Bellanwila at the time the book was published was as cosmopolitan an academic as the authors. He had a British Ph.D. and had traveled internationally, perhaps more than the writers.

The authors see a significant lowering of the Buddha's status when a Sai Baba devotee has pictures of the Virgin Mary, Jesus, Ramakrishna, and a village guardian god, and a Buddha image is kept at a lower level (GombObey 1988 p. 54). But again the authors are probably over-explaining events. Thus, in Cambodia, the present Sangharaja had a picture of the Pope, after a meeting with the latter, hung very high on the wall, higher than the Buddha statues, which were on a platform lower down. Later the Sangharaja removed the picture. When specifically questioned in light of Gombrich and Obeyesekere's remarks, the Sangharaja denied lowering the status of the Buddha.

THE SINHALESE "DARK SIDE"

The authors mention as an implied illustration of the "dark side" of the popular Sinhalese psyche the association of Tamil, astrology, and black magic in the 15th-century poet-monk Totagamuwe Sri Rahula (Gomb-Obey 1988 p. 49). This is a completely false example on several counts. A closer examination shows underlying cultural complexities unsuspected by the authors.

Tamil was a compulsory language for the Sinhala literati at the time, taught in monastic centers of learning. The other compulsory languages, apart from Sinhala, included Pali, Sanskrit, and Apabramsa. Belief in astrology and alchemy was at the time common throughout South Asia. The most important aspect of Rahula's alleged black magic was his search for immortality through chemical means. He himself is supposed to have taken potions for longevity. But this interest in alchemy in the subcontinent also had implications for the development of science in the West, a development that gave rise to some of the very "Protestant characteristics" that were allegedly imported to Sri Lanka.

As I have recalled elsewhere (Goonatilake, Susantha, 1998), a salt-based alchemy—considered a nodal event in the development of science—was being taught in 12th-century South India (Bose et al. 1971 pp. 318, 589). Rahula's interest in alchemy was in this South Indian tradition. The authors' particular reference to Rahula here is thus seen not to resonate with simplistic dichotomies between an allegedly Protestant science and a dark spirit religion. Western as well as South Asian scientific and intellectual history is much more complex than our authors' simplistic assumptions make it appear.

THE "FLIGHT TO THE OCCULT"

Gombrich and Obeyesekere give the impression that there has been a widespread flight to the occult in Sri Lanka (1988 p. 59). As examples of this phenomenon they list palmistry, astrology, and occult newspapers. As a further illustration, they give the example of a sensational headline claiming that a past prime minister had been reborn as a god. The authors overstate and overgeneralize to the entire country when they say of a clairvoyant that he attributes anything the least bit unusual to a supernatural cause. Thus, allegedly, when a bus comes quickly, it is said to have been sent by Kataragama (or Sai Baba), or if a stranger has an effect on one's life, the stranger must have been a deity in disguise. The authors claim that the world has become "de-rationalized" (p. 63).

But such examples of the occult are not necessarily what they appear to signify; nor are they exclusive to Sri Lanka. Sri Lankans are generally down-to-earth. Newspapers such as the *National Enquirer,* although not exclusively devoted to the occult, contain many sensational stories that lay claim to stories of this genre. In the same category are daytime talk shows in the U.S., which offer similar fare. Possibly the share of the U.S. listening and reading market involving the occult is of the same order as that in Sri Lanka. A couple of years before the authors' book came out, a publishing phenomenon hit the Sri Lankan scene. This was the appearance of two fortnightly newspapers, *Vidusara* and *Vidunana,* devoted exclusively to reporting on science. The two newspapers experienced remarkable growth, reaching combined total sales of over 100,000, a figure much higher than the sales of astrological and similar newspapers.

The example given by the authors of a Buddhist woman possessed by the goddess Bhadra Kali who converted to Christianity also shows weakness in the central argument (GombObey 1988 p. 56). To counteract the alleged sorcery used against her, she turned to a Roman Catholic priest-exorcist, and finally to Pentecostalism, and she said that Jesus had spoken to her through Kali. This is not a case of Buddhism transformed into the occult but of a rather idiosyncratic, unstable woman changing her views. It is also an example of Christianity being transformed into the occult. The authors also mention an occult practitioner who worships Mara and whose clients are mainly Roman Catholics (p. 62), again, an example of Roman Catholicism transformed.

The different cult groups of the spirit religion that Gombrich and Obeyesekere claim reveal significant changes in Sri Lanka are, according to the authors' own testimony, small in number. The authors say that the Nawala shrine is a small one (1988 p. 82) but claim that it is part of a phenomenon that gave rise to the many shrines that have mushroomed in and around Colombo (p. 83). They mention Kali shrines but add in the following sentence that these shrines are very small and attract only a few individuals (p. 141). In the area of the urban poor, Colombo 9 and Colombo 10, where, according to the authors' own criteria, the encroachment of spirit cults would have been greatest, they managed to collect information only from ten shrines. They also admit that these shrines serve only "small local areas," and that the numbers of those actually attending them are "likely inflated" (p. 83).

But in keeping with their theoretical premise, the authors assert that in due course "it is likely that some of the shrines *will* become popular" (1988 p. 83, emphasis mine). Munnessarama is one large shrine that the authors have studied. But again the question of its representativeness arises, because it is one of very few large shrines devoted to a deity. Buddhist temples, on the other hand, number in the thousands.

It should also be noted that changes in the worship of gods have not been unusual in Sinhalese history. Thus Natha, one of the powerful gods of earlier centuries, is today not remembered, as Gombrich himself has pointed out (1991 p. 208).

The authors have studied the pilgrimage site of the deity Kataragama, but ignored the more important Buddhist pilgrimage sites such as Anuradhapura, Mihintale, Sri Pada, and Kandy. On Poson days, visitors to Anuradhapura number in the upper hundreds of thousands. The Kandy *perahara* attracts similarly large numbers. The reason for ignoring Kandy is probably that the authors say it is today more entertainment and cultural spectacle than an object of worship (1988 p. 163). But they ignore similar motivations for visiting Kataragama, given by their own respondents (pp. 163, 191–192).

The writings of one pilgrim of forty years who chronicles for the newspapers the facts of "Kataragama pilgrimage for pleasure" are dismissed as the ramblings of a Protestant Buddhist (GombObey 1988 p. 192). And a Western anthropologist, M. C. Hodge, who in a Ph.D. dissertation (1981 p. 299) records his observation that "pilgrims go to Kataragama for vinoda and not for religious purpose," is likewise dismissed by the authors, who label him a Westerner who subscribes to a radical distinction between the secular and the sacred. In fact, a respondent of Gombrich in the latter's earlier study of Buddhism in a village mentioned that he went to Kataragama for fun, *vinodeta*. That respondent also attacked the priests at Kataragama as dealing in lies and drinking alcohol, and Gombrich at that time accepted this view (1991 p. 249). The authors psychologize away these respondents' own commonsensical statements and present instead their own fantasies.

Further, many people come to Kataragama and other shrines only as an adjunct to other instruments for help in exams, job interviews, and the like, not as their first and/or only option. It is merely some added insurance in life, done for the same reasons that top East Asian businessmen pray for success at Mahayana Buddhist temples.

But from ancient times, the Sinhalese have been self-mocking about their practices. We have already noted how the English prisoner of the 18th century, Robert Knox, documents this instrumentality, the Sinhalese villager wanting to "shit in the mouth" of those gods who do not deliver.

According to Gombrich and Obeyesekere's own evidence, instead of Buddhism's being transformed by these practices, Buddhist monks do not approve of the alleged growth in the occult. One monk respondent said that this occult stuff was only for "entertainment" (*vinoda*), while another said that it was "folly" (*modakama*). Further, the authors mention that many of the chief monks do not personally believe in these shrines or are indifferent to them (1988p. 83).

WHAT IS LEFT OUT

Major factors in the authors' constructions include not only the highly selective empirical data but also the significant areas that were left out. I have referred elsewhere to some of these areas, such as socialization processes. But it is necessary to briefly recall a few others.

During the period covered by the book, two important events affecting rural Sri Lanka occurred, namely, the two youth revolts in 1971 and 1987–1989. Young monks were sympathetic to or took part in both these revolts. The book ends in 1987, after the eruption of the second revolt, but not before its end. Such revolts do not appear out of the blue, especially when there is such wide participation. In a book that claims to describe the shift in core values and orientations among the Sinhalese, there are no glimpses of this pivotal change in behavior among the young generation.

The period under study also coincides with a massive enrollment of Buddhist monks in the universities. At the end of the period under study, more than 20 percent of students in the humanities were Buddhist monks. During this time, monks also began to march in May Day parades in support of the working class. At one rally, about 2,000 Buddhist monks walked in sympathy with the working class (the source of this information was Ven. Dr. Wilegoda Ariyadeva of the University of Ruhuna, who was once a chief organizer of such marching monks).

Among the major changes in the village bureaucracy, Gombrich and Obeyesekere cite the replacement of the traditional village headman in 1958 by the *grama sevaka*, a government official (1988 p. 68). But they ignore the sociological realities of that change, including the actual and potential pressures on, and of, that official. The key election of 1956 brought about the gradual politicization of the administrative system. This process has been well-documented in the social science research literature, including the works of the present writer (Goonatilake, Susantha, 1971, 1972, 1973). By the 1970s, positions from the top to the bottom of the government hierarchy were being filled wholly or partially in accordance with political criteria. The period covered by the book was witness to the almost total politicization of *grama sevakas,* who for all practical purposes could be considered extensions of the ruling party apparatus.

The initial period covered by Gombrich and Obeyesekere was a time when most economic life in Sri Lanka was in the hands of the state. Outside of the then Socialist bloc, the Sri Lankan private sector at the time had little participation in the economy. Thus there was tight particularistic control over most economic activities by the ruling parties, including, at the village level, the *grama sevaka.* These politicized officials were thus more potent creators of the everyday reality of most villagers than any religious or other force. Their key activities are completely absent from the authors' narrative.

WHAT SINHALESE BUDDHISTS ACTUALLY LEARN

Sri Lankans use purely secular means to achieve their ends far more frequently than they use what the authors call the "spirit religions" and "transformed Buddhism." An obvious formal means of achieving ends in Sri Lanka is the educational system. The authors pointed out that in the early 19th century, literacy in Sri Lanka was as high as in Britain (GombObey 1988 p. 207). The authors ignore the contents of this formal socialization package.

The authors mention in passing that schools were a major channel for the spread of Protestant Buddhism (p. 11). The question is, how true is this claim? The Sri Lankan school syllabus was modeled directly on British syllabuses. The contents that were not equivalent were those subjects specific to Sri Lanka. These were history (G. C. Mendis, a Catholic, who downplayed the importance of Buddhism according to later university historians, wrote the text *Heritage of Ceylon,* which was compulsory in schools up to the 1960s), geography (not much room for "Protestantism" here), Sinhalese language and literature (which could have given rise to some "Protestantism"), and Buddhism. The authors do not take into account what is included in the largest formal socialization package in Buddhism, namely, the compulsory teaching since the 1960s of the children's own religion in schools. They also do not consider the syllabuses of Buddhism in voluntary Buddhist Sunday schools, known as *daham pasal.*

A "socialization" phenomenon that began to be more widespread in temples around this time was the opening of "shrines" to another type of god. This involved the establishment of "cram shops" on temple premises for students preparing for public examinations. They were advertised widely, with far more students attending them than attended the few spirit shrines. The number of attendees was so large that public address systems were often used to deliver the lectures.

Large temples also often have monastic schools, *pirivenas,* attached to them. Monks in these schools often study for government exams, which are part of the general education system in the country, an educational system not very different from those in Western countries. In fact, this common educational system enables Sri Lankan students to sit for entry examinations into educational establishments in the Western world, including the U.S. and the U.K. The growth in the number of monks preparing for these general secular examinations also coincided with the period covered by the book, and was a much greater and more widespread transformation than those described by the authors.

The Sinhalese use other means of arriving at their goals as well. Thus, there is literature with detailed case studies (including mine—carried out around the same time that Gombrich and Obeyesekere's book was written) on the use of politics and political patronage as a means of achieving ends. Many Sri Lankans have also involved themselves in trade union actions to attain their collective objectives. Sri Lanka had one of the most vocal and militant trade union movements in the world until it was emasculated by mass sackings around the time the book was written, again a theme that is missing from the authors' narrative.

In industrializing Sri Lanka, people have used science and technology as instruments to reach their goals. The authors could well have posed the question, how differently does a Buddhist computer specialist, engineer, or biologist deal with this more mundane sphere of problems? How do these modern professionals relate to so-called transformed Protestant Buddhism and to the ecstatic spirit world? There are far more people working in the different professions in science and technology than there are spirit practitioners. The authors have also ignored other influences on everyday behavior such as mass media, newspapers, radio, TV, and films.

Generally the authors have also ignored what goes on in ordinary life and have deliberately chosen to study the bizarre. They could well have chosen children and adults engaging in meditation at home and in temples rather than the oddballs they did choose. The home and the temple are the major centers where Buddhist tradition is expressed and where significant changes should be tracked. The key actors and factors they have left out of the narrative are more important as guides to contemporary Sri Lankan Buddhist behavior than the ones they have chosen. The authors have insulated their "Sinhalese" from the everyday reality around them and inserted them into an imaginary world of the authors' own construction.

LOCAL AND GLOBAL PROTESTANTISM: PROTESTANTISM TRANSFORMED IN THE WEST

Gombrich and Obeyesekere mention that Dharmapala was the founder of international Buddhism (1988 p. 206), but they ignore the effects of this international Buddhism on the U.S. and the West. Theirs is, therefore, essentially a Eurocentric vision that attempts to see only a one-way flow of ideas from the West to the East, not the other way around.

They say that although Buddhism proper frowns upon the irrational, the supernatural, the worship of gods, and the propitiation of demons, Sinhala Buddhists have always had such practices and beliefs (p. 3). But this is hardly surprising in any society or belief system. At the time the study was being conducted on the alleged spirit takeover of an alleged Protestant Buddhism, there was a similar "takeover" occurring in the West through the counterculture and the New Age. In Britain, the intellectual abode of one of the two authors, there was a resurrection of druidic worship, and in America, the intellectual abode of the other author, there was a renewed interest in the occult. On TV, daytime talk shows and tabloids were highlighting the supernatural, the bizarre, and the irrational. The authors ignore these Western parallels as they make their own tendentious assumptions about Sinhalese society.

OTHER ASPECTS

There are other facets of social change, some of them covering the truer parts of the authors' narrative, that demand comments.

Gombrich and Obeyesekere state that reform movements in the Sangha, for example to expel bad monks and encourage the good, always came from within the Sangha and not from the laity, the latter acting only as the executant (1988 p. 225). This is at best only a partial truth. The best-known reform was carried out under the direct orders of the 11th-century King Parakramabahu 1. The authors also consider it a Protestant import when Dharmapala makes a comonsensical observation that Sri Lankan Bhikkhus are lazy and ignorant, used only to a little Pali grammar and

Sanskrit prosody (p. 226). But such sentiments are part of a continuing tradition, as we noticed in the *Mahavamsa*'s sarcastic descriptions of 12th-century monks' behavior, referred to earlier in this chapter.

The authors mention that Sri Lankan texts were written exclusively by men (p. 457). But this is again an overstatement and ignores some exceptions in the case of Sri Lanka and elsewhere to a general patriarchal truth, "valid" for all religions and all civilizations. The earliest compilation of Sinhalese records into a chronicle was the *Dipavamsa* of the 4th century. Geiger, its German translator, found internal evidence to suggest that the *Dipavamsa* was probably written by a group of nuns. A century later, in the 5th century A.D., Sinhala nuns also took the initiative in spreading the Buddhist nuns' order in China. In the 14th century, a Sinhalese nun, Chandramali, was one of the key writers in the Tibetan tradition. Examples of the Sinhalese women's literary tradition through the centuries include a medieval text on a pilgrimage taken by women, as well as work of the early-19th-century poetess Gajaman Nona.

The authors are correct in criticizing the Sarvodaya movement for blatantly inventing an imaginary tradition, but they describe the movement exclusively through the use of secondary sources, not through observation of their practices. This imagined Sarvodaya past is in strong contrast to the reality depicted both in Sinhala historical writings and in Buddhism. The authors assert that Protestantism was an influence on the Sarvodaya's invented village (GombObey 1988 p. 252), but no Western Protestants would recognize any of this idealized village life which has been attributed to their influence.

Although they correctly refer to the falsification of the Sri Lankan past by Nandasena Ratnapala to create the myths of the Sarvodaya movement (p. 244), Gombrich and Obeyesekere ignore a more telling point. Ratnapala was also a systematic inventor of sociological "facts." In a series of articles in the popular press, he made some wild assertions about prostitution and other social ills. The figures and their implications so boggled the imagination that the Sri Lankan Sociological Association had to warn the public not to believe him.

The extent to which the authors have confused true Christians and Christian (Protestant) Buddhists is seen when they describe, as an example of the prevailing Protestant Buddhist mood, the archaeologist Paranavitana in his dotage seeing inscriptions that no one else could see (GombObey 1988 p. 349). But these hallucinations were not Buddhistic. Although Paranavitana unearthed significant Buddhist ruins in his younger days as archeological commissioner, he was a Christian.

The authors regard changes of names—*Maniyo* for a female priest, and *sami* for a *kapurala,* a male priest—as significant and as paralleling changes in roles (p. 38). But these name changes are actually not very significant. Language usage has been changing rapidly since the 1950s. Thus, the words for father and mother on the coast, *thattha* and *amma,* have become *thatthi* and *ammi* and have also replaced inland forms such as *appochchi.* Teachers and female managers have now become "madame" in Sinhala usage, the equivalent of "sir," and Buddhist monks have become at times *sadhu* in university usage. Looking at isolated changes in language, as the authors do during their brief visits, does not provide adequate support for their argument.

As an example of secularization, the two authors mention that monks today go to theaters but rarely to the cinema (1988 p. 416). But the reason for this is well-known among Sri Lankan university staff. It is not due to Protestantism or post-Protestantism; rather, Sinhala theater is a compulsory subject in the study of Sinhala literature at the universities, and attendance at theater performances is almost mandatory. Sometimes, as part of the teaching, special performances are held for students to watch —several were organized by my wife when she was a university teacher. And monks constitute a significant proportion of those studying Sinhala literature at the university level.

The authors claim that the *Bodhi Puja* (a ceremony that was popular at the time the book was written but has since declined) could have come from Protestantism because the monk associated with the *Puja* was from Panadura. As evidence they point out that Panadura had a powerful Christian presence, including Christian schools, and was the location of the well-known 19th-century debate between Christians and Buddhists (p. 386). This again is fantasy masquerading as science. As for Christian schools, it is impossible that the monk went to such a school, because the only Christian school, St. John's College (which the present writer attended for a short time, decades ago), was made into a non-religious state school in the early 1960s. And as for the Panadura debate where the Christians were trounced, just the opposite of Christian influence is indicated. Anybody who has heard even the folklore surrounding the debates would tend to look at Christianity with contempt. Instead of being an imitation of Christianity, all the evidence is that the *Bodhi Puja* was a development within the local dynamics.

Gombrich and Obeyesekere also make vacuous statements, including, for example, that given urban poverty, conflicts between spouses, parents, children, and siblings are inevitable (1988 p. 85). But such conflicts are not limited to Sri Lanka or the poor world. They are probably more common in richer Western countries, as illustrated by much higher indices of family disharmony such as divorce.

The authors get major facts of everyday existence wrong. In an aside, they mention their admiration of the work done by the government-owned Sri Lanka Transport Board (SLTB) (p. 55). But the SLTB was virtually defunct at the time they were doing their study, as a result of the privatization processes being carried out since 1977. The state of the bus service is everyday knowledge among the very mobile Sri Lankan population, much more so than knowledge of spirit worlds. The authors' lack of awareness of the facts of everyday Sri Lankan existence is indicative of the extent of their reliability on other, less obvious points.

CONCLUSIONS

The book includes several passages that no one could contend with. There are fairly accurate renderings of general Sri Lankan history. Then there are lengthy sections of actual description of various groups, the ethnography of which no one could quarrel with. In the book, the authors mix description with immediate commentary. There is no dispassionate description or explanation arrived at from the facts and presented in a systematic and logical manner. Not only is this tedious to read, but it is indicative of the authors' own thought processes.

Instead of coming to a priori conclusions about Sinhalese society and then selectively choosing characters and events to illustrate them, the authors should have first asked what important social changes were occurring in the country and then sought possible explanations for these in some of the ongoing changes in religion and religious roles.

The authors seem to apologize for the bizarre characters they have selected to study. They say that their narrative is full of colorful facts and detail, and they feel that "theories date but not documents," presumably referring to their field data and attendant odd characters (GombObey 1988 p. xi). But they ignore the core point that their characters and their attendant facts are very selective and not representative of Buddhism in Sri Lanka. Their oddballs could well have found a place among the more colorful clairvoyants and spiritualists in "The Lamasery," the New York home of Blavatsky (Cranston 1993 pp. 169–171).

One glaring omission by the authors is their failure to mention *Bhikshuvage Urumaya*, "The Heritage of the Bhikkhu," by Rahula the monk-scholar (Gombrich 1991 p. 31). Rahula, and his works in general, had been highly praised as a source of help on matters that Gombrich could not grasp in his first research project (1991 pp. x, ix). "The Heritage of the Bhikkhu" would have answered authoritatively many of the assertions of the Buddhist transformation.

The authors also provide no significant reference to the literature and written sources in Sinhala in this highly literate society with a very long literary tradition. But they claim without giving supporting details that what is found today in Sinhala newspapers, school texts, and books is written from the English-language, Orientalist view of Buddhism. In this context, it is significant that the authors state that the Pali Canon, recently translated into Sinhala, is in language so archaic and learned that they could barely understand it (GombObey 1988 p. 448). This is a strange admission about their knowledge of the local language, especially considering that one of the authors, Gombrich, is at present the key official of the once legendary Pali Text Society, founded by Rhys Davids.

The authors also failed to consult theses and dissertations produced at the local universities in social science on the various phenomena they describe. For the last twenty-five years, every sociology student at the undergraduate level has submitted a dissertation. This is apart from the available M.A. and Ph.D. dissertations, several of which have been produced at Western universities.

Gombrich and Obeyesekere make some fantastic claims. They claim that changes in the ethics of society are "anticipated and worked out at Kataragama" (p. 415). The most fatuous claim is that Kataragama priests are "theoreticians whose views seem to anticipate changes in the religion of the Sinhalas" (p. 417). But the contextual information I have presented shows that there are more mundane reasons for, say, the changes in the Kataragama dances. Changes in the society at large feed Kataragama, not the other way around; certainly it is not the mental droppings of Kataragama priests that are providing the theories of the future.

But the biggest contextual problem is that the carriers of alleged Protestantism, the Theosophists, were great believers in the occult and spiritualism, from which the Buddha debarred his followers. The supreme irony of this whole book is that alleged carriers of Protestantism were not Protestants; in fact they were anti-Protestant. Similarly, the recipients of "Protestantism" were against Protestantism and, for that matter, Christianization of any sort.

Toward the end of a very Eurocentric book, the authors say that there have been calls in Sri Lanka for a non-Western sociology-anthropology, without giving the names of these "callers" (p. 456). But let me fill in the gaps. There have been three such callers, Ralph Pieris, Laksiri Jayasuriya, and myself. To my knowledge, the former two contributed one paper each; the bulk of the writing on the genre has come from me. Gombrich and Obeyesekere say that non-Western social science can indeed be carried out, but Sanskrit terms would then have to be first translated into their English equivalents (p. 456). Even in their attempt to search for a non-Western system, their primary reference is thus narrowly Eurocentric, an approach in which they limit themselves to the English language.

Gombrich and Obeyesekere also observe that the dichotomy between classical religion and spirit religion is found in the entire South Asian region. They claim that while the classical civilizing religions emphasized self-control, the spirit religion emphasized possession (p. 457). But this dichotomy is not in keeping with historical reality. Thus, the earliest religious sculpture from the Indus civilization, before the classical South Asian religions crystallized, depicts a Shiva-like figure in a meditative mood. Further, the earliest Vedic literature describes many scenes of loss of self-control, some produced by imbibing the potion *soma*. In more recent Sri Lankan times, letting oneself go was not a practice unknown among persons with a "classical" bent. Monk-poets vividly described drinking scenes, as in the poem *Guttila Kavya,* and amorous dalliances, as in the *Sandesa* poetry genre.

What the authors are therefore attempting in the few paragraphs of presumed non-Western theorizing is nothing of the kind. They do not use South Asian conceptual categories to analyze the Western or Eastern experience. Instead they use existing Eastern descriptions of behavior such as *Bhakti* and apply it to their situation. These are attempts to see analogies between the present they describe and other South Asian situations, but not of non-Eurocentric conceptualizing.

Gombrich observed in his book that Sinhalese Buddhists dislike going beyond the rational. He contrasted this to Christianity, which commends going beyond reason (1991 p. 308). But in this later book, written in a shorter time and describing a haphazardly collected set of oddballs, Gombrich selects only the irrational to examine and "theorize" on with regard to the Sinhalese. In *Buddhism Transformed*, Gombrich and Obeyesekere themselves admit that their study uncovered only a small part of what was actually going on, and was in no way exhaustive (1988 p. xiii). Yet with admittedly such a small part, a very large mountain of tendentious conclusions was created.

The authors' "theory" entails two unrelated concepts, protest and Protestantism. But one of these twin factors is now conveniently forgotten by our theorists. In *Buddhism Transformed,* only changes in alleged Protestantism are examined, not protests. But the protests, as we see many times in this book, continued, not subject to the authors' gaze.

PART III

■

FINDING THE
SINHALESE THROUGH
SORCERY

CHAPTER 6

■

The Sorcerer's Apprentice

Bruce Kapferer is the next anthropologist we address. He has written three books on Sri Lanka: *A Celebration of Demons: Exorcism and the Aesthetics of Healing in Sri Lanka* (first published in 1983; a second edition was published in 1991), *Legends of People, Myths of State: Violence, Intolerance, and Political Culture in Sri Lanka and Australia* (1988), and *The Feast of the Sorcerer: Practices of Consciousness and Power* (1997). His construction of Sinhalese-Buddhist society is very different from that of Gombrich and Obeyesekere, although at times he incorporates their work into his views. Kapferer's first book is of narrow focus, namely, on the rituals of certain Sinhalese groups, as is his third book. The second, however, tries to unlock the social mechanics of Sri Lanka, specifically of Sinhalese Buddhists as a whole. This second book, therefore, will be our main focus. But as he develops the arguments for the whole country as a continuation of his case studies, I will, and necessarily must, deal with his narrower studies, especially the first, which sets his theoretical, methical, and empirical perspective for the other two.

EXORCIZING SINHALESE SECRETS

Kapferer makes his entry into describing the Sri Lankan social systems in his first book by explicitly stating his methodology. He locates it in the anthropological debates of his times. This methodology, however, changes, often implicitly, as he moves from his first field study in Sri Lanka to his two later books. But we can discern the thread from his first foray, and this we will first sketch—a thread to be followed through in the later books.

KAPFERER'S METHODOLOGY

Kapferer lays down explicitly in his first book where his methodology comes from. He approaches the fieldwork and early analysis through considering exorcism ritual as a "drama" or "event" in the manner of the "situational analysis" of Gluckman (1958) and Mitchell (1956) and of the "extended case analysis" of Turner (1957, 1968a, 1968b). As a method, this approach was opposed to the then dominant orientation in British anthropology of structural-functionalism. In this "situational-extended approach" which Kapferer adopts, events and situations are not to be seen as representations or apt illustrations of an embracing structural order that is internally self-consistent, harmonious, and encompassing (Kapferer 1991 p. x). On the other hand, in this extended case-situational approach, the larger social whole does not exist independently of its practices but only in, and through, such practices. In his second edition of the book, published in 1991, eight years after the first, Kapferer also evokes postmodernism in his approach, thus partially shifting his methodological frame from the extended case-situational analysis that he evoked in the first edition (p. xi).

Kapferer's approach in his field study is illustrated by his suggestion about how we should view rituals. The ritual, he notes, is the drama par excellence. Ritual is constructed and defined as a practice in which the participants meet the existential problems of their living. In the ritual process, participants strip away their multiple orientations to reality, thus effecting a deconstruction of the worlds of experience (1991 p. xi). Kapferer states that Sinhalese exorcisms, like rites described elsewhere by Turner, are totalistic. They have a logic and design that can organize a great diversity of meaning and experience. Exorcisms open out to more and more experiential possibilities instead of closing such experiences off. Exorcism, says Kapferer, is efficacious because it progressively explodes the terrifying world of the patient undergoing exorcist healing. The world of the patient is a prison with a demon governing the acts of experience. Sinhalese exorcism removes this world as an oppressive totalitarianism.

Taussig (1987), Kapferer notes, takes a view of ritual different from that of others, emphasizing its radical character. Through the rites of the ritual, the oppressive world of the existing order can be challenged. The rites do this, according to Taussig, by their anti-totalistic character. According to Kapferer, Taussig adopts a postmodernist approach that tries to link the possibilities of resistance in ritual to an essential anti-totalistic quality. Kapferer claims that Taussig conflates totalizing forms with totalitarian orders. According to Kapferer, religion and ritual are always totalizing, which gives rise to their power (p. xii).

Kapferer emphasizes that the exorcisms he describes are to be distinguished from other activities such as rituals for healing and personal alleviation, which are mistaken for exorcism. Kapferer's exorcisms are performed in the house of the ill person. These exorcist performances last all night and are usually performed by members of one caste who are specialists in the field (1991 p. xii).

Gananath Obeyesekere in his studies stated that exorcisms of demons and other rites, such as those of the goddess Pattini, are disappearing. But Kapferer thinks the opposite; the "irrational" and the demonic, he claims, are alive and kicking. He finds such traditional expressions in *gammaduwa* (literally "village shack") ceremonies (1991 p. xv).

Kapferer says that he attempts to combine philosophical and anthropological concerns with ethnography. He admits that anthropological ethnography is not like simply taking a snapshot, making a record; rather, it is constructed. And critical methodological issues are raised in this construction. Anthropologists come with cultural baggage of their own that orients them in the field and determines the conceptual and theoretical positions that they bring to their studies. These orientations are often developed within the metropolitan countries. For anthropologists, the "Others," in the form of their subjects under study, become sites for confirming or contradicting their dominant theories (Kapferer 1991 p. xvii). Kapferer, for his part, uses a variety of approaches, including Marxist, structuralist, and symbolic-interactionist ones. This eclectic mixture is used, he says, because he has not been able to find a total single scheme that is satisfying.

Kapferer says that he is moving away from the dominant position in his discipline, which views theories and analytical perspectives as conceptual elements that can be compared with the evidence given by ethnography and modified, so that the theory becomes not only a representation of reality but reality itself (1991 p. xviii). He moves away from this position to a more phenomenological one. This phenomenological orientation is used to give "full importance to the exorcist understanding and practice." But more importantly, this approach does not allow the interpretation of exorcism to be subjected to external metropolitan authority.

Kapferer believes that all realities are constructions. Realities that are constructed by, say, exorcists cannot be swept away in favor of other constructions, such as rationalist social science theories. To Kapferer no social construction is necessarily more privileged than the others, more true or real than the others (1991 p. xviii).

His methodological approach, he asserts, is similar to that of Evans-Pritchard in his studies of the Nuer. Evans-Pritchard was not interested in the complete recording of reality and organizing that reality in accordance with his own assumptions. In contrast, he was interested in how humans form their realities in living. Kapferer's methodological aim is to assert the ethnographic context's own authority, and not to subjugate it to theory derived from other experiences. His approach, he says, does not therefore categorize the human experience he studies according to the canons of mainstream social science (1991 p. xix).

Although trying to view the world through the reality of his group and so taking a phenomenological position, Kapferer does not accept the phenomenological position of a Mauss or a Durkheim, both of whom brought the compartments of experience into social science. He does not accept that the human world can be divided into such categories as the economic, social, psychological, cultural, or political as determinants of the human condition. He is against such reductions (1991 p. xix).

Kapferer is, therefore, against Obeyesekere's psychologism in the latter's studies on Sri Lanka. Demonic attack in Sri Lanka was analyzed and interpreted through psychoanalytic theory by Obeyesekere (1970b, 1975b, 1977b, 1981). Kapferer believes that this is too reductionist and ignores the fact that human experience is complex. Obeyesekere describes the dynamic interactions between psychological, social, and cultural processes (cited in Kapferer 1991 p. xix). But Kapferer rejects the importance of the psychoanalytic approaches used by Obeyesekere, partly because these lie outside Kapferer's own expertise. Kapferer believes that his own approach does not try to reduce the phenomena he studies to unwarranted assumptions on human personality in a cultural context that is different from his own (1991 p. 14).

Kapferer's approach therefore is radically different from that of mainstream social science, which uses analytical categories. He looks at the lived experiences of people and takes them seriously. This to Kapferer does not mean thinking of these experiences as mere expressions of something else, such as a social scientist's theoretical baggage. Such constructions are a great historical and contextual distance from the lived reality being studied. In Kapferer's approach, the group is studied for its own logics and assumptions. The anthropologist opens himself to the experiences on offer.

Kapferer thus attempts to grasp exorcism within its own logic. When he did his study, he was aware of the fascination in the West in recent decades with non-Western ritual forms and healing practices. These non-Western practices held out the promise of different solutions to problems of humans as well as of different pathways to human liberation (Kapferer 1991 p. xx). They confronted the canons of Western rationalism, which many felt was at the root of much suffering and destruction. Postmodern approaches in anthropology are an extension of such critiques. The approach that Kapferer takes is an extension of attacks on that social science which has come from the mold of Western scientific rationalism. He wants to present what exorcists make of their world according to their own logic, and he does not want to subordinate their knowledge of the world to other forms of knowledge.

Kapferer's book, Victor Turner notes in a foreword, is a pioneering study in an emerging sub-field of "performance studies." There is apparently only one university department, the Department of Performance Studies at New York University, which uses this approach. The approach combines social sciences and arts, so as to shape both theory and method. It is multidisciplinary and cross-cultural in perspective (Turner in Kapferer 1991 p. xxi).

Turner in his foreword also evokes Herbert Mead, whose approach emphasizes that a person is a succession of I's molded by a succession of Me's. The Me is the object one forms of oneself through others' views of oneself (Kapferer 1991 p. xxiv). Turner says that in the possession ritual that Kapferer describes, possession occurs when the I is detached from the Me and becomes involved only in the subjective self—thus becoming aware of only the patient's internal states. At the initial stage of demonic possession, the I is absorbed in the Me. The multiple social selves corresponding to different Me's in different social contexts vanish, and the patient is submerged in his own I. This is similar, Turner points out, to the Western definition of schizophrenia, according to which there is considered to be a disjuncture between emotions and thought processes resulting in the creation of hallucinations and delusions. The patient is cured according to Kapferer by his re-socialization. The patient now becomes like a little child, a blank sheet on which are rewritten the multiple selves, the many Me's corresponding to different social milieus. And, corresponding to the many social and cultural fields, there are many types of demons (1991 p. xxv).

The methodology of Kapferer is also shaped by the phenomenological approaches of Husserl and Schutz. In these approaches, meaning is defined by a context in which both subjective and objective factors are combined (Kapferer 1991 p. 8). Kapferer also believes that exorcisms cannot be understood by confining them within the conceptual boundaries of a particular sub-discipline in anthropology. Kapferer's aim in the study is not just to understand exorcism. The phenomenon has to be studied through its own terms to lay bare what he terms "Sinhalese culture."

One manner in which the "Sinhalese" (generalizing with regard to that social category) can act directly on experiences and meaning of the world is through demon exorcisms (Kapferer 1991 p. 2). Kapferer examines the political and social contexts of these ceremonies as well as the logic of ideas that are included in these performances. He emphasizes the role of the esthetic in exorcism, of music, drama, and song in giving meaning to the world of experience, thus allowing it to be transformed.

In the everyday world, cultural ideas are continuously being reshaped in social interaction. Key cultural ideas are often taken for granted, but in exorcist ceremonies this underlying, pre-reflective world of a taken-for-granted universe is thrown open for examination (Kapferer 1991 pp. 2–3). Kapferer takes exorcist ritual to stand both as a model *of,* and a model *for,* social action. According to him, ideas reach their full potential in ritual, and so can transform the experienced world and the ensuing action through the ritual's illusory and mystifying potential. Sinhalese rituals can be considered in this light as illusory and mystifying because they discover the origins of disturbance, whether individual or social, and aim to restore order by chasing away demons from the human's world. Kapferer says that anthropologists could uncover these illusory and mystifying processes. But, he claims, so also could members of the culture themselves. Exorcism does this for the Sinhalese because they allow for the possibility of demonism (1991 pp. 4–5).

In spite of these broad aims of understanding "the Sinhalese" through his new methodology, Kapferer admits that his study is limited in scope, and he also says that his knowledge of the Sinhala language is "very imperfect" and "fumbling" (1991 pp. xxviii–xxix). Later, in his second edition, Kapferer admits that both the situation on the ethnographic ground and the theoretical situation have changed in the eight years since the first edition (1991 p. ix).

THE EXORCISTS PERFORM

Kapferer's research was conducted in the vicinity of the southern city of Galle (1991 p. xxvii), where for two years he studied a number of patients. He mentions different temple organizations in Galle, presumably because they were influential in his field setting (p. 41).

The number of patients in his study who indulged in exorcist healing totaled 22 males and 35 females, 57 in all. Among those were 17 men and 27 women (a total of 44, amounting to 77 percent of all his patients) who had also previously been to a Western-trained doctor for their ailment, or were concurrently getting Western treatment together with exorcism

(Kapferer 1991 p. 79). Some others, 8 males and 13 females (a total of 21, accounting for 37 percent of the total), had been to an Ayurvedic doctor.

Kapferer says that exorcisms are a regular aspect of everyday life in the western and southern part of Sri Lanka (1991 p. 18). He notes that demon exorcisms are performed primarily among the poor, the working class, and the peasantry, not among the middle classes (p. 18). Kapferer claims that the exorcisms are popular because they enable the working and peasant classes to maintain control over their own religious rites.

Kapferer describes in his case studies the trance dancing of a teenage Sinhalese schoolgirl, the wife of a local police inspector, and a Tamil tea estate employee (1991 p. xv). He notes that the schoolgirl's dancing is less inhibited than that of the others.

He discusses what he claims is the logic of the cultural ideas of the Sinhalese about themselves and about the supernatural (1991 p. xv). The demonic expresses itself in the daily life and experience of the Sinhalese. Suffering, misfortune, illness, and disease can therefore find experience, meaning, and explanation through demons and demonic forces, within a world "commanded and structured by malign demonic forces" (p. 1).

Kapferer discusses the central organizing principles in the hierarchical order of the Sinhalese Buddhist cosmos. Demonic attack subverts this order (1991 pp. 128–155); demons intrude upon the social world of the Sinhalese and disturb their ordering (p. 1). In afflicted patients the "Sinhalese cosmological order" is inverted; the world is turned upside down (p. 155). When the patient engages in exorcism, it helps build up this subverted order again and restore it. Demons, who are the subversives of this order, are masters of tricks and illusion and through these they can fool human beings. But ridding patients of their illusions can remove the power of the demons. This is done by ensnaring demons as victims of their own mischief (pp. 179–245). Kapferer describes how, in these ceremonies, what he considers a reality apart from the everyday world is built around the patient through dance, music, and song (pp. 245–285). The demonic now becomes a theater of meaning for the patient. The later, climactic part of the exorcist ceremony occupies half the time of the drama and uses comic aspects. In this milieu of comedy, the reality of the demonic is shattered (pp. 285–319). The exorcisms are held to honor demons; they are treated as if they are gods. But the ceremony destroys them. They are trapped. What begins as a celebration of demons becomes a means for dishonoring them. The comedy in the exorcist drama laughs at demons and lampoons them, thus freeing the patient (pp. 315–319). The patient now returns to the reality of the healthy (pp. 285–319). This, then, is the final thrust of Kapferer's thesis. The patient experiences a demonological cosmic world, which through the ritual is broken up, restoring the patient to normalcy.

But even in this neat formulation of the rituals and their meaning, there are intruding factors, which Kapferer tries to explain. The first is their class character.

Kapferer claims that according to historians Geiger and Ariyapala, there is some evidence that exorcism was common to all classes before the advent of colonialism (1991 p. 26). But today, the middle classes devalue these exorcisms (p. 25). The ideology of the middle class is against exorcist ceremonies, looking down on them, giving them a class and status inferiority (p. 29).

Kapferer mentions that the Buddhist reformation in Sri Lanka was concerned with getting rid of impurities in ideas and practices (1991 p. 32). He says that in this movement, many practices were frowned upon by the middle class as being those of folk religion. Kapferer states that Anagarika Dharmapala, the main reformer, contrasted Buddhism to the vulgar sciences of "astrology, occultism, ghostology and palmistry," considering them un-Buddhist (p. 35).

Kapferer states that this dichotomy of a purer tradition and false accretions is an invention of the Sri Lankan middle classes (1991 p. 45). Because of particular social processes, the new interpretations of Buddhism are now the new orthodoxy. The practices of the middle classes have therefore become part of a language of domination. But this, he says, should not imply "the veracity of the reformist's religious interpretation" or the "authenticity and purity" of the reformist's practices.

Further, Kapferer believes that the demonic is an "under-view," a view from below, a cultural critique, as it were. This reflects the ideological and class bias of the rituals. This is especially so, as the Sinhalese middle class looks down upon these practices. Kapferer believes these practices are a means of coping with the demonic state. They give voice to the everyday difficulties that Sinhalese workers and peasants face as they are subordinated by the state (1991 pp. 320–323).

There was an insurgency in 1971 in which many thousands were killed by the state. Kapferer says this violence itself was an expression of the demonic (1991 p. 51).

If demons, according to Kapferer, are trapped in the ceremonies, anthropologists for their part, coming as they do from Europe and America—almost as distant as the places demons come from, and almost as exotic—trap their local subjects in categories and concepts. One trap that has given rise to a wide variety of confusion and debate among anthropologists is that there are more females who are subject to these rites than men. Kapferer cites various reasons to explain this phenomenon, there being disagreement among the various anthropological experts. Thus Lewis (1971) took the trance-possession in Somali women to be due to their subordinate position, with the ritual acting as a psychological release for them. Lewis, using some of the work of Obeyesekere, considers this explanation to be applicable to Sri Lanka as well (see Kapferer 1991 p. 129).

Kapferer examines the context of Lewis's remarks, goes back to Obeyesekere's original words, and casts doubt on Lewis's specific interpretation. He also states that both Lewis and Obeyesekere rest their analyses on psychological factors. Kapferer notes that Obeyesekere's position is difficult to either prove or disprove.

Kapferer, in opposing the "subjugation of women" thesis, notes that Sinhalese women are highly independent. They are not prepared to accept without a struggle the submissive role that men may mete out to them. Kapferer also notes P. J. Wilson's (1967) observation that the subordination of females may not account for possession. Wilson believes that possession occurs not so much due to conflicts between men and women but to conflicts between members of the same sex. Kapferer finds Wilson's arguments better than those of the others. Yet he thinks they cannot simply be applied to Sri Lanka. He believes that because of pollution criteria, women are prefigured culturally to become possessed. Exorcisms, he notes, are domestic and household rituals, and women occupy domestic spaces more than men, necessitating the prevalence of women in these rituals (1991 pp. 131–154).

Another intruding factor that Kapferer has to deal with is the fact that even among the poor and women, demonic rituals are not the only means of healing that are resorted to. At time of crisis, Kapferer acknowledges, Sinhalese appeal to a variety of sources of help. These include physicians trained in the Western tradition, hypnotherapists, Ayurvedics, Buddhist monks, astrologers, priests of local deities, and exorcists. So an afflicted person might attend a medical clinic or hospital, obtain Ayurvedic medicine, wear a *yantra* (an amulet to ward off disease), get Buddhist monks to chant *Pirit* (which he calls purificatory and curative), or get an exorcist. Sinhalese may choose from this variety of specialists.

Gombrich (1991 p. 150), noting this phenomenon, stated that Sinhalese will change from one specialist to another in search of a cure. Although Kapferer believes this to be true in a general sense, this search among alternatives, according to him, is governed by a wider search for meaning within the Sinhalese cultural framework. He says that in Sinhalese meaning, there are multiple realities, and the different specialties available emphasize these different realities. Different specialist practices address different facets of the illness. It is through this approach that Sinhalese deal with illness as it is conceived through their cultural ideas (Kapferer 1991 p. 24).

Although some practitioners may view this variety of specialists as characteristic of a pluralistic system, Kapferer does not think so. In the pluralistic view, all practices available are viewed as functionally alternative. To members of the culture they appear as equivalent and subject to free choice. But according to Kapferer, instead of being alternatives, the choices are complementary; the range of alternatives available is less real than it appears to be. Kapferer does not believe that the patient is simply making a "medical" choice. The different choices have cultural and social meanings beyond any medical-technical function (Kapferer 1988 pp. xi, xii).

Kapferer believes that demonic illness cannot be reduced outside of the cultural ideas associated with it. He says that demonic illness *is* the illness. It cannot be broken down into the categories given by Western psychology or biomedical science. These can at best be only partial frameworks for understanding the illness.

THE DEMONS ENTER THE NATIONAL STAGE

In his second book, *Legends of People, Myths of State: Violence, Intolerance, and Political Culture in Sri Lanka and Australia* (1988), Kapferer examines the cultures of nationalism in Sri Lanka and Australia. It is Sri Lanka that gets the more detailed treatment. Its events are explained through the systems that he developed in the earlier book, that is, through the "world view of demons." He examines, from this light, the ethnic conflict between Sinhalese and Tamils. He studies the conflict, considering essentially the actions of one group, namely, the Sinhalese. Tamils do not come into the narrative except as bit players. Kapferer explains Sinhala actions from their nationalist logic, which he says has a hierarchical form (1988 pp. xi, xii). He is aware that although he explains on the basis of his (large) explanatory variables, he could be overtaken by the flow of actual events. Yet he maintains that in a study such as his, the structure of the argument is more critical than events.

Kapferer builds his thesis on a track parallel to that explored by Louis Dumont in *Homo Hierarchicus* and other writings. Here, Dumont tried to show that there were different orientations in European and Indian ideological systems. Kapferer builds on this work, whose central position is that egalitarianism and individualism are not consonant with the hierarchical arrangements in India (Kapferer 1988 p. 8).

Kapferer's central argument, which he says has been partly anticipated by Dumont, is that egalitarianism and hierarchy, separately or in combination, are destructive and dehumanizing. This is seen in the nationalist project, which takes hierarchical or egalitarian directions (Kapferer 1988 p. 9). Dumont excluded Sri Lanka from his hierarchical scheme. But Kapferer takes Sri Lanka to be a variant of Dumont's Indian scheme.

Let me briefly sketch Kapferer's theory of hierarchy.

The hierarchy is a whole constituted of parts. Kapferer introduces the ideas of the demonic, which he learned in his study of rituals, to the hierarchical perspective. He says that the Buddha and the demonic are in polar opposition in this hierarchy; one is reason, the other non-reason; one is pure, the other polluting. The Sinhalese world of existence and its social relations, including relations with supernaturals, exist in a hierarchy determined by their relative distance from the Buddha or from the demons (1988 p. 11).

The logic of hierarchy in Sri Lanka is, therefore, found in rituals of healing. The hierarchical principle implies that what is unified can split into a less unified, more fragmented form. Thus a deity becomes demonic, becoming a lower fragmented form, and can then be re-formed once again into the higher level. Kapferer claims that in the Sinhalese Buddhist cosmic hierarchy, unity can be considered equivalent to purity, and fragmentation to pollution (1988 p. 12).

He says that the nation and the state have a particular significance in the Sinhalese Buddhist hierarchical arrangement. The Triple Gem (the Buddha, Dhamma, and the Sangha) encompasses the state. The state, in turn, encompasses the nation. It is this logic that drives Sinhalese in their relationship with Tamils.

Kapferer says that he explores the growth of ethnic nationalism, its mythic symbolism, the ontology of myth, and the formation of a political ideology based on the hierarchical structure of Sinhalese myths. He says he was driven by only one concern, namely, understanding the escalating ethnic violence in Sri Lanka. This violence includes both the violence of the state and that of rioting Sinhalese Buddhists; both kill Tamils (1988 p. 112).

THE DEMONS COME OUT (IN RIOTS):
THE EMPIRICAL STUDY

The word "demonic" triggered Kapferer into exploring the "hierarchy" theory. He found the violence of the 1983 anti-Tamil riots literally "demonic," and he tries to explain it in terms of the demonic rituals that he studied (1988 p. 29). Kapferer alleges that the demonic passions of the rioters found their driving force in Sinhalese Buddhist nationalism, which included cosmological arguments similar to those in exorcism (1988 p. 29). His central thesis is that the hierarchy dynamic expressed in the historical myths of the Sinhalese had an effect on the 1983 riots. Although he mentions in passing that there was also growing civil strife among the Sinhalese themselves, he claims that the violence was dominated by Sinhalese visions of mythic history and hegemony (p. 115).

Let me first summarize these constructions of Sinhalese history which he makes, and which are central to his position.

Kapferer says that he does *not* dispute the Sinhalese historical chronicles as "repositories of fact in a rationalist empiricist sense" (1988 p. 42). But he says that he shares with Obeyesekere the latter's disagreement with the way historical scholarship proceeds in Sri Lanka. Obeyesekere disagrees with the manner by which history is constructed on the basis of commonsense elements while ignoring those elements that are mythical or legendary. Kapferer says Geiger (1950) (a 19th-century translator of the 6th-century *Mahavamsa,* the most famous of the chronicles) implied that Sri Lankan chronicles were based on folk traditions and not on carefully maintained records (1988 pp. 42–43).

Kapferer implies, quoting Obeyesekere, that the major Sri Lankan archaeologist, Paranavithana (Obeyesekere 1984), tried to interpret inscriptional material to show North Indian claims of Sinhalese origins, suggesting that Paranavithana was involved not in a scientific enterprise but in a myth-building one (Kapferer 1988 p. 37). Kapferer also refers to the statement made by the controversial minister Mathew, of the J. R. Jayawardene government, that 300 sites had been excavated by the Archaeological Department in the North and East of Sri Lanka. Kapferer says such statements are "completely consistent with Sinhalese claims to territorial hegemony that are supported by a reading of the ancient chronicles" (p. 37).

Elsewhere, Kapferer mentions that Sinhala chronicles have ideological content (1988 p. 81). He says historical reality and historical myth are intertwined here, and asserts that the historical material in Sri Lankan chronicles is mostly legend and imagined histories (p. 96).

Kapferer sees the struggles in the chronicles, between what he alleges are fathers and sons and between brothers, not as the simple power politics found in all kingdoms but as grist for his scheme of mythical and cosmic order. In this he differs from another commentator (whose name he does not mention, but it is probably Obeyesekere), who says that these are not raw power struggles, but Freudian-Oedipal struggles (Kapferer 1988 p. 62). Kapferer also claims that the final battle in the form of a duel in the 2nd century B.C. between the local king, Dutugemunu, and the South Indian invader, Elara—whether it took place in the form of direct personal combat Kapferer says is a moot point—was cosmologically ordained (p. 63).

Kapferer claims that Dutugemunu's building of monuments is to be interpreted as an attempt at cosmic stabilization (in the sense in which Kapferer has defined "Sinhalese cosmology"). Through this, the inherent fragmentation of the world order as defined by Kapferer's hierarchical principle is overcome by the affirmation of unifying Buddhist cosmic principles (1988 pp. 57–58). Elsewhere, Kapferer dismisses the entire history of Dutugemunu as an imaginary construct, although he mentions that there is a commitment to the facticity of these events by many Sinhalese scholars (1988 p. 122).

Kapferer says that in the Sinhalese-Buddhist nationalist ideology other groups are held in hierarchical subordination to Sinhalese Buddhists (1988 p. 7). He further says that Sinhalese nationalism is built of what he considers the myths of history and the deeds of its heroes, as the Tamils try to destroy or subsume the Sinhalese. But in the process, the Tamils themselves are destroyed and conquered like demons (p. 2).

Kapferer describes his own invented scheme of hierarchy and then locates the various elements in it as self-evident. He says that evil as depicted in myths finds its chief metaphors in kings and princes "whose actions are antagonistic to Buddhist principles" (1988 p. 71). To give additional credence to his application of this "demon theory" to the past, he mentions that some demons are alleged to be historical figures reborn. For instance, in one exorcist interpretation, Kalu Kumaraya is supposed to be the legendary king Vijaya reborn, while in others he is considered to be Vijaya's son (p. 65).

Kapferer points out that the kings who are the unifiers of the country are also the renouncers. When the cosmic whole is attacked, fragmentation ensues and demonic forces are released. The world loses its hierarchical quality. The former, non-fragmented cosmic situation is ultimately restored by enthroning the hierarchy, with the Buddha at the head and the demonic forces in retreat (1988 p. 12).

In the Sinhalese world, Kapferer states, the individual is conditioned by the way the hierarchical world moves in this overall cosmic process. He says that both Buddhist monks and demons are outside society and orient themselves toward nonexistence. The monks go to *Nirvana* and the demons go to a fragmented annihilation. From the brink of extinction, monks and demons come back to realize the forces in society that their principles embody. Monks reenter the world and reorder it according to their ideals of the cosmic process. Demons in turn enter society as independent beings and recast it in their ahierachial image (1988 p. 13).

The above is a brief summary of Kapferer's views on Sinhalese history and hierarchy. He applies them to the present and near-present.

Kapferer states that the popular invented historical tradition based on myths broke through regional, linguistic, and social restrictions and moved out of the realm of monks to become today's state ideology. In the process, these traditions created a new imaginary community (1988 p. 96). He says, citing Benedict Anderson's (1983) book, that this mythical folk knowledge became widespread in Sri Lanka through the mechanism of printing (Kapferer 1988 p. 94).

Kapferer says, further, that mechanisms such as print capitalism are not the only means by which this type of folk knowledge is spread today. He also gives as examples what he calls "nationalist encouragement of Buddhist worship," such as visiting ancient sites (1988 p. 94). Kapferer says that renewed interest in rituals such as *gammaduwa* and *devol madutwa*, especially as presented by the state in public parks and for mass audiences, shows a marked renewal in the supposed cultural practices of the past. Some of these folk traditions are repeated in school texts (p. 94).

So, this invented past intrudes ideologically into the present and structures it (Kapferer 1988 p. 90). Kapferer says that by "invention of tradition" he means some traditions are created, while others are not, although ultimately he believes that *every* tradition is invented (1988 p. 210).

The nation in history, he maintains, is integral to the psychic unity of the Sinhalese (1988 p. 214). The Sinhalese believe that they have an identity because of their culture. This fetish of culture makes nationalism a religion (p. 98). The hierarchical ideology that he has identified, Kapferer says, stresses the internal unity of the Sinhalese (p. 214). And this internal unity structures the relations of the Sinhalese with non-Sinhalese (p.

xiii), resulting in the present political polarization founded on ethnic identity (p. xiii). There is therefore an association of evil with Tamils, not just through ethnic prejudice but as "threateningly evil" (p. 83). Kapferer says that the "Sinhalese state" defines the dominant principles of the political and social order, ethnic identity, and hierarchy. This, according to him, is a combination that has dreadful possibilities (p. 114). When what he terms the hierarchical Sinhalese-Buddhist state is subject to attack, the fragmentation of the state is considered the fragmentation of the nation, and in turn the fragmentation of the person (p. 7).

Kapferer says that the Sinhalese Buddhist state and the Sinhalese people are therefore in dangerous and reciprocal conjunction. In the eyes of Sinhalese nationalism, the state, its bureaucratic apparatus, and its agents are the guardians of Sinhala Buddhist culture. An "attack on the state, or apparatus of the state is an attack on the [Sinhalese] person" (1988 p. 100).

He also says that although many Sinhalese did not participate in the violence of the 1983 riots, many stood by and watched (1988 p. 34). Further, while some elements of the urban poor defended their Tamil neighbors, others attacked Tamils. The label he uses for the attackers is the derogatory Sinhalese word describing their social function, namely, *rasti-yadu karayo,* "aimless troublemakers"(p. 101).

Kapferer therefore tries to connect the violence associated with contemporary state terror, and violence associated with the ethnic situation, with his demonic logical processes and alleged myths of history. He sees a connection between the passion of sorcery and the furious passion of ethnic violence. He draws attention to an allegation by Obeyesekere that there are murderous sentiments expressed in the sorcery and anti-sorcery practices engaged in by Sinhalese Buddhists. This violence is in the verses that are declaimed on these occasions (Kapferer 1988 p. 33). Pursuing this line of thinking, he claims that Sinhalese rioters fragment their demonic victims (p. 101).

Kapferer gives other examples of the general behavior of the Sinhalese derived from his theoretical construct of hierarchy, history, and demonology. Let me summarize a few of these.

Kapferer connects the 1980s political events in Sri Lanka with the *Suniyam* ceremonies that he studied earlier. He tries to explain the intervention by India at the time by recourse to this *Suniyam* ritual. He sees the overtones of the healing magicians dressed in Punjabi dress in exorcist ceremonies as a comment on the contemporary Indian intervention. He makes a prognosis with regard to the 1987 Indian Accord on the basis of this ritual. He believes that the search for what he calls hierarchical unity by the Sinhalese could lead to further bloodletting *among* the Sinhalese (1988 p. xiii).

He also asserts the significance of Minister Mathew's making nationalist statements during the month of Esala—a time which Kapferer says is high in religious and ethnic consciousness—so that their impact could be high (1988 p. 39). The other examples he gives of the significance of this month is that King Dutugemunu (2nd century B.C.) laid the foundation of the Ruvanweli Seya in this month, that the Kataragama festival popularly associated with Dutugemunu is celebrated in Esala, and that there is also the annual Perehara (a huge, impressive procession whose roots go back centuries, with hundreds of elephants, dancers, and drummers marching by torchlight) takes place during this month. He finds it significant that the 1983 riots also occurred in the month of Esala (p. 39).

Kapferer implies that it is mythmaking at the highest level when the president of the country, J. R. Jayawardene, claims in a speech that there was in Sri Lanka an unbroken line of 2,500 years of monarchs from Vijaya to Elizabeth II (1988 p. 85). Kapferer quotes from the same speech Jayawardene's statement that the last king who came from a Tamil lineage of South India was "wicked and corrupt"; so it was appropriate to rebel against him (pp. 85, 100). Kapferer sees that as an example of the ethnic bias—"the ontology of ideology"—of Jayawardene (p. 100).

In trying to give further evidence of his scheme of historical motivations at the state level, Kapferer mentions yet another speech from a state leader, this time from Prime Minister Premadasa, who says that rebellions start from the South, including those of Dutugemunu, whom Premadasa takes pains to paint as nonracist (Kapferer 1988 p. 86). Kapferer also gives the example of the army commander at his appointment going to worship at the most important temple in the country, implying that this is un-Buddhistic (p. 87). Kapferer complains that Sinhalese regiments fighting Tamil separatists have names like Gemunu Watch, Sinha Regiment, and Raja Rata Rifles, reminiscent of Sinhalese history (p. 35).

Lower down the scale of the state and society, Kapferer gives other examples of current evidence of the hierarchically based bias. One is an article in the Sinhala daily *Divayina* (1988 p. 87). The other is the opinion of the chief monk of the Dutugemunu Viharaya at Baddegama, who stated in a meeting where monks and laity had gathered to pray for an end to terrorism that if these peaceful techniques were not successful, monks themselves should disrobe and take to fighting (p. 87). Kapferer calls the material presented by another monk, Madihe Pannaseeha Thero, before the Sansoni Commission appointed by the government after the 1977 riots, material of fury (p. 36). He also alludes to a slogan that came to prominence in the period of the 1987–1989 revolt, "Death or Mother-land," as another example of the nationalist pathology of the Sinhalese (p. 36).

Kapferer also sees illustrations of the cosmic logic associated with his theories of hierarchy and demons in two newspaper cartoons that he re-produces in his book (1988 pp. 88, 89). To Kapferer, these are illustrative of "the process of a Sinhalese Buddhist cosmic hierarchy" (p. 89).

KAPFERER DISCARDING DEMONS:
ENTER SORCERERS

Kapferer's third book, *The Feast of the Sorcerer: Practices of Consciousness and Power* (1997), explores sorcery. He now discards his foray into the macro social mechanics of the country taken as a whole and returns to a particular aspect of it, as in his first study. As our concern is with anthro-pologists' attempts to decode an entire society, I will not describe this book's contents at length; I will merely summarize it in a few paragraphs.

Among others, Kapferer explores through sorcery (especially a form called *Suniyam)*, the nature of consciousness and how humans create their existential realities and make sense of them. He believes that sor-cery highlights the extraordinary ability of humans to both create and destroy the circumstances of their existence. He is not interested in ex-ploring sorcery either as a reflection of social or political forces or as an expression of internal psychological conflicts, which are the common ap-proaches to sorcery. He rejects these approaches as trying to force-fit sor-cery into categories external to it. His aim is to see sorcery through its own rationality and to expose how humans construct their psychological and social realities. He says that when persons resort to sorcery, they re-center themselves in the world, sorcery having two aspects, cosmogonic and ontogenetic. Through his study, he also wishes to address issues re-lated to contemporary anthropology, such as the nature of human con-sciousness and the embodied nature of mental activities (1997 pp. xi–xii).

Kapferer makes a confession, however, that in his first foray into the irrational in Sri Lankan society (he does not call it the irrational), which was to see the world through the eyes of exorcism, he ignored the exor-cists' own advice on the centrality of *Suniyam,* the current practices that he now studies. His ritual specialists advised him then that the present practices were a key to the whole genre, but he spurned their advice. Now recognizing his error, he follows their advice and studies *Suniyam* (1997 p. xii).

In his second book he also referred to *Suniyam*, but now he says that the ethnography there was only a preliminary sketch. But because in that second book he made certain statements at the macro level, namely, on the ethnic riots, he now makes some "corrections." Apparently there were critics who "misunderstood" him. Kapferer says that contrary to what critics say, he did not argue that Sinhalese nationalism was modeled on exorcism, or that the 1983 riots arose through a causal link from exorcist rites. He says he was claiming only that the rite was a metaphor for the riot. He was, he says, arguing only that the ontogeny of nationalism overlapped with the exorcists because the mythical and imaginary constructions of Sinhala history are also integral to exorcisms such as the form he studies here, *Suniyam* (1997 p. xiv).

Kapferer is still committed to situational analyses and the extended case approach of his teachers. Yet he has shifted his perspective in this book because, he says, almost ten years after his second book there is now a very different climate in both anthropological and general critical discourse (1997 p. xiv). This book, however, builds on the arguments in the first book by expanding them. Whereas in his second book he emphasized the totalizing effects of hierarchy, he now argues for their limitations. He now also wants to move away from human activity as performance, the central theme in his first book, to stressing practice. In his first book he was interested in demonstrating the value of methodological interpretations *then* being developed (emphasis mine). He *now* gives greater importance to the actual discourse on practice and less to abstract reflections on it.

Apparently his earlier work was criticized as Eurocentric. So he says that no ethnography can escape this charge. But he does take into account, he says, recent (implying, since the first book) criticism in anthropology.

The bulk of the 1997 book is an attempt at an ethnography of the *Suniyam* he studies and the surrounding social context, as he considers it to be. It is clearly not meant for a local Sinhalese audience, because it combines selected aspects of the obvious with tedious descriptions of the commonplace together with forays into his own imagination. I will not go into this in detail except to say that the book is boring, patchy, and could well be considered easily and eminently forgettable. It is my considered judgment that no Sinhalese language publisher would have considered it.

We have briefly discussed Kapferer's three books on Sri Lanka. We have seen him move his narrative from a specially laid out methodology, to the study of exorcists on their own terms to explain the macro processes governing the ethnic conflict, and finally to the study of a group of sorcerers. His aim is to reveal the dynamics of Sinhalese Buddhist society. It is time now to see how far he has succeeded. I will do this in two chapters, one devoted to his first book and the second to his last two books.

CHAPTER 7

■

The Apprentice's Illness

Kapferer's methodology for his first book was the "situational analy-sis" of Gluckman (1958) and Mitchell (1956) and the "extended case analy-sis" of Turner (1957, 1968a, 1968b). By the time of his second edition, the debates of anthropology had changed, and Kapferer evokes the by-then-fashionable postmodernism. Explanations of Sri Lanka and its presenta-tion to the external world thus depend on the vicissitudes of the academic constructions of anthropologists and their struggles—including possibly career-related factors—that govern these constructions.

NO MADNESS IN THIS METHOD: ONLY POSSESSION

Kapferer is aware that there is a fascination in the West with non-West-ern ritual forms and healing practices as different pathways to human liberation (1991 p. xx). So his study is partly an implicit massage to the Western psyche in its current state of social and intellectual uncertainty. Metropolitan reality and theory sneak into the description of Sri Lankan reality, in fact into the very choice of the area to be studied as Sri Lankan social reality. More significantly, the exorcist halfway around the world in southern Sri Lanka through his techniques is called in to cure the Western ills of modern times. Kapferer further states that his approach is an extension of attacks on the traces of Western scientific rationalism in social science. But this is a scientistic reading of the Western scientific enterprise and its social, cultural, and conceptual roots. No serious soci-ologist of science today would subscribe to this view.

Victor Turner informs us in his foreword that Kapferer's is a pioneer-ing effort in the emerging sub-field of "performance studies." From what one gathers in the book, this approach is used by only one institution, the Department of Performance Studies at New York University (Kap-ferer 1991 p. xxi). So contrary to what Kapferer says, not only are perspec-tives of the metropolis mapped in his book, but what is mapped is a minority perspective that has not been sufficiently exposed to the regular academic peer review process or been accepted by the rest of Western social science. An unkind person might say that Sri Lanka is not only being viewed through a metropolitan reality but is being viewed through a possiblly crackpot, cranky version of it.

Kapferer says that he uses a combined philosophical and anthropological approach (1991 p. xvii) including Marxist, structuralist, and symbolic-interactionist aspects. But this is self-contradictory, as each of these schemes is conceptually closed; they each try to provide a total picture through which all the variables in the social world are by and large explainable. Symbolic interactionism explores the subjective world as largely a closed field. But the Marxist scheme believes subjective factors are related, and subordinated, to class factors. Kapferer's taking the exorcists' own subjectivist constructions as valid descriptions of reality (p. xviii) is a far cry from a Marxist or any contemporary socially based analysis of knowledge. Kapferer says that all realities are constructions and decries rationalist social science theories, but he avidly and unquestioningly embraces as valid knowledge the statements of a self-styled "Committee for Rational Development."

Kapferer's view that ritual is always totalizing is an assertion that even in allegedly "unadulterated" precolonial Sri Lanka was not true. Robert Knox noted that the average 18th-century Sinhala villager used gods and demons very instrumentally. If the supernatural did not deliver, then the Sinhalese "shat in their mouth" in derision. Kapferer must be aware of this attitude, because he must have read Gombrich, who cites Knox's words. In the village studied by Gombrich, too, there was considerable skepticism expressed about *bali* ceremonies. Some villagers believed that the efficacy was all in the mind. One said that he did not go in for all this *demon* stuff (Gombrich 1991 p. 247). Gombrich also noted that Sinhalese Buddhists do not admit to going beyond the rational, although at times they do go beyond it. He observed that this contrasted with Christianity, which explicitly orders believers to go beyond reason (1991 p. 308). These observations of Gombrich are contrary to Kapferer's assumption of a general "demon point of view" internalized by the Sinhalese. Further, even the exorcists have doubts as to their own efficacy. They refuse to involve their type of healing in the really tricky cases (Kapferer 1991 p. 81). Kapferer also mentions that "Sinhalese are frequently skeptical" (p. 87). They often express suspicion about the legitimacy of a diagnosis in a demonic attack. But apparently Kapferer does not.

A key to Kapferer's thesis is that there is a "Sinhalese cosmological order" governing demons which is turned upside down through demonic possession (1991 p. 155). This could be true for those who know this "cosmological order." Yet no average Sinhalese would know this order, because it is not transmitted formally, as Buddhism is transmitted through temples, homes, and other significant socializing media. This knowledge is held privately by *kapuralas,* the priests who mix Buddhism, deities, and demons into one conceptual whole.

Gombrich also noted in his first study that exorcists derived *pretas,* gods, and demons partly from Buddhism, and that these beings are subsumed to it. They are looked at essentially through the worldview of Buddhism (Gombrich 1991 pp. 190–194). Kapferer, on the other hand, views the world through the worldview of demons. His position is that exorcisms have to be studied on their own terms to lay bare "Sinhalese culture" (1991 p. 2). But in seeing Sinhala culture through exorcist ceremonies, Kapferer is looking through a partially obscured tunnel, in fact even through a distorting prism, focused only on one small aspect—a truly hallucinogenic view of the Sinhalese world. In the exorcist's own hierarchy, the Buddha is placed at the top, demonical theories often being legitimized within an assumed Buddhist framework. So the concept of reality in Buddhism is allowed implicit validity by the users of the very demonic scheme that Kapferer tries to harness for himself. Kapferer thus makes a selective and conscious choice when he chooses exorcists' conceptual fodder for his constructs, whereas he could well have used the more formal and rigorous formulations of Buddhism and still been true to his subjects' own world.

Kapferer says that demonism allows one to uncover illusory and mystifying processes (1991 pp. 4–5). But the main theoretical system that informs Sinhala Buddhists, namely Buddhism, deals explicitly and in a systematic, sophisticated, conceptual manner with the problems of illusion and false perception. Therapies derived from this perspective have been used very successfully in the West. Kapferer also evokes the phenomenology of Husserl and Schutz, which combines both subjective and objective factors (p. 8). But theirs is a position nearer the Buddhist one, which also does not accept the subject-object dichotomy. And Husserl's views, for example, have been compared with South Asian philosophical positions (Hanna 1993). So if Kapferer had really wanted to see the world through Sinhalese eyes, he could have used Buddhist theoretical material instead of the unsophisticated epistemological apparatus of the exorcist.

Kapferer grossly overgeneralizes when he says that in the western and southern part of Sri Lanka exorcisms are a *regular* part of everyday life, and that these village-level ceremonies are increasing (1991 p. 18). In Kandyan provinces which came under colonial rule only in the 19th century, such performances are much rarer. These practices in the Western and Southern Provinces, Kapferer had noted earlier, were limited to the poor. His actual sample reveals how rare they are.

The Sinhalese resort, Kapferer admits, to a multiplicity of healing practices and practitioners: Western medicine, Ayurvedics, Buddhist monks, astrologers, priests of local deities, exorcists, and hypnotherapists (well, I had not heard of that last one before; one continues to be educated by Kapferer). They also change from one to the other. In his own sample of a grand total of fifty-seven souls from, at the time, over 15 million Sinhalese, 77 percent of those undergoing exorcist therapy had gone or were going to a Western doctor. In addition, 37 percent were going to Ayurvedics. Only two or three, literally, went exclusively to exorcists. The question of the typicality of Kapferer's minuscule sample of just two or three patients as a window to the world of "the" (his word) Sinhalese must then be raised in the strongest terms. For the country as a whole, the number of those skeptical of exorcism or using it only as a last resort must be very much larger.

But, in spite of the evidence of therapy switching, Kapferer refuses to consider this as pluralistic behavior. He simply asserts that Sinhalese have multiple realities and that different specialists address these different realities. He says that the choice between treatments is beyond the medical-technical realm and is to be viewed through social and cultural meanings (1991 pp. 24–25).

Kapferer's taking the exorcist's and patient's presumed point of view as the true reality is problematic (1991 p. xix) The fact remains that several other sets of beliefs are held within the internal world of his users of exorcism, namely beliefs in Western medicine and Ayurveda, as well as other bits of knowledge they have imbibed, including science. For example, in a country that has seen near-universal literacy for three generations, the average citizen does not believe that in an eclipse Rahu swallows the moon, the mythical explanation of eclipses given by exorcists. The internal lives of the patients are therefore as much conditioned by modern Western medicine, Buddhism, Ayurveda, or science as by exorcism. This means that if the study of these exorcist followers is a guide to the cultural and inner life of what the author generalizes as *the* Sinhalese, then the study of Western medical practice and Western doctors would provide a better guide.

Such multiple frames of choice exist in a context of rapid change when there is no one agreed cultural frame but a multiplicity of them. A study carried out by the present writer in 1971 of a factory in the same geographical area as Kapferer's study and roughly at the same time indicates this phenomenon (Goonatilake, Susantha, 1971 p. 210; 1972). Thus, members of the organization did not hold that only the formal value system and authority of the organization were legitimate, and hence the only guide for action within the organization. In addition to the formal authority, many other "frameworks of authority" provided rules and norms of behavior that guided the activities of the members. These frameworks of authority were supplied largely by reference groups outside the factory in which factory employees also had membership. These groups included caste groups, kin groups, common-residence groups, and political groups. The factory was a state corporation and was subject to constant intervention by local politicians who acted often on behalf of these outside reference groups and influenced action within the factory organization.

Within the plant there was therefore no common set of rules accepted by all members, all the time, the formal rules being only nominally accepted as common. Not only were different frames of legitimate authority held by different groups of individuals, but often they were held by the same individual at different times. That is, an individual could legitimate one of his actions by one set of rules and another, even opposite, action by another set. In fact members often resorted to claiming legitimacy for actions taken for purely selfish motives by using whatever frame could legitimate these actions. So plurality of values and perspectives was not an uncommon feature in the environs of the authors' study area—and, indeed, one should extrapolate, of the country as a whole.

To give added explanation to Kapferer's framework, Turner in his foreword to the book has evoked the formulation of Herbert Mead, explaining how a succession of I's is molded by a succession of Me's. The "I" detached from the "Me" swims in its own subjectivity, the various social Me's being cast aside. Turner points out that this is similar to what happens in schizophrenia. The exorcist ceremony for its part re-socializes the patient, painting multiple Me's once again on his psyche (Kapferer 1991 pp. xxiv–xxv).

Kapferer wants to understand the world through the eyes of the exorcist, but this is not what he actually does. What he does is take the experience of the ritual as subjectively real and explain, through "I" and "Me," a Western conceptual grid that he himself has imposed. And if Kapferer was searching for a specifically Sri Lankan–inspired Western approach used in psychotherapy, based specifically on the dissociation of the "I" from the "Me" as in schizophrenia, he could well have gone to the theories and practices of his British countryman Laing. Laing's theories of a divided self are partly derived from his experience in Sri Lanka, especially from Buddhist theory (Clay 1996). Kapferer also says that demonic illness *is* the illness, and that it cannot be broken down into medical or psychological categories (1991 p. xxv). But again, there are increasingly effective practices for the treatment of mental illness in the West derived from Buddhist meditative practice. These practices are derived from the view that the self, as the "I" itself, is delusionary.

But today, schizophrenia is not treated through theories of the I and the Me. Such diseases have been increasingly shown to be due to genetic and biological factors, which can be cured by chemical means, or in the future by genetic therapies. In such cases, this whole fancy talk of an I and Me vanishes.

Kapferer says there are different kinds of cultural demons corresponding to the different modes of participation in Sri Lankan social and cultural existence (1991 p. xxv). Extended, this would imply that there are cultural demons corresponding to the different social and cultural roles that the Sinhalese occupy. But these cultural roles are changing, in fact they are multiplying. The sub-roles in today's Sri Lanka number in the thousands, if not tens of thousands, corresponding to the various new social roles that industrialization and contemporary changes in Sri Lanka have brought about. Taking Kapferer's assumptions to their logical conclusion, then, there should be also a proliferation of cultural demons. "Hell" presumably must indeed be an increasingly empty place as demons crawl out to do Kapferer's allotted bidding and fill the new roles.

THE MAGICIAN'S HAT OVERFLOWS

In addition to a highly flawed methodology and a pure sample of three persons on which to build his pronouncements on the Sinhalese, there are many shortcomings in Kapferer's empirical findings. Let me refer to a few.

Kapferer tells us that the trance-like dancing of a teenage Sinhalese schoolgirl at the ceremonies is uninhibited (1991 p. xv). But the probable explanation for the uninhibited trance-like dancing is that, as we saw in Chapter 6, the *baila* had by the 1980s infiltrated almost every school on the island, being performed at celebratory occasions such as sporting events. Apparently, Kapferer's narrow anthropological focus prevents him seeing the obvious in Sri Lankan events.

Kapferer makes a pregnant aside on the role of comedy in exorcism, noting that tourism affected exorcist rituals, which are seen by busloads of tourists. Comedy—the key to successful exorcism—is itself now changed, he says, by gearing exorcist performances to tourists. The key now, it appears, is partly in foreign hands.

The marketing for tourism of exorcism as exoticism was well under way in the 1970s, a fact that I and others had already recorded (Goonati-lake, Susantha, 1978). By the 1970s, exorcist performances were held for tourists not only in houses but also in hotels, and were events firmly built into the tourist calendar. Such tourist, and hence Western, consumption of the local perceived-as-exotic was not limited to exorcism. Traditional art objects such as puppets and masks used in exorcist ceremonies also entered the tourist scene. In the process, arts such as puppetry became bowdlerized. They moved away from their earlier Sri Lankan clientele to the new tourists. The same process occurred with regard to exorcist cere-monies and their paraphernalia, which since the early sixties had been sold in every tourist shop. In fact, the number of demon masks produced for the foreign tourist market exceeds by far the number produced for exorcist ceremonies. Tourists are today the main means of sustenance of mask makers. Such masks are also hung on the drawing room walls of lower-middle-class homes, together with other kitsch paraphernalia. In such drawing rooms, of probably the same lower classes that the author writes about, there are definitely no supernatural connotations or awe in the use of exorcist paraphernalia. The author does not document the im-plications of any of these changes, the movement of the artifacts and cere-monies away from their earlier uses to become both spectacle and deco-rative objects for their new clientele.

Kapferer mentions that demon exorcisms occur mainly among the poor—that the upper classes look down on them (1991 pp. 18, 29). But Gombrich, whom Kapferer has obviously read, makes a contrary class ob-servation, namely, that the upper and middle classes believe more in astrology and in auspicious practices than the lower classes, although Gombrich finds that those with stronger beliefs in Buddhism believe less in astrology (Gombrich 1991 pp. 173–174). Kapferer considers the demonic an "under view," a cultural critique of the Sinhalese middle classes (1991 p. 47). This begs the question of how it was in the past, when, he alleges, the upper classes, too, practiced demonism. Then, which class posture did demonism have; was it a cultural hegemony, the oppo-site of what Kapferer describes? Kapferer also says that these practices are a means of coping with the demonic state, as it subordinates the under-class (pp. 320–323). This begs another question: How did the demonic ex-press itself when the Sinhalese state was not as powerful as the state was in the colonial era? Did the demons creep underground when the state was weak?

In making a special fetish of the class bias of the demonic, Kapferer is being blind to his own Western culture. Contempt by the more educated classes for the "irrational" practices of the lower classes is not limited to Sri Lanka. Thus in the West, football matches, tabloid newspapers, and daytime TV programs that extol the irrational and the bizarre, as well as 900 numbers that provide instant psychics, are all primarily targeted at the poor and viewed with amused disdain by the educated. Nobody in Britain, for example, would dare to say that these newspapers, TV programs, and hooliganism at soccer matches provide a key to *the* British. Further, the knowledge possessed by the British professional classes, in addition to its own intrinsic worth, is also a "powerful ideology of class" and acts as an "instrument of class control" in that those classes who have the knowledge have more power because of it than those who do not.

Kapferer mentions that the insurgency of 1971, in which many thousands were killed by the state, was itself an expression of the demonic (1991 p. 51). The only demonic, meaning exorcist, element that was associated with the 1971 events was a powerful play by the late Dhamma Jagoda, who used techniques of inducing fright and terror found in the exorcist ceremonies as an indictment of the government repression. It should be mentioned that in the 1960s, exorcist ceremonies were explored for their dramatic potential, to be used in the modern stage drama by the leading dramatist Sarachchandra and his followers (Sarachchandra 1953; Gunatilleke, M. H., 1978).

Kapferer mentions the systematic code of lay ethical behavior, written down in the book by Anagarika Dharmapala, asserting that its two hundred rules were a form of class ideology and class domination (Kapferer 1991 p. 35). I have noted in Chapter 5 that unlike the construction given to it by Obeyesekere, Dharmapala's book was not a Protestant influence but a formalization of the percolation of monks' rules to the laity. Kapferer derives the critique of Dharmapala as a Protestant Buddhist from Obeyesekere's faulty construction, which we have discussed earlier. We have shown in Chapter 5 that it was *not* a movement to ape the West or to unconsciously adopt Protestantism. It was a cultural critique. Kapferer also says that the attack on some aspects of tradition placed the new middle classes in the same privileged position as the British rulers. But this ignores the cultural critique dimension, driven by a logic of emancipation. Overcoming servility to the British included a program to determine what was relevant in the tradition while eliminating what was irrelevant. These were strategies widely used by many self-conscious civilizations (which, translated, means those with a strong historical memory). Thus, the Japanese opened up to the West selectively using slogans such as *Wakon Yosai*, "Japanese Spirit, Western Civilization" (Yoshino 1968 p. 21).

Despite being unread in history, Kapferer contradicts the position held by well-read local historians such as K. M. de Silva (1979 pp. 144–47) that such revivals were a continuation of a very old companion to Sinhalese resistance to rule. Kapferer counters this by saying that the Buddhist revival and Sinhala nationalism were born within the structure of colonial British rule. So, he claims, these were class forces, married to class interests, and an instrument of class control (1991 p. 34). He again ignores the context of colonial rule and its subjugation of all classes except those who were allied to it (those the Chinese called the compradors).

Kapferer recalls the reformer Dharmapala's denunciation of "astrology, occultism, ghostology and palmistry," implicitly finding fault with the denunciation (1991 p. 35). He says that the reformation in Sri Lanka was interested in getting rid of impurities in ideas and practices, and so frowned upon many practices, declaring these to belong to folk religion (p. 32). He says that this dichotomy of a purer tradition and false accretions was invented by the Sri Lanka middle classes. He says that this new orthodoxy should not imply "the veracity of the reformist's religious interpretation" or of "the authenticity and purity" of the reformist's practices (p. 45). Kapferer appears unaware that in the Buddhist canon (for example in the *Samannaphala Sutta)* the occult arts are firmly denounced as unfit.

Kapferer fails to mention that this type of cleansing was a regular practice carried out earlier throughout Sinhalese history, for instance, in the Polonnaruwa (11th century) and Dambadeniya (13th century) periods to remove the religion of unnecessary accretions, especially distinguishing "ultimate truths," *parama sacca,* from positions of belief which are considered "conventional truths," *samucca sacca.* The key point to be emphasized is that if Kapferer takes the description of the reality of the exorcist to be valid and true, then he should at least allow the same privilege for the more formal and systematic Buddhist system.

Kapferer mentions that the reflection of social and political boundaries within the temple is a recent phenomenon (1991 p. 37). But this is not a recent phenomenon; careful reading of the earliest chronicles reveals such mapping of social divisions in the city of Anuradhapura in the 3rd century B.C. (see, for this period, Goonatilake, Susantha, 1981). In the same vein, Kapferer mentions different temple organizations as part of the institutional setting of Galle (1991 p. 41). But there are other, equally important or more important institutions that govern the power structure of Galle. (I too lived and did research in Galle at roughly the time Kapferer was doing his study.) Just a walk within a square kilometer around the Galle ramparts would have revealed the Galle Gymkhana Club, the Galle Public Servants Club, the Lions Club, the Gamini Sports Club, and so on. These are places of informal gathering of various key decision makers from different social strata in the city, as significant for the working of the city as are the various temple organizations. Because of his narrow focus—necessarily so because of his short stay and limited socialization into the society—Kapferer misses many of these facts. Galle is far from the remote tribal village of classical anthropology which could be studied in isolation. It is a complex entity with a continuous history of at least two thousand years, the complexity of this history resonating in the present.

By the early 1970s, the period in which Kapferer did his study, Sri Lanka was scoring highly on the development indicator called the Physical Quality of Life Index. This showed that although the nation was poor on the basis of purely economic criteria, it had attained high measures on health, education, and longevity. Further, Sri Lanka had lowered its population growth without the drastic coercive measures employed by China or attempted by India. The central explanatory factor for all these successes was the high literacy and educational standards of Sri Lanka and their effects on behavior. Sri Lankans could rapidly absorb "modern," secular information in a rational manner and act on it. The major factor that influenced the most important aspects of behavior in the environs of Galle, a most literate area, was a very mundane universal education package, behind which was nearly a century of Buddhist agitation. The gremlins that Kapferer deals in are tangential as explanatory factors for Sinhalese society and exist mostly in his brain, or in the literally two (or at most three) people in his sample who frequent exorcists exclusively.

Kapferer criticizes the use of psychoanalytic approaches by Obeyesekere, partly because he (Kapferer) does not want to reduce what he studies to assumptions of human personality that are brought in from an external culture (1991 p. 14). But Kapferer in turn has ventured into gross constructions of his own, which include his own particularistic selections drawn from the external world.

Kapferer explicitly states that his is not a scientific endeavor in the accepted sense. He is shifting away from the standard position of his discipline, in which theories and analytical perspectives are seen as conceptual elements that can be compared with the ground facts delivered by ethnography, checked for matches, and then modified (1991 p. xviii). So

Kapferer does not use the Popperian exercises of verification and refutation which Gombrich admires, because Kapferer rejects the very ground facts that are capable of modifying theory.

In the first sentence of his first chapter, the "Introduction," Kapferer asserts that the social world of "the" Sinhalese is invaded and disturbed by demons. He then goes on to state that he deals with the modalities of the normal and abnormal of "the" Sinhalese Buddhists as they are culturally constructed through demons (1991 p. 1). He says that demon exorcisms are one way that "Sinhalese" act on experiences and meanings of the world (p. 2). These are strong generalizations on "the" Sinhalese to be derived from Kapferer's chosen set of phenomena. For other conclusions, he could also have profitably used existing studies of the educational system, which provide insight into the internal life brought about by socialization, or for that matter the study of an industrial factory in Galle (which I did roughly at the time Kapferer was doing his) (Goonatilake, Susantha, 1971, 1972).

Kapferer takes gross liberties with theory, fact, nature of science, and geopolitical relations in knowledge while admitting that his study is limited in scope and that his knowledge of the Sinhala language, which is the key to his understanding, is "very imperfect" and "fumbling" (1991 pp. xxviii–x). With all these imperfections, he then goes on to make huge generalizations.

CHAPTER 8

■

Kapferer's Exorcist State

The aspects of the Sinhalese that Kapferer claims to have seen in his study of exorcists he projects in his second book to the nation as a whole. The empirical and theoretical edifice Kapferer has constructed in this second book, *Legends of People, Myths of State: Violence, Intolerance, and Political Culture in Sri Lanka and Australia* (1988) has now to be examined as to its validity. The points he makes, as we have seen, are that there is ethnic violence, that this is due primarily to Sinhalese, and that this violence is fed by a mythological history, which is accompanied by a hierarchical worldview that he identified in his studies of exorcism.

Let us see how his empirical findings square with reality.

VIOLENCE AND POLITICS

Kapferer connects the 1983 anti-Tamil riots to his Buddhist-demonic theory (1988 p. xiii).

Yet, the 1983 anti-Tamil riots were only part of a set of horrific disgraces that recent Sri Lanka has been witness to, including the massacres of Sinhala innocents in the southern insurrection in 1971; the 1983 anti-Tamil riots; attacks on civilian Sinhalese, Tamils, and Muslims in the north and east of the country; and the greatest savagery of them all, the mass killings by the state in 1987–1989. The murderous violence in Sri Lanka is, therefore, not only against Tamils but, as in 1971 and 1987–1989, more frequently directed against Sinhalese by the state as well as by other Sinhalese. And more tellingly, Tamil-on-Tamil violence has been much larger in scale than violence by Sinhalese or Sri Lankan state violence against Tamils. And the Tamil attacks on innocent Sinhalese, spiking young babies and pregnant women, as well as the complete ethnic cleansing by Tamils of Muslims from the Jaffna peninsula, are other examples of Sri Lankan violence which are foundationally problematic for Kapferer's formulation of a unique Sinhalese violence against Tamils.

It appears, therefore, that in the 1980s, a large section of the Sri Lankan political spectrum either directly or indirectly indulged in violence or supported groups dealing with violence. Kapferer's book was being edited up to July 1987 (Kapferer 1988 p. xii). By this time the violent actions of the Indian-trained separatist groups as well as their South Indian connections were common knowledge. There were also news reports of violence against the Janatha Vimukti Peramuna (JVP) by paramilitary groups. The contradictions in Kapferer's formulations become more apparent when he mentions that the violence is dominated by Sinhalese visions of mythic history and hegemony, and states that there was growing civil strife among the Sinhalese themselves (p. 115). The question, then, has to be posed: What were the "hierarchical motivating factors" for that violence? Sinhalese cannot have the hegemonic perspective Kapferer imputes to them if they are at the same time killing each other.

Kapferer asserts that what he calls "the Sinhalese state" has as its dominant principles ethnic identity and hierarchy, and that these are the prime movers in the anti-Tamil violence (1988 p. 14). He also equates the state with the Sinhalese when he says an "attack on the state, or apparatus of the state is an attack on the [Sinhalese] person" (p. 100). He also insists that the internal unity of the Sinhalese is maintained by the hierarchical ideology he has constructed for them (p. 214).

But if one takes the amount of Sinhalese-on-Sinhalese violence, or of Sri Lankan-state-on-Sinhalese violence, this internal unity concocted by Kapferer is shown to be false. There is also the subjective belief among the Sinhalese themselves that they are fractious. Further, objective indicators can be given on the fractious nature of the Sinhalese, such as the rate of litigation in disputes over property among them, which is one of the highest in the world. There are also other indicators of social dissatisfaction within the contemporary Sinhalese social order, such as the high rate of suicide, which is a reflection not of violence against others but of the ultimate violence against oneself.

Noting, therefore, that violence from all quarters, from all ethnic groups, including intra-ethnic violence, was endemic in the 1980s, let us now examine how Kapferer sees through his theory one such outbreak of violence, the 1983 anti-Tamil riots.

THE ANTI-TAMIL RIOTS

Kapferer connects anti-Tamil ethnic violence with sorcery (1988 p. 33). Drawing conclusions from his theory, he says that Sinhalese rioters fragment their demonic victims (p. 101). The question is, did such emotions of fragmentation intent actually go through the rioters' minds when they attacked Tamils? On the other hand, what fragmenting thoughts went through the minds of Sinhalese in the much larger-scale violence against other Sinhalese?

Kapferer identifies some of the direct actors in the riots. He mentions as significant that "aimless trouble makers," some elements of the urban poor, defended Tamil neighbors while others attacked them (1988 p. 101). One should also note that these were the lumpen elements that were also activated in political and other riots. Kapferer notes correctly that the police looked on, and even encouraged some of the attacks on the Tamils. But this was not an exclusively Sinhalese-versus-Tamils affair. It echoes the Delhi anti-Sikh riots in 1984, in which elements of the ruling Congress Party as well as the Indian security forces had a hand. And in the massive repression that followed the 1987–1989 uprising in the Sri Lankan south, death squads comprising police and armed forces in civilian clothes were responsible for one of the most brutal events of recent times. The lack of action by police or their involvement in these events was not particularly connected with Sinhala Buddhists.

One of Kapferer's examples, showing the particular ethnic bias of Sinhalese, their "threateningly evil" view of Tamils (1988 p. 83), is the fact that during the 1983 riots many Sinhalese stood by watching. But such behavior does not imply that they were condoning these acts. They probably shared the same motivation that governed the actions of the government M. P. Kapferer mentions, who stood by silently, *unable* to intervene with the rioters. In the much larger-scale violence of 1987–1988 against Sinhalese youth, many persons stood by watching bodies writhing in the last agonies of a painful death. On the other hand, Tamil insurgents have made some of the most brutal attacks on unarmed Sinhalese, but very few Tamils have publicly displayed shock or raised any words against the Tigers.

The major participants in the riots were drawn from those lower classes whose exorcist ceremonies Kapferer depicted as a justified "under view" in his first book. The question is, did he ask his exorcists and their lower-class subjects whether they participated in the riots? Here would be an ideal test group of believers in the demonic with which to try out his thesis of the demonic operating at the macro level. Kapferer, of course, did not ask the question.

TAMIL NATIONALISM:
THE OTHER HAND THAT DOES NOT CLAP

Kapferer searches for reasons for anti-Tamil violence, specifically the riots of 1983, only among alleged Sinhalese mythic elements, working on his hierarchical principles (1988 p. 112). He gives no details of the events leading to the 1983 riots. What set them off? What were the prior social and economic factors? His Sinhalese and Tamils occupy a territory which does not touch base with more mundane facts and acts of living.

Although Kapferer admits that the British colonialists drew the territorial and social ethnic boundaries that now exist, he does not explore the consequences of their actions (1988 p. 90). Examining these constructs, he does not dwell on the most brazen derivative of them, the invention of a fictitious traditional homeland by Tamil separatists, corresponding to the present British-drawn boundaries of the Northern and Eastern provinces. This recent fiction has probably contributed more to present-day ethnic tension than any of the alleged Sinhalese myths from ancient history.

Kapferer's construction of a hegemonic Sinhalese state ignores political history. There is ample evidence that ethnic polarization also grew because of ethnic attitudes among the Tamils, partly through British divide- and rule-policies, and especially through the inflow in the 19th and early 20th centuries of nationalist ideas from South Indian Tamils.

Thus, communally based political representation in Sri Lanka was first introduced by the British in 1833 in the form of a legislative council to assist the British governor. This council included six representatives, three Europeans and one each representing the Sinhalese, the Tamils, and the Burghers (Eurasians), the Sinhalese being hugely underrepresented (Pieris 1996). This type of partisan communal politics was an "integral part of the colonial strategy of knowing, classifying and ruling the nation" (Wickramasinghe 1995 p. 27).

The Sinhalese elite attempted several times to do away with this highly skewed arrangement (Wickramasinghe 1995 pp. 30, 37, 42). In the case of the Tamils, however, one sees a deliberate communal path from the 1920s onward. Ponnambalam Ramanathan, a leader of the Tamils—today considered a "moderate"—had in 1916 made it clear that he was against the democratic politics of rule by majority vote (de Silva, K. M., 1981 p. 393). Tamil politicians requested that communal representation be retained (Pieris 1996). Thereafter Tamils established their communal parties, the All Ceylon Tamil Congress in 1944 and the Ilankai Thamil Arasu Kadchchi in 1949. These were followed by the Tamil United Liberation Front (TULF) and, in the 1970s and 1980s, by a plethora of small separatist parties, spun off from the TULF and often financed and armed by the Indian government. The Sinhalese, in contrast, belonged to national parties such as the United National Party (UNP), the Sri Lanka Freedom Party (SLFP), the Lanka Sama Samaja Party (LSSP), and the Communist Party

(CP), all of which also included members of non-Sinhala communities such as Muslims and Tamils.

Kapferer also mentions the existence in (Tamil) South India of Tamil insurgent training camps, but does not explore obvious questions (1988 p. 85). From colonial times, Tamil nationalism in South India had demanded a separate state—Dravidistan—outside the Indian state, until the advocacy of separatism was banned in the late 1950s by the 6th Amendment to the Indian Constitution. (Historical memories of past Tamil kingdoms seem therefore to have stirred in contemporary Tamil Nadu without recourse to any Sinhala Buddhist chronicles or chronicles of their own.) Sri Lankan Tamil leaders had close ties with their South Indian counterparts, and were active in supporting a separate Tamil political entity. Thus the Liberation Tigers of Tamil Eelam (LTTE)—the "Tigers"—the most intransigent and strongest of the separatist groups, have as their flag the tiger-faced flag of the Chola devastators of Sri Lanka of the 11th century. The word "Tiger" itself as a loaded political epithet actually appeared in 1961 among a group of Sri Lankan Tamil bureaucrats who had decided that Gandhism had no part to play in the Tamil nationalist movement. They consequently called their group Pulip Padai, "Army of Tigers" (Swamy 1994 p. 24).

Kapferer mentions as evidence for his thesis of ethnic bias a speech by then President Premadasa mentioning that resistance begins in the south (1988 p. 86). There is a simple geographic logic for this, in that the deep Sri Lankan south is the farthest from any potential invader. In any other part of the country, resistance could be crushed more easily before it could gather momentum.

The tragic events of 1983 also led to outlandish statements from Tamil ideologues, both in Sri Lanka and in South India. Thus, the book *Genocide in Sri Lanka,* published with exuberant praise from the TULF leadership, stated that "the dimension of [the 1983 violence was] unheard of in the annals of the world, with the only exception of atrocities perpetrated by Nazis in the concentration camps!" (Venkatachalam 1987 p. 21). Under the heading "Butcher Stalls and Severed Tamil Heads," this book also "records" that Sinhalese ate Tamil meat and implies that Muslims collaborated in this cannibalism by lending their butcher stalls for this purpose with signs reading "Tamil meat for sale" (butchers in Sri Lanka are almost exclusively Muslims). The book declares that "the land of Buddhists [had] turned into a land of Cannibals!" (Venkatachalam 1987 p. 29; exclamation marks in the original). Perhaps anticipating Kapferer, in a telling chapter titled "Recent Devil Dance," the book also "records" the existence of a village, "Thembattakudai near Colombo," where two girls were raped at a school by "the Buddhist Priests." There is no such village (p. 21).

Not only, therefore, does Kapferer choose to ignore well-documented Tamil contributions to the conflict, in both Sri Lanka and South India, but he also elects to use loaded expressions such as "Tamil liberationist guerillas" and "Tamil independence organizations" (1988 p. 35). These have the direct connotation that the separatist movement's basis and aspirations are legitimate. He could have used less value-laden connotative words, like Tamil "separatists" or "militants," which, for example, the Western media use in such cases.

POLITICS AND KAPFERER'S SINHALESE STATE

The state is a key element in Kapferer's scheme.

He says that in the pursuance of nationalism, Sinhala Buddhist culture is guarded by the state, its bureaucratic apparatus, and its agents (1988 p. 100). And as he equates the present Sri Lankan state with this nationalism, we must ask how far this view tallies with reality. As for the state bureaucracy, there have been several studies on its peculiarities by social scientists, including the present writer. Let me include only the studies carried out up to the early seventies, when Kapferer did his field study, which also coincided with my own studies (Goonatilake, Susantha, 1971; La Porte 1970; Harris and Kearney 1963).

These studies do not indicate any manifestation of a bureaucracy closely identified with the state and guarding its alleged nationalism. They do reveal a bureaucracy that does not conform to the norms of Western bureaucracies. This is because environmental factors enter in, "distorting" the Sri Lankan bureaucracy (Goonatilake, Susantha, 1971, 1972, 1973). Far from working as a Sinhalese nationalist force, the bureaucracy is involved in fractious infighting because of this inflow of factors. The bureaucracy has political tendencies, and part of the bitter infighting is due to the mapping of inter-political-party interests. The citizenry is often victim to the vicissitudes of this bureaucracy as the latter attempts to serve its overt, stated objectives, which, in spite of departures from Weberian rectitude, it broadly succeeds in doing.

As for the political apparatus serving as an alleged Sinhalese state agent, this often happens only ceremonially. Such attempts to use nationalism are viewed sometimes cynically by citizens. Thus, President J. R. Jayawardene coined a political slogan, *Dharmishta Samajaya*, "Society Based on Dharma," which was a return to the old Buddhist ideas of a just reign. But as his government continued to indulge in repressive actions, *Dharmishta Samajaya* became a term of ridicule. A book with the same title, *Dharmishta Samajaya*, caricatured the government.

As an example of a state ideology, Kapferer mentions Jayawardene's claim of an unbroken line of 2,500 years of monarchy from Vijaya to Elizabeth II. Kapferer dismisses this as mythmaking (1988 p. 85). Vijaya is very probably a legendary figure, but the historical documentation after that period is as strong as in any other country with a recorded history. When Sri Lanka became a republic in 1972, the British establishment newspaper *The Times* editorialized along the same lines as Jayawardene. As an example of the ethnic bias of Jayawardene, Kapferer cites the latter's mentioning that the last king, Sri Wickreme Rajasinghe, who came from a Tamil lineage in South India, was wicked and corrupt (p. 85). But this is a preposterous reading. This line of South Indian kings moved by Sinhalese invitation into the seat of Kandyan royalty so smoothly that historians find it a "sharp contrast" to succession disputes in the earlier kingdoms of Anuradhapura, Polonnaruwa, and Kotte, a time span of approximately two millennia (de Silva, K. M., 1981 p. 144). Sri Wickreme Rajasinghe's unjust behavior is very well-documented by British sources (Wimalananda 1984). In final pursuit of their own goals, the British later attacked the Kandyan Kingdom in 1815, stating that this action was being taken to free the oppressed Kandyans from a cruel king (de Silva, K. M., 1981 p. 229).

Kapferer also complains that names such as Gemunu Watch, Sinha Regiment, and Raja Rata Rifles—names based on historical references—are given to Sinhalese regiments fighting Tamil separatists (1988 p. 35). Anton Muttukumaru, a Tamil Catholic and retired head of the Sri Lankan armed forces, in his *Military History of Ceylon: An Outline* (1987), the only book-length attempt at a history of the Sri Lankan military, gives the dates these units were formed: the Raja Rata Rifles in 1955 (Muttukumaru 1987 p. 163) and the other two units in 1959 (p. 173). The first was formed before Muttukumaru became commander, and the latter two under his watch as commander. These units had historical connotations which Muttukumaru evidently appreciates. When a new prime minister in 1956 wanted to disband the Raja Rata Rifles, saying that the name might have a regional flavor, it was the Tamil Catholic Muttukumaru who dissuaded him (1987 p. 166). Kapferer's interpretation is patently false.

In further exploring the role of the state, Kapferer gives the example, suggesting that it is un-Buddhistic, of the army commander going to worship at the most important temple in the country (1988 p. 87). But going to the temple before important events and appointments is a ritual duty performed by many Buddhists. These events include going to a new class in school, to university, or to a new job. In similar examples of the religious in matters military, there are Christian chaplains in Western armies, church leaders bless army commanders, and the head of the Anglican Church of Britain is the queen, the head of state.

As in countries influenced by other religions, the mixing of religion and defense occurs in many Buddhist countries. In fact, the martial arts were founded by Buddhist monks, Shaolin temple being the legendary birthplace of Kung Fu. The Japanese code of the Samurai, Bushido, and some of the Japanese fighting techniques use Zen Buddhist approaches in fine-tuning fighters. Here some of the very techniques of Buddhist meditation have been used to turn out a good fighting machine, in much the same manner that these techniques have been recently incorporated into sports training (Benson 1987 pp. 138–144; *U.S. News and World Report,* 3 August 1993). There are also recorded instances of Sri Lankan monks' being involved in organizing anti-British revolts (Wimalananda 1970). Thus it should not be seen as unusual (from Christian, Asian Buddhist, or traditional Sinhalese Buddhist perspectives) when the chief monk of the Dutugemunu Viharaya at Baddegama states in a meeting where monks and laity have gathered to pray to end terrorism that if these peaceful techniques are not successful, monks should themselves disrobe and take to fighting (Kapferer 1988 p. 87). But Kapferer misreads this.

Some of Kapferer's statements referring to Sinhala Buddhists to illustrate their perfidy are not local in origin. Thus, he mentions a slogan, "Death or Motherland," which was widely seen during the 1987–1989 revolt (1988 p. 87). It originated in the Cuban revolution, and it probably came to Sri Lanka through JVP sources, which had Cuban ideological influences.

Kapferer sees further confirmation of his cosmic logic for mundane Sri Lankan problems in two newspaper cartoons (1988 pp. 88, 89). The first deals with talks sponsored by the Indian government between Sri Lanka and Tamil insurgents, the cartoon making a parallel with Indira Gandhi's solution to the Punjabi crisis. In both the Punjab and Sri Lanka, Indira Gandhi sponsored insurgents. Punjab insurgents ultimately gunned down Indira Gandhi, and the LTTE killed her son, Rajiv Gandhi.

The cartoonist illustrated his very down-to-earth, matter-of-fact political context by drawing on an exorcist ritual that Kapferer himself had described in his earlier book, because it succinctly illustrated the Indian talks. There was no cosmic logic in it, as Kapferer suggested. Kapferer's second cartoon shows the then president, J. R. Jayawardene, dancing and changing masks. Kapferer finds this illustrative of the operation of the "Sinhalese Buddhist cosmic hierarchy" (1988 p. 89). To any average Sri Lankan reader, it is another satire in cartoon form opportunistically using cultural material at hand, having nothing to do with assumed cosmic principles, demonic forces, or hierarchy.

As another example of Sinhalese ideology, Kapferer refers to an article in the Sinhala daily *Divayina* (Kapferer 1988 p. 83). I will not deal with some of the contentious interpretations he makes. The question I want to raise is, how did he choose this particular article? In the previous book, he admits to his rudimentary understanding of even spoken Sinhala. It is extremely unlikely that in the ensuing years away from Sri Lanka, Kapferer learned to read and write Sinhalese. What would have been his instructions to his informant? If it was his research assistant, did he say, "Give me examples of bias in the Sinhala newspapers"? Or did the academics whom he cites in the book point it out? Kapferer's ignorance and bias are both structured, not accidental.

SINHALESE RACISM RUNNING RIOT

A thread running through Kapferer's narrative is a gut Sinhalese racism that views Tamils as "threateningly evil." Kapferer also says that the hierarchical, ideologically induced, internal unity of the Sinhalese also determines their relations with non-Sinhalese (1988 p. 214), implying that they are antagonistic to outsiders.

But such comments go against even superficial observations coming down from ancient times, which have identified the Sinhalese as friendly lotus eaters. The word "serendipity," derived from the old name for the country, Sinhaladvip—land of the Sinhalese—also expresses this easygoing attitude. Tambiah, even in his own flawed writings, says that the Sinhalese are a people with humor, warmth, and hospitality, more open to outsiders than the people in any other country in South and Southeast Asia, excepting Thailand (Tambiah 1986 p. 1). Gombrich further found that to Western eyes the generosity of the Sinhalese borders on the incredible. He saw monks as hospitable, very kind, and worldly (1991 pp. 311, 379). In fact, in his book on exorcism, Kapferer is effusive about his Sri Lankan contacts. But this ease of association with others can of course coexist, one should note parenthetically, with bouts of violence, against others as well as amongs themselves. But instead of being antagonistic to other religions, Sinhala Buddhists had historically been very accommodating. When the Dutch Protestants replaced the Portuguese as the colonial masters in the coastal areas of Sri Lanka, they persecuted Roman Catholics most inhumanely. Sinhalese Buddhists gave the persecuted Catholics refuge (Malalgoda 1976).

The majority of Tamils in Sri Lanka today, it should also be noted, do not live in the ethnically cleansed regions of Jaffna, where only Tamils live, but in mixed habitats where they live among Sinhalese on a day-to-day, friendly basis. In Jaffna, even before the ethnic cleansing, a customary law called *Thesawalamai* banned the ownership of land by non-Tamils except through an elaborate procedure.

There are also formal studies that reveal a position contrary to Kapferer's construct of gut antagonism. Thus a study by my wife of intercommunal relations in the very same slum areas in which live the *rastiadu karayo*—lumpen troublemakers involved with the riots that Kapferer refers to—showed just the opposite results (Goonatilake, Hema, 1987 p. 265). Here, there was considerable amity between the Sinhalese and Tamil populations. Another study, a large cross-cultural study of personality between Sri Lanka and England, finds that on essential key variables there is no significant difference between Englishmen and Sinhalese (Perera and Eysenck 1984 pp. 353–371).

If the Sinhalese were not antagonistic in a gut sense to other humans, those Tamils who championed the Tamil cause against the Sinhalese themselves had rather dubious attitudes. Thus, the Jaffna *vellala* caste elite, which led the Tamil communal cry, was in its own Tamil areas oppressive. It was only the British colonialists who abolished slavery among Tamils in 1844. Up to that time, the *koviyars* (household servants to the *vellalas*), *chandars, pallas,* and *nallavas* (extractors of alcoholic sap from palms), which are some of the largest non-*vellala* castes, had been slaves of the *vellalas.* Even by the mid-20th century, there had been litttle improvement in their social situation (Russell 1982 pp. 10–11).

Pfaffenberger has noted that the oppressive Jaffna caste system could "be maintained only by force." He observed that in the 1940s and 1950s, oppressed castes were "forbidden to enter or live near temples, to draw water from the wells of high-caste families, to enter laundries, barber shops, cafes, or taxis." This list of forbidden activities was much worse than the restrictions faced by African Americans in the United States or non-whites under apartheid in South Africa. The forbidden activities included wearing shoes, covering the upper part of the body, wearing gold earrings, cutting the hair (males), sitting on bus seats, registering names

to get social benefits, attending schools, cremating the dead, using um-
brellas, owning bicycles or cars, and converting to Buddhism or Christianity. Gangs of thugs were used to enforce these restrictions. These
groups would throw fecal matter, dead dogs, and garbage into the wells
of upstart lower-caste Tamils. They would also burn down the fences of
houses, and beat up and sometimes kill non-upper-caste Tamils (Pfaffenberger 1990). A turning point in this discrimination was the attempt in
the 1960s by the lower castes to enter the temples that were barred to
them.

But in spite of these blatant injustices, Pfaffenberger notes, Federal
Party (FP) leaders such as Chelvanayakam and Amirthalingam "tiptoed
quietly away from [these] issues" (p. 8). Pfaffenberger observes that the
FP's response was "not to develop a coherent and principled position on
the temple entry issue but rather to divert [the] public away from issues"
(p. 8). This attitude of upper-caste Tamils was reflected in their attitudes
toward the lower-caste Tamils. Thus, the leader of the All Ceylon Tamil
Congress, G. G. Ponnambalam, voted for the Elections Amendment Act
of 1949, which disenfranchised lower-caste Tamils (Vittachi 1995 p. 32).

Caste discrimination among Tamils was finally banned only with the
passage of the Prevention of Social Disabilities Act of 1957 by the (Sinhala-
Buddhist majority) SLFP government. This was also in keeping with one
of that government's earliest humane acts, banning the use of rickshaws
because it was considered demeaning for humans to be used to pull other
humans. As it was almost exclusively poor Tamils who were employed
as rickshaw drivers, this was implicitly an act of emancipating poor
Tamils.

Instead of showing gut racism, Sinhalese laymen and monks have, in
fact, intervened on behalf of underprivileged Tamils in Jaffna itself, the
Tamil heartland. In the 1960s in Jaffna, Sinhalese groups—actually including one associated with the monk Madihe Pannaseeha Thero, whom
Kapferer refers to disparagingly in the book—moved closer to repressed
Tamil groups than did the ruling Tamil elite. These Sinhalese groups
reached out to the hundreds of thousands of depressed-caste Tamils, who
were denied entry into temples and schools, by providing schools for
them. Consequently, many lower-caste Tamils became Buddhists, just as
some of the untouchables of India became Buddhists.

Kapferer mentions the Sansoni Commission report on the 1978 riots in
reference to some alleged remarks by Madihe Pannaseeha Thero, but he
misses the central finding of the commission, namely, the blame put
squarely on the Tamil leadership for the ethnic conflict. And this report

was not by a partisan Sinhalese but by a retired Eurasian supreme court judge.

My discussions are not aimed at whitewashing Sinhalese faults. Ethnic antagonisms do exist and have surfaced at times among the Sinhalese, especially during ethnic riots. Similarly, institutionalized ethnic cleansing has occurred among Tamils. But these ethnic attitudes, one should note, are different in flavor from the gut racism that one finds in the West. A film such as *Guess Who's Coming to Dinner?* illustrating American gut racism would never have been representative of Sri Lanka. I remember in the 1970s—at the time Kapferer was working on his first book—the "Paki-bashing" hysteria in London. But in the West, although gut racism was present, it has not broken out recently into major riots, except in pockets, because the socio-legal system has been able to contain it. The socio-legal system in the West has also been able to contain outbursts of intra-ethnic political conflicts, which in Sri Lanka have led to more bloodshed than inter-ethnic violence.

TURNING HISTORY INTO MYTH

Kapferer claims that historical myths from the chronicles feed the Sinhalese. Stories of Tamil invasions and the consequent actions of Sinhalese, destroying the invading Tamils, are key elements in his scheme (1988 p. 2). There are mythic elements in Sri Lankan history, but there are large areas where the chronicles have been shown to be true in great detail and have been corroborated by archaeological finds, epigraphy, and other means, as pointed out by the standard *History of Ceylon* (Perera, L. S., 1959 pp. 46–72); not one of the members of the editorial board for this *History* was a Sinhala Buddhist.

Kapferer (1988 p. 37) also says, quoting Obeyesekere, that Paranavithana tried to interpret inscriptional material to show North Indian claims of Sinhalese origins. But Sinhalese do speak a North Indian–derived language. Paranavithana never claimed that there was a wholesale transfer of population from North India. For him, the transfer was primarily cultural (1967 p. 12).

I myself tried to explain the introduction of this North Indian language as a form of cultural transmission accompanying Buddhism, just as today's Indian elite learned English (Goonatilake, Susantha, 1981). But the most recent excavations in Anuradhapura have extended the North Indian presence to the 6th century B.C. in the form of the Brahmi script, first found in North India. Meanwhile South Indian scholars such as

Raman are propagating the theory that the Brahmi script went to South India from Sri Lanka prior to 500 B.C. (Deraniyagala 1992 p. 739).

In recent studies done in close collaboration with many of the leading institutes in the world, Deraniyagala sums up the archeological confirmation of events before the 3rd century B.C.: "it needs to be affirmed that the nomenclature of Sri Lanka's periodization . . . may now be considered to be on a firm footing: the Early Historic period commences at ca. 500 B.C. and not with Devanampiya Tissa at ca. 250 B.C. . . . The present evidence does indeed vouch for the accuracy of the *Mahavamsa* on this score, which in turn reflects on the core of historical fact that underlies its statements relating to the 'Vijayan' period at over 500 B.C." (Deraniyagala 1992 p. 747).

Sri Lanka's history is not only reliable, it is also the only continuous written history in the whole South and Southeast Asian region with a population of over 1.5 billion. This history is based on historical records kept in monasteries from the 3rd century B.C. in Sri Lanka. These records have also helped mainland Indian history with regard to crucial events; for example, they helped identify the father of Asoka, the great early Indian emperor (Vitharana 1997). Many Ph.D. theses, as well as books, have been based on these chronicles at reputed Western universities; the best such academic work comes from Kapferer's own University of London.

Gombrich considered the *Mahavamsa* of "considerable excellence" (Gombrich 1991 p. 22). He mentions that the *Mahavamsa* described the mission sent by Asoka, the Arahat Majjhantika, to Kashmir. Gombrich notes that dramatic confirmation of the *Mahavamsa*'s accuracy was found after the excavation of a stupa in Kashmir which yielded a reliquary with bones carrying the name of the Arahat (1991 p. 124). More important for an anthropologist such as Kapferer studying local ceremonies would be Gombrich's statement that many of the Buddhist festivals described in the *Mahavamsa* differ very little from what is practiced today, showing the ethnographic accuracy of the Mahavamsa (1991 p. 53).

In cavalier fashion, Kapferer dismisses as a purely imaginary construct the entire history of Dutugemunu (1988 p. 122). The *Mahavamsa,* written in the highest classical Pali, uses literary devices written in the style of an epic, especially when it deals with Dutugemunu. But the core material is historical (Perera, L. S., 1959 pp. 46–72). Dutugemunu's edifices, the ruins of the Ruvanweliseya, the nine-story Lowa Maha Paya, and the Mirisavetiya exist today not as a figment of the Sinhalese imagination but as solid brick, granite, and epigraphic fact.

Kapferer also gets Geiger (1950), the 19th-century German translator of the Sinhalese chronicles, completely wrong when he suggests that Geiger implied that the Sri Lankan chronicles were based on folk traditions and not on carefully maintained records (Kapferer 1988 pp. 42–43). Geiger in fact said just the *opposite*. Geiger in the *first* paragraph of his introduction to the *Mahavamsa* stated, "I have demonstrated that the two Ceylon chronicles [the *Mahavamsa* and the earlier, shorter *Dipavamsa*] are based upon older materials and for this reason should claim our attention as sources of history" (1950 p. ix). Geiger further points out that by no means did the authors of the *Mahavamsa* set out to deceive their audience; nor did they have significant bias. Geiger says that "this is clear from the remarkable objective standpoint from which they judge even the mortal foes of [their] race. That certainly deserves to be emphasized. It is not only true of dominating personalities [such as the main invader, Elara] but also of the two usurpers Sena and Guttika. . . . It inspires confidence at the outset" (1950 p. xv). He goes on to sketch the other sources that support the truth of the *Mahavamsa*.

This Buddhist and Sinhalese view of history stands in contrast to the rest of Indian culture. From Alberuni, the great Islamic writer of the 11th century, to McAuley, the 19th-century colonialist commentator, many have noted the lack of historical writings in the Hindu tradition. In contrast, Rhys Davids observed that "in Sri Lanka, there was a history" (quoted in Ahir 1997 p. 185). Kapferer's key problem is not that, as he claims, Sri Lankan historians believe the *Mahavamsa* to be factual, but that his colleagues in history at his own University of London do.

Kapferer's line of thinking that Sinhalese history is invented bears directly on the present day. Let me illustrate by referring to one of his statements on Minister Cyril Mathew. Minister Mathew was associated with some of the negative aspects of J. R. Jayawardene's rule. Goon squads allied with him are suspected of many attacks on trade unions and intellectuals opposing the government. I have given this background before discussing a statement attributed to Mathew, which is highlighted by Kapferer. It is not the negative treatment of Mathew by Kapferer that I am interested in. I might use much more negative terms. But it is how Kapferer treats material that is problematic, irrespective of whether Mathew or somebody else is quoted.

Kapferer mentions Mathew's statement that three hundred sites were excavated by the Archaeological Department in the north and east, and Kapferer dismisses this as "completely consistent with Sinhalese claims to territorial hegemony that are supported by a reading of the ancient chronicles" (1988 pp. 38, 39). This is a false statement, consistent with separatist propaganda. These sites have been scientifically excavated, their epigraphy has been read, and the sites identified with those have been mentioned in the chronicles, not only by Sinhalese scholars but also by Tamil scholars, as well as European and Asian ones, who have no stake in Sri Lanka's ethnic conflicts. In fact, Mathew's statement was directly based on data compiled by M. H. Sirisoma, later the archeological commissioner.

But in a brazen invention of historical geography, Tamil separatists have recently claimed the entire Northern and Eastern provinces as their "traditional homelands," and have carried out systematic ethnic cleansing on this basis. These blatant inventions have been exposed by reputed scholars consulting original sources. The most authoritative of these exposures are by historian K. M. de Silva (1994) and geographer G. H. Peiris (1991). A similar exercise, taking into account Portuguese, Dutch, and British maps of Sri Lanka, has been conducted by Dennis Fernando, a cartographer. The *Economic and Political Weekly* of India, which had hitherto uncritically accepted the myth, put it this way in 1995: "The theory of traditional Tamil homeland corresponding to the present North-Eastern province is largely a hoax" (Ghosh 1995). Further, even Neelan Tiruchelvam of the TULF admitted in an aside that the traditional homelands concept may be false (interview with Ravi John, 1995).

When Kapferer uses the buzzwords "territorial hegemony" and "Sinhalese colonization," he is implying the truth of the completely mythical inventions of the last few decades. The alleged colonization of traditional land he speaks of is a central part of the separatist falsehoods. Such colonizations of unpopulated or underpopulated areas were actually started in the 19th century by the British, who tried to restore abandoned ancient Sinhalese irrigation works and, through them, open up the fertile lands that had been abandoned to the jungle (Russell 1982 p. 170). These lands, contrary to the impression created by separatist propaganda, had been first offered to Tamil settlers in the area, but there were no takers (Hellmann-Rajanayagam 1990 p. 79). On the other hand, settlers from the land-hungry Western and Southern provinces, predominantly Sinhalese areas, readily volunteered. But Mick Moore, a contemporary British scholar who has studied the peasant colonization of Sri Lanka, shows that colonization when it eventually occurred contributed "less than assumed earlier to Sinhalese migration into the entire Dry Zone" (cited in Hellmann-Rajanayagam 1990 p. 87).

The person who started by believing in the medical effectiveness of exorcist rituals, even when the patients themselves had doubts, now denounces a reliable non-Western formal intellectual tradition. He denigrates the best-attested historical tradition of the entire South and Southeast Asian region. This is the greatest contempt he shows for the traditions of his hosts' culture.

HISTORY AND TAMILS AS EVIL

Kapferer points out correctly instances and examples of ideological content in the epic part of the *Mahavamsa* (Kapferer 1988 p. 81). There *are* ideological elements in this history written in the romantic Mahakavya poetic form. I too have drawn attention to the role of ideology in Sinhala history, especially its use to justify particular social orders (Goonatilake, Susantha, 1981). Ideology, however, exists in all intellectual fields, including science.

The state and the nation, according to Kapferer, have a special meaning for the Sinhalese Buddhist hierarchical arrangement. Kapferer claims that Sinhalese-Buddhist nationalist ideology makes other groups subordinate in the hierarchy. Further, there is an identity of the nation, the state, and the person, so that an attack on the state becomes an attack on and fragmentation of the person (1988 p. 7). And, Kapferer says, evil as depicted in myths finds its chief metaphors in kings and princes, "whose actions are antagonistic to Buddhist principles" (p. 71).

But these are over-interpretations made to fit his own framework. If Buddhist principles depend on *Ahimsa* and non-harming, then those who oppose these principles through invasion and plunder must necessarily be evil. They are not only depicted as evil in myth, they *are* evil. Kapferer claims that in the chronicles, Tamils are associated with evil. This is false. In fact, Geiger, the German translator of the *Mahavamsa*, whom Kapferer evokes positively, attests to the chronicle's fair treatment of invading Tamils (1950 p. xv).

While Tamils have been associated with threatening behavior because of invasions, they have also been associated with the opposite. At the time the *Mahavamsa* was written at the Mahavihara monastery, the institution was host to many South Indians, including Tamils, who came to study and translate into Pali the classical Buddhist texts available in Sinhala. Their texts in Pali today hold a central position in the Sinhalese Theravada tradition. A millennium later, in the 15th century, at the Sunethradevi monastic center in Pepilayana, Tamil was one of the compulsory languages for all monks. Those who did not know these languages were considered "fools" in a very well-known poem of the period —the *Siyabaslakara*.

And of course, the classic case of Sinhala admiration for Tamils was the very invader, Elara, who is defeated by Dutugemunu, the hero of the *Mahavamsa*. Elara is considered an embodiment of just rule not only in the classical literature but also in folk literature, as Gombrich himself has recorded in his foray into anthropology (1991 p. 220). In contrast, the *Mahavamsa's* hero, Dutugemunu, was depicted in a negative light, especially in that part of the text which covers his behavior in his earlier years. In fact, the prefix to his name, "Dutu," meant "wicked" (his given name was Gemunu—Gamini). The addition was made because of his earlier bad behavior. The hero of the epic is shown to be wicked, while the invading villain is shown to be just. The authors of the *Mahavamsa* were far more subtle in their judgments than Kapferer.

But it is Buddhist moral literature, didactic literature such as the *Lowada Sangarawa*, as well as the popular literature such as the Jataka Tales, that governs common folk in their day-to-day activities. This literature is much better-known in detail than the *Mahavamsa*, for example. But this literature is never alluded to by Kapferer as a guide to the behavior of the Sinhalese. Probably he is unaware of its existence.

ESALA'S INFLUENCE ON HISTORY

Kapferer surely overstates when he asserts the significance of Minister Mathew's making nationalist statements in the month of Esala. This, he claims, is a time high in the religious and ethnic consciousness. As support of this contention, he mentions that it is in Esala that the annual Perehara procession takes place, that King Dutugemunu laid the foundation of the Ruwanveli Seya, and that the Kataragama festival, popularly associated with Dutugemunu, also takes place (Kapferer 1988 p. 39). But Kapferer's invention of Esala as an especially significant month for Sinhalese Buddhist nationalism is a blatantly untenable one. This becomes very clear when one considers the other key dates of Dutugemunu. These are the dates of his defiance of his father, his attack on his brother, the beginning of his campaign, his attack on the Vijithapura fort, his laying of foundation stones for his other edifices, etc., which have no connection with Esala.

But there are other key events in Sinhala Buddhist history that have nothing to do with Esala. These include the alleged arrival of Wijaya (in Vesak month) (Geiger 1950 p. 54), the coming of Buddhism (in Poson), the bringing of the branch of the Bo tree under which the Buddha reached Enlightenment (in Il), the setting up of the nun's order (in Il), and work on the great stupa (in Vesak) (Geiger 1950 p. 191). One could add other key events that are as significant as, if not more significant than, the handful that Kapferer has plucked out of the air to give special emphasis to Esala. In fact, key Sri Lankan national and religious events are (as in other countries, and as one would expect) spread throughout the year.

Kapferer finds it significant that the 1983 riots also occurred in the month of Esala. This is preposterous. The riots were triggered by the killing of thirteen soldiers by separatists in the north. If Kapferer attaches special significance to Esala in the riots, he must imply that just as as Esala has significance for the Sinhala Buddhists, it also has significance for Tamil separatists, because it was in this month that they decided to launch the attack that killed the soldiers and triggered the riots. Absurd theorizing leads to absurd counter-questions.

HISTORY AND STABILIZATION

Kapferer explains Dutugemunu's monument-building as an attempt at cosmic stabilization (in the sense in which Kapferer defines Sinhalese cosmology). In this way, he says. the fragmentation of the world is prevented by the affirmation of Buddhist cosmic unifying principles (1988 pp. 57–58).

But monument-building did not begin with Dutugemunu's 2nd-century B.C. Sri Lanka. It has occurred at different times and in different places all over the world. In fact, the Buddhist stupas, which reached gigantic proportions in Sri Lanka, were first constructed in India under Emperor Asoka. His contemporary in Sri Lanka, Devanam Piya Tissa, copied them in his Thuparama (for a sociological explanation of these events, see Goonatilake, Susantha, 1978). Similar monuments have been built in many Buddhist countries—Burma, Nepal, Tibet, China, Indonesia —without the particular cosmology that Kapferer invents for the Sinhalese. There are also other large monuments all over the world. Kapferer attempts to fit the Sinhalese manifestations of this universal urge to build monuments into his exorcist-derived scheme as something unique.

HISTORY AND BATTLE

The chronicle *Mahavamsa* devotes considerable space to the final battle that took place between Dutugemunu and Elara. Kapferer considers it a moot point whether it took place in the form of a direct personal combat, but he says it was cosmically ordained (1988 p. 63). It may not have taken place at all, and the description could be just an embellishment, a chivalrous battle written in *Mahakavya* style. Such duels do, however, take place out of reasons of honor, as, for example, as recently as the 19th century among the upper classes of Europe. After the duel in which Elara dies, continuing in the same chivalrous vein, Dutugemunu orders that a tomb be built for Elara to honor him. Kapferer sees this incident also in his "cosmic" terms. He sees this as the demonic turning into compassionate beneficence.

A somewhat similar case occurred in India, where Emperor Asoka became sorrowful and compassionate after his wars of conquest, turned toward a new struggle, the war for *dharma,* and performed Buddhist acts on a subcontinent-wide scale. Now, the Kapferer explanation for the Indian example would be that this demonic person, Asoka, turns into a person of compassionate beneficence, through Kapferer's hierarchic principles derived from a small, late-20th-century sample of Sri Lankan exorcists. The latter's demonic powers are indeed very strong, and include both space and time travel.

HISTORY AND INTERNAL POWER STRUGGLES

Conflicts have occasionally occurred between fathers and sons and between siblings in the long Sinhalese history. One telling conflict was the killing of his father by Kasyapa, the 5th-century builder of the rock fortress Sigiriya. But Kapferer sees these not as simple power-political struggles that occur in all kingdoms but as mythical grist for his cosmic scheme. Kapferer also begs to differ from a commentator (whose name he does not mention but who is probably Obeyesekere), who also goes out on his own anti-historical limb and asserts that these conflicts are not raw power struggles but Freudian, Oedipal struggles (Kapferer 1988 p. 62).

Kapferer also explains Sinhalese history written in the 4th and 6th centuries through his interpretations of 20th-century folk rituals. His fellow anthropologist Obeyesekere, however, has given evidence that in fact these types of folk ceremonies do change in form and content over the decades-long time span in which Obeyesekere has studied them. Kapferer's rituals have, as his own data suggests, changed in his own short time span of study (1991 p. ix). So it is unlikely that they existed in the remote past in the same form, or if they did, that they had the structure they have today. Such oral rituals, unlike those handed down in a written form—as are Buddhist rituals—are subject to change.

HISTORY AND DEMONS

Some of the demons that are encountered in Kapferer's study are accompanied by historical allusions. Thus Kalu Kumaraya is considered to be Vijaya, the legendary pre-historical king Vijaya reborn. But this type of local folk story alluding to alleged past events is very common in Sri Lanka. There are, for example, many places where folk belief links a site with the Ramayana epic, which, in contrast to the Buddhist Jataka stories, is not widely known in the country. Linguists will relate scores of such stories by which people try to explain the origin of particular words through folk-etymological local historical allusions. So, the fact that current beliefs come with historical allusions is not extraordinary and is not the outcome of a grand hierarchical theory. Sinhalese—and other people around the world—have made up such stories for a long time for more mundane reasons.

CULTURAL TRANSMISSION

A central element in Kapferer's thesis is his recourse to Anderson's (1983) ideas of the imagined community, alleging that in Sri Lanka, printing made folk knowledge widespread (Kapferer 1988 p. 94). But here he contradicts himself, because elsewhere he records that historical knowledge, including the alleged myths surrounding history, was widespread. That is, folk knowledge built around history was known very widely. And if this live folk knowledge refers to events that took place more than two thousand years ago, it must mean that it is ingrained deeply in the population.

Models of the spread of knowledge that compare pre-printing knowledge in Europe with the post-printing phase cannot be facilely transferred to countries outside Europe. This would imply making sweeping assumptions that societal mechanisms for knowledge dissemination both inside and outside Europe were identical. This is not the case. There is strong evidence that the extent of literacy before the advent of the print media in Sri Lanka and other Theravada countries was at least equal to that which obtained in Britain in the 19th century *after* the widespread use of print media and after the Industrial Revolution had taken hold (Gombrich and Obeyesekere 1988 p. 207). The reasons for this have to be seen in the knowledge production and dissemination processes in Theravada countries, which were centered on temple schools. Each temple also had a library, with those in the larger monasteries having thousands of manuscripts. Monks and lay persons were taught in these schools, learning religious knowledge as well as secular subjects such as languages, literature, history, and medicine (Mirando 1985 pp. 11, 17). The temples also have a form of discourse between monks and lay audience—preaching and discussion—which imparts knowledge of religion and similar matters in an interactive seminar-type mode. Knowledge is also imparted when the monks preach on their visits to houses of the laity.

The historical material is therefore found to be widespread all over the country, both in its formal manifestations as chronicles and in its more bowdlerized, oral forms. These types of cultural transmission must have increased in intensity with the introduction of print. But print capitalism is not the only medium through which Kapferer says that imagined histories are spread.

Kapferer sees exorcist ceremonies sponsored by the state for mass audiences as wrong, calling them a return to the *supposed* cultural practices of the past by the masses (1988 p. 94). He contradicts himself here. In his first book, which is the foundation on which his present edifice is built, he mentioned that official circles looked down upon such non-Buddhist performances.

Kapferer mentions that "folk knowledge" (equated here with the Sinhalese historical tradition) is spread not only by print capitalism but also by what he calls "nationalist encouragement of Buddhist worship," such as visiting ancient sites. He implies that visits to ancient sites are the result of recent developments and had no earlier precedents. He gives the example of a secular site, Sigiriya, saying that the visitors are "pilgrims" (1988 p. 95). But once again his ignorance is very apparent.

Sigiriya, which was built in the 5th century with elaborately laid-out gardens and galleries of paintings, was soon abandoned. But even from as early as the 6th century, people from all over the island began touring this site, as evidenced by their scribbled comments on a major wall (Ariyapala 1956 p. 18). These comments show that the visitors came only for pleasure. The wide range of social strata represented in these writings attests also to the fact that literacy was widespread at the time.

But the idea of Buddhist pilgrimage actually began with King Asoka (Dhammika 1997 p. 50). And, the fact that Sinhalese in the past traveled widely is revealed by several other indicators. Thus a well-known 16th-century book, *Nam Potha,* gives a catalogue of sites to be visited by Buddhist pilgrims. The list includes almost all the sites that are popular today. Gombrich mentions that pilgrimages had taken place in Sri Lanka from time immemorial (1991 pp. 128–129). Gombrich also describes a

Sinhalese book, *Bauddha Adihilla,* with texts from the medieval period onward, that also gives the particular forms of worship to be performed at the different pilgrimage sites in the country, indicating again the richness of the culture of pilgrimage (1991 p. 383).

The extensive literature in Sinhalese called the *Sandesa Kavya* of the 15th century is also replete with descriptions of pilgrimages. And an entire genre of minor works, many written by ordinary men and women, describes such pilgrimages (Deraniyagala, P. E. P., 1954 p. 100; 1955 p. 245). Foreign travelers—from East and West—also have described the centers where Sinhalese go for pilgrimages. These foreign sources include many in Chinese (for example, Fa-Hsien, in Beal 1993 pp. 399–414). For a good summary of the more than two-thousand-year global reach into and out of Sri Lankan pilgrim sites as attested to by foreign visitors, an excellent source is Heinz Mode (1981).

So pilgrimage as an ancient practice among the Sinhalese has been very widespread. And the recent increase, which Kapferer notes, is probably nothing more than the proportionate increase of general mobility in the country due to recent improvements in the transport system.

KAPFERER IN PERSPECTIVE

Kapferer's thesis of hierarchy is derived from Louis Dumont's *Homo Hierarchicus,* from which Dumont specifically left out Sri Lanka. The central tenet of Dumont was that egalitarianism and individualism did not agree with Brahmanist India (Kapferer 1988 p. 8). Buddhism as an ideology, on the other hand, was highly egalitarian and individualistic. Further, the legitimacy of the king differs formally in the two systems. In the Hindu system, the ruler's legitimacy is divine, derived from "God." In the case of the Buddhist ruler, it is derived from the people through the well-known ideology of *Mahasammata,* the "Great Elect," and the *dasaraja dharma,* the rules governing the just king and emphasizing benevolence. However, it is not Buddhism that Kapferer is writing about but the ideology that he himself has conveniently constructed *for* his subjects from his study of a small sample of exorcist rituals.

Dumont's approach is against the evolutionist position of much Western social and political philosophy (Kapferer 1988 p. 219). But the persons whom Kapferer uses as his Sri Lankan academic mentors were, at the time he was writing his book in the mid-1980s, Marxists of the old-fashioned variety. They included Leslie Gunawardene, who had been a politburo member of the Sri Lanka Communist Party (for most purposes, a branch of the Soviet Party). Newton Gunasinghe and Kumari Jayawardana were also Marxists of the old left. So one wonders how Kapferer's anti-evolutionist and therefore anti-Marxist perspectives sit with the others whom he cites, admires, and evidently agrees with.

Rituals similar to those observed by Kapferer, Obeyesekere has pointed out, are also performed in other parts of India and Southeast Asia (Gomb-Obey 1988 p. 457). Kapferer also admits that his Sinhalese hierarchical myths could have come from North Indian Mahayana Buddhism (1988 p. 11). So, the North Indian antecedents of the Sinhalese hierarchy must have left some residue in North India itself. Dumont's views on the Indian hierarchy must now be quickly modified in light of Kapferer's Sinhalese hierarchy's presence in India. Further, if the Sri Lankan riots were motivated by an assumed Sinhalese hierarchical motivation, were there then Sinhalese demons, complete with their hierarchical schemes, lurking in the thick of the anti-Sikh riots in Delhi? The theoretical possibilities in Kapferer now multiply dramatically.

Kapferer says that his central argument, partly derived from Dumont, is that egalitarianism and hierarchy are destructive and dehumanizing (1988 p. 9). Here he ignores again the fact that the Dutugemunu story, which forms part of his central thesis, has the parallel story of the invader, Elara, being considered just, in fact, the Sinhalese epitome of humanism.

Kapferer says that the Sinhalese believe that they have an identity because of their fetish of culture that makes nationalism a religion (1988 p. 98). He sees something exceptional when Sri Lanka's past intrudes into the present, affecting it (p. 90). Pride in a Greek cultural heritage drove Westerners into the study of Greek history and archaeology in the 19th and 20th centuries. What was sauce for the European goose, then, is now denied to the Sinhalese gander. Further, Sinhalese do not make a special fetish of their culture; any cursory glance at contemporary Sri Lanka would reveal evidence to the contrary. One would today see a fascination with cricket, probably more people watching cricket on TV than going to the temple. None of the older traditional games are played today. The dress is Western. What is taught in school is mostly Western-derived syllabi. Kapferer thus makes his grand pronouncements without even the barest of obvious observations.

Further, the Sinhalese historical memory that he finds fault with can at crucial times be very short. Thus, after the Indian proxy invasion of Sri Lanka that culminated in the Indian-imposed Accord of 1987–1989, the

American ambassador to Sri Lanka, James Spain, told a reporter, "We [Americans] still blame the Japanese, but ironically in Sri Lanka, the people do not blame India" (Gunaratne 1993 p. 210).

Sri Lanka is a complex society with a literary tradition much longer than those of many West European countries. Yet, although it is a theory that depends on the persistence of literary traditions in a highly literate society, Kapferer's bibliography does not have a single Sinhala-language source. There are also virtually no English-language texts that approach the subject from an angle sympathetic to the perspective of his hosts, the Sinhalese. Kapferer makes all his grand analyses of the country and its culture, admittedly without a proper understanding of the language, relying entirely on dubious secondary material, antagonistic to the culture he studies. Dumont's work, on the other hand, was sympathetic to his subjects, unlike Kapferer's relentless attack on his subject matter through his own "hierarchical scheme," essentially a fairy story constructed by him. This denigration of the broad culture Kapferer studies is in contrast to previous generations of European scholars, including those of the colonial era, who celebrated Sinhalese achievements.

Kapferer's spurious constructions now affect Sri Lanka neocolonially at the international level, because international decision makers who want to know what is happening in Sri Lanka read the handful of books on it, of which Kapferer's is one. His writings, because they present the Sinhalese in this partial light, help justify the Indian indirect and direct proxy invasion of the country and current international interference by virtually every foreign embassy in the country. So much for taking seriously the local subjects and their views of the demonic.

THE RETURN OF THE DERANGED TO SORCERY

The above has been a rather extensive discussion of Kapferer's attempt to decipher the whole of Sinhala Buddhist society through his second book. Let us now quickly move into his third book, *The Feast of the Sorcerer: Practices of Consciousness and Power* (1997), written twenty-five years after his first foray into Sri Lanka. In this third book he returns to the more modest ambitions of his first book—to the study of the irrational. I will deal with this book rather succinctly.

Let me begin with his methodological approach here, as his first odyssey into Sri Lanka began with explicit and self-righteous methodologies. As we saw in his first book, as well as in the second, these methodologies were often contradictory. He also shifted, in his second edition of the first book, the methodologies with which he started in his first edition. The second book had an entirely different methodology. The winds in the anthropological world had changed, and he was now trimming his sails. In the third book he keeps to form.

He says that he still adheres to his earlier situational analyses and the extended case analysis. But he shifts the eyes through which he says he sees Sri Lankan reality from his first band of exorcists to a second band—those who perform *Suniyam*. Why? Because he did not follow advice earlier that *Suniyam* was the most important exorcist ceremony, and hence the key to Sinhalese reality. But his contortions as he tries once again to force-fit Sinhalese reality into his imagined and contradictory frames are embarrassing to behold.

Kapferer now recognizes that the Buddhist and Hindu worlds were familiar with the phenomenological approach he uses. Western phenomenology, in his words, is "very much a Johnny-come-lately." He, however, says that the phenomenology he uses has no "ultimate truth in itself" (1997 p. xv).

Again his stated intentions are noble. He says the anthropology of sorcery has been "an important area where anthropologists have attempted to overturn colonialist and other forms of dominant knowledge and practice" (1997 p. 9). But sorcery, as he himself acknowledges in his first book, is looked down upon by the local educated class. He says the five senses become in Sinhalese sorcery the channels through which humans are malevolently influenced by others (p. 2). But the man who grudgingly acknowledges Buddhist possibilities in his art of phenomenology is unaware of the vast Buddhist literature on mental functioning and, therefore, on human behavior. This literature uses the five senses as variables together with the Buddhist sixth sense of mind.

Elsewhere, Kapferer waxes evocatively on sorcery, saying that sorcery is the irrationality of the rational, flowing within worlds that are committed to rationalism. This he says is the Zen of sorcery (1997 p. 15). It is not. Kapferer shows absolutely no understanding of first Buddhist principles, let alone philosophical variants such as Zen. The Buddhist variant Zen philosophy is derived from the 1st-century A.D. Madhyamika philosophy of Nagarjuna and his principal disciple, Aryadeva, a Sinhalese. It is interesting to note that when Kapferer uses the word Zen (in its pop usage), it illustrates the fact that international Buddhism launched by Dharmapala's reforms, which Kapferer denigrated in his second book, had now seeped into the popular imagination of the West and has come back to him in a corrupted form to analyze falsely the cultures of its origin.

Kapferer says that exorcism, which was looked down upon earlier, is today re-evaluated positively in view of the "acute cultural reaffirmation" among the Sinhalese because of the Tamil-Sinhala ethnic conflict (1997 p. 18). In fact, the re-evaluation arose in the fifties and early sixties simply to see whether there were theatrical elements in these practices that could be used for contemporary drama. Prominent in this re-evaluation were Professor Sarachchandra and his students, such as M. H. Gunatilleke (Sarachchandra 1953; Gunatilleke 1978). But although these dramatic elements were borrowed, exorcist ceremonies continued to be looked down upon by the educated as well as by Buddhist theory—again just the opposite of what Kapferer says.

In his two earlier books Kapferer examined the *whole* of Sinhalese society through the lenses of his exorcist ceremonies, frequently referring to "the" Sinhalese society. He now backtracks in his third book. He says he uses the current "sorcerer's perspective" only as a metaphor to describe the Sinhalese, emphasizing that in "no way" can the social and political events in Sri Lanka be subsumed to the arguments of his current interest, *Suniyam* (1997 p. 24).

Kapferer has some interesting observations that contradict his central positions. He says that people practice *Suniyam* "routinely," although there is "widespread moral abhorrence" against it (1997 pp. 45, 268). This goes against his earlier statement in the book that people now accept it (p. 18). But in contrast to his first book, he does not give any figures to indicate the extent of this practice that everybody frowns upon.

His emphasis is on the practice of Sinhala Buddhists, but he says that there is a widespread demand for "innovative" or foreign sorcery. He describes pluralistic practices in which the Sinhala Buddhists borrow from Maldivians, Hindus, and Muslims (1997 p. 46). Things foreign, he says, are very useful and prized among these borrowers. But unfortunately he does not give us any numbers of his practitioners to help us come to any conclusion. In the first book, we noticed that his practitioners were a minuscule part of the population, and, more significantly, that they often selected exorcism as a healing approach after more regular approaches such as Western or Ayurvedic medical systems were exhausted; even his exorcists did not have much faith in their own rites. But on the strength of that sample's skewed views, he went on in his second book to describe the whole dynamics of Sinhalese society. Now unfortunately, according to him, his sorcerer-heroes, too, display a plurality. They, in fact, also import their practices. So sorcery is not the firm definitive art he had assumed it to be. As "innovative foreign sorcery imports," they could even import some New Age practices. But this and the example of the

Maldivian, Hindu, and Muslim imports raise the question, how can one theorize on "the" Sinhalese condition from such a tainted sorcery rite?

Even in 1997 Kapferer quotes as true Gombrich and Obeyesekere's spurious assertion in their 1989 book, which was based on fieldwork done earlier, that there was a growth in the number of ecstatic priests (Kapferer 1997 p. 52). He again takes as true the Protestant Buddhism thesis (p. 92), and, on several occasions, refers approvingly to Tambiah (pp. 8, 9, 285, 312).

This time around, Kapferer also explores philosophical and psychological themes, for example, consciousness (1997 p. xii). He examines consciousness as associated with activity, as chained, as being in the world, as perception, and as speech and sound. But consciousness has been the subject of systematic philosophical and psychological study in Buddhism, some of its findings corroborated by Western scientific study.

Kapferer says that humans are conscious of their selves because they are embodied. He is therefore against the dualism of Western Cartesian philosophy (1997 p. 222). But the concept of an embodied consciousness is a very central facet of Buddhism, found not only in its Sinhalese classical literature but also in many popularly available English-language books and pamphlets written by both contemporary Westerners and Sinhalese.

Kapferer says that the passions of sorcery demonstrate that a reflective consciousness is already integral to the knowing body which is situated and active in the world (1997 p. 224). He writes a long harangue describing this view, completely unaware that it is a central and elementary feature of Buddhist philosophy and psychology.

In his foray into consciousness, Kapferer evokes Sartre favorably, although he has reservations about him (1997 pp. 231, 259). He also refers to Merleau-Ponty, saying that Merleau-Ponty and Sartre brilliantly describe the condition of being-in-the-world. He also refers to Heidegger and Nietzsche, saying that the latter has an approach to power similar to the sorcery that Kapferer describes (pp. 271, 289). But Sartre and the other more influential existentialist, Heidegger, have again been compared with Buddhism. For a specific Theravada treatment of similarities with Sartre, there is Phramaha Prayoon Mererk's *Selflessness in Sartre's Existentialism and Early Buddhism* (1988). As for Heidegger, there are many sources that explore the Buddhist parallels (Smith 1965 p. xii). And for Merleau-Ponty there are again many descriptions of parallels with Buddhism, the book by Varela being one recent effort (Varela et al. 1993). Nietzsche, too, had a Buddhist connection (Faber 1988 pp. 25–45).

Kapferer also goes international—saying that Sri Lankan sorcery resonates with New Age dabblers in New York, London, and Sydney (1997 p. 267). But he ignores the fact that the New Age and its derivatives are not only the irrational and the occult. The New Age heralded, and was part of, a broad counterculture which also saw an upsurge in studies of Asian philosophies and psychologies, specifically in our case Buddhist psychologies from Sri Lanka. The New Age itself was partly opened up, as we showed elsewhere, by the activities of the Theosophists, Madame Blavatsky being the New Age's alleged mother, and by the international Buddhist movement launched by Dharmapala. The Theosophists' heritage was that of the irrational, while Dharmapala exemplified the more rational and the more scientific, well-illustrated by the publicized split between the Theosophists and Dharmapala.

Kapferer, unlike in his earlier book, now depicts the LTTE in negative terms, saying that it probably ordered the assassination of President Premadasa (1997 p. 243).

In this third book he says that more persons died in the few short months of the 1989 insurrection, largely because of the cruel government repression, than died in the entire ethnic conflict (1997 p. 30). He relates this to class forces. But nowhere does he examine these epochal events among the very groups he claims to have studied for twenty-five years. The insurrection and its massive repression was strongest in those very southern areas he studied. I am certain that there were a number of deaths among the groups he studied. When the admittedly lesser number died in the ethnic riots, he wrote an entire book to explain the deaths through his exorcist logic. But significantly, his own admitted informants listed in his preface were supporters of the Indian incursion, which was the main trigger of the 1989 insurrection and, hence, its aftermath.

Kapferer mentions that the number of women who go to the shrines he studied has increased because of the number of deaths due to the barbaric government crackdown (1997 p. 248). He mentions that because of the closure of all other avenues, it was only in these shrines that people could vent their feelings (pp. 253–254). Although he says that there were many more deaths among the Sinhalese than in the ethnic war, he does not do a sociological analysis. In fact, he says that he will not attempt it (p. 287).

He then retracts much of the thrust and content of what he said in the second book, now claiming falsely that he did not say that "the cultural ideas and meanings of civilizations long dead were alive" and influencing the actions of the present Sinhalese (Kapferer 1997 p. 287). This is after going on at length in his second book about the effects of allegedly imagined histories in the Sinhalese historical documents.

In his contortions, trying to wriggle away from his foray into violence in Sri Lanka in his second book, Kapferer appears sympathetic to the JVP. His description of the organizational mode of the JVP is, however, illustrative of his lack of contextual knowledge even of basic social science. He is blithely unaware that the JVP is a classical Marxist-Leninist organization and gives his own idiosyncratic descriptions (1997 p. 292). He says that the JVP operated in the night, organized strikes, declared curfews, put placards around the necks of those killed by them describing the reasons for the executions, and warned their targets, whom they considered antisocial, by anonymous letter, saying that they would meet with punishment unless they changed their ways. Kapferer considers all these acts "the instrumentality of the war machine and of sorcery" (p. 293). He says that some of these acts were "not unlike that of the sorcerer" (p 293). He also designates the crackdown of the state as assuming "the garb of the Sorcerer" (p 294).

This is rank nonsense. The "technology" of the revolution that he describes is all drawn from classical Marxist-Leninist-Maoist sources. All his examples of sorcery can be found in the Chinese and Vietnamese revolutions. The government crackdown itself, although vicious, was standard operating procedure drawn from the manuals of counterinsurgency, with parallels found in many contexts in Indonesia in the early 1960s, Vietnam in the 1960s and 1970s, and several Latin American contexts. These counterinsurgency techniques have been taught to the Sri Lankan armed services, especially by the Israelis, with technology mastered in the Arab experience.

One is truly at a loss to summarize Kapferer's gross failings.

PART IV

■

SINHALESE
FRATRICIDE

CHAPTER 9

■

Tambiah's Sinhala Buddhists

Tambiah has written three books relating to Sri Lanka: *Sri Lanka: Ethnic Fratricide and the Dismantling of Democracy* (1986); *Buddhism Betrayed? Religion, Politics, and Violence in Sri Lanka* (1992); and *Leveling Crowds: Ethnonationalist Conflicts and Collective Violence in South Asia* (1996). All three deal with macro issues pertaining to Sri Lanka. Let me briefly describe each of them.

ETHNIC FRATRICIDE

Tambiah says that his first book, *Sri Lanka: Ethnic Fratricide and the Dismantling of Democracy,* is meant to be an engaged work, a mixture of theory and practice. It was completed immediately after the 1983 anti-Tamil riots in July 1984 (Tambiah 1986 p. 1). Yet Tambiah is confident that he is "in fact, correctly comprehending, both theoretically and scientifically," the movement of ethnic relations in the country (p. ix).

In this first book Tambiah takes a positive view of Sri Lankans as people with humor, warmth, and hospitality. He looks positively at Sri Lanka's ancient ruins and monuments. No other country in South and Southeast excepting Thailand, he says, is more open to outsiders. He asks how could such a people, implying here the Sinhalese, be responsible for the horrendous acts of the 1983 anti-Tamil riots (1986 p. 1)?

In examining this question, he places before us some pertinent facts. He debunks the racially exclusive categories of Sinhalese and Tamil and shows the two groups to be social constructs. The two had been built up through repeated contact with India, especially in recent centuries with South India. But in saying this Tambiah does not want to belittle the Sinhalese civilizational attainments. What he wants to debunk is the view of an "age long, permanent confrontation" between two ethnic blocs of Sinhalese and Tamils. He believes that this view of a long confrontation was given support by the *Mahavamsa.* He believes that over the previous

three decades (1956–1986) there had been an increase in ethnic polarization and mobilization on a previously unknown scale (Tambiah 1986 pp.
1–13).

Tambiah mentions the earlier riots in 1958, 1977, and 1981 that led to
the major uprising in 1983. He mentions that all these riots of unruly
mobs abated in a short time, like similar Hindu-Muslim and Hindu-Sikh
riots in India. He also notes the JVP insurrection in 1971 as another violent episode. He begins the book and makes his points in the neutral and
nonracial way of a Tamil brought up in an elite school in pluralistic
Colombo. The non-communal attitude inculcated in these schools is in
fact mentioned by Tambiah as having shaped his own attitudes as well
as those of an earlier generation of Sri Lankan leaders (1986 pp. 13–17).

He describes in detail the 1983 riots and the involvement in them of
organized gangs (Tambiah 1986 pp. 19–33). He mentions that the armed
forces had prior experience, in 1971, in quelling local groups, in this case
Sinhalese insurgents, but were inactive on the worst days of the riots (pp.
14, 25). He refers to them as a "total solution," evoking images of the Nazis (p. 33). He mentions the inaction of leading politicians as the riots
raged. But he considers this "not so much a racist indifference and lack
of pity" but cowardice (p. 27).

Tambiah gives economic factors, especially the tensions caused by the
new economic schemes of the post-1977 government, as partial reasons
for the riots. He documents the tendency toward increasing authoritarianism in the country, including postponing elections through a rigged
referendum, making members of Parliament puppets by getting them to
sign prior letters of resignation, rewarding policemen who broke the law
on behalf of the government, eroding the independence of the judiciary,
and so on (1986 pp. 19–65). He mentions that despite appearances, the
country still is not a monolithic despotism. He attempts to describe factions within the government. Although he does not reveal or even hint at
his sources, he lists three factions that are said to have existed at the time
of the riots (pp. 46–48). He describes what he perceives as the disadvan-
tages of Sri Lankan Tamils.

Tambiah describes in very negative terms the form of affirmative action introduced in university examinations to give a more representative
ethnic and rural-urban intake (1986 p. 29). He emphasizes that this affirmative action in education, taken to correct colonial wrongs, was itself
wrong (p. 77). He is of the view that economic imperatives and tensions
in Sri Lankan society were not based on class factors but became de-
flected toward the Tamils as a target. He mentions as contributing to the
fragility of the present situation the banning of the TULF because under

the 6th Amendment to the Constitution all members of Parliament had to take an oath that they would "not directly or indirectly, in or outside Sri Lanka, support, espouse, promote, finance, encourage or advocate the establishment of a separate State within the territory of Sri Lanka" (p. 44).

The book is peppered with statements alluding to pathological Sinhalese attitudes as responsible for the crisis. At times Tambiah describes historical reasons for the emergence of such Sinhalese attitudes. He mentions "millenarian politicized Buddhism" and "a dangerously simplified racism" as giving rise to aggressive action against the Tamils (1986 p. 34). He mentions that the riots were due to populism, chauvinism, and militant Buddhism (p. 57). He says that increasingly in the 1970s and 1980s a formulaic Buddhism took root. During this time, to be a Sinhalese was to be automatically a Buddhist and an Aryan and to make a total claim over Sri Lanka, territorially and politically. He says that to be Buddhist is in turn to be Aryan and Sinhalese, and to be Sinhalese is to have the right to exclude and even exterminate other ethnic groups in Sri Lanka, especially Dravidians (pp. 58–59). As illustrative of the Sinhalese fixation on their heritage, he states that Sri Lanka, unlike Pakistan and India, has been parochial with regard to its prehistory, limiting its archaeological digs to the historic Buddhist period (p. 88).

Tambiah mentions that these are tragicomic uses of Buddhism and Sinhala identity, and that they go together with other contributing features. These include what he claims to be the growth of fundamental devotion to ecstatic cults (1986 p. 59). His evidence here refers to *Bodhi Puja* ceremonies documented by two American-based Sri Lankan social scientists (Seneviratne and Wickremeratne 1980). Another feature that Tambiah cites as contributing to the current situation is the increasing prominence being given by the Sinhalese to the worship of Kataragama, a god common to both Sinhalese Buddhists and Hindu Tamils. The extent of Sinhalese attraction to Kataragama has resulted in Sinhalese priests replacing Tamil priests. He sees this as an ethnic takeover and as another example of the unfair and unhistorical monopolistic ambitions of the Sinhalese. Tambiah sees the Sinhalese as searching for a homogenizing, militant national identity. He considers their actions with regard to Kataragama a Sinhala colonization of a Hindu god (p. 62).

Tambiah enlivens his narrative when he describes ceremonies that clearly appear to be the same as they were when he himself saw them in person in previous years, such as the annual Hindu *Vel* festival. He mentions in a positive tone how in earlier years Sinhalese rubbing shoulders with Tamil devotees had broken coconuts in propitiating the Hindu god Murukan. He notes that Sinhalese, in intensifying their worship of Kataragama, simultaneously also deny the heritage of Murukan. He says that the historian/anthropologist (meaning himself) observing this feels as if he were "standing on the shifting sands of [the] ethnic fantasies" of, evidently, the Sinhalese (1986 p. 63).

He mentions that in the past, Sinhalese Buddhism was a rich and complex civilization that celebrated differences and complementarity. In contrast, he claims that there is a current Sinhala Buddhist racist nationalism propagated by extremist politicians. As the exemplary propagandist of this racist dogma, he picks out the minister of the United National Party (UNP) at the time, Cyril Mathew. Mathew voices support, Tambiah says, for the Malay nationalist position on *bhumiputras*, "sons of the soil." He says that there is a prevalent feeling that Tamils have been given too much. This, he believes, is brought about by the frustrations of a deprived majority. He does not ascribe willful intent to such views, which he believes are the cries of dashed collective hopes (Tambiah 1986 pp. 63–64). In presenting statistics on ethnic ratios, he reproduces in the body of the text only figures for 1980 to indicate that the ethnic representation in the country had become more even, but no base figures to indicate what the situation was before (Tambiah 1986 p. 77).

Tambiah states that the Sinhalese and Tamils were two indigenous ethnic communities, previously separate but brought together by the British administration (1986 p. 65). He also notes that the Tamils were not homogeneous. There were differences between Jaffna Tamils, Eastern Province Tamils, and Indian Tamils, as well as within them (pp. 65–68). Throwing cold water on a key propaganda point of the separatists, he also mentions that the Sinhalese Kandyan Kingdom ruled the Eastern Province, although not the Tamil Jaffna Kingdom (pp. 1–13).

Tambiah says that in the socio-politically significant events of 1956, the protesting social groups who were arraigned against the English-educated elite were hostile to Western clothes, Western films, Western sex mores, and Western recreation (Tambiah 1986 pp. 68–71). The Protestant attitudes of the Theosophists were borrowed by these groups. Tambiah states that the package of nationalism set off by this renaissance was an exclusionary one. It excluded and alienated groups speaking other languages or professing other religions. This new cause was exemplified by the Sinhalese race, the Buddhist religion, and the Sinhalese as an Aryan "race" (pp. 68–71). He describes white-collar Tamils living in Colombo in self-made ghettos in the Wellawatte, Dehiwela, and Ratmalana suburbs and the reaction of Sinhalese to them (p. 107).

The Sangha—the monks' order—Tambiah says, has resisted attempts by the state to control its affairs, implying that it is a monolithic body. He says that the Sangha has harbored militant, chauvinist, and demagogic monks. But he claims that the Sangha is no longer the torchbearer of militant political Buddhism. He says that the present stage is characterized by contentless flag waving that has no philosophical and ethical grounds (1986 p. 83). He finds extremist elements, referring to them as "shapeless, hungry ghosts and monsters" of militant Sinhala Buddhist nationalists who limited the actions of President J. R. Jayawardene (p. 117).

Tambiah mentions that parallel to nationalist developments in the 19th and 20th centuries among the Sinhalese, there were similar developments among the Tamils. Such was the case of Arumuga Navalar. Navalar had worked in South India and was associated with a "Jaffna School," which at that time dominated the literary scene in Madras (1986 p. 109).

He mentions that after repeated rebuffs and relegation to second-class status, Tamils have opted for separation and have developed links with South Indian ethnic parties, the Dravida Munnetra Kazhagam (DMK) and the Anna Dravida Munnetra Kazhagam (AIDMK). This in turn enrages the Sinhalese. He believes that these are acts of desperation by the Tamils (1986 p. 77). But he says that the connections of Tamil Nadu politicians with Sri Lankan Tamil politicians would not lead to the invasion that the "Sinhalese hysteria" predicted. He stated that New Delhi would be noncommittal (p. 111).

Tambiah describes the acceptance of Tamils by the Sinhalese when Tamil kings were imported by the local ruling strata to keep the European colonialists at bay (1986 p. 97). He mentions other aspects of South Indian influence, such as the arrival over the centuries of different caste groups as well as families to be absorbed and become Sinhalese. He mentions the establishment of a Tamil polity restricted only to the Jaffna peninsula. He mentions that this kingdom had no control of the Eastern Province, which was under the Kandyan kings (pp. 101–104). He observes that Jaffna Tamils, cut off from South Indian Tamils for centuries, have begun to be perceived by the Sinhalese as clannish and communal-minded. He mentions that there are stronger caste divisions in Jaffna than among the Sinhalese. He says that this exclusivity and experience of caste dominance by the (upper-caste) Tamils made them less prone to accept a subordinate position to the Sinhalese because these Tamils felt they were purer in customs and had more talent, and they accepted no historical claim to be ruled in their own lands (pp. 103–106).

The minority Tamils, Tambiah says, are now "inventing a new history of their past" (1986 p. 117). He says that Tamils must realistically accept Sinhalese as the "only viable and economical language" for much of the country's administration (p. 125). He advises the Sri Lankan Tamil diaspora not to engage in vicarious revenge by giving financial and moral support to Tamil extremist politics. To the Sinhalese he mentions that causing a Tamil diaspora will itself have a boomerang effect. He appeals to both factions (pp. 111–113).

Tambiah says that he is a "distant observer [who] ruefully and despairingly delineates" the Sri Lankan case (1986 p. 117). He remembers how in his youth things were much better and tensions were much lower. In the mid-1950s he had feared that the freezing of ethnic and communal boundaries would be counterproductive to a pluralistic society (p.136).

With this rueful comment, we should now move to Tambiah's second book, in which he pursues the ethnic conflict further and attempts to identify the actors and dynamics behind the crisis.

BETRAYING BUDDHISM

In his second book, *Buddhism Betrayed? Religion, Politics, and Violence in Sri Lanka* (1992), Tambiah continues his examination of his main actors in Sri Lanka, the Sinhala Buddhists.

Tambiah states that this second book "is not written for Sri Lankan specialists, but for general readers, both inside and outside academia" (Tambiah 1992 p. 136). Yet it attempts to subject the violence in Sri Lanka to a sociological/anthropological examination. The special question he poses, as the book's flier rhetorically asks, is, "How can committed Buddhist monks and lay persons in Sri Lanka today actively take part in the political violence against the Tamils?" He poses the further question of "whether the framework of current Buddhist nationalism can in the future stretch and incorporate a greater amount of pluralist tolerance in the name of Buddhist conceptions of righteous rule."

Tambiah states that as a methodology he "must look at the universe, so far as possible, through the eyes and practices of Buddhist actors situated in history and in their local contexts" (1992 p. 3). But whether or not he adopts the viewpoint of the Buddhist actors, one of the features of Tambiah's book is that he generally does not give sources for his information, whether they are his own anthropological observations or published primary sources.

Tambiah specifically mentions that he has left out one key actor in the conflict, namely, the Tamils. He says that in the list of riots and insurrections he has omitted from his "account the impulsions and motivations behind the insurrections and the civil war begun and continued unabated since the 1970s by the Tamil militant youth" (1992 p. 46, n. 3). He mentions that he also leaves out the activities of the Indian army in Sri Lanka. He says that he is has omitted these actors from consideration "because I am primarily concerned with the nature of the involvement of Buddhism in recent politics and in the occurrence of civilian violence" (p. 46, n. 3). Tambiah says that his mission is also to trace the roots of the problem in the "legacy of the deep past" (pp. 129–183).

The book has a foreword by Lal Jayawardena, the then Sri Lankan director of the World Institute of Development Economic Research (WIDER) in Helsinki. Jayawardena states that Sri Lanka's problem is an "ethnic and religious conflict" become "endemic." Jayawardena, in sponsoring the book, seeks in it answers to the violence that has wrecked development in the country, including the violence of the JVP, which was, according to Jayawardena, "drawing sustenance from the slogan of Sinhala Buddhism and anti Indian sentiment" (Tambiah 1992 p. x). Lal Jayawardena says that the aim of the book is "to explain how Sri Lanka's ethnic and religious conflict reached its present pass of being able to completely frustrate the development process" (p. xi). The reasons for this condition, Jayawardena says, are "embedded in history, the political process and the ideology of religion and nationalism." Jayawardena intends to explore this field with Tambiah "in the company of other scholars" (p x.).

The book is divided into several parts. In the first the author raises the key questions he wishes to explore. First he examines the period of Buddhist revivalism and protest from 1860 to 1946. He then goes back, in a chapter titled "The Period of Buddhist Revivalism, 1860–1915," to the alleged origins of the recent conflicts at the time when reformers were spearheading the anticolonial movement. Here Tambiah directly and indirectly blames the reformer Anagarika Dharmapala for the later tragedies, describing Dharmapala as "an uncharitable propagandist" (1992 p. 7).

Tambiah describes those who became members of the Theosophical Society, which later spearheaded the Buddhist Renaissance. He says that together with several wealthy Sinhala traders, arrack renters (licensees to sell coconut spirits), and coconut planters, Gunananda became a member of the Theosophical Society (1992 p. 6). Tambiah also notes that the monks Hikkaduve Siri Sumangala, Walane Siddharta, Weligama Siri Sumangala, and Ratmalane Sri Dharmaloka participated in key Buddhist revival activities. These activities included the formation of Buddhist schools and involvement in the temperance movements of 1904 and 1912 (p. 6).

He next covers the rise of radical monks who wanted to reverse colonial inroads; the key election of 1956 and its aftermath, which saw the restoration of Buddhism and the transformation of education; the deepening crisis of the 1970s; and the violence-stricken 1980s. In the last three chapters, he addresses "the issue of Sinhala historical consciousness as a composite exercise" (1992 p. 4).

In the first few chapters, Tambiah describes the early history of Buddhist agitation and its conceptual basis. The influence of 19th-century reformers, the 19th-century debates between Christians and Buddhists, and the confluence of the Theosophists and Buddhist revivalist Anagarika Dharmapala are briefly described. More detailed are the descriptions of the 1940s and 1950s, when a marriage between Sinhala Buddhist nationalists and radical leftist monks took place.

It is the 1980s, however, when most of the Sri Lankan violence occurred, that Tambiah concentrates on. And it is this section that naturally attracts our attention. He says that Sinhalese were against the devolution of political power (1992 p. 123).

The Maubima Surakhime Vyaparaya (Movement for Protection of the Motherland, or MSV) was a leading umbrella organization of monks in the 1980s. Tambiah identifies it as the major monastic organization of the time. The MSV, Tambiah claims, was "totally opposed to any devolutionary solution to the [ethnic] conflict" (1992 p. 85). And he says that "sections of the *sangha* [were] engaged in political protest against the alleged division of the country and compromise of the supremacy of Buddhism" (p. 84). To protest the Indian-imposed "Peace Accord" on the island, he claims, a "mass rally of protest organized by the MSV deteriorated in a horrible riot in Colombo" (p. 89). The MSV monks were also "for Islandwide propagation of Buddhism" (p. 88) and preferred a "homogenising national identity" (p. 92). He mentions that the targets of the MSV monks also included Catholics, quoting a statement from a monks' journal, *Vinivida*. Cracks, however, appeared later within the MSV, Tambiah notes, but he does not explore this phenomenon further, in terms of the reasons for and the outcome of the cracks (p. 98). He claims that "'monk ideologues'... have also primordialized and romanticised the 'unity' of the country to a pristine homogeneity devoid of differences of political party and the divisions of party government" (p. 86). Tambiah claims that many Sinhalese patriotic organizations freely used the expression "sons of the soil" (*bhumiputra*) in their rhetoric (p. 86). To illustrate the present attitudes of monks, he quotes a 1989 book by James Manor that describes monks' attitudes in the 1950s (Manor 1989). He claims the existence of "Buddhist universities," to which young monks are drawn and where presumably their ideas are formed (p. 94).

In describing the turbulent 1980s, Tambiah considers three leading

Buddhist monk-activists of the period, Maduluweve Sobitha, Palipane Chandananda, and Muruttetuwe Ananda, who together with the SLFP "offered powerful resistance to the Peace Accord." Sobitha, he mentions, was a popular preacher who was banned from the state radio for his critical views of the government; Tambiah claims that this ban was an important ingredient in Sobhitha's support of the SLFP and hostility toward the UNP president's "attempt to settle the ethnic conflict" (implying here the Indian-imposed, so-called "Peace Accord" of 1987) (Tambiah 1992 p. 85).

Describing these monks further, he mentions that "Muruttetuwe became opposed to the UNP when President J. R. Jayawardene thought it improper for a monk to be president of [the nurses'] union and wanted him removed" (1992 p. 84). Muruttetuwe's career, he claims, now "took a radical turn, leading militant strikes staged by the nurses union, a specially successful one being that conducted in 1978" (p. 85). Muruttetuwe's sympathies, Tambiah says, gravitated ultimately toward the radical but chauvinist rhetoric of the JVP (p. 85).

Tambiah gives the example of a thousand monks walking under the banner of the JVP in the May Day parade in 1982 as an example of the transformation to "sons of the soil" (1992 pp. 90, 96). The JVP is described as egalitarian, nationalist, anti-Tamil, especially anti-Indian-estate-labor, adding that the Sinhala Buddhist charter of the JVP appealed to young monks (pp. 90, 96). He also mentions that the JVP was banned after the anti-Tamil riots of 1983.

Later, Tambiah mentions that the JVP directed its violence not against Tamils or Indians but against political groups among the Sinhalese (Tambiah 1992 p. 98). He also mentions that younger monks criticized their elders and the clerical authorities, and that they condoned passively, and even perhaps collaborated in, the assassination by JVP-allied forces of senior monks opposed to them. He notes that later these younger JVP-oriented monks were themselves killed. Although mention is made in passing to a class character and a larger social agenda to the younger monks' activities, this is not followed up (p. 99).

Tambiah says that after the armed forces' violence against civilians, bystanders, and nonmilitary targets, the Tamil rebels started acting violently, attacking Sinhalese sacred sites; he adds that through these attacks, the Tamil rebels were "only" making a statement (1992 p. 76).

Tambiah in his narrative uses expressions such as "Buddhist nationalism and chauvinism" (1992 p. 59), "Tamil homeland" (p. 59), "Sinhala army in the north" (p. 19), and "army of occupation" (p. 70). He says that colonization of Tamil traditional homelands had occurred (pp. 68–70), adding that Tinneveli, "the heart of Sri Lankan Tamil territory in North Sri Lanka," had been occupied by "a Sinhalese army for some time" (p. 71).

LEVELING CROWDS

Tambiah embarked upon his third book, *Leveling Crowds: Ethnonationalist Conflicts and Collective Violence in South Asia* (1996), in order to find common features in ethnic violence in South Asia in general (p. x). In this book, unlike his last, Tambiah takes into account the fact that ethnic riots do occur in other countries as he looks at riots in South Asia as a whole. He also finds such ethnic conflicts worldwide (1996 p. 25). He now finds "chauvinism," "identity panic," "racism," "discrimination," and "attacks on foreigners" in Western Europe and considers them "disturbing" (p. 5). He observes that as a result of ethnic conflicts there have been large-scale expulsions of Asians from Uganda (p. 5).

Apart from the Sri Lankan riots, Tambiah examines the riots in Pathan-Bihari and the Sindhi-Muhajir clashes in Pakistan, and the Sikh-Hindu and Muslim-Hindu clashes in India, including the destruction of the Babri Masjid at Ayodhya. He notes that instead of being long-lived, such riots are "mercifully short-lived." He finds that all over the region, "in country after country, police, army, other security forces, paramilitary groups recruited by the state, and even some public officials [have] participated in riots" (1996 p. 214). After this spasmodic bloodletting, the civilian destroyers return to the humdrum routine of everyday life (p. 215).

Tambiah says that among the factors that aided the development of the Western nation-state was a loyalty to secularism. But he says there is in India now a "subaltern" resistance to secularism (1996 p. 14). By "subaltern resistance," he means Hindu nationalism. He says that this is linked to a fear of cultural extinction in the region. He includes Hindu nationalism, Islamic fundamentalism, and Buddhist "nationalism" under this general subaltern rubric in the region. He says that these movements, including Buddhist "nationalism," were against many Western inroads, including the celebration of sex, Western economic affluence, political supremacy, and privatization of religion (p. 14).

He finds that the replacement of the colonial language, English, with local languages, *Swabasha*, has created problems in countries as varied as India, Pakistan, Burma, Sri Lanka, and Malaysia. This is also related to ambitious educational and literacy programs which create large numbers of job-seeking young people who vie for the available slots (Tambiah

1996 p. 17). He takes note of and looks positively at the affirmative action through legislation taken on behalf of disadvantaged groups such as the Harijans of India (p. 24).

Tambiah notes that communalism was in fact constructed by the British as part of a divide-and-rule policy in the region. He observes that some recent commentators on the British period, such as Gyanendra Pandey (1990), show that the British used grand narratives like that of a Hindu-Muslim communal divide as deliberate master narratives (Tambiah 1996 p. 23). He mentions that recent commentators on subaltern studies have said that British accounts of riots have been dressed up in the language of counterinsurgency. Pandey had noted that a variety of protest movements were reduced to a master principle of a permanent divide between Muslims and Hindus and so justified the use of deadly force to suppress them (Tambiah 1996 p. 29).

Tambiah considers ethnic conflict to be a complex issue (1996 p. 27). He says that in this universal phenomenon there is more at play than either primordial features of a natural-instinct kind or constructionist features that are only imagined by the new literate intelligentsia (p. 25). He considers the need to study the victims of ethnic cleansing (p. 27). He observes that militant groups such as those of the Sri Lankan Tamils have international networks of collaboration with other militant groups, not unlike the networks of sovereign countries and great powers (p. 6). He also notes that there was armed intervention by India in Sri Lanka in 1987, which was facilitated by the secessionist movement (p. 5).

Let us now concentrate on Tambiah's approach in his third book on Sri Lanka. He details four riots, the Buddhist-Catholic riot in Kotahena in 1883, the Muslim-Buddhist riot in 1915, and the Sinhala-Tamil riots in 1956 and 1983.

Tambiah says that in colonial Sri Lanka, both Buddhists and Hindus reacted angrily to the activities of an English-speaking, Christian local elite who had a stranglehold on education. This resulted in a revival among the Buddhists and Hindus led by what he calls "famous charismatic and innovative leaders" such as Angarika Dharmapala and Arumugam Navalar. He says that later Muslims also came together in their own revival (1996 p. 38).

Tambiah says, following the Protestant Buddhist line, that the Sinhalese Buddhists borrowed propaganda techniques and institutional forms from the Protestant missionaries, including the use of the printing press. He describes as an important episode the debate at Panadura, in which he says local enthusiasts gave the victory to the monk Gunananda. He says that it was during this time that Colonel Olcott arrived and Dharmapala emerged under Gunananda and Olcott's "patronage and tute-lage" (1996 p. 47). Tambiah calls Migettuwatte Gunananda a "presiding eminence" who organized the Society for the Propagation of Buddhism in imitation of the society for the Propagation of the Gospel. He says that Gunananda's views "are alleged to have stimulated the arrival of Colonel Olcott" (p. 48).

He informs us that the Buddhist revivalism associated with Dharma-pala was not marked by any desire for deep economic and social reform. There was no attempt to advocate land reform, or to become involved in eradicating caste discrimination and establishing capitalist enterprises. Tambiah quotes Sarath Amunugama, and says that the lay ethics pro-nounced by Dharmapala were derived from the monks' rules of behav-ior, the *Vinaya* (Tambiah 1996 p. 40). He says that there is no indication that the youth inspired by Angarika's exhortations were encouraged to incorporate science and technology for development. For Tambiah, Dhar-mapala was "more a propagandist than a creative or profound thinker-reformer" (p. 41). Tambiah quotes approvingly the writings of Kumari Jayawardena, who claimed that the Buddhist Renaissance aroused Bud-dhists only to a "holy war" instead of to an anticolonial struggle (p. 48).

Tambiah claims that Buddhist revivalism resulted in majoritarian domination. This resulted in monopolistic gains for the Sinhalese. Wher-ever local businesses sprouted, he says, it was under state patronage with subsidies to fend off rivals (1996 pp. 41–43).

The Kotahena riot of 1883 that he describes pitted Catholics against Buddhists. Tambiah says that "the question has been raised whether the reformist monk Gunananda deliberately chose the month of March" for his Buddhist activities to provoke the Christians in Kotahena that re-sulted in the riots (1996 p. 50). In looking for the reasons for the Kotahena riot, Tambiah says that it should be considered an expression of early Sin-hala Buddhist nationalism, which he says the British authorities "failed to recognize at that time" (pp. 52, 53).

However, Tambiah cannot run away from the British colonialists' own inquiry, which squarely blamed the Catholics for the riot. He now quotes the conclusions of this inquiry, which said: "we have no hesitation in stating that we believe the illegal assemblies, both on Good Friday and Easter-day were thoroughly organized and previously arranged by the Roman Catholics, with the express purpose of attacking Buddhism [*sic*] processions" (1996 p. 54). Tambiah says that it was likely that the Brit-ish officials were prejudiced against the Catholics. He says that the Bud-dhists, "protesting that they were the victims of attacks by Catholic mobs," had insistently asked that the rioters be apprehended. Tambiah implies that this request was somehow wrong.

Tambiah mentions that the British did little to address Buddhists' grievances over the Kotahena riots. He notes that this incident resulted in Buddhist religious, political, and economic hopes beginning to be articulated. But he also says that the British over-read the anticolonial nature of the Sinhalese-Muslim riots of 1915—another riot he studies—which he says was not an example of resistance to colonial rule (1996 p. 55).

The immediate trigger for the Muslim riots of 1915 was a Buddhist procession in Gampola that passed in front of a mosque playing music. Tambiah says that the riots may have been due to the centenary of the Convention of 1815, which ceded the country to the British. He says that a contributing factor may have been "the alleged non observance of certain understandings" in this treaty to safeguard the position of Buddhism (1996 p. 57). The riots were brought under control by floggings and shootings by British volunteers, which, Tambiah admits, "were worse than anything the rioters did" (p. 56). A Britisher, Fraser, wrote that the "Moors had brought the attack on themselves by their religious intolerance" (quoted in Tambiah 1996 p. 61).

Tambiah now mentions that, corresponding to the Buddhist revival of Dharmapala and the Hindu revival of Navalar, there was also a Muslim revival. He quotes the Muslim Sri Lankan writer Ameer Ali, who says that this revival aroused an exclusivist and separatist image of Muslims among the Sinhalese. It was the recently arrived "Coastal Moors," unlike the earlier assimilated "Moors," who championed this Islamic fundamentalism (Tambiah 1996 pp. 74–75). The "Coastal Moors," numbering only about 12 percent of the total Muslim population in the country, had recently come from South India (p. 46).

Tambiah uses only secondary sources for the Muslim riots, and for a significant part of his account he uses Kannangara's exhaustive study (1983). When the latter points out that there was no link between the Buddhist Renaissance and Sinhalese commercial interests, Tambiah disagrees. He says that such commercial interests "*could* have fused their revivalist religious enthusiasm with a Sinhala nationalism" (1996 p. 79, my emphasis).

Tambiah goes on to discuss two other riots, the anti-Tamil riots of 1956 and 1983 (1996 pp. 82–101). These two riots he had in fact discussed to varying degrees in his two earlier books. Tambiah's general descriptions of the anti-Tamil riots of 1958 and 1983 generally keep to well-known facts. In the case of the 1983 riots, I was a partial witness, trying to rescue many Tamil friends. I would have used even stronger language in the descriptions (pp. 82–101).

In discussing the riots of 1956, Tambiah begins by taking the issue of settlement of lands in the underpopulated areas in the north and east—abandoned to the jungle since about the 14th century. He also says that the Tamil separatism of the Federal Party of Chelvanayagam developed only after the rise of Sinhalese nationalism in 1956.

Tambiah also follows up to some extent in this third book the events of the turbulent post-1987 period. He refers to the Pettah meeting protesting against the Indian incursion. He mentions the Movement for the Defense of the Motherland and Prins Gunasekere, Muruttetuwe Ananda, and Maduluwawe Sobhita—all of whom we met in his second book (1996 p. 271).

Having completed this summary of Tambiah's descriptions ("from within") of, principally, Sinhalese Buddhists in a time of great turbulence, let us look at how well his descriptions square with reality.

CHAPTER 10

■

Ethnic Fratricide Turns to Death of Facts

Let me begin examining Tambiah's writings by looking at his first book.

In a book that attempts to unravel complicated problems in a very complex society, nowhere does Tambiah give details of his sources to show how he arrives at his "facts." The recent problems of Sri Lanka have seen the appearance of many books, including by non-academics. None that I have come across, other than Tambiah's, do not provide sources so that the truth of the statements can be checked.

Tambiah has many positive things to say of Sri Lankan society; he remarks on its humor, warmth, hospitality, and openness to outsiders (1986 p. 1). Here he must be alluding largely to Sinhalese, because elsewhere he says the Tamils are perceived as clannish and caste-bound (1986 pp. 103–106). The question he poses is, what were the underlying reasons for the 1983 anti-Tamil riots?

He says that an "age long, permanent confrontation" between the Sinhalese and the Tamils was given support by the chronicles. This is not true. I have dealt in fair detail with the alleged primordial anti-Tamil attitude of the Sinhalese in Chapter 9, and shown it to be a false construction. (For a more popular Sinhala-language source at a time of ethnic tensions over the coexistence of Sinhalese and Tamils in the predominantly Sinhala society, see the articles of Mendis Rohanadeera [1983a, 1983b].)

Tambiah correctly mentions the ethnic polarization that has occurred over the last three decades. But he ignores the contributions to it of Tamil groups, concentrating only on Sinhalese actions. He mentions that the Eastern Province, which was until recently largely jungle, and which is claimed by Tamil separatists as their "traditional homelands," was part of the Sinhalese Kandyan Kingdom until it was ceded to the Dutch and the British, and was never under Tamil rule (1986 pp. 1–13). But Tambiah does not carry this observation to its logical conclusion by identifying the traditional homelands hoax as one of the deepest causes of ethnic tension in the country. He quotes Virginia Leary on the riots and human rights violations (pp. 20, 45), but ignores the fact that she implicitly accepts the traditional homelands hoax, especially its application to the Eastern Province (Leary 1981).

Tambiah's descriptions of the riots, the involvement in them of organized groups, and the inaction of the politicians are generally correct. One also notes a sense of detachment in his presentation of these facts. One even gets the feeling that in some instances, Tambiah is too accommodating of local politicians when he excuses their inaction as the response of cowed politicians swept by a tidal wave of Sinhalese mob action (1986 p. 27). As an angry and futile witness to the riots, I myself would not excuse these politicians in the same casual way—although I agree they were not racist. When Tambiah appears to be making excuses for the completely unprincipled actions of the then president, J. R. Jayawardene, as a cowed politician, this particular remark seems out of place.

Tambiah's descriptions of the growth of authoritarianism, including the postponement of elections, the forcing of members of Parliament to sign letters of resignation in advance, and the subversion of the independence of the police and judiciary by the government itself, are also correct (1986 pp. 19–65). But these were well-known analyses and criticisms at the time, covered by the Sinhala press. In a different context, Tambiah mentions class factors as reasons for the 1971 Sinhalese uprising (1986 pp. 46–48). He also gives economic reasons for the 1983 anti-Tamil riots. But just two years after the publication of his book in 1986, a much larger bloodletting in the south occurred, for which there are no sociological pointers in his book.

He finds fault with the 6th Amendment to the Constitution, which bans all members of Parliament from supporting, espousing, promoting, financing, encouraging, or advocating separatism (1986 p. 44). Coming at a time when Tamils were reeling under the impact of the 1983 riots, the timing of this amendment was appalling. But the content of the amendment itself was not unique to Sri Lanka; it was similar to the 16th Amendment to the Indian Constitution, introduced in 1957 to combat Tamil separatism in India. Indian Tamil separatism died soon thereafter.

Although Tambiah's book contains strong statements about alleged pathological Sinhalese attitudes, such as "millenarian politicized Buddhism," "dangerously simplified racism" (1986 p. 34), and the right to exclude and exterminate others, especially Dravidians (pp. 58–59), nowhere does the author give evidence for the existence of these attitudes and perspectives. There are no citations, no newspaper or other reports supporting these allegations. Instead of evidence, he offers assumptions.

When he says that in the 1970s and 1980s a formulaic Buddhism took root whereby to be a Sinhalese was to be automatically a Buddhist and Aryan (pp. 58–59), in fact just the opposite was occurring. Monks' attitudes were turning rapidly away from their 1950s nationalist agenda.

Tambiah says that the tragicomic use of Buddhism and Sinhala identity is accompanied by an increase in *Bodhi Puja* ceremonies and the worship of Kataragama (1986 pp. 58–59). His sources are studies by Obeyesekere and Wickremaratne. These studies are examined in Obeyesekere's *Buddhism Transformed,* and we have shown them to be unrepresentative of change in the country. The same stories are recycled by both authors, but for their own uses and for their own interpretations. The social reality that has been left out of the original studies, which I have dealt with in detail, is also left out in Tambiah's interpretations. A narrative tangential to the total reality is now built up on the basis of the original partial truths.

Tambiah sees Sinhalese going to Kataragama as a Sinhalese takeover, illustrative of the unfair ambitions of the Sinhalese. But to Obeyesekere, Buddhists' attraction to Kataragama represented a transformation in Protestant Buddhism. Yet, as we have seen, the events reported by Gombrich and Obeyesekere, on which Tambiah depends, are, from their own internal evidence, flawed. The result is contradictory interpretations by both Obeyesekere and Tambiah, based on faulty evidence. But when those who go to Kataragama are asked why they do so, many of them say they do it for *vinoda* ("pleasure"), not exclusively for a religious purpose, for a Sinhala takeover, or to transform Protestantism.

Tambiah does not present evidence of how the Sinhalese priest practicing Hinduism actually performs this alleged Sinhalese homogenizing act and brings about Sinhala colonization of a Hindu god (1986 p. 62). On the other hand, Sinhalese adopting a Tamil Hindu god as their very own could be interpreted as Sinhalese Buddhists internalizing the worldview of Tamil Hindus, a Hindu colonization of the Sinhalese Buddhists, the reverse of Tambiah's interpretation.

Tambiah says that Sinhalese pilgrimage to Kataragama denies the heritage of Murukan (the Tamil name for the Kataragama god), and that the historian/anthropologist, meaning he himself, is "standing on the shifting sands of [the] ethnic fantasies" of the Sinhalese (1986 p. 63). Again he does not describe any connections between the alleged ethnic fantasies of the Sinhalese and these presumed changes. Significantly, Tambiah does not deal at all with the greatest threat to Tamil—as well as Sinhalese—culture, namely, the threat arising from the massive inflow of Western culture.

If these are Tambiah's fantasies, he is on surer ground when he describes the Hindu *Vel* festival, celebrated by Sinhalese and Tamils together, which he himself must have seen when he was living in Sri Lanka. If, as he says, the two communities rubbed shoulders at this Hindu festival, one cannot understand his objection to their doing so at Kataragama.

Some of the descriptions Tambiah gives of white-collar Tamils living in what he describes as self-made ghettos in Colombo suburbs and perceived by the Sinhalese as clannish and communal-minded seem also to be from the 1950s, the time when Tambiah lived in Sri Lanka and knew the place well (1986 p. 107).

Films have been a great cultural influence on the Sinhalese since the 1950s. Initially, Sinhalese films were directly modeled after South Indian Tamil cinema. This Tamil influence on the Sinhalese film was possibly a much deeper cause of cultural change than those identified by Tambiah. But Madras politics, one should add parenthetically, was also influenced by this cinema, both by its Tamil nationalist themes and by its leading stars, who were all allied with South Indian Tamil nationalism. Hero figures from this nationalist cinema became chief ministers of the Tamil Nadu state, and at one time all supported the LTTE cause.

When Tambiah says that the Sinhalese and Tamils were two separate indigenous ethnic communities that the British brought together, he is repeating the fictitious propaganda, put out by separatists, of two distinct nations from time immemorial until they were brought together by the British (Tambiah 1986 p. 65). Here Tambiah ignores his own prior statements, in which he mentioned that the Eastern Province, now "claimed" by separatists, was under the Kandyan kings, and that Tamils are now inventing a new history (p. 117). There has been immigration of different ethnic groups to both Sinhalese and Tamil areas, resulting in the Sinhalization and Tamilization of areas which are today largely Sinhalese or Tamil, a process that gives the lie to the Tamil separatists' "two-nations" theory. I wrote on this in a popular newspaper article in the early 1980s (Goonatilake, Susantha, 1985).

A key aspect of this false history is the invention of the myth of "traditional homelands" encompassing the present Northern and Eastern provinces. Tambiah ruefully remembers his youth, when he feared the freezing of communal and ethnic boundaries (1986 p. 117). The invention of history that he mentions in passing, with its fiction of traditional homelands and the separatists' "two nations" theory precisely freezes such categories.

Tambiah also over-reads the events of 1956 when he says that the groups that came into power were hostile to Western films, sex mores, and recreation (1986 pp. 68–71). This is the first time that I have heard that they were against Western films and Western recreation. Western clothes, however, exemplified at the time a great social divide. Those who wore them were considered "gentlemen" (*mahattaya*) and were addressed as such. Those who wore national dress were considered socially lower, tending to be addressed with the derogatory "you" (*umba*). I have briefly described the social and cultural aspects of the 1956 movement elsewhere (Goonatilake, Susantha, 1982 pp. 163–189). The "1956" social movement was not just "anti"; it was also "pro." Out of its initial phases came new experiments in theater, short stories, the arts, and film.

SINHALESE MONSTERS AND HUNGRY GHOSTS

Tambiah again over-reads when he says that the Buddhist Renaissance excluded and alienated groups speaking other languages or professing other religions and was exemplified by the Sinhalese "race" as an Aryan "race" and professing the Buddhist religion (1986 pp. 68–71). This is a very selective reading of the Buddhist Renaissance.

In Chapter 5 I have dealt at considerable length with the Buddhist Renaissance, its roots, and the attitudes of its key figures, such as the scholar-monks and Anagarika Dharmapala. I showed them to be very big-hearted and in agreement with the Sinhala tolerance Tambiah had already mentioned.

This tradition of Sinhalese Buddhist tolerance toward nonthreatening foreigners and religions was well documented in earlier centuries. The Dutch, who replaced the Portuguese in the coastal regions, forbade Catholic priests to work in their territories, where most of the Catholics lived. The Catholic priests were then given refuge in the Kandyan Kingdom. From this safe haven, they went in disguise to the coastal areas to minister to their flocks (Malalgoda 1976 p. 35). Robert Knox records that the King of Kandy "honored and esteemed" Christianity, and in his kingdom "Protestants and Baptists" gave up their differences and were happy to call themselves "We Christians" (Knox 1911 pp. 67, 304).

Further, although the Brahmins in India shunned Europeans with the same disgust with which they viewed the lower castes, the Sinhalese Buddhist monks did not look at Christian missionaries as adversaries. They were very open, willing to share their knowledge. Their generosity extended to two of the ablest monks helping the Colombo Bible Society in 1812 to translate the Bible. Some of them helped in preparing places of Christian worship; they even offered the hall of the Buddhist temple itself as a place for Christians to preach. Missionaries on their preaching rounds in the countryside often stayed at temples. But when the monks occasionally reciprocally requested the use of missionary school houses, they were turned down (Malalgoda 1976 pp. 210–211).

As the presumed racist attitudes of the Buddhist Renaissance form a backdrop to Tambiah's thinking in both this and his later book, I will digress to discuss this at length, giving more attention to the modern Buddhist movement's key figure, Dharmapala, adding to my discussion in Chapter 5.

BUDDHIST RENAISSANCE'S INCLUSIVENESS

Dharmapala, the key figure of the Buddhist Renaissance, was tolerant of other religions. He objected only to their misuse for domination. He said, "Religion is a thing of the heart, and it is beyond the power of man to go into the heart of other people. To oppress a human being for his inner conviction is diabolical" (Guruge, ed. 1965 p. 271). Dharmapala's broad tolerance of religions is revealed in the topic of his very first lecture in Calcutta, which was on the kinship between Hinduism and Buddhism (p. xxxvi).

Dharmapala's view of Christianity was not the blind hate of an Olcott or Blavatsky. Speaking to an American audience, Dharmapala mentioned that Christianity, in the way it had been practiced in recent centuries in the East, had gone against its own injunctions. He suggested that Christians with the "spirit of self sacrifice, spirit of charity, spirit of tolerance, as well as the spirit of lowliness and meekness which characterized Jesus Christ" should be sent to the East (p. xlvii).

Dharmapala wanted positive coexistence among all faiths. He had "exalted hopes for the brotherhood of man and for a Utopian period, not too far distant, when Christian and Jew, Muhammadan, Brahman and Buddhist would associate with joyous understanding, purged of the prejudices and hateful passions that an intensity of religious belief invariably inspires in the narrow-minded and ignorant of any race, nation or creed" (quoted in Guruge, ed. 1965 p. 690). He wanted Christians and Buddhists to unite to elevate the condition of the common people, giving the example of the Christian Sun Yat Sen, who worked for the benefit of the Chinese people (p. 510).

Dharmapala was also concerned with the interests of other oppressed groups in other parts of the world. He said that everywhere in Europe capitalism was introducing class hatred (p. 394). Iriyagolla, who was one of his disciples, summarized Dharmapala's position: "To him the depressed class children of India or the Negro children of Harlem, or even the dead end kids of East End slums, were as close to the heart as the children of Ceylon. . . . He decried and deplored the exploitation of the weak and the under-privileged by the stronger and the powerful, be it in Ceylon, India or America." (Iriyagolla, Gamini, 1965 p. vii).

According to British colonial sources, Dharmapala was suspected during one of his visits to Europe of trying to link up with Indian Marxist revolutionary groups. The colonial government of Ceylon warned about Dharmapala's visit, saying:

> It may possibly be that he is making this trip with the object of getting into touch with M. N. Roy, a notorious Indian Bolshevik and publisher of revolutionary papers in Berlin. (Quoted in Guruge, ed. 1965 p. lxix)

I have mentioned earlier that, in addition to the European rulers, Dharmapala sometimes castigated those intermediate groups such as Boras (a small Indian minority), Tamils, and Muslims who acted in an exploitative role in Sri Lanka. I pointed out that this criticism was parallel to nationalist criticism elsewhere of similar intermediary groups, such as those in Burma, Africa, Indonesia, and China. (One should also note that Dharmapala castigated the Sinhalese for their negative qualities in much stronger terms.) Dharmapala's other negative references to Tamils were in respect of earlier invasions, described only in a historical sense, not a racial one. Dharmapala also mentioned the British importation of Tamil workers to man European plantations, displacing Sinhalese peasants en masse from their homelands (Guruge, ed. 1965). These were not subjective racial attitudes, but examples of objective social criticism. In fact, Dharmapala considered Tamils and the Tamil language as friends. Thus, writing from his exile, he urged that "a special class . . . be formed to teach Tamil and Hindustani" (771–772).

Dharmapala's frequent use of the Buddhist term "Aryan" was very different from the use of the term in its modern connotation. He used it for many people, including all the people of India. *Arya* was a common appellation in the 19th century. The name of the Indian reform movement, Arya Samaj, included it. And the house associated later with the one-time Theosophist Krishnamurti—a South Indian Tamil—in California was called Arya Vihar, the House of the Aryan (Washington 1993 p. 220).

Olcott used the word *Arya* similarly, founding a magazine titled *Arya Bala Bodhini* ("Understanding of Arya [Noble] Power") and forming the

youth organization called the Aryan League of Honor. Olcott also promoted a Hindu *Epitome of Aryan Morals* (Prothero 1996 p. 145) in the Tamil
heartland of Adyar in Madras, hardly an anti-Dravidian use of the word.
In a letter to Sumangala Thero urging the propagation of Buddhism in
India, Olcott stated, "If the assistance of good and well-disciplined monks
could be obtained, hundreds of thousands of Aryan people, who are
learned and righteous, could be made Buddhist devotees," including here
all Indians as Aryans (quoted in Guruge 1984 p. xxxix).

In his riveting speech before the Parliament of Religions in Chicago,
Dharmapala said, "The Sinhalese followers of Arya Dhamma, miscalled
Buddhism by western scholars greet the delegates" (quoted in Guruge
1984 p. xlvi). In fact, foreign Buddhists used "Aryan" in the same sense.
Thus a Britisher ordained as a Buddhist monk with the name Bhikkhu
Ananda Metteyya authored a book on Buddhism titled *The Wisdom of the
Aryas* (p. cxliii).

Dharmapala distinguished between "European" and "Aryan," saying
that Christianity, a religion of Europeans, was "a system utterly unsuited
to the gentle spirit of the Aryan race" (quoted in Guruge 1984 p. 441).
He identified India as "the land of Aryan culture" (p. 399). He wrote:
"Indian-Aryan women were always free. Today [they are] free in the
provinces of Bombay, Madras and other provinces where the Moslem influence did not penetrate" (p. 342), thus defining Tamil Madras as Aryan.
In the inaugural meeting with the Dravidian untouchables, Dharmapala
declared that Buddhism was "a pure Aryan religion founded upon the
Aryan Dharma, promulgated by an Aryan, preached by the Aryans to
the Aryans" (quoted in Prothero 1996 p. 141). Clearly, he saw no difference between Aryans and Dravidians.

Dharmapala spoke evocatively of Madras, the Tamil heartland, equating it with Bombay and Bengal. Thus he said that patriotism "is now active and working as a leaven in the whole body of Indian thought, to
thrill through all hearts the feeling of kinship and brotherhood, Madras
is linked with Bengal, Bombay with Northern India" (Guruge, ed. 1965
p. 369). At Madras he convened a meeting of Buddhist delegates from
Burma, Chittagong, Sri Lanka, and Japan. This was to consider what
steps should be taken for the propagation of Buddhism in the West (p.
649). For his publication, *The Buddhist,* he obtained type from Madras
(p. 704).

On another occasion he wrote ebulliently of scholars in Madras, talking proudly of "Pandit N. Bashyacharya, and the late T. Subba Row, a
great Vedantin scholar, both of Madras" (p. 372). When a Buddhist procession was stopped in Colombo by the authorities, he gave Madras as an

example of rectitude, saying, "in Calcutta, Bombay, Madras and other great cities in India where a diversity of races and religions exist, no attempt is ever made to stop processions" (p. 526). On another occasion he advocated sending Sinhalese youth to Madras instead of to local schools, saying of the latter, "High Schools [in the then Ceylon] are a sham. One must send . . . Ceylonese youths to Poona, or Pusa or Madras" (p 536).

Dharmapala and Olcott also formed in South India a Dravidian Buddhist Society for untouchables to learn about Buddhism and so overcome the indignities of caste. The inaugural meeting was addressed by both Olcott and Dharmapala. High-ranking Sinhalese monks responded positively to this Dravidian Buddhist Society. Soon two untouchables from Madras left for Sri Lanka, and at a "monster meeting" they—as Olcott and Blavatsky had done before them—became Buddhists by accepting *pansil,* the five Buddhist precepts (Prothero 1996 p. 141). It should be noted that large crowds greeted the two Tamil untouchables in Sri Lanka, as did the Americans. In the 18th century, similar large crowds had greeted the Thai monks. All this illustrated nonracist attitudes toward all those who wanted to advance Buddhism.

Although Dharmapala was devastatingly critical when Buddhist and national interests were involved (Guruge, ed. 1965 p. xxiii), he was as critical of his own countrymen and co-religionists as he was of others. He attacked wealthy locals for being indifferent to the plight of the poor and destitute (p. 510). Sir Ponnambalam Arunachalam, the leading Tamil of the time, defending Dharmapala against the charge that he was anti-British, throws light on Dharmapala's character. In a letter to the British colonial secretary, Sir Ponnambalam Arunachalam spoke on Dharmapala's behalf, saying, "He is an ascetic but caustic also, not sparing his own countrymen and priests" (quoted in Guruge ed. 1965. p. xlviii). And as a final rebuke to his countrymen, one should note that Dharmapala spent thirty-four of his forty years of active life in India away from the Sinhalese in voluntary exile (p. xxi).

Tambiah makes blanket statements, for example, that monks today are characterized by content-less flag waving with no philosophical or ethical groundings (1986 p. 83), and that "shapeless, hungry ghosts and monsters" of militant Sinhala Buddhist nationalists were limiting the (then) president's actions (p. 117). Tambiah does not provide any evidence for these colorful statements. By "monsters," he probably means the likes of Minister Mathew, who was widely believed (including by the present author) to be involved in unsavory activities. But, things are not that simple. It was also widely believed at the time that thugs of Minister Mohammed, a Muslim, took part in the riots. The involvement of

Mathew's thugs is likewise just a suspicion, in the absence of any judicial inquiry. Mathew and J. R. Jayawardene also attacked Sinhala Buddhist nationalist groups, including the Sinhala Bala Mandalaya, dragging key speakers across a stage. And Jayawardene got his troops to besiege the nationalist monk Ven. Labuduwe Siridhamma (a Ph.D. from Oxford) at the Getambe temple in Kandy.

THE SOUTH INDIAN CONNECTION

Tambiah mentions that Sri Lankan Tamil nationalist developments arose parallel to Sinhalese nationalist developments, primarily through the writings of Arumuga Navalar, and that Navalar was influential in Madras (1986 p. 109). But having noted this, Tambiah does not explore this early Tamil Nadu connection further, especially its later effects on the Tamil movements in Sri Lanka.

Tambiah also believes that it was only after "repeated rejections" that Sri Lankan Tamils linked with the South Indian ethnic parties, the DMK and the AIDMK, and began a separatist campaign (1986 p. 77). He also asserted (this was before the Indian interference) that these links would not result in an invasion of Sri Lanka, which he calls a figment of Sinhalese "hysteria." He further said that, in addition, the central government in New Delhi would be neutral with regard to Sri Lanka (p. 111). This prognosis was far from the truth. Not only did political links between Sri Lankan Tamils and South India predate the present, they also led to a proxy invasion of the country. At the time Tambiah was writing, the Indian central government in New Delhi was arming and coordinating Tamil guerilla groups in the indirect attack on Sri Lanka.

Contrary to Tambiah's assertion, the political links of Sri Lankan Tamils with Tamil Nadu predate these events. I have already given some details in Chapter 9. Let me add some further salient facts from a recent book by two Indian Tamils documenting these connections (Palanithural and Mohanasundaram 1993). From its formation, the Indian Tamil Party, the DMK, and its offshoot, Nam Tamizhar ("We Tamils"), strongly championed secession from the Indian Union and the establishment of a separate "Dravidanad." The Nam Tamizhar went further, demanding the creation of a "greater Tamil Nadu," to include the Tamil-speaking parts of Sri Lanka. Meanwhile, the DMK established a working relationship with the Sri Lanka Tamil Federal Party, the forerunner of the separatist TULF (Palanithural and Mohanasundaram 1993 p. 45). The Sri Lankan Tamil opposition to the Official Language Act of Sri Lanka had strong resonances with the DMK's opposition to the Indian official language, Hindi. From its beginnings, "the fervent nationalistic ideals of D.M.K. had an appeal to the Tamils in Sri Lanka" (p. 65).

The political and personal links between the DMK and the Sri Lankan Federal Party were seen in other examples. Thus, in 1971, chief minister of the DMK, M. Karunanidhi, participated in a celebration of the birthday of the Federal Party leader, S. J. V. Chelvanayagam. Karunanidhi said on this occasion in 1975 that Sri Lankan Tamils "look to us for support: when we ourselves are fighting for autonomy, there is no way out except to sink together" (Palanithural and Mohanasundaram p. 73). As part of this support, DMK personnel went to Sri Lanka to actively work for TULF candidates in the 1977 elections, a clear interference in the internal affairs of a sovereign state. When the TULF contested on a separatist platform, the Indian High Commission in Sri Lanka itself became worried about this development (p. 81). The support in Tamil Nadu for armed Tamil groups from Sri Lanka finally broke out into the open in 1981 as a result of a shooting incident in a Madras street between rival Sri Lankan Tamil separatist groups (p. 82).

A book authored by two Sri Lankans who had worked for a long time in India adds further information (Piyasena and Senadheera 1986). They describe how "Tamil Nadu politicians who failed to establish a separate Tamil State in India focussed their attention to aggravate the ethnic crisis in Sri Lanka" (p. 13). The dream of a separate Tamil state, which had become more difficult to achieve in India, became a distinct possibility with the creation of the Tamil United Liberation Front in Sri Lanka. The authors go on to point out that as a consequence, "the movement of separatism in Sri Lanka was guided more from Madras and Madurai than from Jaffna or Trincomalee" (p. 14).

As a result of these connections, and later as a result of India's strategic perceptions and the active support of the central Indian government, there was a massive arming of Tamil groups. Meanwhile, the different Sri Lankan separatist groups had developed their own links with different Tamil Nadu groups (Gunaratne 1990).

Every Sri Lankan militant Tamil group thus had its links with different Tamil Nadu nationalist groups. The LTTE had links with the Dravida Kazhagam (DK) of K. Veeramani and the Kamraj Congress of Nedumaran. The People's Liberation Organization of Tamil Eelam (PLOTE) had links with Prof. Perinchitharan's Thani Tamil Iyakam ("Pure Tamil Movement"), another Tamil Nadu separatist group. The Tamil Eelam Liberation Organization (TELO) had links with the DMK (Gunaratne 1990 pp. 76–77). Gunaratne describes how, when the DMK came to power in Tamil

Nadu in 1967, the Federal Party's links with Tamil chauvinists in the DMK intensified. And in May 1973, two Indians and a Sri Lankan Tamil, S. Yogachandran, alias Kutimani, were found transporting 20,000 detonators to Jaffna (Gunaratne 1990 p. x).

These links are amply collaborated by books written by the Indian generals who came to Sri Lanka in the wake of the Indo-Lanka Accord. Thus, Lt. General S. C. Sardeshpande points out that the Tamil Nadu government "pointedly lionized" the LTTE. There were large posters of LTTE leaders on the main beach of Madras, and LTTE cadres in return participated in Tamil Nadu election campaigns (Sardeshpande 1992 p. 147). Another Indian commander in Sri Lanka puts it bluntly: "Mr M. G. Ramachandran, the then Chief Minister of Tamil Nadu, was a powerful supporter of the LTTE" (Singh 1992 p. 61). And the most celebrated Indian general, the hero of the 1971 war with Pakistan, Field Marshal Sam Manekshaw, describes how the Tamil insurgents were "supplied with large quantities of arms and equipment, money and moral support from Tamil Nadu" (Manekshaw 1992).

BLINKERED ARCHAEOLOGY

Tambiah also mentions—seemingly illustrative of Sri Lanka's Sinhala Buddhist bias in archeology—that unlike Pakistan and India, Sri Lankan archaeology and prehistory have been limited to the Buddhist period (1986 p. 88). This is simply not true. Tambiah mentions in passing the work of Siran Deriniyagala, the present (2000) archaeological commissioner, but ignores Deriniyagala's truly magnificent work on Sri Lankan prehistory, which was well-known at the time Tambiah was writing his book. In fact, access to this material would have been only a short distance away from Tambiah's own room in Harvard because Deraniyagala's material—some of which had been published elsewhere—was submitted as a Ph.D. thesis in the Department of Anthropology right there at Harvard, Tambiah's academic home. Tambiah relies to a large extent for his archaeological interpretations on an essay written by the present author in 1975, giving nearly a page of quotes from my article (Tambiah 1986 pp. 90–91). My article was based on the archaeology of Deraniyagala.

Further, the recent work of Deraniyagala, which I referred to in an earlier chapter (Deraniyagala 1992, especially pp. 739–749), indicates that my own claim, which discounted the Sinhalese chronicles prior to the 3rd century B.C., that dominant North Indian cultural influences came only with the introduction of Buddhism in the time of Emperor Asoka (3rd century B.C.), was wrong. But now these new hard archaeological finds seem to vindicate the early chroniclers and disprove the views of theorists like myself. Deraniyagala had found North Indian influences in the form of the Brahmi script dated to the period 600–500 B.C., a date given by the chronicles as the period of the arrival of North Indian influences. More interesting, an inscription has been found on a shard bearing the word "Anuradha," giving confirmation to the early dates in the chronicles for the establishment of Anuradhapura, "the City of Anuradha," as given by the chronicles. Further, it also appears that in the exploration of prehistory using the most modern techniques, Sri Lanka, instead of being a laggard, is ahead of other South Asian nations such as Pakistan and India.

Sri Lankan prehistory is also relatively well-known among contemporary Sinhalese—in contrast to Tambiah, who is ignorant of the developments in Sri Lankan prehistory at his own university. The work of Deraniyagala—going back to times when there were neither Sinhalese nor Tamils—has been regularly featured in the Sinhala printed and electronic media. In contrast to the Sinhala archeological findings, there have been consistent attempts by Tamils to destroy sites of Buddhist remains, as recorded by the Archaeology Department.

MAKING SENSE OF FRATRICIDE

In his first book, Tambiah appears at times to be a genuinely concerned person. Many of the observations he makes about the negative features of the then government had appeared in the press, especially the Sinhala press. But still there are huge gaps in his treatment. He demonizes only Sinhalese acts while trying to explain Tamil positions as reactions to the Sinhalese acts. His book was written after the 1983 anti-Tamil riots, and so this is understandable as the emotional response of a Tamil but not as a scholarly reflection. The major villains he identifies are Sinhala Buddhist groups, but since he does not give any significant sources for his "facts," one is left with the feeling that he is repeating gossip from a few Colombo drawing rooms.

He makes some sensible suggestions together with some contentious ones. He calls for the return of the rule of law. He rejects a separate state as nonviable and in fact reproduces, as an illustration, a government propaganda brochure that shows its lack of viability. Thus he calls for devolution of power on a variety of issues. But he ignores the most vexed area, namely, land settlement, which is tied in with the fictitious traditional homelands concept of Eelam propagandists.

Tambiah describes ruefully the era of the 1940s and early 1950s, when under the UNP of D. S. Senanayake there was relative ethnic calm, which was broken by the 1956 election of Bandaranaike. Tambiah describes Bandaranaike in generally negative terms (1986 pp. 129–132). But for a student of Buddhism and politics, he makes no adequate reference to the monks' movement in the 1940s, or to the debates at the time on the role of Buddhist monks in politics, which led to many of the subsequent social changes. These social changes included the granting of free education to all children in the country, the advocacy of *Swabasha* (national languages—meaning both Sinhala and Tamil), and a unilateral declaration of independence by the Sangha for the country. These omissions are all the more remarkable because the most internationally prominent Buddhist monk, Walpola Rahula, was involved in these monks' activities. Rahula was the author of *What the Buddha Taught*, which was translated into a score of languages and can be found in virtually every major university library in the world. Rahula's book *Bikshuvage Urumaya* ("The Heritage of the Bhikkhu"), published in the 1940s, was both a participant's view of these events and a charter for the monks' involvement. Recently H. L. Seneviratne, one of Tambiah's informants, has said of *Bikshuvage Urumaya*, "it is a unique document because it launched the only successful grassroots revolution in the history of Sri Lanka . . . it is the finest synthesis imaginable at the time . . . between Buddhism and Marxism, between young monastic intellectuals of the Vidyalankara Pirivene and the young Trotskyite intellectuals trained in the West" (Seneviratne 1994 p. 30).

Tambiah also ignores the findings of the Sansoni Commission, a judicial inquiry into the riots of 1978. Sansoni was a Eurasian and very probably known to Tambiah's brother, who is a respected judge in Sri Lanka. Sansoni could even have been a family friend. This commission laid a major share of the blame, if not the main responsibility, for the ethnic conflict on Tamil separatist ideology and the political actions of the TULF.

Tambiah does not mention the political violence immediately after the elections of 1977. In that violence, UNP thugs systematically attacked the homes of opposition supporters. Many were killed, and others were assaulted. This was a systematic attack, not a random one. It presaged the systematic attacks on Tamils by UNP thugs six years later, as well as the much more aggressive attacks on JVP suspects a decade later.

Tambiah gives figures for ethnic representation in the country for the different professions only for 1980, providing no figures for the earlier period, when Tamil representation was much stronger (1986 p. 77). And this is in spite of Tambiah himself having published a study in 1955 giving details about the over-representation of Tamils from 1870 to the time of independence.

Although Tambiah attacks the Sri Lankan version of affirmative action to right historical wrongs, he works in the United States, where affirmative action was implemented to undo historical wrongs. In the U.S., at the time when Tambiah was doing his study, there were different quota-based minority hirings to favor not only African Americans, but other ethnic groups as well. Affirmative action was practiced at Tambiah's own university, Harvard. His informant, Devanesan Nesiah, wrote a Ph.D. thesis on the subject at Harvard, now published as *Discrimination with Reason: The Policy of Reservations in the United States, India and Malaysia* (1997).

Having surveyed Tambiah's analysis of ethnic fratricide, we should now move on to discuss his view of Sinhalese Buddhists in his *Buddhism Betrayed* (1992).

BUDDHIST REVIVALISM REFORMULATED

Before commenting, I should mention that when Tambiah's book *Buddhism Betrayed* appeared in Sri Lanka, it provoked many adverse comments and reactions. Some were scholarly, considered reactions that detailed serious shortcomings in Tambiah's writing. Some were emotional. One of the most detailed and informed refutations of some of Tambiah's facts appeared in five articles in the *Island* (Colombo), written by Gamini Iriyagolla, a lawyer initially trained as a historian. In addition to comments of my own, I will cite some of the material that Iriyagolla and others first publicized, after checking its veracity for myself.

Central to Tambiah's thesis is what he alleges to be the origins of the conflict during the anti-colonial period dealt with in his chapter "The Period of Buddhist Revivalism, 1860–1915." In his treatment he does not describe—as in his first book—in any meaningful way the events during the colonial era that led to resistance by the locals. He does not delineate these social dynamics, on which there is very wide documentation, especially in Sinhala. It appears that his sources for these events are almost exclusively the English-language pamphlets of Kumari Jayawardena, one of his informants and a strong critic of the Sri Lanka Buddhist Renaissance.

The flavor of Jayawardena's views is seen in the following quotation:

Buddhist revivalism in Sri Lanka (in the late 19th and early 20th century) used slogans of religion, culture and temperance, to mobilise people in anti-Christian agitation. . . . Through popular agitation, including invective against Christians in the press, some blasphemous, others scurrilous and novels where the heroes were Buddhists and the villains were Christians. Christians were ridiculed. (Jayawardena 1985 p. 6)

In Chapter 5, I described in some detail the oppressive background within which the Buddhist Renaissance occurred and its emancipatory nature. Tambiah, following Jayawardena, does not recognize the oppression under which Sinhala Buddhists suffered, and which led to the anti-Christian stance. Tambiah mentions the Buddhist Commission Report but does not refer to the detailed material it contains on the colonial persecutions. Not only were the Sinhala Buddhists subject to colonization, but the treaties that their last king entered into with the British were broken. White men not only spoke with forked tongues but, in the fashion of the times, indulged in forced religious conversion through monetary and other incentives. These abominations went against the 1815 treaty between the British and the Kandyan Kingdom whereby the British undertook to respect the position of Buddhism.

But, in spite of the British rulers' acceptance of the continuation of Buddhism, Buddhism appeared to the Christian missionaries to be a "massive evil structure that had to be destroyed before conversion proper (the inflexible goal) could begin" (Malalgoda 1976 p. 204). J. Gogerly, chairman of the South Ceylon Wesleyan Mission, wrote in 1831, "at present, it is by means of the Press [that] our principal attacks must be made on this wretched system. . . . We must direct our efforts to pull down this stronghold of Satan" (quoted in Iriyagolla 1994). At that time, all the presses were in the hands of the Christians.

The level of cultural oppression was so severe that not only were lucrative jobs reserved for Christians, but one had to be a Christian to have any safeguard for one's basic legal rights. For several decades of British rule, the registration of births, deaths, and marriages, with all the legal implications that this implied, was a Christian monopoly. Direct pressure by the Christian hierarchy and its interests resulted in a high degree of discrimination and, at times, direct persecution of Buddhists. Instead of the false construction that Tambiah, following Kumari Jayawardena, gives to the anti-Christian feelings at the time, a contemporary Tamil Christian historian of the church and a past chairman of the National Christian Council, D. Kanagasabal Wilson, conveys a sense of what really happened (1975). Wilson describes how the attempt in the 1850s of the colonial government to sever connections with Buddhism led to several religious disputes. The Buddhists were also indignant at the Christian instruction given in mission schools to non-Christian children. "In fact, many of the Buddhist monks believed that their religion was in danger," notes Wilson. (1975 p. 1).

Tambiah makes gross unforgivable errors in basic facts central to the history of the time. Thus, he contends that the leading monks, Hikkaduve Siri Sumangala, Walane Siddharta, Weligama Siri Sumangala, and Ratmalane Sri Dharmaloka, took part in the formation of Buddhist schools and the temperance movements of 1904 and 1912 (1992 p. 6). But three of these monks were dead by this time (Malalgoda 1976; Bechert 1970). Tambiah's basis for this misinformation is again Kumari Jayawardena (1979 p. 13). These three monks that Tambiah refers to and then forgets were not lightweights who could be ignored by any chronicler. As I have already described in detail in Chapter 5, they belonged to a generation of truly broad-minded scholar-monks—well-read men with vision and learning.

One of the most important objectives of the program of education in the English schools was clear. It was in the spirit of the notorious McAuley, whom we quoted in Chapter 5, to remold South Asian inhabitants as Europeans. The European administrators in Sri Lanka described this program as follows:

> to associate the natives with European civilization and gradually raise them to a higher level which eventually might lead to the creation of a new nation [and] their absorption in the controlling European nation. . . . One of the important features of the education in both the missionary and government schools at that time [i.e., the 19th century] was the stress laid on the teaching of Christianity. (Wilson, D. Kanagasabal, 1975 p. 120)

The Wesleyan Mission for 1849 summarized the project vividly:

> The education given in the institutions is essentially a Christian education. Instruction is so communicated that Christianity is made to appear the end for which all mental processes are conducted. (Quoted in Wilson, D. Kanagasabal, 1975 p. 120)

Migettuwatte Gunananda, "the acclaimed orator" of the Panadura debate in 1873, is a special target of Tambiah. This debate has been represented by Kumari Jayawardena, Tambiah's source, as a mischievous Buddhist action to inflame aggressive anti-Christian sentiments. In her reading there was no prior Christian oppression that sparked the anti-colonial sentiment. It is important to quote her at length:

> Bureaucrats and missionaries were attacked for their religion and the campaign was directed against the Christian power rather than against British colonialism. It had the effect of arousing the Buddhists to a holy war instead of an anti-colonial struggle. One can note that the creation of an ideology based on traditional values, emphasizing the ethnic, religious and cultural identity of the Sinhala Buddhists, resulted in an aggressive campaign against Christians. The battles, both non-violent and violent, were fought at several levels. Through public debates between Christians and Buddhists as occurred in Panadura in 1873, when Bhikkhu Migettuwatte Gunananda aroused Buddhist popular opinion by confronting Rev. David Silva and launching a searing attack on Christianity. (Jayawardena 1986 p. 16)

But the truth was entirely different from this account by Jayawardena on which Tambiah relies.

The Panadura debates were the culmination of a series of debates. The proceedings of the Panadura debates were published in the organ for British mercantile and plantation interests on the island, *The Times of Ceylon,* by its British editor, John Capper. Later, the debate was published in the form of a book by Capper. The English translations were taken to America by Dr. James Martin Peebles. He then had them reprinted there with his own introduction and comments (Abhayasundara, ed. 1990 p. x). The reports of the debates then reached English, French, Russian, and American audiences, and reached the Theosophists (Abhayasundara, ed. 1990 p. xi).

Peebles describes what actually happened as follows:

> The Rev. David Silva stated that before engaging in the controversy it was necessary to explain the reasons for holding it. On the 12th of June last he delivered a lecture on the teaching of Buddha with reference to the human soul, on the 19th of the same month it was taken exception to by the Buddhist party, and denounced as untrue. The present occasion was, therefore, appointed to show that the doctrine of Buddhism was with reference to the soul, and he hoped that the Buddhist party would, if possible, meet his argument properly. (Quoted in Abhayasundara 1990 p. 21)

Kumari Jayawardena distorted these events in her description, converting a reasoned, albeit heated, debate into an unprovoked attack by the Sinhala Buddhists. The facts were just the opposite.

In the Baddegama debate in 1865, which preceded the Panadura debates, the Christians were, according to their own descriptions, *primarily* interested in attacking Buddhists: "we felt that our victory would be more triumphant and complete" by attacking Buddhism (Abhayasundara 1990 p. 80).

In the Panadura debate itself, the Christian priest had called Migettuwatte, the latter noted, *viruddhakaraya*, "the opponent," although Migettuwatte himself had been very polite. So, Migettuwatte said, his intention was to use the same epithet toward the Christian debater, and he wished his hearers to distinctly understand the reason. Migettuwatte went out of his way to say that although the two speakers belonged to two different religions, they had come forward to take part in the controversy solely with the view of ascertaining which was the true religion. He said that there was no personal enmity between them, which the word "opponent" or "adversary," used by the opposite side, would seem to imply, but now that it had been used, he regretted to say that he had no other alternative but to do the same (cited in Abhayasundara, ed. 1990 p. 80). So this was completely contrary to Tambiah's and Kumari Jayawardena's construction of the debate's context, of a bellicose Migettuwatte and an accommodating Christian.

Olcott on his arrival in the country confirms the mood of the Buddhists as the seriously aggrieved party when he mentions that "the missionaries, in anticipation of our arrival, had been spreading all kinds of calumnies against us [i.e., the Theosophists], and on the previous evening had been preaching bitterly against Buddhism in the streets of Kandy. Being white men, the timid Sinhalese dared not confront them, but brought their complaints to us" (Olcott 1974 p. 181).

Tambiah, depending on Jayawardena, casts aspersions on the key Buddhist figure, Gunananda, by lumping him together with arrack renters and coconut planters as members of the Theosophical Society (1992 p. 6). But Olcott himself describes how in fact Migettuwatte Gunananda became a member of the Theosophical Society:

> [I] addressed another huge audience [at Panadura]. Migettuwatte [Gunananda] presided. . . . [T]he next day I initiated as members [of the international Theosophical Society] Migettuwatte, Sri Weligama [Weligama Sri Sumangala] . . . and Waskaduwe Subhuti. (Olcott 1974 pp. 177, 179)

One of the worst distortions of Kumari Jayawardena, which Tambiah follows, is to blame Gunananda for the riot on 25 March 1883 at Kotahena, whose date Jayawardena gives as April, not March (1986 p. 24).

Jayawardena says, under the subhead "Violent Clashes," that "the militant bhikkhu Gunananda," whose temple was near St. Lucia's Cathedral, organized Buddhist ceremonies during Easter week. "The Catholics took this as a provocation and a serious riot occurred; the street fighting caused one death and 30 injured, including 12 policemen." The British commission of inquiry that followed flatly contradicts Jayawardena and Tambiah:

> We are convinced that the Buddhist Perahera [procession] started from Borella on Easter day without the least intention of offering insult to the Roman Catholics, and certainly without any anticipation of a riot, and also that they carried with them nothing of an objectionable character. . . . We have no hesitation in stating that we believe the illegal assemblies both on Good Friday and Easter-day were thoroughly organized and previously arranged by the Roman Catholics, with the express intention of attacking Buddhist processions. The ringing of the church bell on Sunday was evidently a preconcerted signal. . . . Blame attaches to the Roman Catholic authorities in allowing the bell to be rung, and in failing to show the least inclination to hand over those who rang it to justice. . . . The fact that these persons have not been handed over to the police for exemplary punishment is, we consider, a standing reproach to the Roman Catholic authorities at Kotahena." (Kotahena Riots 1883, paras. 33, 35, and 36)

SINHALESE ACCOMMODATION

Tambiah has laid the blame on Dharmapala for the ethnic tragedies that followed. He describes Dharmapala as "an uncharitable propagandist." But in his earlier book, written only four years earlier, he had compared Dharmapala positively with the Jaffna revivalist Arumuga Navalar, saying that the Hindu revival protesting Christianity had preceded the Buddhist one.

In Chapter 5, we have shown Dharmapala to be very well-read in both Eastern and Western traditions and well-traveled. Instead of being against Tamils, he extolled their cultural center, Madras, as the place the Sinhalese should go to. He organized many events there. Instead of blindly attacking Christianity as the Theosophists did, he wanted a Christian presence in Asia nearer to the spirit of Jesus Christ. Instead of blindly supporting the Sinhalese, he castigated them, as the Tamil nationalist Ponnabalam Arunachalam testified. Instead of defending the flawed country, "right or wrong," in blind patriotism, he spent more than thirty years of his active life in self-imposed exile in India, away from his Sinhalese Buddhists. Dharmapala was a complex, driven man. But he was hardly the "uncharitable propagandist" that Tambiah derives from Kumari Jayawardena's biased constructions.

TAMIL REACTIONS AND SOUTH
INDIAN CONNECTIONS

The development of resistance to Christian oppression by the Buddhists was paralleled by the resistance among Hindus. As a present-day Christian historian, D. Kanagasabal Wilson, puts it, "the hostility and bitterness towards Christianity also reared its head amongst the Hindus" (1975 p. 5). The aim of the Hindu revivalists was to sponsor and develop Saivism. Arumuga Navalar, the Tamil Hindu revivalist (1822–1879), carried on for more than thirty years a strong campaign against Christians.

In 1884, Sir Ponnambalam Ramanathan also opposed Christian schools. A member of the Legislative Council waxed eloquently on the greatness of Hindu civilization and culture, and this encouraged the Tamils immensely. Wilson notes that the British missionaries' view that the Christian religion was superior led to the denationalization of both Sinhalese and Tamils (Wilson, D. Kanagasabal, 1975 p. 5).

Tambiah admittedly and consciously omitted the role of Tamils from his description. But there is ample evidence that Tamil Saivite revivalism provided the background for the present Tamil extremists' close links with South Indian Tamil chauvinist groups. I described some of these links earlier. The late K. Kailasapathy, professor at the (Tamil) University of Jaffna, has noted:

> As a writer of polemics Navalar was unsurpassed. Consequently by the 1880s, Tamil opinion makers in both South India and Sri Lanka became enthusiastic about Tamil-language, history and culture. . . . The language had been declared divine and thereby sacrosanct. (1984 pp. 110–113)

Navalar led a movement in South India and Sri Lanka extolling the Saiva Agamic faith as the core religious thought of the Tamils. Tamil was declared a "goddess" and was considered divine and sacrosanct in South India (Kailasapathy, 1987 pp. 34–39). Sri Lanka Tamils contributed greatly to these developments in South India. Indian Tamil journals included many quality contributions from Sri Lankan Tamils. A Madurai Tamil Sangam ("Tamil society of Madurai"), formed in 1901, drew inspiration from the Jaffna Tamil Academy. In turn, South Indian Tamil scholars came to Tamil conferences in Sri Lanka (Kailasapathy 1987 pp. 34–39).

It is also significant to note that Tamil Christian scholars in India and Sri Lanka played active roles in Tamil nationalism. They included Savariroya Pillai, L. D. Swamikannu Pillai (1865–1925), Fr. S. Gnanapiragasar (1875–1947), T. Isaac Tambyah (1869–1941), and Rev. Fr. X. S. Thani

Nayagam. This led to accusations by some Hindus that the Tamil cultural movement had been infiltrated by Christians. A Sri Lankan Catholic, Xavier S. Thani Nayagam, founded the journal *Tamil Culture* (1952–1966). Its contributors included Sri Lankan Tamils such as A. J. Wilson, Thani Nayagam, W. Belendra, and S. J. Gunasegram (Kailasapathy 1987 pp. 34–39). Recently these strong Christian connections have led to the LTTE being called "a private army of the Christians" by the Indian Hindu nationalist, Vishwa Hindu Parishad, the ideological arm of the Indian Hindu nationalist party, Bharatyiya Janata Party (BJP) (Sinha 1998).

Kailasapathy noted that the linguistic and cultural consciousness of the Sri Lankan Tamil community was "always" influenced by South Indian developments. This influence applied to both politics and culture. South Indian regional movements that resulted in the Dravida Munnetra Kazagham (DMK), as well as the political Tamil-language movement, contributed to and affected the cultural and linguistic consciousness of Tamils in Sri Lanka (Kailasapathy 1984).

The details of this South Indian/Jaffna-Tamil link connecting events in South India and Jaffna are very revealing. Thus, the Ponnambalam fifty-fifty demand in Sri Lanka arose in parallel with the growth of the Indian separatist Tamil Justice Party under Ramasamy Naicker in the 1930s. The Federal Party of Sri Lanka (in Tamil called the Tamil State Party) was formed in the same year—1949—as the DMK was formed in India. Chelvanayagam, the founder of the Federal Party, the precursor of the separatist TULF, had as early as 1941 declared the Tamils' right to secede from the then British Empire and to federate with a South Indian Tamil state. Tambiah knew of these intimate links between South India and Sri Lankan Tamils as he knew of Kailasapathy's article, which he had described in 1988 as a "remarkable" essay.

These links led to the more aggressive South Indian/Sri Lanka-Tamil joint political and military activity from at least the early 1970s, giving way ultimately to the proxy invasion of Sri Lanka. I documented these events earlier.

Hellman-Rajanayagam, a pro-separatist writer, notes that although there was a close association of Sri Lankan Tamil chauvinists with those of South India, there was a major difference. In India, the separatist cry never went to the extent of demarcating exact boundaries of Tamilnadu or Dravidanadu. In fact, for the Indian Tamils, the idea of a Dravidian territory "receded before the all-encompassing claim of the Tamil language." This was in strong contrast to the TULF, whose slogan was "Language and territory are the most important factors for a Nation" (Hellmann-Rajanayagam 1988 p. 56). As a follow-up to this territorial claim, the Jaffna Tamils also invited up-country Tamils of Indian origin to settle in the northeast (Hellmann-Rajanayagam 1988 p. 57).

During the 1965 anti-Hindi protests in Madras, the Federal Party leader, Chelvanayakam, expressed solidarity with the DMK, saying that there was an "identity between your great struggle and the resistance we are putting up here in Ceylon" (Gunawardene 1986 p. 75). An organization titled the Dravida Munnetra Kazhagam of Ceylon arose among the Indian Tamils in the hill country but was banned in 1962.

The formal training of Tamil cadres by the Indian state in camps in Tamil Nadu began no later than November 1982; some training camps were set up in early 1983, others in 1984. This training also occurred in eight North Indian locations (Gunawardene, Victor, 1986). An Indian newspaper gave details in 1983 of a planned Indian invasion of Sri Lanka. A secret meeting had been convened by the Indian prime minister and her top advisers on this, but the plan was dropped (Dua 1983 p. 8).

The leading Indian weekly, *India Today*, in an article titled "Sri Lankan Rebels: Ominous Presence in Tamil Nadu," on 31 March 1984 described vividly dozens of training camps set up by the Lankan Tamil insurgents inside Tamil Nadu, where new recruits received "ideological grounding from rebel theoreticians" as well as advanced arms training. They were "driven by a strong emotion of ethnicity"—that is, by Tamil chauvinism —the journal noted. Mrs. Gandhi's own daughter-in-law, Menaka Gandhi, provided information about the Indian proxy invasion in the September 1984 issue of her magazine, *Suriya* (cited in Gunaratne 1993 p. 27) giving details of the involvement of RAW (the Indian equivalent of the CIA).

So Tambiah's constructions of Tamil reactions and South Indian connections are completely at variance with the truth on the ground.

THE VIOLENT EIGHTIES

The chapters on the violent 1980s are the highlight of Tambiah's thesis on violence and Buddhism, but unfortunately, the thesis he builds on, as any cursory reader of Sri Lankan newspapers of the time can see, is a brazen travesty of the truth. The basic facts are very much at variance with Tambiah's presentations. Let me give a few illustrations.

Firstly, the Sinhala/Tamil violence, in spite of the popular image in the outside world, was not the major violence during the period. Of the possibly 65,000 to 85,000 people killed in Sri Lanka in the eighties, between 15,000 and 25,000 were killed in ethnic-related conflict. This occurred in the predominantly Sinhala areas during the anti-Tamil riots of 1983, sparked by army casualties in the separatist civil war, and since then primarily in the north and east, where there were Tamil, Sinhala, and Muslim civilian casualties, as well as casualties among various armed combatants including different shades of Tamil guerrillas, and Sri Lankan and Indian troops. The remaining number of deaths, possibly between 40,000 and 70,000, were almost exclusively Sinhalese and occurred in the south in the uprising of the JVP and its allied groups in the late 1980s, subsequent to the Indian-imposed "Peace Accord" of 1987 and the repression by the state of those involved in the uprising.

The major direct anti-Tamil actions of a racist nature were the 1983 riots. Yet even here there are strong indications that it was more organized factions in the government, as opposed to a generalized anti-Tamil feeling, that were behind the violence. In fact, in his first book, Tambiah alludes to this. Thondaman, the leader of the Estate (Indian) Tamils, speaking at Parliament of the 1983 riots, mentioned that the vast majority of Sinhalese condemned the atrocities. He said, "The vast majority of the Sinhala people condemn these atrocities on these innocent Tamil people and have shown sympathy and understanding . . . and have braved [the dangers] and given shelter in their own homes in spite of intimidations and threats" (S. Thondaman's speech in Parliament, 4 August 1983, quoted in Iriyagolla, Gamini, 1994 p. 7).

Since 1983, there have been virtually no Tamil casualties of any significance in areas outside the civil-war areas of the north and the east, that is, not in the predominantly Sinhala areas where the *majority* of Tamils live. This is in spite of continuing massacres of Sinhalese villagers by Tamil separatists. So, Tambiah's rhetorical question, why Sinhalese are engaging in violence against Tamils, is a question that covers only a small part of the violence, as Sri Lankans as a whole were engaging in mutual slaughter, albeit sometimes with the help of their external "friends," including India and Israel. Tambiah has also consciously left out two key actors in the violence, the Tamil militants, whose efforts began in the 1970s, and the Indian army (1992 p. 46, n. 3), whose activities began at least in the early eighties with the training of Tamil separatists and intensified on Sri Lankan soil in the period after 1987. Clearly Tambiah's project is not an impartial one.

Further, Tambiah in effect justifies murders of Sinhalese by Tamils when he says that Tamils started attacking Sinhalese sacred sites after the Sri Lankan military attacked civilians, bystanders, and nonmilitary targets (1992 p. 76). This is patently untrue. The Tamil rebels began attacking civilian targets before there was any military presence. These attacks were first aimed against Tamil civilians who did not agree with the ideas of the rebels. Religious violence was adopted as a policy by Tamil insurgents, and in its execution they have massacred both Buddhists and Muslims and desecrated their places of worship.

Tambiah also uses terminology drawn straight from Tamil separatist propaganda when he writes such loaded words as "Buddhist nationalism and chauvinism" (1992 p. 59), "homeland" (p. 59), "Sinhala army in the north" (p. 19), "army of occupation" (p. 70), and "the heart of Sri Lankan Tamil territory" (p.71). He also uses the canard of traditional homelands to argue that colonization of these lands had occurred (pp. 68–70). His flaunting of the fiction of the traditional homelands goes against what he said in his earlier book. There Tambiah noted that the Eastern Province (1986 pp. 1–13) was never under Tamil sovereignty, although he now claims it as part of the Tamil traditional homelands (1992 pp. 68–70). Recently, some of the settlers have come from the areas of the former Sinhalese Kandyan Kingdom itself, whose lands were declared "wastelands" by the British and converted to tea plantations. Here it is illuminating to read Tambiah's own words on the dispossession of this Kandyan peasantry of their lands, the words taken from perhaps the only field study that he did in Sri Lanka, in 1957. He described

> the chain of events which reduced the Kandyan peasantry to chronic landlessness and overcrowding [by] the sacrifice of village interests to [colonial] plantation agriculture. A phenomenal loss of [village] land took place. . . . [Further] the newly opened estates moreover were run by immigrant South Indian labor [and so provided no employment for the Sinhalese]. The process worked remorselessly and within a generation or two produced a large landless or semi-landless class in [the Kandyan Sinhalese] rural areas. (S. J. Tambiah in Sarkar and Tambiah, eds. 1957 pp. 79, xi)

MONKS AS FAVORITE VILLAINS

The monks he describes—even the most politically active—were not all aligned along political lines based on the "primordial romanticism" he ascribes to them. The monks had different affiliations; many were nonpolitical, and those with political affiliations at times changed their sympathies.

Thus even the monks' group, the MSV, was not the monolithic organization Tambiah makes it out to be; it included many factions, and later split up. One of the major reasons for the split (as documented in the Sinhala media at the time) was precisely the fact that the major faction, made up of younger monks—many with JVP sympathies—was critical of previous ethnic policies, including language policies, as alienating the Tamils. One objection to the younger monks was that they presented Tamils among their principal speakers at the monks' public meetings.

The JVP was never a Sinhalese militant force, as implied by Tambiah and Jayawardena. Its tract on the ethnic conflict is both broad in its scope and specific in its details (Wijeweera 1986). Its program in response to the Tamil demands included the creation of an autonomous region, the abolition of special privileges brought about by such legislation as the Official Languages Act, the Standardization of Education Program, and the Constitution. Chandraprema, a Christian editor of the local journal *Christian Worker*, which documented, based on security records, the elimination of the JVP—hardly a JVP or pro-Buddhist ideologue—wrote that the JVP was a secular party, not a Sinhalese-Buddhist one (Chandraprema 1988).

The MSV meetings were not held only to protest against the loss of sovereignty in the country brought about by the Indian Accord, but also to advocate the re-democratization of the country, calling for elections to reverse the effects of the rigged referendum of 1982 that had postponed regular elections. They were not, as Tambiah claims, for the island-wide propagation of Buddhism. Instead of the meetings being anti-Catholic, as he asserts, several Catholic clergymen also spoke on the MSV platform, which was received with enthusiasm in the predominantly Catholic areas. Further, all the major monks who spoke at the main (Pettah) rally, which Tambiah refers to as the culmination of the MSV efforts, emphasized in their speeches that their movement was not anti-Tamil and that Sinhalese, Tamils, and Muslims had all suffered a loss of sovereignty because of the Indian Accord. And, in the anti-Accord-related violence that followed, which saw tens of thousands of Sinhalese killed, no Tamils were hurt.

The nurses' strike of 1987 (not 1978, as Tambiah dates it), led by the monk Muruttetuwe Ananda, which Tambiah looks at askance, was notable in that it was the first trade union action to successfully challenge the repressive J. R. Jayawardene regime. In his first book, Tambiah provides some details of Jayawardene's repression, although he does not deal with the mass sacking of workers, a pernicious act that virtually brought all trade union actions to a standstill. Also at variance with Tambiah's construction is the fact that Jayawardene castigated Ananda for leading a trade union only *after* the trade union militancy emerged. Important also, for the light it sheds on Tambiah's knowledge of simple but key facts, is that Abeyaramaya (in fig. 5, on p. 95), which he misspells as Abeyramana, was the temple of this monk, Ananda, not, as he states, of Sobhitha.

Missing from Tambiah's whole narrative are the two large Sangha Sammelanayas (Monks' Congresses), which thousands of monks attended in the late eighties; they were among the largest gatherings of Sri Lankan monks since the 12th century, which were very indicative of the changed mood of monks. These congresses signaled a sea change from the 1950s decolonization agenda of monks with its assertive Sinhala Buddhist rhetoric. The younger monks were in revolt, calling for increased democratization in the monastic order. And the resolutions on the ethnic problem that ensued in these congresses, including the resolution calling for compulsory education for all citizens in both Sinhala and Tamil languages, were a far cry from the "Sinhala Only" rhetoric of the majority of monks in the 1950s (*Lankadeepa* 11 November, 13 November 1988; *Kalaya* [Colombo] November 1988 pp. 8–10).

There are also major and obvious contradictions in Tambiah's formulation that he does not pursue. For example, why did the allegedly anti-Tamil militant JVP and its allies, who had stood for revolutionary violence as a means of changing society, do no violence to Tamils? Nowhere is any evidence given for the JVP's alleged anti-Tamil chauvinism. The JVP's views on the ethnic questions were not unknown, having been published in a rather convoluted JVP book at the time, in which one cannot detect racism. The government falsely blamed three left-wing parties at the time, including the JVP, for the anti-Tamil riots of 1983, but no informed observer took that charge seriously; all the evidence points to elements of the state apparatus being to blame.

In fact, the charge against the JVP-oriented monks in the MSV, as we have already noted, were that they were too pro-Tamil. During 1988, an aborted eight-party opposition political coalition, in which JVP elements were prominent, produced one of the largest devolution packages for the Tamil areas, a package denounced at the time by the ruling United National Party as being too pro-Tamil. The JVP-oriented monks' organizations produced in the 1970s and 1980s many socially oriented publications, such as *Vimukti Maga,* "Liberation Way," which were very different in flavor from the 1950s monks' writings. The thousand monks walking under the JVP banner in the 1982 May Day rally, which Tambiah mentions, partly signaled this change, and there was no mention of "sons of the soil" at this rally, as Tambiah claims. And, in a well-known press interview, the late Sri Lankan president Premadasa, who later was the destroyer of the JVP, asserted in 1988 that the JVP wanted "to do away with racialism and the class system" (*Island* [Colombo], 16 November 1988).

Although Tambiah says that the Sinhalese are against devolution (1992 p. 123), he does not mention anywhere in the book that a 13th Amendment to the Sri Lankan Constitution was passed, which completely recast the system of government. Tambiah makes other gross errors: the "Buddhist Universities" (presumably Vidyalankara and Vidyodaya), which he says the young monks are drawn to, in fact, do not exist. More than thirty years ago, they were made into Western-type universities functioning in accordance with the same academic and other criteria as all other universities, and today they have absolutely no religious affiliations.

Although Tambiah states, following standard undergraduate anthropology texts, that he "must look at the universe, so far as possible, through the eyes and practices of Buddhist actors situated in history and in their local contexts" (1992 p. 3), his book hardly exemplifies this laudable injunction.

The Buddhists that Tambiah has constructed live in an insular world. They receive only messages from the past. Reading this book, we see no evidence about the extent to which today's Buddhists believe the myths that are ascribed to them. One is also at a loss to understand from Tambiah's flawed thesis why since 1983 there have been no major anti-Tamil actions by the general Buddhist population. The reason, which cannot be discussed in detail here, is that a large constituency of younger, noncommunal monks has in fact now emerged. A monks' human rights organization, whose journal was *Vinivida* (referred to in Tambiah's book), was formed after younger monks became disgusted with anti-Tamil feelings and defended Tamils against marauding mobs in the 1983 anti-Tamil riots, as, for example, recorded in the then Jaffna-based newspaper *Saturday Review.* Many of the younger monks were at the regular universities (not "Buddhist Universities"), and monks constituted at the time of these incidents nearly 20 percent of humanities students at universities in the predominantly Sinhala areas. These non-communal Buddhists are edited out of Tambiah's book; no information is provided on their discourses, which were relatively well-publicized.

The discourses of these non-communal Buddhists show that although their debates were sometimes simplistic, they were in fact engaged in extending "the framework of current Buddhist nationalism . . . [to] . . . stretch and incorporate a greater amount of pluralist tolerance in the name of Buddhist conceptions of righteous rule," as Tambiah (1992 p. 3) had wished. Some of them may in fact have even condoned violence as an avenue to social justice, which to my personal knowledge, because of my wife's acquaintance with hundreds of young student monks in her classes, probably came from their reading of Christian liberation theology. I recall monk-students asking me questions about the Latin American revolutionary priest Camillo Torres.

There is a strong selectivity in Tambiah's concern with Buddhist matters (and remember that Tambiah is a person who also wrote on the Buddhism of another Theravada country, Thailand). Thus, he does not ask what was the nature of the violence that killed Buddhist monks themselves (more than six hundred are recorded to have been killed, the overwhelming majority being young monks); who killed them and for what reasons are topics significantly not discussed in what purports to be a tract on Buddhism and violence.

Tambiah's construction also leaves out interactions between ethnicity, class, and geopolitics. "Outsiders," including various Tamil groups, are simply reacting to monolithic Sinhala Buddhists.

There is, for example, no mention of the Indian government's perception of the Sri Lankan United National Party (UNP) government as pro-Western, leading to the Indian sponsorship, training, indoctrination, and arming of various Tamil groups so that the line between local Tamil insurgency and a proxy invasion became nonexistent. There is no mention of any Tamil writings or movements that inspired Tamil groups, only assumed reactions to Sinhala actions. The writings on Tamil movements, one should note, are freely available in the Indian press—especially for the period after Rajiv Gandhi's assassination by Tamil Tigers, and include descriptions of elaborate plans by the Liberation Tigers of Tamil Eelam (LTTE) for a proposed Greater Eelam that would include South India.

Tambiah's limited construction does not answer such necessary questions as, Where were the social psychological origins of the violence within the different Sri Lankan minds? Within the training camps of Israel, where both elements of the Sri Lankan army and some of the Tamil militants were trained? Within the Indian training camps, where different, rival Tamil groups were trained? Or within local and probably informal settings, where the JVP's allied grouping (the DJV), which was without international sponsorship, presumably got its training?

Tambiah's false data touch on elements that Tambiah should know well. Gamini Iriyagolla in his newspaper articles has provided some useful information about Tambiah himself that allows us to put Tambiah's ideas into perspective. (It appears that the two knew each other earlier.) Tambiah is a Tamil Christian and was educated at St. Thomas' College, which was owned and managed by the Church of England through the

Church Missionary Society (CMS). His father contested a parliamentary seat in 1947 in the Jaffna Peninsula, as a candidate of the United National Party whose leader then was D. S. Senanayake. The latter, following in the footsteps of the Britishers, opened up the abandoned heartlands of the Sinhala civilization, restored the ancient irrigation networks, and launched the modern Gal Oya scheme in the same underpopulated area. The settlers in these irrigated areas came predominantly from the over-populated Western and Southern provinces. In 1949 Tambiah's father also became an officer of the Order of the British Empire, a British honor. An older brother, H. D. Tambiah, was appointed by President J. R. Jay-awardene to the Court of Appeal set up according to the new Constitu-tion of 1978. Jayawardene later promoted him to the Supreme Court. Tambiah thus comes from a family that benefited from the Sri Lankan establishment.

Iriyagolla points out errors and sloppiness even when Tambiah gives details about his own father and his connections. These details relate to two well-known politicians, the brothers Sir Ponnabalam Arunachalam and Sir Ponnabalam Ramanathan—one of whose sons had been a friend of Tambiah's father. Tambiah claims that these two brothers led the Cey-lon National Congress in the early decades of the 20th century. Iriyagolla points out that Ramanathan was not even a member of the Ceylon Na-tional Congress, and that Arunachalam, elected its first president, was in the Congress for only three years (Iriyagolla, Gamini, 1994 8 March p. 7).

TAMBIAH'S SOURCES

The sources given for this book are almost exclusively secondary ones written in English, many of the authors being social scientists living out-side Sri Lanka. There are no references to any Sinhala-language primary source, although such works are the almost exclusive channel of Sin-halese Buddhist discourse in Sri Lanka, except for one single unpub-lished English translation by a Western social scientist. So the gross fail-ings in this book may perhaps be attributed to ambiguous or false data.

A lecture was given by Tambiah on the broad topic of the book at the Graduate Center of the City University of New York in 1990, long be-fore the book was released. My wife, a Ph.D. from London University, a scholar of Sinhalese Buddhism, and a faculty member at a Sri Lankan university, attended the seminar. She herself had written of the violent 1980s in Sri Lanka as the Sri Lankan chair of the World University Service (WUS) in the series of books produced by WUS, *Academic Freedom.* During question time, she pointed out that Tambiah's central points were seriously at variance with what really happened. So Tambiah had prior information about his inaccuracies.

Tambiah's acknowledged key informants are Kumari Jayawardena (the wife of Lal Jayawardena, who commissioned the study), Sarath Amunugama, and H. L. Seneviratne. For his information on the Movement for the Protection of the Motherland and the violence that arose after the Indian Accord, Tambiah has limited himself to only a few sources, principally to two articles by Peter Schalk (1988) and Sarath Amunugama (1991). Amunugama, however, was the chief government official in charge of "information" in Sri Lanka, the government propaganda apparatus, including the state-owned radio and TV, being under his jurisdiction. For a time, Amunugama was also the actual government censor. We will return to the reliability of Tambiah's other sources in a later chapter.

Tambiah's purported role in this second book, the role of a sympathetic observer of the society he studies, actually becomes the opposite. Later, when a storm broke out in Sri Lanka over the many inaccuracies in this book, he mobilized his friends in Sri Lanka to apologize to a monk he had falsely maligned. A lawyer, Prins Gunasekere, living in exile in London, wrote to Tambiah and reported his book to the American Anthropological Association and to Harvard University for falsifying data about Gunasekere himself and an organization, the Movement for the Protection of the Motherland (MSV), with which he was associated. These reverberations, which are in the public domain, will be dealt with in Chapter 11 in the discussion on the sociology of Sri Lankan anthropology.

LEVELING TRUTH

In his third book, *Leveling Crowds: Ethnonationalist Conflicts and Collective Violence in South Asia* (1996), Tambiah moves away from his earlier foray into ethnic violence in Sri Lanka, in which he saw unique features among the Sinhalese Buddhists as the major actor in the Sri Lankan ethnic conflict (1996 p. x). He is now moving to study the general phenomenon of ethnic conflict, and the comparative examples before him necessitate that he move away from single-actor causation in Sri Lanka (causation that perhaps only coincidentally fitted into his own Tamil ethnicity) (p. 6).

Tambiah now says that Hindu nationalism, Islamic fundamentalism, and Buddhist "nationalism" are common features in the region (1996 p.

14). He finds that his thesis of a peculiar "disease" shared only by Sinhalese Buddhists, as readers of his earlier book would have been led to believe, is a more universal one. Now he finds the negative characteristics, which he ascribed almost solely to Sinhala Buddhists in his earlier two books, targeted at a Western audience, also in Western Europe. Tambiah now finds that ethnic conflicts are worldwide, and that they are not due to primordial factors or brought about only by a new history invented by a recently literate intelligentsia (p. 25). And riots, Tambiah finds, are not limited to Sinhalese Buddhists but also occur among other groups both inside and outside Sri Lanka. He also finds that the police, the army, other security forces, and public officials have participated in riots in other countries of the region (p. 214).

Tambiah recognizes, as he did not in the first two books, that the Sinhala-Tamil conflict is partly externally based, not just homegrown and due to the work of one actor, the Sinhalese Buddhists. Tamils, he now emphasizes, also have extensive external networks (1996 p. 6). He now finds Indian intervention in Sri Lanka being helped by the secessionist movement (p. 5), again an emphasis that was lacking earlier. The language cry that he earlier saw as primarily a peculiarly Sinhalese disease is now seen as a more general demand accompanying decolonization found in all the countries in the region (1996 p. 17).

Tambiah admits that he writes in English and addresses an audience in both West and East. But he stoutly rejects the idea that his narrative is preconceived by Western categories of thought and grounded in a myopic Western milieu (1996 p. 34). Yet this third book, although less partisan than his last, turns out when he deals with Sri Lanka to be at times of the same colonial genre—the "natives are misbehaving."

Even while recognizing that ethnic attitudes are a common feature, he misunderstands what he calls Buddhist "nationalism." Here once again, he inadvertently simplifies and falsifies the Sri Lankan Buddhist situation. Sinhalese Buddhists were not and are not monolithic. The roles of Buddhists and Buddhist monks have varied on the social goals spectrum. Some Sinhalese Buddhists were, especially during the Cold War, advocates of socialism; others were supporters of capitalism. Buddhist monks themselves have been accused of lives of luxury, an echo of similar charges that have reverberated periodically through Sinhalese history, while some, in contrast, have lived frugal lives meditating in the forest. They were not simply angry repositories of subaltern views.

Tambiah now changes his views on Dharmapala. In his earlier work, Angarika was an "an uncharitable propagandist" (1992 p. 7), but now he is seen as a "famous charismatic and innovative leader" (1996 p. 38) and as part of a larger anticolonial cultural movement in which various disadvantaged groups participated.

Although Tambiah revises somewhat his earlier negative views of Dharmapala, he also now says that Dharmapala was not interested in deep economic and social reform or in incorporating science and technology for development. To Tambiah, Dharmapala was far "more a propagandist than a creative or profound thinker-reformer" (1996 p. 41). This was far from the truth. Dharmapala, as we have already seen, assiduously exhorted the people to follow the path of development and industrialization as seen in Japan and America. He visited industrial schools in several countries and advocated that similar schools be set up in Sri Lanka. He was associated with reformist Buddhist movements such as those of the Amarapura and Ramanna Nikayas, which had no caste bias; in fact, their leading cadres came from the lower castes.

Dharmapala exhorted the Sinhalese endlessly to rise from their stupor and be active, his choicest words of contempt being aimed at the Sinhalese and not at any other group. He did not advocate a deep class revolution except in his lampooning of the dependent imitative bourgeoisie, which was equivalent to the comprador bourgeoisie of Maoist terminology. But his actions led the British to believe that he was plotting revolution together with the "notorious Indian Bolshevik M. N. Roy" (quoted in Guruge, ed. 1965 p. lxix). As for Dharmapala's lack of profundity of thought, he was well-versed not only in Eastern and especially Buddhist thought but also in Western classical thought as well as its more recent scientific literature. His writings reveal a facility and familiarity with these works, much more, in fact, than I have detected in Tambiah.

Tambiah finds that Dharmapala transferred monastic rules to the laity. But Tambiah forgets that the relationship between monks and laity, unlike those of the Christian priest and his flock, was very close. This led to a continuous process of Buddhist monastic codes percolating to the laity. This is witnessed, for example, in the similar forms of deliberate eating and other social acts in Southeast Asian Buddhist cultures such as the Thai, Cambodian, and Lao. I have drawn attention to this earlier.

Tambiah again repeats the canard that locals borrowed Protestant propaganda techniques, that Dharmapala emerged only under the tutelage and patronage of the Theosophists, and that it was only local enthusiasts who gave the victory of the Panadura debate to the Buddhist monk (1996 p. 47). But these assertions, as we have seen, are heavily flawed, Eurocentric views. Buddhist texts in China and Korea were the first printed books ever, yet no one talks of that technology's appearance in Europe as a Buddhist phenomenon. And it was not the local Sinhalese who gave victory to the monk in the Panadura debate but British news-paper editors. Olcott came to the country only after he had admired a report of the debate. His relationship with the locals, including Dharma-pala, was not one of tutelage. The tutelage was in the opposite direction, beginning with the correspondence of the Theosophists with local Bud-dhists before the Theosophists had even thought of coming to Sri Lanka, through their having to obtain permission before publishing anything se-rious on Buddhist thought, and ending with the estrangement of the lo-cals, including Dharmapala from Olcott and Theosophist thought.

Tambiah errs when he says that the education and literacy programs had some common features in all South Asian countries (1996 p. 17). The Tamils, as Tambiah himself had so vividly shown forty years pre-viously, were the educationally privileged group in Sri Lanka during co-lonial times (Tambiah 1955). But decolonization opened up education (and white-collar jobs) for the Sinhalese. It was partly the competition for jobs among the educated that drove the Tamil secessionist movement, as Sinhalese in the postcolonial era were making inroads into the Tamil hold on most white-collar jobs. The key year was 1972 with its Vaddukodi resolution, which was a partial response to demands for affirmative ac-tion to correct colonial imbalances. Tambiah in this book finds affirma-tive action to be a positive thing in India (1996 p. 24), although earlier he found it unacceptable in Sri Lanka (1986 p. 77).

But access to education varies widely in the region. Predominantly Hindu India and predominantly Muslim Pakistan are the greatest pro-ducers of illiterates in the world today, with literacy rates lower than those of many sub-Saharan countries which had no written language or sophisticated written literature until these were introduced by the colo-nial powers. On the other hand, Buddhist Sri Lanka has near-universal literacy, due primarily to Buddhist influence, its literacy figures in the 19th century being higher than those of many Western countries.

Now that he finds ethnic conflict everywhere, Tambiah finds that eth-nic conflicts are neither primordial nor imagined (1996 p. 25). Still, for Sri Lanka, he mentions only the riots in which Sinhalese Buddhists par-ticipated (p. 39) and ignores other clashes such as Tamil-Muslim riots. Ethnic conflict now appears complex to Tambiah, and he consequently finds the need to study ethnic cleansing (p. 27). He mentions ethnic cleansing in Uganda (p. 5) but does not mention the equivalent large-scale expulsion of Sinhalese and Muslims by the LTTE from the areas under their control. This was the only ethnic cleansing of note in recent South Asia.

Tambiah now finds that the British used divide-and-rule policies in the region (1996 p. 23). But he ignored this fact or underplayed it in his earlier books on Sri Lanka. His attention to the contribution of Tamils to the Sri Lanka conflict as beneficiaries of British divide-and-rule policies was virtually nonexistent. Tambiah notes approvingly that recent commentators on subaltern studies have pointed out that colonial authorities had a master narrative of a permanent ethnic and religious divide between the subject peoples. This divide justified the use of deadly force by the colonialists (1996 p. 29). But Tambiah's earlier emphasis on "primordialism" among Sinhala Buddhists flirted dangerously with this master narrative.

The riots that Tambiah discusses are, except for one in Sri Lanka, all located in the post-independence period. Among other sources of information he uses official and unofficial commissions of enquiry for his narrative (1996 p. 33). Yet he leaves out the one comprehensive study on a single recent riot in Sri Lanka, that of the Sansoni Commission on the riots of 1978. This commission was headed by a Eurasian Supreme Court judge, Sansoni, who had no ethnic affiliation with either Sinhalese or Tamils. The proximate cause was the actions of Sinhalese rioters. Sansoni's conclusions on the non-proximate reasons for the riots laid full blame on Tamil political parties for a long racist campaign.

Tambiah again repeats the misconstructions that appeared in his second book. He uses the highly derogatory expression "presiding eminence" to describe Migettuwatte Gunananda (1996 p. 48), an expression that even the British colonialists would have been reluctant to use. The Society for the Propagation of Buddhism, which Tambiah claims was formed by Gunananda in imitation of the Society for the Propagation of the Gospel, was, as we have seen, only the English version of the Sinhala original name, Sarvajna Sasanabhivrddhidayaka Dharma Samagama, which directly translates as "Dharma Association Contributing to the Advancement of the Omniscient Sasana." And Gunananda was not "alleged" to have stimulated the arrival of Olcott, as claimed by Tambiah. The ample documentation points not to "allegations" but to direct inspiration for Olcott to come to the country. Tambiah's own inspiration seems to be colonial anthropology at its worst.

Tambiah's quoting the British judicial inquiry in the present book (which found the Buddhists to be the offended party) is a major departure from his first book, in which he blames the Sinhala Buddhists for the riot. Yet he seems to find fault with the Buddhists for wanting justice, demanding that the Catholic perpetrators be arrested (1996 p. 54). Tambiah claims that the "question has been raised" whether the monk Gunananda deliberately chose the particular Easter month of March for his celebration in order to provoke the Christians (p. 50). But he does not reveal by whom the "question" has been raised. The British found that the provocation came squarely from the Catholics. Tambiah goes beyond the British colonialists' findings.

Tambiah also blames the colonialists for not recognizing the Kotahena riot as an early sign of Sinhala Buddhist nationalism (1996 pp. 52, 53), implying probably that they should have nipped it in the bud. Again, Tambiah is faulting the colonials for not being colonial enough. And adding worse insult to the real facts of the case, the neocolonial Kumari Jayawardena's mischievous writings, which claim that the Buddhist Renaissance was not an anticolonial struggle but only a holy war, are quoted approvingly by Tambiah (pp. 48, 55). Again taking his cue from Jayawardena's writings, Tambiah seems to fault the stage plays on heroic Sinhala kings and "the provocative anti-British dialogue" of one satire (p. 71).

In his search for causes of the riots that would show Sinhalese as the villains, Tambiah says that a trigger may have been the centenary of the ceding of the country to the British and the "the alleged non-observance of certain understandings" by the latter (1996 p. 57). But these were not "alleged" non-observances; the British directly violated the understandings. All these are apologies for colonial rule, and they deny and denigrate the efforts of cultural resistance to colonial rule.

Tambiah finds the 1915 riots to be due to the rising Islamic consciousness of "Coastal Moors" coming into conflict with Sinhala Buddhist attitudes (1996 p. 43). Again it is now no longer just one hand—namely, the Sinhalese Buddhists—clapping, as he tried to show in *Buddhism Betrayed*. The fundamentalist "Coastal Moors" had come recently from South India, and in orientation they were very different from the integrationist Muslims who had lived in Sri Lanka for centuries. The integrationist Muslims had very close relations with the Sinhalese. Thus when the Portuguese on their arrival drove the Sri Lankan "Moors" away from the coast, the Sinhalese king found them refuge in villages he granted them, and gave them the opportunity to build their mosques and to freely practice their religion. The Sri Lankan Moors' mosque at Gampola was on the route of the Buddhist procession, and they used to pay respect to the host country's culture by remaining silent when a Buddhist procession passed by. The newly arrived "Coastal Moors'" response was just the opposite. They wanted the procession's music—which for millennia had been integral to the procession—stopped when it passed the mosque.

Tambiah depends on secondary sources, mainly the exhaustive study of Kannangara. He describes an alleged connection between the Buddhist Renaissance and Sinhalese commercial interests as the indirect motivation for the riots, which Kannangara specifically denies. But without evidence, Tambiah writes that commercial interests "*could* have fused the ... revivalist religious enthusiasm with a Sinhala nationalism" (1996 p. 79, emphasis mine).

Tambiah again says, as in his second book, that Tamil youth took up arms "in desperation" after 1956 (1996 pp. 81, 86, 286). But even in this milder third book he ignores the roots of Tamil nationalism in a South Indian–Sri Lankan Tamil nexus going back to the 19th century. There have been enough books published in the 1980s and 1990s that show these connections with South Indian separatism. But ignoring these, Tambiah again uses loaded expressions like Tamil youth taking up arms "in desperation," a "Sinhala army of occupation," and "Sinhalese chauvinists had been frustrated and flustered over the puncturing of their virile right of domination, established by Dutthagamani" (p. 286).

In this more nuanced book, Tambiah mentions, quoting a local author, a fact well-known at the time, that one of the worst massacres in 1983 was triggered by the rumor that Tamil Tigers had infiltrated Colombo and were marching down to where Sinhalese lived (1996 p. 283). This resulted in a hysterical orgy of killing suspected Tigers—which in actuality meant killing hundreds of innocent Tamils. Tambiah now finds that it was fear of suspected Tigers marching on Sinhalese in Colombo—not simple hatred of Tamils—that led to these killings. Instead of the simplistic reading of brutal Sinhalese, fired by their primordial past, killing Tamils, which was his crude construct in his second book, he now finds that these killings were caused by a combination of "anger" (at Tamil killings) and "panic" (at the alleged approach of Tamil Tigers). But the 1956 riots were also similar, preceded by false gruesome stories that trains were arriving with bodies of slain Sinhalese women with their breasts cut off.

Tambiah says he is not Eurocentric and is not guided by Western categories (1996 p. 34). But this is hardly true, because his series editor is Juergenmeyer, whom we show later as part of the larger matrix of writers who have deliberately distorted Sri Lankan reality. I wrote to Juergenmeyer requesting his evidence for some completely false information he presented on Sri Lanka. In spite of several reminders, he could not present the evidence, and his excuse was that he had forgotten because he wrote the book some time earlier—in reality, barely a couple of years before my correspondence with him (for details see Chapter 11).

Tambiah says that Buddhist domination resulted in majoritarian domination and monopolistic gains for the Sinhalese under state patronage (1996 pp. 41–43). These are again tendentious, partial interpretations. Sri Lanka has scored very high on the Physical Quality of Life Index (PQLI) in such categories as literacy, infant mortality, and life expectancy. Although at a low level of income, Sri Lanka has characteristics for which its scores are as high as those of Western industrial nations. The primary reason for this has been widespread literacy arising from educational reforms and to some extent participation in the electoral process. But in both these transformations, the heritage of the Sinhala Buddhist revival was a direct catalyst.

As for Tambiah's charge that Sinhalese Buddhists gained from state patronage, he must be referring to the post-independence period, when the state was in Sri Lankan hands and industrialization was attempted through import substitution. But the facts are not so simple. In fact, the Tamils have also been prime beneficiaries of the import substitution regime probably getting the lion's share, at least initially. This was because when the import substitution program was started, it was Tamils who were in the import trade or were clerks in the import business who had access to information and were quick to make use of the new incentives. As a result, notable houses like St Anthonys, which had its origins during that period, are Tamil-owned. The largest conglomerate today, Maharajas, is also Tamil-owned. The Sinhalese who benefited from that period of import substitution and who were widely believed to have had political patronage, like the Dasa group, are hardly heard of today because their businesses did not take off.

Tambiah says that his evidence for his last book is based on archival and other data, so that the data can be verified, challenged, or confirmed (1996 p. 34). But nowhere in this book is there an inkling that his earlier works on Sri Lanka have been challenged and shown to be partly fictitious, or that he himself has apologized for aspects of them. This is all the more surprising in that his second book was the most widely discussed anthropology book in Sri Lanka. There is no reference to any of the "facts" that he presented earlier that were subsequently disproved.

Tambiah recalls once again institutions and individuals, such as the Movement for the Defense of the Motherland (MSV) and Prins Gunasekere, Murututuewe Ananda Thero, and Maduluwewe Sobhita Thero, that featured prominently in his second book (1996 p. 271). But there is no mention that his earlier references to them had created a furor and that there had been very public charges that he was blatantly inventing facts. One charge was the complaint by the secretary of the MSV, Prins Gunasekere, whom Tambiah now describes positively as "a civil rights lawyer who had defended many people accused by the government of subversive activities" (1996 p. 271).

Tambiah makes a correction on another matter.

There is a strange admission hidden away in Tambiah's endnotes. In the first book, he stated that he and his Sri Lankan students were caught up in the 1958 riots at Gal Oya. Now he says in an endnote that "it was mistakenly stated" [in that book] . . . "that I [Tambiah] and the students were caught up" in the riots (1996 p. 351, n. 2). This is a very strange admission. A Tamil caught up in an anti-Tamil riot would not have forgotten it. It would be indelibly stored in his memory. If he did not get caught, then it is not a slip but a deliberate invention. It is probable that in the debate on his second book, this falsity was pointed out; hence his present backtracking. But he backtracks under cover of an endnote. This duplicitousness is similar to his mentioning in his second book—again hidden away in an endnote—that in his discussions on the ethnic conflict he is, apart from the Sinhalese, avoiding discussion of other key social actors like Tamils and Indians.

PART V

■

THE SOCIOLOGY OF
THE ANTHROPOLOGIST
TRIBE

CHAPTER 11

■

Toward a Sociology of Sri Lankan Anthropology

We have seen in the previous chapters that the reality depicted by the four leading anthropologists on Sri Lanka is highly tangential to the truth. They have mostly created a set of contradictory fictions. The questions we have to pose now are, How could this happen, apart, of course, from the different authors' own private failings? Can we demarcate a set of social factors—in summary, a sociology of Sinhalese Buddhist anthropology that helps throw light on these constructions?

This sociology of the anthropology of Sinhalese Buddhists would contain certain elements. These would include what the anthropologists say about each other, the impact of their studies on other social commentators on Sri Lanka, and the indirect impact of their work on perceptions of Sri Lanka. Another aspect would be the identification of a social cohort which acts as a social filter for our authors' findings and perceptions.

THE AUTHORS SPEAK ABOUT EACH OTHER

Let us first see what the authors think of each other's work. My exercise does not exhaust all they say about each other, but it provides adequate indicators.

Kapferer says of Tambiah that the latter's "understanding of the modern politics of Buddhist states is unsurpassed" (Kapferer 1988 p. 213). He also reviews favorably Tambiah's *Buddhism Betrayed?* in the *Tamil Times*, the Tamil ethnic and separatist newspaper (1993 p. 20). He calls *Buddhism Betrayed?* "a masterly follow-up" to Tambiah's earlier book on Sri Lankan ethnic violence, *Sri Lanka: Ethnic Fratricide and the Dismantling of Democracy.* Evidently he admires the first book, too. Kapferer mentions that some of Tambiah's arguments have been confirmed by the increasingly murderous factionalism and violent practice of monks due to the extension of the political party process to temples. Kapferer says approvingly that Tambiah supports the unpopular view that Sinhala ethnic con-

sciousness appeared only in about the 12th century A.D., thus supporting the denial of any history of the Sinhalese prior to the 12th century.
But despite this, nowhere does Kapferer revise his own central thesis of
an "ontological" Sinhalese hierarchical drive that goes back to ancient
times, a historical perspective that Tambiah himself accepted in his *Buddhism Betrayed?*

Kapferer disagrees with Obeyesekere's use of Freudian categories, but
he accepts unquestioningly Gombrich and Obeyesekere's highly questionable findings on Buddhism transformed (see Kapferer 1991 p. 387 for
nearly thirty largely favorable citations to Gombrich and Obeyesekere;
Kapferer 1988 p. 262 for more than twenty largely favorable citations
to Gombrich and Obeyesekere; Kapferer 1997 p. 364 for twenty-seven
largely favorable citations to Gombrich and Obeyesekere). Kapferer views
Gombrich's work favorably but ignores Gombrich's view that the Tamil
invader Elara was considered a righteous king in the *Mahavamsa* (Gombrich 1991 p. 220).

Tambiah, in turn, admires the writings of Kapferer. He mentions that
Kapferer utilized the ideas of hierarchy and the demonic to explain Sinhalese behavior. He says that these imply a deep-seated cosmology governing Sinhala Buddhist behavior (Tambiah 1992 p. 2), and that Kapferer's
ideas show how Sinhalese nationalism is structured (p. 106). Tambiah
also evokes Kapferer in discussing Dutugemunu (1992 p. 150). He pays
"tribute" to Kapferer's *Legends of People, Myths of State* (Tambiah 1992
p. 170).

Yet, Tambiah does harbor some doubts. He specifically wonders how
the hierarchical logic and model presented by Kapferer on the basis of his
studies of contemporary exorcism can be applied to a 6th-century text,
the *Mahavamsa*. Tambiah also rejects Kapferer's view that the Sinhalese
state attempts to absorb all in its path, removing fragmentation and developing hierarchy and inclusion. Tambiah's view is that in earlier times
the Sinhalese state was loosely structured, inclusive, flexible, and incor-
porationist (1992 pp. 168–178). His thrust here is that of a person who
grew up in the country, not that of a short-term visitor like Kapferer.

Tambiah subscribes in part to the Protestant Buddhism thesis of Obeyesekere (Tambiah 1996 p. 38). He also takes Obeyesekere's descriptions as
given reality, saying that the intensified involvement with spirit cults and
deities that Obeyesekere "records" possibly signals a religious change in
the country (1992 p. 93). But Tambiah adds that such a transformation of
Buddhism, which does not take into account the political transformation
in the country, including a transformation in the political role of Buddhism, becomes "gravely distorted and deficient" (1992 p. 93). He also
criticizes Obeyesekere and Gombrich for ignoring the importance of the

monk Gnanasiha, although Gombrich called him one of the most erudite and influential of monks. Tambiah further criticizes Gombrich and
Obeyesekere for a "lack of serious discussion" on the role of monks.

A CHAIN OF CITATIONS

The four authors, as the anthropologists who have written the most
on the country, have also been frequently cited by other authors on Sri
Lanka. It is useful to explore this act of legitimization by examining a
few books by other anthropologists. The journal literature would give us
more citations, but as indicators of the impact of our authors' constructions, the books are sufficient.

Stirrat, in his own foray into Sri Lankan anthropology, studies a different group of Sinhalese—Sinhalese Catholics—and cites both Obeyesekere
and Gombrich (Stirrat 1992 pp. 103, 150–151, 181). He takes for granted
the Protestant Buddhism thesis as well as Obeyesekere's view that there
was a shift to *Bhakti* and an increase in possession. He also uses Obeyesekere's *Medusa's Hair* (not covered in this book because its arguments are
not central to the macro social reality of the country per se) and shows
that several of the priestesses of (Buddhist) gods were originally Catholics (p. 104). (This is actually a case, one should note parenthetically, of
Catholicism transformed by cults, not of Buddhism transformed.) Using
these constructs of Gombrich and Obeyesekere as a partial guide, Stirrat
goes on to explore Catholicism in Sri Lanka.

Stirrat also regards Kapferer's descriptions of exorcism as valid (Stirrat
1992 p. 91). He accepts Kapferer's reasons for the greater representation
of women in possession. Yet Stirrat has this revealing perspective on Kapferer's sprawling and contradictory constructions: "Summarizing Kapferer's argument is extremely difficult because of the way in which cave-
ats and modifiers are scattered throughout the text, often denying what
appears to be the main thrust of his argument" (1992 p. 211). Stirrat also
points out that Kapferer is not persuasive, citing, as an illustration, the
fact that Kapferer has said that even the simple and essential act of cook-
ing by women was considered polluting, a plainly preposterous idea (pp.
110, 211).

Bond, in his own monograph on the Buddhist revival, devotes thirty
pages exclusively to the topic of Obeyesekere's Protestant Buddhism thesis (1988 pp. 45–75). Elsewhere he also positively and approvingly refers
to the Protestant Buddhism thesis (pp. 7, 38, 39, 101, 77, 81, 90). But Bond
is led astray.

For example, there were two major projects associated with the 2,500-

year Buddhist anniversary—Buddha Jayanti—namely, the translation of the *Tripitaka*, the Buddhist "Canon," into Sinhalese and the *Encyclopedia of Buddhism* project. These, say Bond, "clearly had a Protestant or reformist purpose" (p. 80). This is clearly not a correct interpretation. The Cambodians completed the translation of the *Tripitaka* into Khmer in the 1960s, before the Sinhalese and unrelated to any Protestant impulses. The *Encyclopedia of Buddhism* project in Sri Lanka was launched almost simultaneously with a *Sinhala Encyclopaedia*, again revealing a universal urge and not a Protestant one. Similarly, there are many 20th-century Indian encyclopedias on a variety of topics, again launched without any Protestant infection.

Jonathan Spencer, in an exploration of social change in a rural setting, makes positive use of all four of our authors, Gombrich, Obeyesekere, Kapferer, and Tambiah (Spencer 1990). He accepts the Kapferer-Obeyesekere thesis that sorcery and possession have grown in recent years (p. 207). He takes as given Obeyesekere's Protestant Buddhism hypothesis (pp. 20, 69). He similarly accepts Kapferer's descriptions of exorcism as true (pp. 175, 206, 226). Spencer also takes Kapferer's explanations of nationalism as valid, although he says it is unnecessary to consider Kapferer's ideas on hierarchy and ontology as correct (pp. 246, 253). Kapferer's 1988 fictional explanations are considered by Spencer to be an "important contribution" (p. 284, n. 2). Spencer also approvingly cites Tambiah on the ethnic issue (pp. 95, 254) and calls Tambiah's second book an "excellent summary" (p. 284, n. 2).

A recent American biography of Olcott by Stephen Prothero (1996) accepts some of Obeyesekere's "Protestant" explanations of Sinhalese Buddhism. Prothero derives his ideas from Obeyesekere's thesis of Protestant Buddhism. Prothero claims that Olcott wanted to liberate the Buddhists from "sectarianism, superstitions and unseemly rituals" (p. 7). But, blinded by Obeyesekere, he ignores the fact that such attempts at "purification" were made several times in Sri Lankan history, and in fact are embedded in key texts of the Buddha.

Holt, in his study of the transformation of Avalokitesvara into the god Nath in Sri Lanka, also assumes the premises of Protestant Buddhism as true, although he has a reservation about the extensive monasticization of lay life that the Protestant Buddhism thesis implies (Holt 1991 pp. 9–10, 219, 225). He also accepts as true Gombrich and Obeyesekere's concept of transformed Buddhism in the form of *Bhakti* and religiosity (Holt 1991 pp. 9–10, 219, 225). In addition, he takes as true some of Kapferer's descriptions of exorcist ceremonies (Holt 1991 p. 132). Although Holt himself relies heavily on Sinhalese historical material for his essay, he also uses Kapferer's and Tambiah's views on nationalist history (Holt 1991 p. 125). Holt's study has some perceptive sections—his recourse to the four authors seems to be incidental. Holt's book, in fact, is richer than those of our four authors. This is because Holt seems to have been immersed in the local intellectual culture and based himself at a local university for his study. The individuals he acknowledges are all bona fide teachers and students deeply involved in the Sri Lankan literary, historical, and religious traditions.

A book by another American, William McGowan, *Only Man Is Vile* (1992), although not exactly a scholarly work, is in the genre of gross distortions of Sri Lanka. It deliberately drew its title from a 19th-century Christian hymn by Bishop Heber, which had the racialist refrain on Ceylon, "where every prospect pleases and only man is vile." McGowan uses much of the false construction of our four authors. For example, he repeats the usual distortions of Protestant Buddhism, including the story about Olcott inventing the Buddhist flag (1992 p. 139).

McGowan also maintains the fiction that Dharmapala invented a mythical history, that Dharmapala used "Aryan" in its Hitlerian usage, in fact predating Hitler (1992 pp. 144–147), completely ignoring the South Asian definition of "Aryan" as noble and the fact that as "Aryans," Dharmapala also included South Indian Tamils. McGowan says that with the spread of this Aryan view, Nazi propaganda "poured into the country and comparisons between the Thousand-Year Reich and the multimillennial reign of the Buddha outlined in the ancient myth" were made (p. 146). He refers to this alleged Nazi connection and to Hitler many times (pp. 97, 99, 146, 234, 269, 279, 327). Unfortunately McGowan does not give any sources for these preposterous nuggets of completely unfounded "information."

McGowan also refers to Jathika Chintanaya ("National Thought") as a Hitlerian movement. Sinhalese racism is referred to on numerous pages (McGowan 1992 pp. 7, 12, 16, 26, 96–100, 118, 146, 169, 191, 216, 256, 273, 278), but Tamil racism on only two pages (pp. 173–174). McGowan also assumes that the memory of the ancient Sinhalese cities was only a recent invention, after the British "discovered" them. The sources McGowan cites approvingly include the International Center for Ethnic Studies (ICES), Colombo (on pp. 277, 280), Reggie Siriwardene (pp. 277, 280), and Tambiah (p. 7), writers who, we note elsewhere in this book, distort Sinhalese reality. McGowan (1992 p. 280) refers to Reggie Siriwardena as a "Buddhist," although the latter publicly admitted that he knew little about the religion, saying, "I am deeply conscious of my lack of scholarship in this field" (Siriwardena, "Where Are the Radical Buddhists?" p. 17).

Another American academic, Mark Juergensmeyer, wrote *The New Cold War: Religious Nationalism Confronts the Secular State* (1993) on a presumed new cold war that would replace the old and would be driven by ethnic and religious divisions. Juergensmeyer made some completely misleading statements on Sri Lanka which are clearly representative of, or derived from, the literature discussed here. He wrote, for example, that the JVP harked back to the past, that the Sri Lankan government was democratic, and that Buddhist monks propagated Buddhist socialism (Juergensmeyer 1993 p. 104).

Reading this misinformation, I wrote to Juergensmeyer asking him for the primary or secondary sources for his statements. After a third reminder sent by certified mail, he replied that he had written the book some time ago—actually only a couple of years prior to my correspondence —and so he could not identify the sources. My construction is that he acquired this skewed view of reality from the available literature and his Sri Lankan sources. This suspicion is further strengthened by the fact that Tambiah published his last book, *Leveling Crowds,* in a series edited by Juergensmeyer.

Writing in the same vein, Benjamin R. Barber in his more popular book, *Jihad vs. McWorld: How Globalism and Tribalism Are Reshaping the World* (1995), says that the Tigers' ethnic revolt also led to an extremist counter-jihad in the Sinhalese majority (meaning here the JVP) (pp. 190–191). This is, of course, again complete nonsense. Barber does not give sources for this assertion, but it clearly comes from our authors, since theirs are the major works on the ethnic issue published in the West. Brow (1996), another anthropologist who uses demons as a gateway to Sri Lankan reality, refers approvingly to all four of our authors, as does Michael Roberts (1994) in his own take on matters ethnic.

So our authors do reverberate. Especially when, at times like the present, Sri Lanka is in the throes of major turbulence and civil war, their texts are referred to when outsiders want to make sense of the fast-moving events in the country.

THROUGH THE *NEW YORK TIMES* PSYCHEDELICALLY

A good illustration with many epistemological and civilizational reverberations of how anthropology has constructed Sri Lanka in the external world is a 1996 report in the *New York Times* by Daniel Goleman, the author of the bestseller *Emotional Intelligence* (1988). He reported on the Vanniyala-etto—better known as Veddahs—the aboriginal residents of

Sri Lanka before the coming of the Sinhalese in the 6th century B.C. The Veddahs now number only in the hundreds. The report was based on a meeting of the American Anthropological Association at which a new Committee for Human Rights decided, on the basis of an initiative taken by Wiveca Stegeborn, a graduate anthropology student at Syracuse University, to make a protest to the Sri Lankan prime minister. This was because a twenty-year-old irrigation scheme had turned the traditional hunting-grounds of the Veddahs into farmland. The American Anthropological Association asked that the Veddahs be allowed to "live in their original lands" (Goleman 1996 p. 11).

Shortly after the report was published, a correction was made by the *New York Times*, saying that the original report misstated the position of the Anthropological Association. The correction stated that although "some" anthropologists had stated that the Vanniyala-etto people, or Veddahs, had been excluded from their traditional homelands, and the Association's Committee for Human Rights had been asked to send a letter of protest, it had in fact not acted on the appeal (*New York Times*, 27 March 1996 p. 2). It was clear that Wiveca Stegeborn was included among "some" anthropologists, if not solely implied.

A few days later, the *New York Times* carried a letter to the editor by Gananath Obeyesekere, in which he identified himself as a professor of anthropology at Princeton. It said that he had been working "in Sri Lanka for more than 40 years and this is the first [he had] heard of a 'tribe' of that name [the Vanniyala-etto]. There are no tribesmen in Sri Lanka, and no one uses bows and arrows." He said that instead of trying to reconvert the Vanniyala-etto "into tribesmen with bows and arrows," anthropologists interested in human rights ought to address themselves "to such things as the 20,000 or so Sinhalese youths killed in the recent rebellion" (Obeyesekere 1996 p. 24). Incidentally, Obeyesekere did not mention that he was ethnically Sri Lankan. His identity was given only as that of an anthropologist at Princeton who had "worked" in Sri Lanka for forty years.

Goleman, the *New York Times* reporter, was no stranger to Sri Lanka. He had written a book, *The Meditative Mind* (1988), one of whose chapter headings described the Sinhalese 5th-century classic *Visudhdhimagga* as a "Map for Inner Space." He had also published a small book with a Sri Lankan Buddhist publisher, titled *The Buddha on Meditation and Higher States of Consciousness* (1980). This was before he began his career in the United States. Some of his U.S. publications compare Eastern psychology (including Sinhalese Theravada Buddhist psychology, which he knew at first hand) favorably with Western psychology (Goleman 1981 pp. 125–

136). So with this prior Sri Lankan connection, it seems natural that Goleman would highlight the Sri Lankan case.

Obeyesekere, in contrast to Goleman, one should note parenthetically, had no use for Sinhalese psychology anywhere in his work. As we have seen, he used loaded, inaccurate terms such as "hypnomatic states" to describe the key mental transformative process of Sinhalese Buddhist psychology, "meditation." Obeyesekere also used Freudian psychoanalytic approaches to the Sinhalese condition. During this period, however, Freudian approaches were being increasingly questioned as to their validity and scientific worth, and were fast descending into the category of folk psychology. With mounting negative evidence, there have been a spate of recent books attacking the scientific basis of Freud and reducing his approach to a pseudoscience. Channel 4 TV in Britain presented a special documentary on Freud with the title, "Bad Ideas of the 20th Century" (reported in *Time,* 29 November 1993, p. 55). Freud was now being called a "witch doctor" and a "quack" (p. 53). American health authorities and insurance companies were also refusing to pay for Freudian treatment because it was ineffective (see p. 51). In contrast, one should note that Buddhist-derived techniques of mental therapy were being recommended by U.S. health authorities. And Buddhist psychology was encroaching on the American psychological mainstream; the numbers of scientific papers on the therapeutic use of meditation-derived techniques today exceed by a very wide margin those on psychoanalysis (Walsh 1992 p. 32).

Obeyesekere is thus now seen to be using a rather soiled, Freudian, Western approach to study his own Sinhalese society, while Goleman and some other Westerners were enthusing about Sinhalese psychology as suitable for use in Western society. Having sketched the comparative background of the intellectual roots of Goleman and Obeyesekere, let us now return to the *New York Times.*

Obeyesekere had mentioned in his *New York Times* letter that anthropologists, instead of talking of the Vanniyala-etto, should concentrate on the 20,000 or so Sinhalese who had died at the hands of government death squads. Now these death squads were sent out to suppress a massive uprising in the country against the so-called Indian Accord. But Obeyesekere himself had been in the forefront of welcoming the Accord. So not only did Obeyesekere as an anthropologist reject the approaches of his countrymen on mental processes—that is, in fact, "on how natives think," the natives here being the Sinhalese—but he also gave unconscious and indirect legitimation for the death squads by endorsing an aggressive accord, which gave away Sri Lankan sovereignty.

The subject of "how natives think" has cropped up more recently in Obeyesekere's work. He has written a critique of the outsider's anthropology in the form of a book-length reply (1994) to a monograph written by Sahlins on Captain Cook. Obeyesekere asserted that Sahlins had misunderstood the entire Cook episode and expressed a colonial-era perspective. Sahlins himself has written a reply with the title *How Natives Think* (1995), a tongue-in-cheek title in which the "native" is Obeyesekere, who claimed a special social epistemology because of his non-Western origin.

But Obeyesekere entered the field of anthropology in the 1960s, a time when "natives" were becoming restless everywhere as they achieved their independence from colonial masters. There were predictions that anthropology would soon die as the anthropologists' hunting-grounds vanished. Obeyesekere himself had not taken part in this questioning of anthropology. Other Sri Lankan sociologists/anthropologists, including the present author, wrote on the need to decolonize the subject, efforts that Obeyesekere acknowledges obliquely in his *Buddhism Transformed*. So in the Sahlins incident, Obeyesekere was stepping away from the unmitigated Eurocentrism of his entire career.

In the preface to his book on Sahlins, Obeyesekere also describes in sorrow how his Sri Lankan driver of several years, Wijedasa, "a gentle and dignified man," was killed during the massive state repression in 1988–1990. He was killed because he was shielding his son, who had been accused of being a terrorist. Obeyesekere wanted the book to be a memorial to Wijedasa so that it would encourage those back home who "refuse to keep silent" (1994 p. xvi).

This is interesting because the driver's son was protesting the very same sovereignty-reducing accord, signed literally under the threat of Indian gunboats, that Obeyesekere and his cohorts so vocally endorsed. In the eyes of the son and the tens of thousands who protested at the time, any foreigner's "crimes" of Sahlins-type misrepresentations would have paled in comparison with Obeyesekere's misrepresentation of the accord as good for the country. If endorsing a foreigner's designs on a country is the standard against which actions are to be measured, then Obeyesekere's actions are far more serious than Sahlins's.

But the *New York Times* episode reveals deeper truths for us in the person of the Swedish "anthropology student" Wiveca Stegeborn, who first alerted the Anthropological Association, requesting it to protest on behalf of the "Vanniyala-etto." Although Obeyesekere denies it, the Vanniyala-etto do exist. "Vanniyala-etto" ("those from the Vanniya region") is the name that the Veddahs call themselves. They number today perhaps in the hundreds, the rest having been absorbed into the general Sinhala

society. They do possess bows and arrows, having used them at an earlier time. Today these weapons are paraded in front of visitors for money
—predominantly Sinhalese visitors, with an occasional Western tourist
thrown in. The Veddahs show their collective solidarity in a procession
at the ancient (pre-Christian) Buddhist city of Mahiyangana. These facts
are well-known among the Sinhalese; the term "residents of the Vanniya"
occurs among others in medieval Sinhalese literature, and the word
"Veddah" is found in the much earlier literature dating back to pre-
Christian times. When in 1998 a Veddah chief died, there was virtually
a national day of mourning. There was extensive media coverage together with high-level state patronage of the event. So Obeyesekere is patently wrong in his letter to the *New York Times*.

But the story spins on further. In the early 1980s, I knew the alleged
graduate student of anthropology Wiweka. She comes from Sweden, and
is a member of the Saami, the Laplander community. On her visits to Sri
Lanka, she on occasion stayed in my house. In fact, the first time she tried
to take Veddah representatives to an international conference, she stayed
with me.

She knew the Veddah language, as well as Sinhala, which she spoke
with a Veddah accent. At the time she also spoke English with a high
Veddah-Sinhala accent. When, on her suggestion, I visited the Veddahs,
I found them split into two camps, the majority wanting to settle as
agriculturalists (for which the state had given them land), go to school,
and integrate with the rest of the rapidly changing Sri Lankan society.
There was a small minority who would perform Veddah rites and speak
the Veddah language, largely for money from curious outsiders. Among
the latter group were a few who genuinely wanted to continue their earlier life.

But Wiweka was not the concerned "anthropologist" she claimed to be,
as I soon found out. She was, she told me, a Swedish nurse who had come
to Sri Lanka as a tourist and decided to stay among the Veddahs. There
is nothing wrong with that. In fact, it could even be admirable—except
that she was soon publicizing her story in the popular Swedish press.
Some of the press coverage that she showed me was sickening because of
the projection of a "Tarzan-Jane" image that deliberately evoked a white
queen among hunter-gatherer "natives."

This was well over ten years before her appeal as a graduate student in
1996 to the American Anthropological Association. But when I met her
in the early eighties, she had already acquired the status of a graduate
student, at Uppsala University. Discussions with her at that time revealed
that although her love for the Veddahs, and especially for one Veddah

man, whom she referred to frequently, was unquestionable, her knowledge of anthropology and the social sciences was at the time extremely rudimentary. Nearly fifteen years later, it appears, she was still an anthropology student.

I have dwelled on the *New York Times* story because in capsule form it summarizes the problems of anthropology in trying to capture the reality of Sri Lanka, a complex entity with its own contributions to the study of the human condition. There are, in this incident, multiple stories jostling with each other, trying to describe both the "true social reality" of Sri Lanka and the social truth of those trying to describe the country.

ONE DOMESTIC REACTION

If the stories told above exemplify how the anthropologists' construction of the Sinhalese reverberates in the international media, can we detect similar reverberations in the Sri Lankan media? Unfortunately, anthropology texts generally do not reach the Sri Lankan public, either English-language readers or Sinhalese-language readers. Kapferer, for example, admitted that his *Legends of People, Myths of State* was not easily available in Sri Lanka (Kapferer 1989). In fact, such books do not generally reach even the academics in sociology and anthropology departments. However, our authors have occasionally been featured in the local English-language journals, most prominently those funded by foreign money.

Writing in the journal *Lanka Guardian*, which he co-edits, Dayan Jayatilleka says, "Prof. Kapferer who our friend Newton Gunasinghe rightly considered to have done the most exciting and original research on Sri Lanka in recent times, brilliantly uncovers aspects of our socio-cultural matrix" (Jayatilleka 1989 p. 21). Clearly both Gunasinghe and Jayatilleka admire Kapferer. Dayan Jayatilleka, one should note here, is a minor populist academic whose group, Vikalpa, was convicted for waging a separatist war. He has also gone on record as justifying the "traditional homelands" fiction of Tamil separatists (*Lanka Guardian*, 15 May 1979; *Lanka Guardian*, October 1982).

An expatriate Tamil academic, Perinbanayagam, again writing in the *Lanka Guardian*, argued that ethnic violence was due to frustrations and contradictions in Sri Lanka's political economy, and not due to Kapferer's fanciful reasons (Kapferer 1989). He dismissed Kapferer's fanciful constructions of the demonic, evil, and ritual sorcery practices (Perinbanayagam 1989). In response to Perinbanayagam's criticism, Kapferer said that he had only caught hold of the "elephant's tail" by saying that "at times in recent Sri Lanka history the tail, ridiculously tiny though it may be, appears to control and direct the elephant!" (Kapferer 1989). In Kapferer's response, he also seems to approve of the Indian intervention in the country, saying that India blocked Sinhalese nationalist urges.

Although our authors' anthropology texts are generally unknown to their subject matter, Sinhalese Buddhists, one book did reach directly into the general Sinhalese discourse, and its trail is both illustrative and instructive.

This was Tambiah's second book, *Buddhism Betrayed*, which created a major controversy in Sri Lanka because of its gross distortions. The reaction to this book must rank as one of the strongest public condemnations ever of an anthropological study. There were more than fifty articles in the Sri Lankan press. There were also public meetings criticizing the book (although not calling for it to be banned). Let me convey a sense of the debate by sampling some of the coverage in the English-language press. (The reactions in the Sinhala-language press were even stronger.)

Piyasena Dissanayake showed that Tambiah's book contained many distortions and factual inaccuracies. Nalin de Silva wrote a small, highly critical book in reply to Tambiah, *Budu Dahama Paava Dima*, "Betraying Buddhism" (see Nakkawita 1994). Ranjith Soysa wrote of Tambiah "maneuvering" history to speak ill of the Sinhalese (Soysa 1993). This was a sentiment echoed by others. Tissa Jayatilaka noted that Tambiah had relied for almost the whole of his material on English-speaking Sri Lankan contacts, Sinhala-language informants and key decision makers being left out (Jayatilaka 1993). This criticism was echoed by a Catholic, Jehan Perera, normally a strong critic of Sinhala Buddhists (1993).

Following this storm of reactions, fifty-two academics and non-academics wrote a joint public letter in Tambiah's defense. However, it seemed that they had not read the book, because they said "we are not primarily concerned with the content of the book" (Fernando 1993). They did not answer any of the criticisms of the book. One of the signatories to the letter was Gananath Obeyesekere, who also wrote a published open letter to the minister of Buddhist Affairs asking that the book not be banned (1993). The signatories, however, were not disinterested observers. Some of them, especially the key signers, also appear as constituents of the interpretative matrix of the Sri Lanka anthropology project that we discuss later in this book. They include Gananath Obeyesekere, Carlo Fonseka, Sarath Amunugama, Neelan Tiruchelvam, Reggie Siriwardena, Jehan Perera, Radhika Coomaraswamy, Charles Abeysekera, Sassanka Perera, Rohan Edirisinghe, Pradeep Jeganathan, Kumari Jayawardena,

I. V. Edirisinghe, P. Saravanamuttu, J. Uyangoda, and Sunil Bastian. They were individuals who as an identifiable cohort had consistently taken public positions greatly at variance with popular opinion. Several of them had also been signatories to statements welcoming the Indian incursion into the country; others were members of the foreign-funded non-governmental organizations (NGOs) that we refer to later.

These signatories' views on Tambiah's book were largely misrepresentations, as many commentators who were opposed to the book's contents, as well as neutral observers, soon pointed out. These included the columnist "Jayadeva" in the *Island* ("Jayadeva" 1993 p. 15). Rajpal Abeynayake, a columnist for *The Sunday Observer,* wrote that neither those who protested Tambiah nor those who supported him had read the book (Abeynayake 1993). The columnist Sena drew attention to the fact that no one had advocated banning the book, as had been implied by Obeyesekere's open letter to the Minister of Buddhist Affairs protesting against an alleged plot to ban *Buddhism Betrayed?* (Sena 1993). Sena also confirmed that after the furor, Tambiah wrote to the monk Sobhita Thera, apologizing for his depiction in the book. A letter Tambiah wrote to a newspaper defending himself as not antagonistic to Buddhism found Pathiravitana responding that judging by the letter alone, Tambiah was hardly the best proponent of Buddhism in the West (Pathiravitana 1993). The *Island* newspaper editorialized that "Books are not for burning" and called on all sides to cool the situation (28 November 1993 p. 10). It also pointed out that this was not the first religion-related controversy, offering me as an example of someone who had suffered persecution.

One of the most interesting documents to come out of the Tambiah controversy was a letter to Tambiah by Prins Gunasekere, a human rights activist who had fled the country to escape death squads, escorted for his safety by the British ambassador. He was an organizer of the Maubima Surakhime Vyaparaya (MSV), which had been referred to in very disparaging terms by Tambiah in his book (1992 p. 85).

Prins Gunasekere's letter to Tambiah, with copies to the president of Harvard University, the chairman of the Anthropology Department at Harvard University, and others, was reproduced in a full-page article in the largest-circulation English-language paper in Sri Lanka, the *Sunday Observer* ([Colombo] 16 January 1994 p. 11). In addition, the letter sent by Gunasekere to the president and council members of the American Anthropological Association, after he failed to get a response to his first letter, and the "Statement of Ethics" issued by the Council of the American Anthropological Association were also published in the newspaper (American Anthropological Association 1990).

Gunasekere's letters pointed out truly unforgivable errors of fact in Tambiah's book, which often depicted the MSV as just the opposite of what it actually stood for. Gunasekere's correspondence also alleged that Tambiah's book was a transgression of the established ethics of anthropology as detailed by the American Anthropological Association, and showed the exact points where Tambiah had transgressed the code.

Apparently he did not receive a reply from Tambiah, Harvard, or the American Anthropological Association. As this incident is a telling indicator of the state of Sri Lankan anthropology itself, I offer below extracts from Gunasekere's article as published in the newspaper. I reproduce only Gunasekere's charges, leaving out, for reasons of space, the many factual errors that he points out. Here are some of Gunasekere's charges:

> I write to protest against the gross inaccuracies of fact, false and malicious statements and innuendos contained [in] *Buddhism Betrayed?* . . . If I were to enumerate all instances where your diachronic recital of events has failed to include the most obvious, relevant and readily available data that would give a more accurate and realistic picture of the cause of political violence in Sri Lanka, and point to all inaccuracies of fact you have indulged in, this note will be at least half as long as your book! . . . In particular, your portrayal of the Mavbima Surekime Vyaparaya MSV (of which I was the Organizing Secretary) is misleading, unjust and unrelated to actualities.

> . . . That the ideology of the MSV . . . was directed at another suspected enemy—the Catholic Church is false and mischievous. In fact several members of the Catholic clergy spoke at MSV meetings; several MSV public meetings, attended by thousands of enthusiastic Catholics, were held in Catholic [areas].

> . . . You are again economical with the truth when you state that when a banned rally outside the temple was broken up by the police, a student was shot and killed. The rally was not banned, it was not outside the temple, it was not broken up by the police, two persons were shot and killed inside the temple premises, one inside the shrine room, both after the rally was over. The government in its ultra democratic concern for the security of the people, had banned all public meetings that day. The rally referred to was a Labour Day meeting organized largely by students, held inside the temple premises simply because the police did not issue permission for public meetings. The police/state violence against a peaceful May Day Meeting within the temple premises was the subject matter of protracted and public, legal proceedings in the High Court of Colombo: yet your informants have got the facts all wrong.

> . . . Did not your sources tell you that over 20 human rights lawyers were killed by unknown gunmen and over 36 other lawyers fled the country from state death squads during this period? Your methodology . . . is . . . erratic, leading to pseudo scientific generalizations against a singled out com-

munity of people in Sri Lanka—the Sinhala. You ignore the horrendous violence perpetrated by the State on the whole composite community, the majority Sinhala and minority Tamil and the Muslims.

. . . You significantly overlook the unprecedented violence by another section of the community—the exclusively Tamil, LTTE suicide death squads, on the Sinhala and the Muslim communities.

. . . The primary source you acknowledge was incidentally the official government news censor during the period you cover. Need I say more?

. . . I am sending a copy of this letter to the head of your University to initiate an inquiry into possible scientific fraud which undoubtedly your book in many ways is.

. . . Please make amends. (Gunasekere 1996)

I myself, together with Hema Goonatilake, a Buddhist scholar, had written a review of the book in the University of London journal *South Asian Review,* and so was curious about the outcome of Gunasekere's published letter to the Ethics Committee of the American Anthropological Association. I therefore wrote from my New School for Social Studies, New York, address in 1994 a letter of inquiry about the outcome of Gunasekere's complaint to the Ethics Committee, now made very public in the Sri Lankan press, but I received no reply. Later I also telephoned the chairman of the Ethics Committee, who talked to me for more than half an hour but evaded giving a direct answer about Gunasekere's letter. A year later I sent a written reminder, again with no reply. Mystified, in April 1996 I wrote once more by certified mail to the Ethics Committee but still got no reply. So in this silence, I must assume the worst, that not only had Tambiah perhaps transgressed basic academic ethics and norms, but the governing bodies that oversee such issues were themselves silent bystanders. It is my strong belief that if such a transgression had occurred in natural science research at Harvard, it would have been subject to an inquiry with regard to scientific fraud.

Tambiah's controversy did not end there. The book was eventually banned by a new government in which some of the author's key supporters were either senior officials or to which they were formal or informal advisors. Recalling that they had publicly objected when there was no cry for a ban, I wrote a long newspaper article asking that the ban be lifted and, furthermore, that the book be translated into Sinhala to encourage a better dialogue (Goonatilake, Susantha, 1997). I also mentioned that lifting the ban would be easy because the key signatories who earlier had advocated no ban were now key advisors to the government. The ban remained in place.

But Tambiah's brand of peculiar anthropology spun further on.

Tambiah relates in his first book how he began to write on the ethnic conflict in Sri Lanka, resulting ultimately in his three books on the subject. It is interesting now to recall what exactly he said in that first book about his involvement. He said that in 1958, while he was leading a research team of university undergraduates in a sociological study of peasant colonization in Gal Oya, ethnic riots unexpectedly broke out around him. "And at Amparai, Sinhalese public works laborers went on the rampage in hijacked trucks, attacking Tamil shopkeepers and Tamil peasant colonists. My students, very solicitous for my safety, insisted that I stay behind closed doors while they stood guard. And I was later hidden in a truck and spirited out of the valley to Batticaloa, a safe Tamil area." This experience traumatized him; it was the first time the ethnic division was so directly thrust into his life (1986 p. 137).

But Tambiah, in a comment tucked away in a footnote to his third book, makes an interesting revisionist statement on this breathtaking incident. He says that "it was mistakenly stated in my book *Sri Lanka Ethnic Fratricide and the Dismantling of Democracy* (1986) that I and the students were caught up in the Gal Oya riots" (1996 p. 351, n. 2). He now admits that this entire incident, replete with detailed ethnography, as it affected him personally, was not true. That is, he had mistakenly invented the whole incident in which he was allegedly personally involved. (The reason for this backtracking I cannot fathom, except to surmise that one of his students had surfaced and had exposed the lie either publicly or privately to Tambiah.) If this is how Tambiah "presents" alleged observation of incidents in which he is directly involved, one can well imagine what he does with less immediate events.

In our trail of the social context of our anthropologists, we have traced their view of each other, their impact on other writers, their impact on the international scene, and their impact on Sri Lankan debates. We have shown how their faulty constructions have wound their way through these different social domains. But this does not exhaust the social context of Sri Lankan anthropology. An important consideration remains. This is the set of individuals and institutions in Sri Lanka that provide encouragement for our authors, generally approve of their findings, provide the authors with "facts" and other support, and generally constitute an intermediary social layer between these authors and Sri Lankan reality. It is this intermediary layer that we now have to examine.

CHAPTER 12

■

Key Players in a Cognitive Matrix

PRIOR STUDIES, SOURCES, GUIDES, AND PEERS

There is an easily recognizable intermediary social layer of individuals and institutions that acts as a cushion between our authors and the Sri Lankan population at large. These individuals and institutions take the role that a truly organic interaction between anthropology and local academia should take. In the exercise below, I present their views not just for "colorful facts and detail" (GombObey 1988 p. xi), or as a "charge to the text" (meaning to dramatize the text; Tambiah 1992 p. xvii), but as necessary detail to identify anthropologically this filtering group.

In his first book Kapferer describes the social scientists who were helpful to him. He gives the name of Michael Roberts as a person who was extremely useful to his work (Kapferer 1991 p. xxx). Malsiri Dias also helped him (Kapferer 1991 p. xxviii). In his second book Kapferer identifies the Sri Lankans who discussed the ethnic situation with him and who he says "continue to do so." They are Mahen Vaithyianathan, Newton Gunasinghe, I. V. Edirisinghe, Charles Abeysekere, Kumari Jayawardena, and Leslie Gunawardene. Michael Roberts, another Sri Lankan, was also, as in the first book, "invaluable" to Kapferer (1998 p. xiv). Among those whom Kapferer acknowledges in the third book as being useful are Mahen Vaithianathan, who constantly contributed in the way of discussion; Newton Gunasinghe, I. V. Edirisinghe, and Niloo Abeyeratne, who "reacted usefully" to his arguments; and S. J. Tambiah, who was "always supportive" (1997 p. xviii).

Tambiah identifies those who helped him by reading the manuscript as well as those whose work he used. They include the Committee for Rational Development (CRD) and its Radhika Coomaraswamy (Tambiah 1986 pp. xi, 147–167), H. L. Seneviratne, Devanesan Nesiah, A. J. Wilson, G. Obeyesekere, and Jehan Perera (1986 p. xi). As key informants for the other book, *Buddhism Betrayed?*, he identifies Kumari Jayawardena and Sarath Amunugama.

Obeyesekere and Gombrich do not provide much information on their methodology and academic contacts, except that Obeyesekere has had close ties with the International Center for Ethnic Studies, Colombo (ICES), and the Social Scientists' Association (SSA), for example publishing in SSA (Obeyesekere 1988).

Many of the names that the authors cite are also members of organizations that constitute the foreign-funded private sector—the so-called "NGO" sector—in Sri Lankan academia. Examples of the latter are the Committee for Rational Development (CRD), the Marga Institute, the Social Scientists Association (SSA), and the International Center for Ethnic Studies, Colombo (ICES). Radhika Coomaraswamy, Reggie Siriwardene, and Newton Gunasinghe are members of CRD. Charles Abeysekera, Michael Roberts, Radhika Coomaraswamy, Devanesan Nesiah, and Jehan Perera have all been closely associated with Marga. Radhika Coomaraswamy and Reggie Siriwardene are key members of ICES, while Uyangoda, Charles Abeysekera, and Newton Gunasinghe have been closely associated with it. Newton Gunasinghe, I. V. Edirisinghe, Charles Abeysekera, Kumari Jayawardena, and Leslie Gunawardene are members of SSA. The membership of these organizations often overlapped, especially the leading lights. The extent of this interlocking in 1987, for example, is revealed in the fact that the same person, Charles Abeysekera, was president of the Movement for Inter Racial Justice (MIRJE), president of the Committee for the Release of Political Prisoners (CROPP), and coordinator of the Social Scientists Association; he was also at one time the chief researcher at the Center for Society and Religion and the key researcher for the Marga Institute. So what appeared to be different voices often came from the same mouth.

These foreign-funded NGOs, which form a partial filtering screen for our anthropologists, have taken very explicit anti-national positions. Thus, contrary to the popular outcry against the loss of sovereignty of the country, these foreign-funded NGOs were also about the only group, apart from the Indians themselves, to back the then government on the so-called "Peace Accord" imposed by the Indians in 1987. With hindsight we now know, because of subsequent statements by J. R. Jayawardene, then president of Sri Lanka (see, for example, the Sunday *Lankadeepa*, 7 January 1996), that the then UNP government itself was not in favor of the accord. The government's arms had been twisted by the Indians, literally under the pressure of gunboats and overflying aircraft, to accept the accord. But the leading lights in the following organizations backed the accord very eagerly: the Center for Society and Religion, the Social Scientists Association, the International Center for Ethnic Studies (Colombo), the Committee for Rational Development, the Marga Insti-

tute, MIRJE, and CROPP. Our filtering group had overlapping membership in all of them.

Several of the key figures in our filtering net publicly praised the ac-
cord. The signatories to a statement welcoming it included Gananath
Obeyesekere, Radhika Coomaraswamy, Charles Abeysekera, Kumari
Jayawardena, Carlo Fonseka, H. L. Seneviratne, Newton Gunasinghe, and
Sunil Bastian. This was in addition to statements they issued through
their organizations.

Some of them made revealing statements extolling this invasive and
sovereignty-eroding accord. Charles Abeysekera decried those who opposed it as "chauvinists" (*Sunday Times* [Colombo], 3 August 1987). The
Committee for Rational Development (of Radhika Coomaraswamy and
Reggie Siriwardene stated that "for a long time now, we Sri Lankans have
refused to accept the realities of our geo-political situation" (Gunatilleke
1987), implying the need to bow to Indian pressure. Godfrey Gunatilleke
of Marga commented implicitly on the need to manage and control public opinion when he said, "leaders who are confronted with this problem
would have to . . . go forward with a solution which they thought was the
most feasible one, *and then* attempt to mobilize support for its wider acceptance and for its implementation" (Gunatilleke 1987). Translated into
less obscure language, what this meant, in effect, was "ignore the wishes
of the people," impose a "solution," and ram it down their throats by
propaganda and other means.

This group's support for the erosion of sovereignty in the country was
not an isolated instance restricted to the Indian Accord. Several members
of the group continued to invite foreign intervention. Thus, in another of
the appeals published by some members of the group, they invited either
the neighboring countries in the form of the South Asian Association of
Regional Cooperation (SAARC) or the United Nations (UN) to intervene in the country on lines suggested by them. The signatories also included Gananath Obeyesekere, S. J. Tambiah, Carlo Fonseka, and Qadri
Ismail. Many have supported, directly and indirectly, some of the separatist propaganda, specially the traditional homelands hoax of the Tamils. Thus according to the *Tamil Voice* (Summer 1995), the Tiger organ
in the United States, some members of this group, including MIRJE—
another organization in which Charles Abeysekera had a leadership role
—accepted the Tamil homelands hoax. And when government troops
captured land held by the Tigers, some in this group bemoaned it. Thus
on 4 December 1995, Radhika Coomaraswamy was reported in a Reuters
dispatch from Colombo, reproduced in the *Island*, regretting the government capture of Jaffna from the Tigers.

Public attitudes toward the foreign-funded NGOs, however, have been very negative. Real civil society was at odds with them. As an ethnically Tamil journalist, Periathamby Rajanayagam, editor of the *Tamil Times,* put it: such "NGOs should not be expected to provide the basis for broad-based representative groups on issues . . . because the NGOs are small and have a history of taking up positions for which there was little popular support" (quoted in Jayaweera 1990 p. 127).

Newspaper articles have criticized and lampooned them. A series of detailed articles by Sisira Paranavithana called them "Nameboard Organizations," shells empty of members, restricted to high-sounding names. These attitudes were dramatically illustrated when these foreign-funded NGOs met with their foreign supporters at a tourist resort and were attacked by a large crowd of irate villagers. However, this example of people's power over the NGOs ended on an ominous note, with a statement by the foreign head of these NGOs. (The local leader of the NGOs was Charles Abeysekera.) The foreign head issued a threat. "[The incident] had sent shock waves through the entire NGO community and could have grave consequences, both within Sri Lanka and abroad. It was a stigma that must urgently and publicly be removed" (*Island,* Sunday 19 November 1995 p. 9). It was a direct warning.

An anthropological journey through the published attitudes of some of these individuals and groups is instructive in delineating the sociology of Sri Lankan anthropology.

MARGA: "FOR ALL SEASONS"

A key foreign-funded NGO that has acted as an indirect clearinghouse for our filtering matrix is the Marga Institute. Marga's leadership has supported several of the anti-sovereignty interventions in the country, including the Indian Accord. Marga is a private company formed on the initiative of a retired government bureaucrat, Godfrey Gunatilleke. It has done some unobjectionable work; for example, in its early years it translated some foreign-language books. The rest of its work is generally humdrum. One of its funders, the Swedish aid agency SAREC, noted that the funding agency was "struck by the general impression of most documents [of Marga] being rather descriptive and/or policy oriented": that is, the studies were hardly remarkable (Thornstrom 1986 p. 44).

A convenient way to see the real thinking behind Marga is by way of a travelogue on Sri Lanka written by the late Caribbean novelist and essayist Shiva Naipaul, in which he records a remarkable and insightful encounter with a Gunatilleke, easily identifiable as Godfrey, the founder and head of Marga (Naipaul 1987).

Naipaul observes Godfrey Gunatilleke seeking sanctuary behind his bureaucrat's desk and soon realizes that he will "get nothing of intrinsic value out of him." For Naipaul, Godfrey Gunatilleke was "not [an] unfamiliar type." He had met many such "touchy mandarins" in other poor countries. Yet Naipaul persists and continues his discussion. He notes that the head of Marga was both a supporter of the then [antidemocratic] government and its policies, and so could be labeled rightwing. But he had also lavished praise on the Soviet dictatorial system. Naipaul calls him bluntly "a man for all seasons" (1987 p. 88).

Like some other mandarins in similar poor country situations, Godfrey Gunatilleke admits that he "spends half my life in airports," going from one conference to another presenting "papers" (quotation marks in the original). (On a visit to Marga in the eighties, I saw dramatic confirmation of this. There was a branch of the travel agency Thomas Cook at Marga.) Naipaul mentions that such mandarins keep themselves well-supplied with choice duty-free liquor bought on their way home. He has read some of this "paper" genre and finds it trite, not describing anything recognizable about the reality of the worlds portrayed. These "papers," Naipaul says, delineate "fairy realms of diagnosis, prognostication and prescription. . . . [T]hey inhabit a fourth dimension of reality . . . a Fourth World clamped down on the Third" (1987 p. 88). Naipaul further says that "fine names" are used to "justify this counterfeit" (p. 89).

Soon Naipaul grows "weary of the man" (1987 p. 91). He wonders at the "chimerical constructions" that Godfrey Gunatilleke must be displaying on the international conference circuit. Naipaul asks "how was it possible for him [Godfrey Gunatilleke] to take himself seriously . . . and did the principle of self interest necessarily have to be so blind . . . necessarily have to coexist with delusion and deception" (p. 93)? At one stage of the discussion Naipaul is so dumbfounded that he is left in "almost open-mouthed astonishment" (p. 92). Naipaul then falls silent.

A contrast to Godfrey Gunatilleke is a Sinhala-language writer, Tissa, whom Naipaul meets. There is no doubt from Naipaul's description that poor, shabby Tissa is a much better intellectual and observer of the local scene than Godfrey Gunatilleke is or, given the temperament and attitudes described by Naipaul, can ever hope to be.

KUMARI JAYAWARDENA AND THE SSA

Kumari Jayawardena is a nodal player with Charles Abeysekera in the SSA and has close personal ties with almost all the other players in our filtering matrix. Kapferer also identifies her as a key figure. Tambiah cites her as an informant. As a key figure in the SSA, she has published Gananath Obeyesekere's work. She has in turn also quoted Obeyesekere's *Buddhism Transformed* affirmatively (Jayawardena 1992).

(I should mention that I was a founding member of the SSA, but I have had no contact with it since its first few years because of its serious organizational, financial, and academic shortcomings, which, as a member of several transparent national organizations, I found unbelievable and unbearable. From my experience, I found that it had agendas of its own, including its own brand of very peculiar internal democracy, and a lack of both financial accountability and open discussion among its members. The only open general meeting of its members after its formation, according to the information I have been able to gather, went on until the early hours of the morning amid serious charges of improprieties, including considerable financial shortfalls.)

It is instructive to explore Kumari Jayawardena's positions.

She, as we have already noted, provided the mischievous attitude toward the Buddhist revival that fed Tambiah. Elsewhere, trying to give only an economistic gloss on it, she has played the revival basically as a conflict between, on the one hand, weak, incipient local capital supporting the nationalistic movement, and, on the other, external capital, British (for the larger infusions of capital) and Indian (for the lesser capital). She says that it "was during this period that [Sinhalese] communalism took on its modern form" (Jayawardena 1987 pp. 19–25). She gives a host of reasons for this, including the revival of an early mythical history that describes the alleged arrival of the North Indian prince Vijaya, the alleged visits of the Buddha to Sri Lanka, the emphasis on Sinhalese history and the insular view as the Sinhalese were threatened by external forces, an alleged Aryan myth of the European Hitlerian variety, the new discovery of ancient Sinhalese cities, and the lack of rationality among the nationalists as Sinhalese capital was not associated with industrialization (1987 pp. 19–25).

But such constructions were far from the truth.

The early history was not a recent invention but was continuously present over the millennia in the Sinhalese imagination. Awareness of the alleged visits by the Buddha was, again, not new. The sites of these visits were included in the sixteen necessary pilgrimage sites continuously visited for more than 2,000 years. "Aryan" was meant not in the Hitlerian sense, but in the original Hindu-Buddhistic sense, meaning noble. Buddhist reformers such as Anagarika Dharmapala in fact applied the appellation "Aryan" to Madras Tamils. In the same issue of the journal in which Jayawardena writes her accusations, a Tamil, Kailasapathy, describes nationalist developments among Tamils in India and Sri Lanka, in reference to the Hindu revivalist "Arya Samaj," developments which strongly influenced Sri Lankan Tamils (1987).

Instead of being insular, those associated with the Buddhist revival were, as we have seen, men of high learning possessing a cosmopolitan nature, as noted by their European colleagues. As for rationality, we have seen in Chapter 2 how key Buddhist ideas were in fact deeply resonant with the emerging philosophical views of the new scientific world. We mentioned also a host of philosophers, makers of the 19th- and 20th-century Western consciousness, who were partial to Buddhism. Instead of being out of tune with industrialization, the leading Buddhist reformer, Dharmapala, was a strong advocate of industrialization and science, asking Sri Lankans to emulate Japan and America. Furthermore, he took the lead in visiting factories and industrial schools in the West and attempted to establish similar schools in Sri Lanka. In contrast, those Theosophist Westerners such as Madame Blavatsky who came to Sri Lanka and were associated with the Buddhist revival were noted irrationalists.

But Jayawardena herself makes a retreat from this excursion to rationalism and science and becomes the chief advisor to a book (*The Unmaking of the Nation*) with an alleged post-rationalist, postmodern methodology. Now postmodernism and deconstruction, one should note, have also had their share of favorable comparison with Buddhism. A flavor of these comparisons is seen in recent articles in the journal *Philosophy East and West*, with titles such as "Nagarjuna and Deconstruction," "Indra's Postmodern Net," "Speech versus Writing in Derrida and Bhartrhari," and "Paramartha and Modern Constructivists on Mysticism: Epistemological Monomorphism vs. Duomorphism" (Mabbett 1995 pp. 203–225; Loy 1993 pp. 481–510; Coward 1991 pp. 141–162; Forman 1989 pp. 393–415). (If it seems strange that Buddhist philosophy was associated with the growth of both modernism and rationality, as well as with postmodernism, one should note that this congeniality is due to Buddhism's denial of an abiding substance, or self, and an emphasis on process and impermanence.)

Jayawardena also mentions that Sinhala Buddhist ideology developed only on communal lines and did not develop into a progressive, anticolonial movement. This is a gross travesty. The two anti-British revolts that she mentions in the article, of 1818 and 1848, both had monks in leading roles, a fact she herself had acknowledged elsewhere (Jayawardena 1979a pp. 16–18). She had also mentioned on an earlier occasion that the leaders of the independence movement *all* came out of Buddhist schools that were direct creations of the Buddhist revival. Similarly, the Sri Lankan left-wing movement itself had emerged from this stratum educated in

Buddhist schools. The strikes that heralded the trade union movement, as Jayawardena had likewise mentioned earlier, all had links with the Buddhist revival (Jayawardena 1979b pp. 10–11). The leading revivalists, Dharmapala and Harischandra, she mentioned, had helped both financially and organizationally in these strikes (Jayawardena 1979b pp. 10–11). Later this Buddhist movement would make its own unilateral declaration of independence.

An article by Jayawardena claiming that there was no anticolonialism in Sri Lanka appeared in the journal *Seminar*'s special issue on the "Indian Accord," the Indian incursion into Sri Lanka (1987). But the article neither makes reference to this Indian incursion, which she had publicly welcomed, nor mentions that there had been a prior, major Indian conspiracy to subvert the country. And while Jayawardena blamed all the communal tensions in the country on Sinhalese alone, two of the Tamil writers in the same issue in fact described details of Tamil racism (Kailasapathy 1987; Coomaraswamy 1987).

The 1987 Accord evoked countrywide opposition and a JVP-led revolt. The JVP had their own multicultural prescriptions for the ethnic issue, described in a nearly 300-page book (JVP 1986 pp. 239–242). Jayawardena features heavily in it.

She is accused in the book of distorting the JVP view on the ethnic question by mischievously adding the word "Sinhala" whenever the JVP referred to "Jathiya." In Sinhala, as well as most South Asian languages, "Jathiya" could stand for caste, "race," or nation. In Jayawardena's hands, when the JVP wrote "nation" (meaning Sri Lanka) it had become "Sinhala race" (ibid.).

The agenda of Jayawardena and the SSA is explicitly presented in a recent book by the SSA, titled *Unmaking the Nation* (Ismail and Jeganathan, eds. 1995). Jayawardena had been its guide "at every stage" (1995 p. 9). The editors stated openly, " . . . we suspect the nation," and so their project is evidently to break up the Sri Lanka nation, hence coinciding with the separatist project. Jeganathan's chapter, "Authorizing History, Ordering Land: The Conquest of Anuradhapura" (Jeganathan 1995), both denigrates the nationalist renaissance in Sri Lanka and, worse, denies the historical importance and facticity of Anuradhapura, the ancient Sinhalese capital (5th century B.C.–1100 B.C.). The chapter places colonialists as "discoverers" of Anuradhapura and nationalists as villains because they used Anuradhapura for anticolonial projects. The author's special targets are the anticolonialists Harischandra and Dharmapala. He lists Benedict Anderson—the scholar who popularized the expression "imagined communities"—as a person who commented on the master's thesis on which this chapter is based (p. 131). When I asked Anderson in a taped discussion whether he had seen Jeganathan or his thesis, he could not remember such a person. After prodding, he said it might have been a student he remembered meeting once for, at the most, a total of fifteen minutes.

David Scott (1995), a non–Sri Lankan, also has a contribution in *Unmaking,* titled "Dehistorizing History," another attack on the local heritage. In it he claims that "Sinhalese" was an appellation given to the people of the country, "only" after the 12th century. This is the farcical misreading of another SSA member, R. A. L. H. Gunawardene. Scott refers to only one local counter-voice to Gunawardene, namely, K. N. O. Dharmadasa, ignoring the barrage of counter-voices who laughed at Gunawardene. Significant for Scott's highly skewed view are some of the persons to whom he acknowledges his "principal debt" (p. 24) One is Reggie Siriwardene, who has openly admitted a lack of knowledge of the main local religion, Buddhism (Siriwardena 1979). As again illustrative of the interlocking networks among foreign-funded academic NGOs, one should note that Scott did this work for the SSA as a visiting fellow at the International Center for Ethnic Studies (Colombo), where the paper was first presented.

Another contributor to *Unmaking* is P. L. de Silva, who was earlier convicted of waging a separatist war. Although his present article is on the Tigers, his major prior academic work was an M.A. thesis at the Institute of Social Studies, The Hague, on "Sinhala-Buddhist Chauvinism" (1992). This thesis (which I have read), presented to a Dutch academic audience unfamiliar with the details of Sri Lanka, gives a completely distorted view of Sri Lankan reality—indirectly justifying the separatist armed stand its author took earlier.

The attitude and methodology of Jayawardena are seen again in *Embodied Violence: Communalizing Women's Sexuality in South Asia* (Jayawardena and de Alwis, eds. 1996), on communal tensions and women's sexuality in South Asia. Here Jayawardena speaks of the "alarming spread of fundamentalism" among Sinhalese Buddhists and describes the Sri Lankan ethnic conflict as only "between Tamils and Sinhala Buddhists" (p. x). She further says that (a) for Sinhala Buddhists the ideal woman is a *pancha kalyani* (having the five attributes of physical beauty) (p. xi); (b) the spread of modern education, demand for women's rights, and entry of women into the professions led to the denunciation of these women as foreign-influenced (p. xiv); and (c) Sinhala Buddhist chauvinists had double standards, which from the late 1970s were being exposed by the feminists (p. xiv).

But nowhere have the large majority of Sinhala Buddhists acted in the way the book ascribes to them. In the first place, *pancha kalyani,* which the authors refer to, is only an ideal of female beauty, not of women as such. In fact, the advances for women in Sri Lanka are in strong contrast to the rest of the South Asian region. Apart from the general effects of the gender-equal Buddhist cultural background, gender equality in Sri Lanka came largely through free compulsory education brought about by the agitation of Buddhist monks. The impact of the "feminist movement" (there was no such mass movement) was marginal; at most they kept up with the educational system and may have helped open the doors as the educated females climbed the ladder.

Hema Goonatilake did a detailed survey in the 1980s of the newspaper responses to the "movement" of which she was a part (1981 p. 982). One telling conclusion was that the stronger attacks came from the English-language press, the Sinhala press being, in contrast, matter-of-fact and less ideological. The goals of equality as such were never questioned in the Sinhala-language media.

Embodied Violence also contains two individual chapters on Sinhalese Buddhism, which again carry distorted images, and both of which Jayawardena endorses. In one, the ethnic war is again designated as one of "a Sinhala Buddhist State against the Tamil community and quasi-LTTE state." Further, it is argued that the Sinhalese view themselves as having "Aryan purity" and have been moving toward a "pure homogeneous ethnic, or racial group consciousness" (de Mel 1996 pp. 168–169). These were again mechanical repetitions of the distortions that we have already identified, drawn broadly from Jayawardena's attitudes. (The persons acknowledged in this chapter are, significantly, Jayadeva Uyangoda, P. Jeganathan, and Qadri Ismail, all members of the interlocking filtering group.)

The second chapter, "Sexuality in the Field of Vision: The Discursive Clothing of the Sigiriya Frescoes" (de Alwis 1996 pp. 89–113), is a Eurocentric tract about the "discovery" of the Sigiriya frescos, which again tries to make out the ruined cities to be only part of an imagined history constructed primarily through colonial discoveries. The chapter distorts the reformer Dharmapala's request for those women wearing European dress to adopt the common dress of South Asia, the saree. The anticolonial protest is distorted, and the request is considered only an attempt to "clothe the female body" (de Alwis 1996 p. 104). Dharmapala's anticolonialism is downgraded and considered almost a disease. Also forgotten in the process are Dharmapala's efforts toward the equality of women, as in his advocating the resurrection of the Buddhist order of nuns, which had died out in Sri Lanka in the 11th century.

If these neocolonial positions of Kumari Jayawardena sound strange, we should note one other salient feature in discussing her overtly anti-Sinhala rhetoric. It was her husband, Lal Jayawardena, who commissioned Tambiah's book *Buddhism Betrayed?*, which has an underlying anti-Sinhala tone to it. He also wrote a foreword to the book in which he bemoaned the alleged Sinhala Buddhism of the JVP. The father of Lal Jayawardena, however, is well-known as having proposed an exclusivist Buddhist international bank and later launched a local private Sinhala Buddhist–oriented bank, the Sampath Bank. From all accounts, the son was also part owner of this bank, and so indirectly Kumari Jayawardena as a family member was a beneficiary of the bank, which was popularly identified with a Buddhist and "sons of the soil" image. Kumari Jayawardena's father, A. P. de Zoysa, was in turn a Sinhala Buddhist nationalist, having founded and campaigned as a member of the Buddhist Republican Party (de Silva, G. P. S., 1979 p. 75), a Sinhalese-Buddhist party. Kumari Jayawardena's mother was British and, from all accounts—I myself met her a few times—was a kind, rational woman, not at all anti-Sinhala. Although the actions of the parents and parents-in-law cannot be blamed on the children, it is significant that Kumari Jayawardena in her anti–Sinhala Buddhist rhetoric does not refer to these particular well-known Sinhala Buddhist actions in her own family.

CHARLES ABEYSEKERA: SSA

Charles Abeysekera directly and indirectly figures as a member and key gatekeeper in many of the organizations referred to earlier. Abeysekera also co-edits the foreign-funded political journal *Pravada*. He reveals a very instructive public character. Let me describe it using the published record.

In the early 1970s, Abeysekera, as chairman of the state-owned Steel Corporation, was the subject of a series of strikes directed against him for alleged corruption. He was subsequently locked out of the factory for eight months by irate workers demanding his removal. This was the first time that workers in Sri Lanka had physically forced out an executive. Later he was sacked ("Unions Want Officers Removed," *Daily News*, 26 June 1970; "Steel Corp Men Storm Ministry," *Observer*, 29 June 1970). But the image he now presents is different.

Thus, in the respectable *Index on Censorship* (1992), Abeysekera introduces himself as a "sociologist," although he has no sociological training, and as "a retired civil servant," although he was "retired" for wrongdoing. His *Index* article referred to one of his articles being shortened before being published in a state-owned newspaper, the *Sunday Observer,* among other reasons, for considerations of space. This trivial incident was not significant enough to be included in the *Index.* Regular editorial cuts are made in newspapers, both state and otherwise, usually for space and stylistic reasons. The same fate has befallen me several times. (Worse, on complaints made by a foreign-funded NGO, I was suspended for one year from my job as the founding editor of a journal, *Economic Review,* for allegedly insulting the Buddha.)

The list of contributors to Abeysekera's journal *Pravada* reads like a who's who of our interconnected interpretative web, with names such as Uyangoda, Kumari Jayawardena, Sunil Bastian, and Coomaraswamy (*Pravada* February 1992, May 1992). *Pravada* is notorious for its many anti–Sinhala Buddhist articles. But instances critical of Tamil, or of the South Indian designs on Sri Lanka for a Greater Eelam, or of the LTTE's Indian connections are hardly found. Abeysekera repeated in *Pravada* Jayawardena's invention that the Buddhist reformer Dharmapala "generated a strong social ideology of ethnic exclusivity" (Abeysekera 1992 p. 21). Further, Abeysekera on several occasions has taken a strong neocolonial stand on issues of sovereignty. Thus, he supported the Indian incursion into the country (Abeysekera 1987) and supported the separatist traditional homelands hoax (*Tamil Voice,* Fall 1995).

COOMARASWAMY:
MODERNIST AND POSTMODERNIST

Radhika Coomaraswamy and her Committee for Rational Development (CRD) and International Center for Ethnic Studies (Colombo) (ICES) are used by Tambiah and Obeyesekere. Kapferer, who evokes a post-rational, postmodernist epistemology, also takes the CRD as authoritative. Both the CRD and ICES (Colombo) have welcomed foreign interference. Some of Kapferer's obvious mistakes, such as his statement that Dutugemunu was found to have fought with Sinhalese "kings" (actually, not with kings but with a prince, his brother) as well as Tamil "kings" (actually, only one king, Elara) and had allied with Tamil lords in his fight against Elara (untrue), are due to the CRD (Kapferer 1988 p. 219).

Coomaraswamy has revealed herself as having a very uneven sense of right and wrong. I have already referred to her political stands, especially vis-à-vis Sri Lankan sovereignty. Coomaraswamy has distanced herself from LTTE groups pointing out the demeaning life of Tiger women cadres (1997 p. 12). She appears to agree that the so-called traditional homelands of the Tamils were a falsehood (1986). Yet, she says that those who study Sri Lanka's history can be divided into two camps, those who have "a desire for *modern* solutions to contemporary problems of justice and democracy and those who argue from a vantage point of historical right" (ibid. p. 23; emphasis mine). In saying this, Coomaraswamy ignores the point that the false Tamil separatist claim is also the product of allegedly "historical facts."

After the brutal repression of youth by President Premadasa, she was appointed to a Presidential Commission on "youth problems." The commission's findings adduced a variety of reasons for the youth unrest (*Island*, 29, 30, 31 January 1990) but ignored the basic one, namely, that the alleged "youth unrest" was an uprising against the Indian Accord. This accord was welcomed, supported, and legitimized by the very Coomaraswamy who was now appointed to diagnose the cause of the uprising after Premadasa's death squads had dealt with it.

For a key member of the self-styled Committee for Rational Development, which had been wedded to the idea of "rational development," Coomaraswamy has taken a peculiar epistemological turn to postmodernism and so is in the company of Kumari Jayawardena, who made a similar switch. Coomaraswamy recently co-edited a rather humdrum book titled *Introduction to Social Theory* (Coomaraswamy and Wickramasinghe, eds. 1994), which attempts to take a postmodernist view of knowledge. But what she implies in the book is not that, in spite of attempts at objectivity, subjective biases always creep in. She says that in (research) writing, there is a formal "privileging [of] one voice over another" (p. 112). And as an example, she says that "in this course on social theory, we are privileging Western voices over Eastern, modern thinkers over the ancient texts" (Coomaraswamy 1994 p. 112). And, she adds ominously, she privileges *"generally those who interest ICES staff over those who irritate them"* (p. 112, emphasis mine). As an example of exclusiveness, she gives the JVP, which, she says, excludes cosmopolitan persons. Coomaraswamy had on another occasion chastised the JVP as "Ethnopopulist" (Siriwardena and Coomaraswamy 1987). But this new statement goes further.

The allegedly exclusionist attitudes of the JVP have recently been refuted in some very revealing tape recordings of A. J. Ranasinghe, a former minister in the government of President R. Premadasa (Ranasinghe 1996). These recordings show that the JVP, instead of being exclusivist and anti-cosmopolitan, had, in fact, once suggested Radhika Coomaraswamy herself for the presidency of the country.

JAYADEVA UYANGODA: KEY PLAYER

Jayadeva Uyangoda is one of the other key links with several formal and informal positions in different foreign-funded NGOs.

A revealing glimpse of Uyangoda's reliability is seen from a published stricture on him by a senior judge, Alles, who tried the suspects in the 1971 JVP insurrection in which Uyangoda was involved (Alles 1990). Judge Alles's book recalls that Uyangoda, who was to lead 800 schoolchildren and university students in an attack on Colombo, failed to turn up either to lead them or to ask them not to take part in the attack. Uyangoda had left a young boy—as Judge Alles put it—"with the responsibility of performing the impossible task of trying to capture Colombo with about 200 students armed with 75 bombs." The judge was horrified, and he denounced, with "the severest condemnation," "the callous irresponsibility" of Uyangoda (ibid. p. 107). If this behavior is a window into Uyangoda's general attitudes, his other actions place him squarely with other members of the filtering matrix. Thus, in the journal *Serendipity,* Uyangoda gives a platform to Peter Schalk, a Tiger supporter, to falsely claim that a well-known statue found in Jaffna early this century and given to the king of Siam was not a Sinhala statue but a Tamil one (Schalk 1993). *Pravada,* which Uyangoda edits, describes the Buddha as sexually weak (Perera, Ranjith, 1994 pp. 22–28) and repeats the Jayawardena distortions of the Buddhist Renaissance. Uyangoda has also regularly welcomed foreign intervention in the country, including the Indian incursion.

JEHAN PERERA:
SOVEREIGNTY AND DEMOCRACY AT ANY COST

Jehan Perera is a key person who helped Tambiah. Let me illustrate the extent of Jehan Perera's commitment to the laudable anthropological exercise of "looking at the universe . . . through the eyes . . . [of local] actors," which Tambiah advocates (Tambiah 1992 p. 3).

The Indian Accord was seen on the international stage as a crude projection of Indian power. Thus, the British *Guardian* newspaper declared that "India's pact with Sri Lanka is the most infamous contract imposed on a small country—short of military occupation—since the Munich

Agreement of 1938. The Island's ethnic conflict and her relations with India have drawn comparisons with many post-war situations. There are no more striking parallels, however, to the course of events in Sri Lanka than those which preceded the Sudeten-German crisis of the 1930's" (*Guardian* [London], Third World page, 21 August 1987). The London *Evening Standard* said, "India . . . is a colonial power in the region today." The *New York Times* editorialized about "Mr. Gandhi's . . . big-stick diplomacy in Sri Lanka" (quoted in *Lanka Guardian*, 1 March 1994, pp. 260–261). The *Wall Street Journal* described India as "a rogue elephant trampling upon its neighbors" (ibid.).

Jehan Perera was of a different mind. He wrote in the government newspaper, *Ceylon Daily News*, that it was now time "to tell Sri Lankans some hard truths about their Island, its geography, its multi ethnic population and its limitations." He said that any government would now have "to confront the reality of the Indo-Lanka Accord and the presence of the Indian army in the North and East. . . . [They] are unlikely to leave should the Accord be dishonored by Sri Lanka. . . . [Our] governments have been presented with a fait accompli. . . . [They have no] choice but to honor the Accord. Given the Indian presence in Sri Lanka, it would be reckless not to do so" (Perera, Jehan, 1987). This is clearly a man who looks at the world through the eyes of the local actors.

Before the flawed presidential election that followed the uprising after the Indian Accord, several organizations and individuals called for a set of preconditions to make it a fair and free election, to avoid a repetition of earlier malpractices. These preconditions included the removal of the state of emergency, the dissolution of Parliament so that parliamentarians could not use their considerable informal and formal power to unduly influence the election results, the disbanding of paramilitary groups, and the holding of elections under a neutral figure, such as the chief justice. These demands were put forward by, among others, the leading religious dignitaries and organizations, the Organization of Professional Associations—an umbrella organization for more than twenty professions—the senates of several universities, the Federation of University Teachers Associations, many trade unions, and almost all the opposition parties. The election was later boycotted by the JVP, which gave as its reason the nonfulfillment of these preconditions. They "advised" others to do the same, with more than a hint of violence—in fact a definite threat.

The resulting election resulted in a very low poll, with serious allegations of rigging (*Bangkok Post*, 22 December 1988). The result was that the winner, Mr. Premadasa, received only 27 percent of even these disputed votes. This, of course, did not necessarily mean that in a free vote he would not have won. He might have; but the nature of the boycott and the heavy-handed attempts to both impose it and counter it removed much of the legitimacy of the election.

Immediately afterwards, Jehan Perera wrote to the government newspaper, *Ceylon Daily News,* praising the role of the armed forces in the election (1988). He said that the army was "the envy of Asia" as it was fighting for "democracy." He added exultantly, "let us wish the new President well. . . . Let us be proud to be in Sri Lanka and stop looking abroad for countries to emulate or emigrate to" (ibid. p. 10).

And this was during the period when the most intense violations of human rights were occurring in the country, perpetrated by special elements of the armed forces and other death squads, resulting in more than 60,000 disappearances. This was also the period when Obeyesekere lost his driver, Wijedasa, in Sri Lanka to these very same death squads, as poignantly related in the preface to his *Apotheosis of Captain Cook: European Mythmaking in the Pacific.* Our filtering matrix had curious attitudes toward the welfare and voices of our anthropologists' subject matter.

LESLIE GUNAWARDENE AND
THE DISAPPEARING SINHALESE

Leslie Gunawardene has influenced the distorted constructions of Kapferer and Scott through a highly contentious paper, " 'People of the Lion': The Sinhala Identity and Ideology in History and Historiography" (1979 pp. 1–36). Gunawardene's claim is a highly idiosyncratic minority opinion reminiscent of the hallucinatory writings of the archeologist Paranavithana in his dotage. Gunawardene's "thesis" has been roundly rejected by all other historians, being greeted with derision. Many have responded angrily in the newspapers, both English and Sinhalese. These newspaper articles are incidentally more scholarly than, say, Scott's highschoolish essay, which uses Gunawardene's arguments as an anchor. One series, written with scholarly depth, wit, and dismissive sarcasm, is by Mangala Ilangasinghe (1996, 1997, 1998, 1999).

These writers have pointed out the overwhelming evidence, both local and foreign, indicating that the country's inhabitants as well as the language spoken were named Sinhala. This is also evidenced by records in Indian languages—including Tamil—in Chinese and other foreign sources. The oldest epigraphic record to describe the inhabitants of the country as Sinhala comes ironically from a 3rd-century Tamil source in present-day Tamil Nadu, which gives the Tamilized word Eela (the Tamil pronunciation of Sinhala) when it refers to a family from the island, directly stating that the inhabitants of the island were known as Sinhala. In fact, in an act of supreme irony, today's Tamil separatists use the word Sinhala in its Tamilized form of Eelam in describing the whole island.

The pre-Christian *Valahassa Jataka* says that two merchants came to Sihaladipa, the land of the Sinhalese (Weerasinghe 1995 pp. 1–2). A 4th-century inscription at Allahabad of the Emperor Samudragupta also refers to the island as Sainhalaka, land of the Sinhalas. The Greek historians called it Salike—a word derived from Sihala, meaning the land of the Sinhalas. The Roman literati referred to it as Serendivi, the island of the Simhalas (ibid. p. xv). The Romans, in the description of Pliny the Elder (77 A.D.), give the name of the country as Taprobane and its inhabitants as Salike or Salai (Sinhala) (ibid. p. 23). A Sinhalese embassy to the Byzantine court of Emperor Julian in 361 A.D. refers to the country as Seren Devi, a corruption of Sinhaladvip, "island of the Sinhalas" (Guruge 1993 p. 13). Cosmas (6th century A.D.) also noted that Taprobane is known in India as Sieladiba—island of the Sinhalas (ibid.). The Chinese names for the country were Seng-Kia-lo (Simhala, the Kingdom of Lions) or Seih-lan (Simhale) and Simhaladipa (Sri Lanka). And to the Chinese of the 5th century, as well as present-day Chinese, those who live in Lanka were known as Sinhalese (Weerasinghe 1995 pp. viii, 20).

The 9th-century Arab geographer Ibn Khurdab and the 10th-century Arab author of *Ajaib al-Hind,* Ibn Shahriyar, knew that the island was known as Saheelan, another corruption of Sinhala, but they used the more popular corruption, Sarandib, pronounced as either Selendip or Serendip. Other Arab authors, including the authors of the Arabian Nights, used this latter form, the most popular literature on Serendip being found in the adventures of Sindbad the Sailor. The English word "serendipity" is derived from this Arabic word for Sri Lanka, and so literally means "Sinhala-ness" (Guruge 1993 p. 13).

R. A. L. H. Gunawardene, who goes against this overwhelming evidence, is also a professional politician. He was a politburo member of the Sri Lanka Communist Party (CP), for many purposes an appendage of the Soviet party. The Soviets were projected by Gunawardene's Communist Party in Sri Lanka as having solved their ethnic problems. This was in spite of the fact that the Soviets under Stalin deported entire ethnic communities from one part of the then Soviet Union to another, and later the Soviet Union unraveled into warring ethnic groups. Gorbachev's last important foreign policy speech in Vladivostok in the late eighties also referred to Sri Lanka and came out in support of Eelam-type demands such as the traditional homelands hoax. Gorbachev undoubtedly obtained the material from the local CP.

A. J. WILSON: TAMIL PARTISAN

One other person who helped Tambiah is A. J. Wilson. But he is hardly neutral, as far as Sri Lankan politics is considered, especially on the subject of the Sinhalese. He is the son-in-law and sympathetic biographer of S. J. V. Chelvanayagam, who was closely linked to South Indian separatism and was the founder of the Federal Party, which later developed into the separatist TULF. (Kinship alone does not necessarily mean the same political attitudes, although in this case it does. One of Chelvanayagam's sons, Vaseeheran, one of my closest friends, was a man with absolutely no communal bias. Vaseeheran—who died a couple of years ago—also had decided views on his brother-in-law, which now make sense to me years later.)

Wilson's statements supporting separatism appear in the *Tamil Voice,* the organ of the LTTE in the U.S. Thus he is quoted: "the war may take several years for a final decision. . . . [But] the partition of Sri Lanka is already a fact of history" (Wilson, A. J., 1988 p. 4). Wilson was also an active participant in a conference called by the World Federation of Tamils, a front organization of the LTTE. According to its published record, "the Conference was unanimous in its recognition of Velupillai Prabhakaran [the ruthless leader of the LTTE, convicted of murder in India] and the LTTE as the true leaders of the struggle for Tamil Eelam."

TRACKING THE MATRIX EXTERNALLY

Our matrix filters information to the external world indirectly through our four anthropologists. But the members of the matrix spread their disinformation through other organizations they are involved in. Space does not permit me to explore in detail these external expressions of our matrix. But two examples suffice as illustration.

After the massive repression in the south by death squads in the period 1988–1990, key members of this filtering group were also associated with a meeting allegedly on "human rights" that was held in Bangkok in May 1990. Its reverberations are instructive. Members of this Bangkok group included Charles Abeysekera, Kumari Jayawardena, Carlo Fonseka, Fr. Paul Caspersz, Yohan Devananda, Kumar Rupesinghe, and Peter Schalk, some of whom we have already met as members of the filtering matrix.

Other organizers included leading members of MIRJE, CROPP, CRD, ICES, and SSA, all institutional members of our filtering matrix.

The secretaries of this so-called "World Solidarity Forum on Sri Lanka for Justice and Peace" were Yohan Devananda and a Buddhist monk, Baddegama Samitha, both with very interesting backgrounds. Devananda and Samitha were among those few who supported the Indian Accord. Yohan Devananda was a Christian priest, the head of a foreign-funded NGO, Devasarana, which was funded largely by foreign Christian money and operated in an area of almost 100 percent Buddhist population. Baddegama Samitha, although presently a human rights worker, was better known as a chief suspect in the murder of a visitor to Kelaniya University, for which he spent several years in jail awaiting trial, although he was later released because of insufficient evidence. He was later trained by the church in England, from all accounts through funds arranged through Yohan Devananda.

The meeting in Bangkok was severely criticized in Sri Lankan newspapers. The background document circulated at the forum now denounced the accord as one "which largely revolved on the security interests of India" (Bangkok 1 1990 pp. 1–2). Yet it was silent on the fact that almost all the Sri Lankan organizers of the forum were once vociferous and vehement supporters of the accord, which indirectly led to tens of thousands being killed. The background document also blamed the revolt in the South—like the Youth Commission of Radhika Coomaraswamy—on a variety of causes but failed to mention the central one, the uprising against the accord (Bangkok 1 1990 p. 13).

The organizers' general response to Sri Lankan social reality was symptomized by their forbidding the attendance of key human rights activists who wanted to attend this meeting. This included Sri Lanka's best known human rights lawyer at the time, Prins Gunasekera, who had been personally invited by a British human rights activist, Martin Ennals (personal communication from Gunasekera). Gunasekera had filed the largest number of *habeas corpus* applications in the country and was now living as a refugee in London after several of his law partners had been killed by death squads and he himself had been threatened.

The other significant denial of participation was to a monk, the editor of the largest-circulation human rights journal in Sri Lanka, *Vinivida*, who was living as a refugee at the time in Bangkok (personal communication from Gunasiri Thero). The group of monks editing *Vinivida* was created initially out of concern for Tamil victims of the 1983 anti-Tamil riots (referred to earlier in the text). This journal had reported on the death squad activities of the so-called People's Revolutionary Red Army

(PRRA), and the monk had fled to Bangkok. During the state crackdown, the mere possession of this journal was sufficient reason for a security force visit, possible arrest, and disappearance. The temples where the monk editors of the journal resided were often raided (as recorded, for example, in a British Channel 4 TV program, "Dispatches Sri Lanka," July 5, 1990).

The extreme lack of awareness of Sri Lankan reality was again seen in a project proposal for training Buddhist monks, which came informally out of this meeting. Sri Lankan Buddhist monks were to be trained in "Buddhism and Reconciliation" (Bangkok 2 1990). Sri Lankan monks, it was claimed, had "horizons" which had "inevitably narrowed," and they found "it difficult to see beyond the short term" (Bangkok 2). It was implied that the monks' "religion can lead to polarization through righteous fervor or rigid dogmatism" (Bangkok 2). The assumption was that Sri Lankan monks were not capable of internal debate and change, requiring in essence a missionary force from outside so that they "will lose some of their present rigidity of views" (Bangkok 2). The proposal ignored much of the recent history of Sri Lankan monks, even the changes that had occurred since the 1950s, and mischievously assumed that the monks' main concerns were "the survival of a tradition." The aim of the proposed course was "to offer members of the Sri Lanka Sangha a regional and global perspective" (Bangkok 2 p. 7). And this was to be done by "two trainers from Oslo."

This training of monks by the "Oslo missionaries" in 1991 evoked a firestorm in Sri Lanka. The delegation of monks was led by a layman, Raja Dharmapala. A monk, Maduruoya Dhamissara, writing on behalf of thirty other monks who had been taken to this meeting, exposed the events there in a newspaper article. It mentioned that Dharmapala had distorted key facts at the meeting, seeming to address an unseen host, Tamil separatism, and had taken the participants to a local Bangkok separatist office. Dharmapala, who is closely linked to foreign-funded NGOs, has in his foreign-funded news sheet, *Dhammavedi* (1 February 1997), recently viciously attacked both Sri Lankan history and monks, especially singling out the monk Walpola Rahula, who was in the forefront of this country's democratization. In the 1940s, Rahula led social movements, including one that helped usher in free education.

Devasarana, which runs as a thread through these meetings, is informally allied with many of the filtering groups mentioned here. A published record, an internal Devasarana Sinhala-language document of 108 pages titled "Devasarana Evaluation Report," dated December 1993 (Devasarana 1993), is very revealing as to what Devasarana stands for.

The report is an international evaluation of Devasarana by two foreigners and one local. The document is obviously a translation; the original would have been in English.

The need for this "evaluation," according to the report, had been decided on by representatives of Devasarana's aid donors. They are all Christian groups: I.C.C.O. (Netherlands), Christian Aid (U.K.), the Commission on Participation in Development in the World Council of Churches (Switzerland), Bread for the World (Germany), and Christian World Service (New Zealand). The report contains some cryptic hints as to why the need arose for an evaluation. It mentions the effect on "Devasarana: 1989–1990" of the "Reign of Terror and the Organizational Crisis" (Devasarana 1993).

The report says that Devasarana was at that time "increasingly . . . descending into a dangerous area." It says, "Devasarana was attacked by the JVP since it gave refuge to certain groups within its Center." And it says that "this attack was not conducive to the credibility and the public image of Devasarana" (ibid. p. 24). Now anybody would expect a victim of an attack to be received with sympathy and to have his or her credibility and public image enhanced. Victims of the activities of the death squad, PRRA, did find sympathy, as did victims of JVP-associated assassination groups.

There could, however, be a very significant reason for this strange aspect.

"Certain groups" and similar euphemisms had been used for armed groups, including the death squads active at the time. If that is indeed the case, then here may be the explanation for the refusal to allow Prins Gunasekera and the *Vinivida* monk, who had fled PRRA threats, to attend their Bangkok meeting. Devasarana, a staging post for "certain groups," now goes international, with several other members of our filtering group, as a defender of "Justice and Peace" for the country. The links of our filtering group become increasingly "curiouser."

WIDER: EXTERNAL HOST TO THE MATRIX

Another key external link of our filtering matrix was WIDER, the sponsor of Tambiah's book, and which we have referred to earlier. The WIDER Institute was a UN-sponsored academic body supported financially as a prestige project by the Finns. WIDER was headed at the time by Lal Jayawardena, the husband of Kumari Jayawardena. Several other members of our social filter had close links with WIDER. Thus the list of those hired as consultants by WIDER included Stanley Tambiah, Charles Abeysekere, Sunil Bastian, Carlo Fonseka, Newton Gunasinghe, Sitra Managuru, and Jayadeva Uyangoda (personal communication from Tuomao Pietilainen, a reporter for *Helsingin Sanomat;* and *Helsingin Sanomat*).

WIDER itself was embroiled in an international controversy and alleged scandal. A brief overview of that controversy has considerable import for the sociology and social psychology of our social matrix.

The story was broken by *Helsingin Sanomat,* Finland's leading newspaper, and given top billing. The main charge in the controversy, very vehement at times, was against Lal Jayawardena. *Helsingin Sanomat* (Saturday, 6 February 1993, main news page) charged that expensive consultants and wastefulness ate up WIDER'S resources. It said that Lal Jayawardena hired helpers in a particularistic, biased manner, especially from India and his homeland, Sri Lanka. Some were friends of Jayawardena and his wife. Those hired, it said, had ill-defined, often very minor tasks, which brought them large tax-free incomes.

It was alleged that the institute had funded research which had already been half completed before the researchers were hired, and which would have been completed without WIDER. For eight years, WIDER had produced studies that could have been done elsewhere much more cheaply. The institute, the newspaper added, sometimes resembled an embassy more than a research institution. The newspaper asserted that the short history of the WIDER Institute was an exotic story of easy living on aid given by Finns. In the newspaper's eyes, Lal Jayawardena had made WIDER "an independent state in the middle of Helsinki, pretending to suffer from constant shortage of money."

Jayawardena's hirelings, the newspaper charged, included "colourful secretaries, consultants and scholars" who received top fees for vaguely defined tasks. They gave as an example the hiring of Sri Lankan professor of physiology Carlo Fonseka—whom we have already met as part of the filtering matrix—for social science work. Fonseka had received a tax-free monthly salary of tens of thousands of markka for about three years. And, after a few years' work, Fonseka produced a booklet on Sri Lankan society, which consisted of introductory readings on his particular outlook on Sri Lankan society, meant as an introduction for university undergraduates in his country. The cost of the booklet was about one million markka.

Subsequent to this furore, there was an official audit of WIDER by the United Nations (UNIAD 1993). Couched in the usual obtuse UN language, it tended to confirm some of the Finnish allegations.

The picture the Finns present is of a socially unresponsive incestuous group from Sri Lanka helping to produce material of doubtful quality and without organic links with the reality of either its host society, Finland, or its targeted beneficiaries in the developing world. But this incestuous WIDER group overlapped strongly with our filtering matrix. WIDER, as far as its Sri Lankan interests were concerned, was part of our filtering group projected externally to Finland. It filtered facts particularistically and its organizational behavior was reminiscent of many of the questionable acts of this filtering matrix back in Sri Lanka.

IN RETROSPECT

We have looked at some very colorful characters with some very idiosyncratic perspectives. Our anthropologists channel their information to and from their Sri Lankan "victims" partially through this filtering net that forms this identifiable group. As we have now seen, they constitute a very interesting group.

This filtering matrix includes the following:

Jeganathan, a strong anti-national who denies the importance of the ancient city Anuradhapura and its restorer, Harischandra, a greater attack on Anuradhapura than the one the LTTE itself perpetrated in killing pilgrims there; Kumari Jayawardena, who attacked Anagarika Dharmapala, a fountainhead of anti-European Asian nationalism in the 19th century and founder of the world Buddhist Renaissance (Kumari Jayawardena's father and her father-in-law, both strong advocates of Sinhala Buddhist nationalism, being ignored in the process); Charles Abeysekere, who was chased away by angry workers for financial impropriety, reengineering himself to falsify Sri Lankan history; Uyangoda, another falsifier of history, who was admonished by a judge for cowardice and irresponsibility; Radhika Coomaraswamy, who endorses the Indian incursion, indirectly helps legitimize the incursion by denying the reasons for the revolt against it, and distorts both the JVP and social science methodology; Reggie Siriwardene, who admits his ignorance of Buddhism but pronounces on Sinhalese Buddhism; Leslie Gunawardene, for whom even the country of the Sinhalas did not exist; Carlo Fonseka, disgraced publicly in Finland for obtaining large sums of money to publish a small pamphlet on advice to undergraduates; Qadri Ismail, who wants to unmake the nation; P. L. de Silva, who was convicted of an insurrection trying to establish a Tamil state; and Sunil Bastian, who accepts a falsified history.

Some of these have misrepresented the facts; some have fought against Sri Lankan sovereignty; all supported the Indian incursion into the country; many have invited further foreign intervention and often do not seem to see anything good about Sinhala Buddhists. They form a very biased filter to Sri Lankan reality, especially to that of Sinhalese Buddhists, a filter which colonialists of old would have admired. It is a very strange collection for anthropologists to rely on to "observe from within" the Sinhala Buddhists.

These individuals are also key figures in several organizations which collectively hold strong positions against historical fact and Sri Lankan sovereignty. Many of these organizations, however, are not really open. Seemingly in favor of civil society, they are afraid of truly open, democratic politics and open academic discourse. They have never been seen in the open academic bodies in the country that act as clearinghouses for local academic civil society. Seemingly open, their journals reflect a uniform view. They epitomize the social equivalent of the closed mind; in fact, their search for the newly fashionable post-Soviet cliché of "Civil Society"—now fashionable in aid-giving countries—has been embraced by them only within their closed groups. The supreme example was when some members of this filtering group advertised in the local newspapers a seminar they were sponsoring on civil society with the note, "for invitees only." This particular advertising slot in the newspapers is the space in which local academic bodies advertise their lectures for public attendance, this being the whole point in such advertisements. But our "civil society advocates" wanted it known only that they were having this meeting, although it was for private members only. In this, they were keeping to form, projecting privately held beliefs onto the world as public fact. A definable group, they are hardly a reliable or sympathetic guide to Sinhala Buddhists, the subject matter of our four anthropologists.

CHAPTER 13

■

The Anthropology of Sri Lanka at a Dead End

As anthropologists, Kapferer, Obeyesekere, and Gombrich use direct fieldwork at a village level for their results. Tambiah uses indirect means. Tambiah disclaims two of his books as not being strictly academic. But they are published by academic publishers with the academic fig leaf, "not sociology" and "engaged." Yet other academics, including, for example, Kapferer, take them to be truly academic works. Kapferer says of Tambiah that his "understanding of the modern politics of Buddhist states is unsurpassed" (Kapferer 1988 p. 213), and Spencer also approvingly cites Tambiah on the ethnic issue (Spencer 1990 pp. 95, 254), calling Tambiah's second book an "excellent summary" (p. 284, n. 2). Tambiah's more recent book, *Leveling Crowds,* refers in the blurb on its cover to his *Ethnic Fratricide,* giving it normal academic respectability.

But our four authors deliver a highly flawed anthropology, partly derived through their intellectual social matrix. Contradictory views of what constitutes the Sinhalese and what makes them behave emerge through these studies. It is like the old Buddhist story, which every Sinhalese child learns, about blind men trying to describe an elephant. Let me enumerate a few of these contradictory results as our authors survey their target—Sinhalese Buddhists.

According to Kapferer, Sinhalese Buddhists pursue the irrational; according to Gombrich's first study, the rational. Gombrich mentions that *pretas,* gods, and demons are viewed by Sinhalese Buddhists through the lens of Buddhism, and so are looked down upon (Gombrich 1991 pp. 190–194). Buddha warned against such beliefs, and Gombrich's Sinhalese respondents in turn laugh at them. Kapferer, too, admits that the Buddha is at the top of the belief hierarchy, but he deliberately chooses to view the Sinhalese through the worldview of demons, and not through the ideas of the Buddha or of Buddhist monks. Kapferer mentions that demon exorcisms occur mainly among the poor, and are looked down upon by the upper classes (1991 pp. 18, 29). Gombrich, whom Kapferer has read, makes a contrary class observation, namely, that the upper and middle classes believe more in astrology and auspicious practices than the lower classes. Yet, Gombrich finds that those with stronger beliefs in Buddhism believe less in astrology, giving credence to his other observation of Buddhism as emphasizing the rational (Gombrich 1991 pp. 173–174).

When Kapferer considers the contending views of Lewis and Obeyesekere on why women are more afflicted by demon worship, he notes that Lewis's position is difficult either to prove or to disprove (1991 p. 129). This is not an acceptable mode of inquiry from a Popperian position—the approach favored by Gombrich—which rests on criteria of disprovability, of conjecture and refutation. But Gombrich claims his methodology to be rational science, whereas Kapferer rejects scientific rationality. Obeyesekere uses Freudian approaches, while Kapferer scorns them.

Allusions to language drive both Obeyesekere and Kapferer to their studies. "Protest" and "Protestant" drive Obeyesekere; riots being "demonic" drives Kapferer into his grand theory (Kapferer 1988 p. 29). This is a magical explanation of the most primitive (in the derogatory sense of the word) kind, the power of accidental words given explanatory power. Magical words—"Open sesame"—trying to prise open Sri Lankan reality. Others, including Tambiah, and some members of the filtering matrix such as Kumari Jayawardena, have argued that the motivations for the riots came from the followers of Anagarika Dharmapala and their alleged communalism. But Tambiah also subscribes in part to the "Protestant Buddhism" thesis, an allegedly modern social and cultural invention, and so the motivation should come not from "primordial Sinhala Buddhism" as he alleges, but from an American cultural transplant.

Kapferer uses exorcists as theoreticians for the dynamics of Sri Lankan society. Obeyesekere and Gombrich use *Kapuralas*—deity priests—as their "theoreticians of the future" (GombObey 1988 pp. 415, 417). But these two sets of anthropologists come up with contrary results with respect to the dynamics of Sinhalese Buddhist society. Gombrich (1991 p. 150) notes that Sinhalese will change from one specialist to another in search of a cure. Kapferer gives a quasi-mystical explanation for this commonsensical practice, saying that although seemingly plural, for him it shows the opposite—the demonic *is* the illness. Kapferer speaks ill of the *Mahavamsa* (Kapferer 1988 p. 96), and Tambiah is ambivalent about it. Gombrich considers it a work of "considerable excellence" (1991 p. 22). Obeyesekere wants to subject the Sinhalese historical tradition to the same analysis that Malinowski uses for myth (cited in Kapferer 1988 pp. 41–44).

Gombrich finds that the virtues most valued among the Sinhalese are *santa danta*—politeness in the largest sense, and *karunawe*—compassion, kindness. He finds that Sinhalese generosity borders on the incredible, and that monks are very kind, hospitable, and worldly (1991 pp. 311, 379). Tambiah in his first book speaks of the Sinhalese in similar words. Kapferer praises the practitioners of exorcism and the Sinhalese generally for their hospitality (Kapferer 1997 p. xix). But by the end of their books on Sri Lanka, Kapferer and Tambiah paint an opposite picture of the Sinhalese as uncompassionate.

Seager (1995), in his civilizational analysis of the relationship of Buddhism to the West, uses the same idea of social drama of Victor Turner that Kapferer used. But whereas Kapferer used it to study only a microcosm, a cultural outcast of a civilization, Seager uses the technique to explore the large East-West civilizational canvas (1995 p. xxv). This, however, yields some weird echoes. Thus Seager in his civilizational analysis of the World's Parliament of Religions in Chicago acknowledges Tambiah as one who showed him how to appreciate the dynamism of Christian and post-Christian modernity (1995 p. xiii). That is, Tambiah comes out as an advocate of the (Buddhist) East. Seager says appreciatively that Dharmapala was a key Eastern figure at the Parliament. But it was this same Dharmapala whom Tambiah earlier falsely described as an uncharitable propagandist. In 1995, Tambiah apparently wants to ingratiate himself on Dharmapala's side.

The four authors' misconstructions of Sinhala Buddhism, reminiscent of the worst colonial anthropology, have been produced since the 1970s, by which time both colonial anthropology and Sinhala Buddhist nationalism had passed their respective zeniths. They were therefore dated. Further, these false constructions fed the myths of other actors in Sri Lanka's social conflicts. The Sinhalese Buddhist world, however, was not the isolated social pocket of the classical anthropologist. It had never been so. Historically, Sinhalese Buddhists, as we saw in Chapter 2, had a global reach as well as deep philosophical and scientific views on the human condition, that area of discourse which anthropology in its academic cloak pretends to address.

We have shown that the Protestantization thesis is a fatally flawed perspective. And as Prothero points out in his book, the issue is not just one of alleged Protestantization or Americanization of countries such as Sri Lanka but also the reverse—that is, the locals' resistance to attempts at Protestantization and Americanization (1996 p. 11). Further, "the discovery of Buddhism by the West . . . coincided with the rediscovery of Buddhism in Sri Lanka, and the two movements reinforced each other" (Bond 1988 p. 48). The West flowed into the East and the East into the West. So the best way to view the Sinhala Buddhist condition would have been as an East-West civilizational dialogue through which both parties shed their own ethnocentricities.

In depicting a very complex civilizational social entity, what is left unsaid about it is as important as what is said. For example, the assumptions on which Gombrich based his questionnaire for the book, he says, were so complex that if he had sketched them, it would have taken up much space in the book (1991 p. 3). This means that anthropological inquiry into a complex society such as Sri Lanka is only the tip of an iceberg; the unsaid facts and context assumed by the locals in this civilizational entity constitute the hidden parts of the iceberg.

In a complex societal situation, small-group anthropological studies have to be supplemented by a lived experience, wide reading, a sensitivity to the culture, and awareness of a large number of social statistics. But all four of our authors' methodologies, including some drawn from the irrational and using different skewed samples of data, claim to decipher a total society. They then come to different conclusions about the nature of this one society.

Gombrich and Obeyesekere live in Western societies that since the 1960s—that is, since the various authors began their practice of anthropology—have seen much change in their belief systems and practices. These changes in the U.S. and Europe could well be described as Christianity transformed. Because of these changes, some Christian practices are today influenced by Buddhism—for example, the use in the church of Buddhist-derived meditation practices. So, one could explore in the West a Buddhist Christianity, an influence of Buddhist substance rather than form, a contrast to the spurious Protestant Buddhism, which the authors claim is restricted only to a Protestant form. But our Eurocentric authors do not follow this line of reverse influences.

Tambiah, although Sri Lankan in origin, was hardly an insider to Sinhalese culture. He was never a fluent Sinhala speaker, according to the sociologist Dr. Dudley Dissanayake, who in the late 1950s, as a student, acted as interpreter for Tambiah. In the meantime, Tambiah's knowledge undoubtedly deteriorated in his decades outside the country. Tambiah also has a selective memory, ignoring his own early studies in Sri Lanka that documented the over-representation of Tamils in public services and the eviction of the Kandyan peasantry from their homelands due to the establishment of British plantations.

Gombrich and Kapferer are both outsiders to the local culture and language. But Gombrich is a linguist. Yet, as we have seen, he requires help even in translating the contents list of a popular Sinhala book. In Gombrich's book there is another indicator of how even a linguist can fail abysmally in the key test of having the minimal understanding of the local language that is essential for anyone making major pronouncements about the country. The preface to his first book, which he dedicates in "gratitude and respect" to his informants, includes a statement written in Sinhala script. It says, *Samadenavahanseta nivan sapa labewa* (1971 p. ix), which translates as "May you all [monks] attain *nibbana*" (the Pali word for nirvana)—a rather odd statement, to say the least, normally made to monks and not to lay persons. This is a gross and fundamental misunderstanding of the local cultural context that no proper linguist, let alone an anthropologist, would make.

We have also seen how the entire edifice of Kapferer is built on perhaps just two persons who believed in the exclusive efficacy of exorcists. We have also seen how haphazardly Obeyesekere and Gombrich went about selecting the oddballs for their study. The four authors also leave out key items. These include national politics (Gombrich and Obeyesekere), the principal socializing agencies such as the schools (all four), the major discourses in the printed literature in this highly literate culture (all four), and scientifically valid local windows into human behavior in the from of Buddhist psychology (all four).

The Buddhist resonance with key Western philosophers, which we saw in Chapter 2, extends also to those who influenced key anthropologists. Thus, all our four anthropologists have evoked Malinowski as part of their intellectual heritage (see Gombrich 1971, 1991 pp. 4, 13; Gombrich and Obeyesekere 1988 pp. 423, 431, 449; Kapferer 1983, 1991 pp. xviii–xix; Kapferer 1988 p. 223; Kapferer 1997 pp. 3, 4, 5, 8, 12, 265, 303; Tambiah 1990 pp. 1, 42–84). Newly found material shows that Malinowski's functionalism had its roots in Mach's positivism (Paluch 1980). If Mach, with his strong resonances with Buddhist thought, was a key influence on Malinowski, then one does not have to go far to find aspects of Buddhist thought resonating with Malinowski's philosophical base. That is, Buddhist "epistemological technology" potentially has uses for even the flawed anthropology of our authors. Buddhism could become a tool for anthropological exploration, not just a subject of exploration.

Gombrich mentions that religion can be studied by psychologists, who vary from social psychologists to behaviorists to psychoanalysts (1991 pp. 1–3). He mentions the importance of Buddhism to psychologists, implying that there are conceptual elements in Buddhism of possible use to psychology. He does not explore this further, even though by the time he was writing the book, there had been many works written on the usefulness of Buddhism to psychology, including the work of his own countryman R. D. Laing.

Anthropology of the type our authors practice clearly has the power to shut them off from observing and recording the everyday Western society around them, especially when it interacts with the East. In this, they are a much lesser breed of ethnographers than the colonial ones, who always compared events that they saw in their exotic lands with situations back in their Western homes—albeit often displaying in the process the arrogant European *Zeitgeist* of the time.

Elementary observation, elementary logic, essential knowledge, and context are all lost sight of by our anthropologists. They have to be contrasted with the more inclusive colonial non-anthropological tracts. The founding fathers in scholarly Western interpretations of South Asia, the likes of William Jones, Max Muller, and Rhys Davids, went about their work fascinated by ideas derived from the region. The 19th-century Western scholars who undertook the difficult task of translating and understanding the ideas of Buddhists treated Sinhalese Buddhist monks as their teachers and equals. This is in strong contrast to our present anthropologists, who either ignore them or treat them with barely concealed contempt. Part of this contrast between sympathetic colonialist and antagonistic postcolonialist lies in the sociology of the present anthropology of Sri Lanka.

THE SOCIAL STRUCTURE OF FORMAL
SRI LANKAN SOCIAL KNOWLEDGE

There are social factors affecting the Sri Lankan knowledge community that may explain the flights of fancy indulged in by our writers on Sri Lanka and their ability to get away with spurious nonsense. Let me explore this social context.

Compared with, say, India, Sri Lanka has near-universal literacy. Yet unlike India, it has a lesser flow of information and resources at the tertiary levels and above—essential for informed debates. This is partly because in several disciplines, university education has for more than a generation been delivered in the national languages of Sinhala and Tamil. This process has democratized access to education but has tended to strongly compartmentalize the knowledge available to the English, Sinhala, and Tamil readership. It has also restricted access to knowledge, largely because the literature in the local languages on current developments and disciplines is very limited and dated. In India, by contrast, debates at the tertiary and post-tertiary level are conducted after exposure to current international debates, largely through the use of English-language works. In Japan and Korea, on the other hand, a flood of translations have kept the local intelligentsia well-informed about developments elsewhere.

In the 1970s, due to a combination of factors, Sri Lankan academia was subject to more restrictions on access to information than perhaps any Western country, even in wartime. Subscriptions to many journals were stopped. Orders for books slowed to a trickle. Certain academic departments were curtailed by "rationalization." The practitioners of one discipline, history, were among the most seriously affected. Historians, many trained at the best universities in the world, had to switch in a hurry to subjects such as anthropology and sociology without specialized training in these fields.

If this is the situation in terms of information inputs in general, there are other contextual factors that skew the knowledge system.

In a Western university milieu, institutional mechanisms exist that are designed to ensure truth (although truth may not always be reached). These are mechanisms such as examination of articles by peers, seminars and conferences of peers, and academic promotions tied to certain criteria, such as publications in refereed journals. In the West, social science findings are also subject to discussion in an informed press, and so indirectly in the society at large; and afterwards, if need be, these findings can be corrected. Such mechanisms are the context within which the academic system works.

Further, in the natural sciences, transgressions such as false data would be immediate grounds for dismissal. If Tambiah had been a natural scientist at Harvard, he probably would have been, especially after the complaint by Prins Gunasekere, subjected to scrutiny for falsifying data, a charge that carries severe penalties, including dismissal. But the forlorn letters of Prins Gunasekere to the American Anthropological Association and Harvard, charging serious lapses, went unacknowledged. The intellectual upheaval that unconfirmed "cold fusion" created in the natural sciences could not occur in anthropology—a subject that deals with intellectually subject peoples.

In an open and organic social science milieu, there are thus two feedback loops that try to promote accuracy of facts and findings. One is in the academic community, and the second lies with the public. In Sri Lanka, in works such as those of our authors, both these feedback processes are lacking. Tambiah, thus, can conveniently ignore his earlier studies in the 1950s on ethnic over-representation of Tamils or on displacement of Sinhalese by the British. He can also change with impunity his positions in his last book without reference to the challenges that his earlier books, especially *Buddhism Betrayed?*, brought about. And Kapferer can, unabashed and unchallenged, totally change his methodological approaches in the four editions of his three books.

Further, none of the groups that the authors quote, including the ICES, CRD, and SSA and their members, are subject to the normal open criteria of science. And others such as Satchi Ponnambalam and Jayarajan, whom Kapferer quotes as authorities, have no academic credibility. There are national structural reasons why marginal groups like these have come to the fore.

A major reason is that Sri Lankan social science research, unlike that in India, has had only lukewarm support from the state, or, in the absence of a significant local bourgeoisie, from local benefactors. Major funding has generally come from external Western donors, largely to private organizations.

By the late 1980s, the university system had approximately 400 persons on staff who were certified capable of independent social research, that is, with graduate degrees. But at the time the last comparative study was carried out, the *total* research money available annually for this social science community was just over $10,000! In contrast, a private company, a so-called NGO—Marga—with a staff of only six with comparable backgrounds, was getting over fifty times that amount from foreign sources (Goonatilake, Susantha, 1990). Hettige in a perceptive essay has described in detail how the growth of such groups outside the university milieu of relative rigor has led to serious distortions in Sri Lankan sociology and anthropology (1997 pp. 85–93). Consequently, essential resources in the form of, say, reading material and access to travel to meet other colleagues are denied to those with the best potential to use them in the highly literate Sri Lankan milieu. The result is that the collective social imagination of those who otherwise would have the training to do social research has been reined in.

There is also no formal financial support for Sri Lankan academics to enable them to travel to each other's meetings within the country. At a time of increased internationalization of the knowledge-creation enterprise on Sri Lanka, the increasing barriers to external travel by Sri Lankan academics create further problems. The average Sri Lankan academic today cannot travel, unlike his Western counterpart (or even the latter's undergraduate student), without what is in effect a difficult-to-obtain entry permit to the accepted discourse. Obtaining entry to the debates depends on travel money and an invitation—often from agenda-setting Western academics. So the international gatekeeper to knowledge becomes a double gatekeeper, in the local company he keeps in and keeps out, a fact easily demonstrated by a simple analysis of the participants in the international conferences on contemporary Sri Lankan conflicts.

But legitimate truth in the globalized world is also formed by the structure of the citation of earlier work. The earlier Sri Lankan anthropologists and sociologists working abroad came to prominence at a time when colonial anthropology was being criticized. None of our anthropologists are known to have taken part in that criticism. Those of Sri Lankan origin among them performed, as it were, an intellectual Uncle Tom function, what some African Americans might have derisively called a "house nigger" function in the global division of knowledge, delivering false over-interpretations for an essentially external audience. The unabashedly neocolonial role is enhanced by the fact that they are or have been resident at influential universities in the West, such as Cambridge (Obeyesekere), Princeton (Obeyesekere), and Harvard (Tambiah). (Gombrich and Kapferer, the two non–Sri Lankans, were at Oxford and London, respectively—again, two influential universities.)

In the meantime, the anticolonial thrust went out of anthropology, and some of the objections were internalized by Western anthropologists, the intellectual heirs to the 1960s social unrest. The Sri Lankan anthropologists of yesteryear, who have now become senior anthropologists in the Western world, have in the meantime largely set the citations that juniors now have to refer to. As is normal in scientific practice, the juniors—often Western graduate students with at most a couple of years' exposure to the complex Sri Lankan reality—now have to lock onto the categories and problems set by their predecessors.

Nor has the role of over-interpretive categories changed in the later writings. These include some of the Sri Lankan writings that come from very mechanical Marxian approaches. None of these reveal the significant stand against cultural colonialism that was part of the New Left elsewhere. The dead weight of dependence is perhaps more apparent in this mechanical left than elsewhere. Over the last twenty years, I have observed the Western left increasingly include in its discourses non-Western aspects and developing-country critiques of the West, including at times my own descriptions of the knowledge enterprise. But none of our commentators or their local social matrix have taken that route. In the words of Coomaraswamy, they generally "privilege western academic voices over others." None of these dependent left authors deal seriously with the biggest cultural assault on the Sinhalese and Tamils, which is Western culture. For contemporary Sinhalese (and Tamil) society, it is not print capitalism that is important, as Kapferer has alleged. What is central is the new print and other cultural colonialisms, among which are the writings of our anthropologists.

But there is evidence that (some) other externally based commentators of Sri Lankan origin also engage in this skewed postcolonial Orientalist discourse on Sinhalese Buddhists. My analysis of the social science journal literature on the ethnic conflicts in Sri Lanka strongly pointed to a particular trend in this literature. These external Sri Lankan commentators were themselves almost exclusively members of groups such as Eurasians (Burghers), Christians, and Jaffna Tamils who had enjoyed colonially derived prerogatives and then migrated to the outside world after the development of Sinhalese nationalism (Goonatilake, Susantha, 1993). They now pontificate from the belly of the metropolis in a highly biased manner from a position of structural strength that they would not have had in Sri Lanka.

A key element in the insulation of the anthropological system from informed public discussion is also to be found in the journalistic structure of the country. Sri Lanka has in addition to near-universal literacy an intense competition to enter the universities. There has also been chronic unemployment and underemployment of graduates. Many university graduates end up as clerks. Yet in spite of this situation, several holders of leading positions as editors and similar gatekeepers to the national media are non-graduates or even high school dropouts. These, for example —at the time of writing in 1998—included the key gatekeepers to the leading government-owned organs which have the widest reach. Thus the *Sunday Observer* editor has barely a high school background, while the *Daily News* editor is similarly handicapped. The chief executive of one leading government-owned TV channel does not even possess a high school certificate. Their appointment as gatekeepers to the Sri Lankan consciousness has much to do with the politics of the ruling party at any given time. Under such circumstances, in addition to the local and international features of academia that I have sketched, the local media act as partial, ignorant filters that prevent necessary feedback.

The effect of these pervasive social mechanisms is that today, Sri Lankan thinking of the formal social sciences kind is very much governed, in spite of a few laudable local attempts, by external definitions. Thus, a mid-1990s meeting in Amsterdam on Sri Lankan studies that I attended saw only a handful of Sri Lankan writers and nearly fifty Westerners, who between them have written a relatively large amount of the literature. Their works preempt the "international" and, hence, in a dependent situation, also the local academic definition of formal Sri Lankan social knowledge.

On the other hand, some of the local Sri Lankan debates, because of the lack of access to information across different islands of partial discourse, local as well as international, fall into the most provincial of genres. A good example is a debate that raged on the so-called Jathika Chintanaya ("National Thinking") movement, a search for a noncolonial discourse on which I did a formal study (Goonatilake, Susantha, 1991). This debate, I found, was characterized in the arguments of both protagonists and antagonists by a heavy provinciality, the opposing actors in the debate being unaware of the local intellectual debates on the topics as well as the international ones. Some of the members of our filtering matrix, notably Uyangoda, participated in the debate as antagonists, in the process displaying a barely disguised neocolonial attitude toward local culture.

The extent of the barrier that prevents outsiders from accessing local discussions because of the particular disjuncture of local and global is seen not only in access to local debates in the Sinhala medium but also in discussions in the English medium. Thus Gombrich and Obeyesekere —we noticed—says that local sociologists have been calling for a non-Western sociology-anthropology without naming them or detailing their arguments (GombObey 1988 p. 456). The local context is left out and essentially ignored.

Similar limits to the anthropological perspective in the coverage of recent debates that appeared in the press are seen in the discussion by Jonathan Spencer on Sri Lanka in a book on "Occidentalism." Occidentalism is billed as the opposite of Orientalism (1995 pp. 234–261). Now that anthropology has gone through the phases of decolonization rhetoric and postmodernism, this book goes to the next step, attempting an exercise that is the reverse of Occidentalism, an exercise in which the world is seemingly looked at through non-European eyes.

Spencer attempts in this work to cover the protagonists in the recent Jatika Chinthanaya ("National Thought") debate, but has almost totally ignored both its details and its context, as well as less populist, more formal discussions. This failing cannot be attributed to Spencer's own perverseness. It is caused by the simple fact that no visitor to the country who tries to describe Sri Lanka with the tunnel vision derived from a small village study that makes him an "expert" on the country can get the total picture. He cannot grasp the millennia-long collective accumulation of knowledge and experience in the various Sinhalese subcultures. Unable to grasp the inputs from the various Sinhala-speaking subcultures, he is not even aware of the debates going on in the Sri Lankan English-language discourse in academic circles, which one would have thought would be his first stop.

The general conceptual confusion typical of a weak dependent intelligentsia extends also to our anthropologists and their local filtering group. Thus, uncertainty is the hallmark of postmodern analysis, but Kapferer, who claims a postmodern position, describes his Sri Lankan case study with the utmost certainty, filling in with imagined fiction where he lacks firm knowledge. It is the same with the alleged postmodernists in their Sri Lankan filtering peer groups. Some of them, including Dayan Jayatilake, once diehard Stalinists, now become admirers of the postmodernist Kapferer. Extreme Stalinists turning to deconstruction! Reggie Siriwardene and Radhika Coomaraswamy, who a few years ago extolled rationality, now evoke with the utmost certainty postmodernist social science imagery where there is no certainty, no single rationality. And in the process, truth is lost sight of, not through the inevitable bias that may creep in unconsciously but through a deliberate bias and conceptual confusion that is brought in.

The limited nature of discourse is typical also of most political discussion today. A good example would be that of the JVP, which in spite of its laudatory opposition to the erosion of sovereignty was characterized not only by brutality (far exceeded by most state security and allied actors) but also by an unawareness of actualities in the outside world. These limited discourses, stuck in their parochial local islands more suited to the times of pure colonialism, are now struggling to inadequately picture the reality of a heavily dependent country within a multidimensional globalized world.

Because of the play of these particular dynamics between the different islands of discourse, one also finds within the country some bizarre occurrences, unheard of perhaps anywhere else in the world. As we noted, the apologist Youth Commission appointed by the brutal President Premadasa, under whom tens of thousands of young people were massacred, included a key member of our filtering matrix, Radhika Coomaraswamy. This Youth Commission cited all sorts of imagined indirect causes for the student unrest of the late eighties, except the very causes that were so bitingly displayed in the students' protest slogans. These slogans all referred to the loss of sovereignty brought about by the Indian incursion, which was supported by Coomaraswamy. The defense of sovereignty was the only reason for the revolt which the apologist commission glossed over. In another such example of truly perverse social dynamics, one co-editor of the leading English-language, allegedly "alternative," journal

(*Lanka Guardian*) was, at the time of the highest number of human rights violations, brought in to advise the state on its foreign image and sent to Sri Lankan embassies abroad (personal communications from two senior officials in Sri Lankan embassies in the West). The other co-editor of this supposedly "alternative" journal, Dayan Jayatilake, on the other hand, wrote pseudonymously the principal political column supporting the ruling (right-wing) party in the government-owned newspaper. This writing was so partial that one faction of the ruling party, which was out of favor, successfully sued him for the largest amount of money in Sri Lankan libel history.

The choice of a question to be studied by any researcher demarcates a universe of discourse. It also preselects the broad area of answers to be given to the question: What is Sri Lankan reality? When these answers enter the print stage of a publication and are studied by the proponents of the dominant anthropological discourse in Europe and America, they become "reality" for those who read the book, and later go on to influence policies in Sri Lanka. The anthropology that our authors construct for their subjects is a reality apart, an external reality, an artificial reality that hangs over the subjects in distant corners of the world and categorizes them, judges them, and operates on them through academic discussion, citations, and foreign government actions. Those who take in this manufactured "reality," for example, include those who give aid to the country and, in the context of the severe civil turmoil in the country, those who want to "understand" it and directly or indirectly intervene in it.

This artificial anthropology has survived and grown influential because it is not tied to local reality and practice. Its results do not reach the audience of the country's intelligentsia or the subject matter of the studies. There is no reality check built into the social system. As Hettige (1997) has suggested, there is no viable social science community. I personally put tremendous energy over two decades into building such institutions. They included the Sociological Association, the Social Sciences Section of the Sri Lanka Association for the Advancement of Science (SLAAS), and the Social Scientists' Association. The first two sputter on at times; the last has turned itself into a private neocolonial enterprise. One other institution, outside academia, that I helped build up in the early 1970s, the Catholic Center for Society and Religion, is flourishing, but it churns out the same type of tangential information that this book has discussed.

Therefore, no general open center of discourse for relaying the different social information available in Sri Lanka exists today except in closed islands. I can vividly recall the fervent call by a former Tamil member, now residing in Australia, of Sri Lanka's premier academic body, the Sri Lanka Association for the Advancement of Science, asking the association to organize a comprehensive scientific dialogue on the ethnic problem. I also remember how this organization did organize seminars on the topic, some with as many as three hundred participants, only to find that some of the key academics described here, who were writing on the topic, avoided them. Hettige (1997) vividly describes this avoidance of open public discourse by the artificial islands.

None of the social science literature on Sri Lanka in the external world, it should also be noted, is fed back to those studied. The locals, including local academics, are left out of the loop. First, there is the language barrier in that the books are in English, an impenetrable barrier to some. Very rarely are the books and articles that have been referred to reviewed or discussed in the English, Sinhala, or Tamil newspapers in the country, or even known among the vast majority of university faculty members. Very few of the books are read; of many, even the titles are not known. Certainly the direct village subjects (and ultimately the victims) of these studies are unaware of them. The geographical arena of discourse is mostly abroad or at local institutions outside the public sphere of local academic discourse. It is in the tightly closed cliques that Hettige describes. So a tangentiality to truth can persist in these islands barely touching each other or the ground reality.

In contrast to anthropology, economics in Sri Lanka has a connection with reality. Government decisions, whether in the Ministry of Finance or the Central Bank or through the IMF, the World Bank, and aid givers, are brought into a loop that touches people, and so can be debated and discussed, as both practice and theory. If somebody were to present a spurious theory, it would be carefully tested by different layers of academia— which go up to the IMF, universities, and also the IMF's critics—as well as at the ground level of real economic life.

But it is not economics, politics, or the sociology of Sri Lanka that has dominated Western scholarship on the country in these very troubled times. A heavily flawed anthropology has colonized the social science discussions and so influenced Western perceptions. This is in spite of realistic sociological studies, many done in Western universities (see, for example, Hettige 1984: Perera, Jayantha, 1985; de Silva, Tudor).

Given the sad state of anthropology in Sri Lanka, we could prescribe better conditions. The ideal social science approach would have been to take actually observed phenomena, including reliable reports in the press, generalize from them in historical and civilizational context, and then go on to make theoretical constructs. In addition, studies of *all* the social actors impinging on the country, including the extra–Sri Lankan ones, could have been very useful. Cross flows of information between the present islands of discourse would also result in a reduction of the present social science solipsism.

To break open this social science insularity, there are more direct measures that could be taken. The villages studied by our anthropologists could be identified, their social science anonymity broken (the names of the villages are no secret to the Sri Lankan anthropological community), and the anthropological results conveyed to those studied—the victims. Thereafter a debate, if need be, should be held among those studied, and those studying would be held accountable to those that they study.

ANTHROPOLOGICAL FUNDAMENTALISM RE-ENTHRONED

In Chapter 2 we described the state of anthropology in the world as our four intrepid anthropologists were about to embark on their foray into Sri Lanka. In the context of what we have seen of their work, it is now germane to discuss the state of anthropology then and what is being delivered to us now. In doing so, we should keep in mind that the subject matter of our anthropologists, as well as their less prolific colleagues and their filtering matrix, is *not* the whole population of Sri Lanka. It is an anthropology almost exclusively of Sinhalese Buddhists.

Many of those who criticized anthropology in the 1960s and early 1970s emphasized its connection with the domination of those studied.

Asad (1973) said that anthropology was the result of an unequal power encounter between the West and the Third World; Hooker (1963) spoke of the subject as the handmaiden of the colonial project; Maquet (1964) described how anthropology was completely involved with the colonial system and was useful ideologically to colonial exploitation; Lévi-Strauss (1966) said it was a body of knowledge that legitimized the colonial relationship; Gjessing (1968) found its subject matter ideologically useful to justify colonial domination; Anderson (1968) discussed anthropology's dual role as advisor and ideologist to the system of domination; Kathleen Gough (1968) found it "a child of Western imperialism" that interpreted the non-Western world within the value system of capitalist society; Goddard (1969) pointed out that the principal concern of anthropology was the problem of social order in a colonial context; and Berremen (1968) was concerned about the use of research material, under the cloak of a value-free science, against the people who were studied.

Colonial anthropology in this role also created multiple fictions in the name of science. Mafege (1971) pointed out that the ideology of tribalism was *created* by anthropologists. Magubane (1971) spoke about how anthropology misinterpreted African reality by the use of concepts such as "Westernization" and "modernization."

All of these charges against the bygone anthropology, we have seen, can be directly applied to the anthropology of our four authors, to the other less prolific ones spun off from them, and also to the interpretative matrix that feeds them and feeds off them. Generally they have welcomed the political domination of those studied, welcoming the sub-imperial Indian Accord and continuing to call for further foreign intervention in the country. They have used categories such as "rationalism" and "postmodernism" to obfuscate the reality that is Sinhalese Buddhist society. These constructions helped justify those desirous of intervening in the country, implying that the Sinhalese Buddhists could not understand their own problems. The authors and their matrix have ignored more telling influences on the country, such as the covert war against it as well as such factors as modern schools being its major socializing engine.

Peter Worsley (1966) said of the old anthropology that the Third World would challenge the assumptions under which it grew. Lévi-Strauss (1966) said that the suspicion anthropology aroused was justified, and that for it to be viewed as legitimate by its victims, it should dissociate itself from the colonial system, so that "by allowing itself to perish another [could] be born again in a new guise." Onwuachi and Wolfe (1966) said that if anthropology did have a future, it would be only after genuine and careful reorganization. Stavenhagen (1971) called for the decolonizing of the applied social sciences, and Jones (1970) suggested a "native anthropology."

These debates in the 1960s and 1970s on "outsider's knowledge," "colonial anthropology," and "Orientalism," and the resulting partial apprehension of truth and direct or indirect falsifications, now become central to Sri Lanka. Sri Lanka never went through a general phase of questioning colonial anthropology except for a few contributions like those of the present author. Colonialism passed into neocolonialism without question. The debates that raged in the late 1960s and 1970s on the social sciences of the Third World should now be raised once again in Sri Lanka.

At the end of the 19th century and the beginning of the 20th, a remarkable set of Sri Lankan scholars interacted with the outside world. These were the scholar-monks referred to earlier in this book. They interacted as men of learning, liberality, and deep knowledge with leading Orientalist scholars of the day. They were versed in Sinhala, Pali, Sanskrit,

English, and French, and were cast in the mold of the European Renaissance. If their European counterparts translated, interpreted, and popularized the Buddhist texts in the world, then these scholar-monks were "The Living Fountains of Buddhism," as one Western scholar put it, which guided the Europeans. It was they who were responsible in an ultimate sense for the efflorescence of interest in Buddhism in the world today.

In the 1980s and 1990s, a similar situation of interpreting Sinhalese Buddhism arose. Once again there were Westerners who came for a stay in Sri Lanka in an attempt to understand it. They, however, were of a different breed from the earlier Western visitors. They were not driven scholars like the Orientalists of yore. They came on visits of about a year on academic grant money. During this time they had to attempt to learn the language. (From all accounts, their efforts resulted only in a pidgin knowledge of the language; they often thank their interpreters.) The intermediaries they met as intellectual counterparts were a strong contrast to the living fountains of earlier years. Some were heavily flawed as to their integrity; their role was functionally to downgrade the local heritage. They were far from erudite. These local intermediaries could get away with their roles because the new Westerners were in a grant-induced hurry that did not allow them the luxury of getting to know the country better. Instead of being the living fountains for a renaissance, the locals invited an invasion and were set on "Unmaking the Nation." An odyssey of a distinctly colonial flavor. It is also of a definitely obscurantist flavor.

BIBLIOGRAPHY

∎

Abeynayake, Rajpal. 1993. "The Academics Defend the Author of *Buddhism Betrayed:* Why Tambiah Should Not Be Massacred." *Sunday Observer* (Colombo), 5 December.

Abeysekera, Charles. 1987. "The Indian Accord." *Sunday Times* (Colombo), 3 August, p. 8.

———. 1992. "Sri Lanka: The Limits of Space." *Index on Censorship* 7, p. 21.

Abhayasundara, Pranith, ed. 1990. *Controversy at Panadura or Panadura Vadaya.* Colombo: The State Printing Corporation.

Ahir, D. C. 1997. "Buddhism in India: From Asoka to Ambedkar." In *Asoka 2300, Jagajiyoti: Asoka Commemorativeion Volume,* ed. Hemendu Bikash Chowdhury. Calcutta: Bauddha Dharmankur Sabha.

Alles, A. C. 1990. *Insurgency 1971.* Colombo: Lake House.

Alvi, M. A., and Rahman, A. 1968, 1989. *Jahangir: The Naturalist.* New Delhi: Indian National Science Academy.

American Anthropological Association. 1990. *Statement of Ethics.* Arlington: American Anthropological Association.

Amunugama, Sarath. 1991. "Buddhaputra and Bhumiputra? Dilemmas of Modern Sinhala Buddhist Monks." *Religion* 21, pp. 115–139.

Anderson, Benedict. 1953. *Imagined Communities.* London: Verso.

Anderson, P. 1968. "Components of the National Culture." *New Left Review* (London), no. 50.

Ariyapala, M. B. 1956. *Society in Medieval Ceylon.* Colombo and Kandy: K. V. G. de Silva.

Asad, Talal. 1973. *Anthropology and the Colonial Encounter.* Ithaca, N.Y.: Cornell University Press.

Axelson, Bjorn, and Jones, Michael. 1987. "Are All Maps Mental Maps?" *GeoJournal* 14, no. 4.

Balding, John William. 1922. *One Hundred Years in Ceylon.* Madras: Diocesan Press.

Banaji, J. 1970. "The Crisis in British Anthropology." *New Left Review* (London).

Bangkok 1. 1990. Paper presented by the Sri Lankan Coordinating Committee at the World Solidarity Forum, Bangkok, May. Mimeograph.

Bangkok 2. 1990. Documents titled "Buddhism and Reconciliation in Sri Lanka" and "Additional Explanation of the Project Proposal on Buddhism and Reconciliation in Sri Lanka." Thai Inter-religious Commission for Development (TICD) and the Peace Research Institute of Oslo (PRIO), Bangkok, May. Mimeograph.

Barber, Benjamin R. 1995. *Jihad vs. McWorld: How Globalism and Tribalism Are Reshaping the World.* New York: Ballantine Books.

Basham, A. L. 1953. *The Wonder That Was India.* New York: Grove Press.

Beal, Samuel. 1993. *Travels of Fah-hian and Sung-yun, Buddhist Pilgrims from China to India.* New Delhi: Asian Educational Services.

Bechert, Heinz. 1970. "Thervada Buddhist Sangha: Some General Observations on Historical and Political Factors in Its Development." *Journal of Asian Studies* 29, no. 4 (August).

Beck, Aaron T., and Emery, Gary. 1985. *Anxiety Disorders and Phobias: A Cognitive Perspective.* New York: Basic Books.

Bennet, J. W. 1843. *Ceylon and Its Capabilities.* London: W. H. Allen and Co.

Benson, Herbert. 1987. *Your Maximum Mind.* New York: Random House.

Berremen, Gerald D. 1968. "Is Anthropology Alive? Social Responsibility in Anthropology." *Current Anthropology* 9.

Bishop, Donald H., ed. 1925. *Indian Thought: An Introduction.* New York: John Wiley & Sons.

Blackburn, John T. 1972. "Mach and Buddhism." In *Ernst Mach: His Work, Life, and Influence,* ed. John T. Blackburn. Berkeley: University of California Press.

Bograt, Greg. 1991. "The Use of Meditation in Psychotherapy: A Review of the Literature." *American Journal of Psychotherapy* 45, no. 3 (July).

Bond, George D. 1988. *The Buddhist Revival in Sri Lanka: Religion, Tradition, Reinterpretation, and Response.* Columbia: University of South Carolina Press.

"Books Are Not for Burning." 1993. *Island* (Colombo), 28 November.

Bose, D. M., Sen, S. N., and Subbarayappa, B. V. 1971. *A Concise History of Science in India.* New Delhi: Indian National Science Academy.

Boxer, C. R. 1963. *Two Pioneers of Tropical Medicine: Garcia D'Orta and Nicholas Honardes.* London: Hispanic and Luso-Brazilian Councils.

Brow, James. 1996. *Demons and Development: The Struggle for Community in a Sri Lankan Village.* Tucson: University of Arizona Press.

Buddhism and Science. 1980. Kandy: Buddhist Publications Society.

Chandraprema, C. A. 1988. "The JVP and Gunadasa Amarasekera: Two Sinhala Buddhist Tendencies." *Lanka Guardian* (Colombo), 15 August.

Chowdhury, Amiya Kumar Roy. 1988. *Man, Malady and Medicine: History of Indian Medicine.* Calcutta: Das Gupta & Co. (P) Ltd.

Christophersen, Axel. 1988. "Big Chiefs and Buddhas in the Heart of the Swedish Homeland." In *Thirteen Studies on Helgo.* Stockholm: Museum of National Antiquities.

Clay, John. 1996. *R. D. Laing: A Divided Self.* London: Hodder.

Collins, William. 1998. *Grassroots Civil Society in Cambodia.* Phnom Penh: Center for Advanced Study.

Committee for Rational Development. 1987. *Statement on the Accord.* Colombo: Committee for Rational Development.

Coomaraswamy, Radhika. 1986. "Nationalism: Sinhala and Tamil Myths," Part III. *Lanka Guardian* (Colombo), 15 June.

———. 1987. "Ethnic Myths." *Seminar* (New Delhi) (September), p. 337.

———. 1994. "Madness, Sexuality and Crime: Reflections on Society's Margins." In *Introduction to Social Theory,* ed. Radhika Coomaraswamy and Nira Wickramasinghe. Colombo: International Centre for Ethnic Studies, in association with Konark Publishers Pvt. Ltd.

———. 1997. "Women of the LTTE: The Tigers and Women's Emancipation." *Frontline* (Madras), 10 January.

Coomaraswamy, Radhika, and Wickramasinghe, Nira. 1994. *Introduction to Social Theory.* Colombo: International Centre for Ethnic Studies, Colombo, in association with Konark Publishers Pvt. Ltd.

"Correction." 1996. *New York Times,* 27 March, Sec. A., Metropolitan Desk.

Coward, Harold G. 1991. "Speech versus Writing in Derrida and Bhartrhari." *Philosophy East and West* 41, no. 2 (April).

Cranston, Sylvia. 1993. *H.P.B.: The Extraordinary Life and Influence of Helena Blavatsky, Founder of the Modern Theosophical Movement.* New York: G. P. Putnam's Sons.

de Alwis, Malathi. 1996. "Sexuality in the Field of Vision: The Discursive Clothing of the Sigiriya Frescoes." In *Embodied Violence: Communalizing Women's Sexuality in South Asia,* ed. Kumari Jayawardena and Malathi de Alwis, pp. 89–113. New Delhi: Kali for Women.

de Mel, Neloufer. 1996. "Static Signifiers? Metaphors of Woman in Contemporary Sri Lankan War Poetry." In *Embodied Violence: Communalizing Women's Sexuality in South Asia,* ed. Kumari Jayawardena and Malathi de Alwis. New Delhi: Kali for Women.

Deraniyagala, P. E. P., ed. *Sinhala Verse (Kavi).* 1954. Collected by the late Hugh Nevill (1869–1886). Ceylon National Museums Manuscript Series, vol. V, Ethnology, vol. 2. Colombo: Government Press.

———. *Sinhala Verse (Kavi).* 1955. Collected by the late Hugh Nevill (1869–1886). Ceylon National Museums Manuscript Series vol. VI, Ethnology, vol. 3. Colombo: Government Press.

Deraniyagala, S. U. 1992. *The Prehistory of Sri Lanka: An Ecological Perspective.* Memoir vol. 8, parts 1 and 2. Colombo: Department of Archaeological Survey, Government of Sri Lanka.

de Silva, G. P. S. 1979. *A Statistical Survey of Elections to the Legislatures of Sri Lanka 1911–1971.* Colombo: Marga Institute.

de Silva, K. M. 1979. "Resistance Movements in Nineteenth Century Sri Lanka." In *Collective Identities: Nationalism and Protest in Modern Sri Lanka,* ed. Michael Roberts, pp. 144–147. Colombo: Marga Institute.

———. 1981. *A History of Sri Lanka.* Delhi: Oxford University Press.

———. 1994. *The "Traditional Homelands" of the Tamils: Separatist Ideology in Sri Lanka—A Historical Appraisal.* Kandy: International Centre for Ethnic Studies.

de Silva, Nalin. 1994. *Budu Dhama Paavadeema (Betraying Buddhism).* Navala: Samanala Graphics.

de Silva, P. L. 1992. "Dynamics of Sinhala Buddhist Chauvinism and the Contemporary Ethnic and Political Conflict in Sri Lanka." M.A. dissertation, Institute of Social Studies, The Hague.

de Silva, Padmal. 1984. "Buddhism and Behavior Modification." *Behavior Research and Therapy* 22, no. 6.

———. 1985. "Early Buddhist and Modern Behavioral Strategies for the Control of Unwanted Intrusive Cognitions." *Psychological Record* 35, no. 4 (Fall).

———. 1990. "Buddhist Psychology: A Review of Theory and Practice." *Current Psychology Research and Reviews* 9, no. 3 (Fall).

Devasarana. 1993. *Devasarana Evaluation Report.* Devasarana: Ibbagamuva.

Dewaraja, Lorna. 1989. *Sri Lanka through French Eyes.* Kandy: Institute of Fundamental Studies.

Dhammapada, The. 1988. Translated by K. Sri Dhammananda. Kuala Lumpur: Sasana Abhiwurdhi Wardhana Society.

Dhammavedi Newsletter (Colombo). 1997. Untitled editorial, 1 February.

Dhammika, S. 1997. "An English Rendering of the Edicts of Asoka." In *Asoka 2300, Jagajiyoti: Asoka Commemoration Volume,* ed. Hemendu Bikash Chowdhury. Calcutta: Bauddha Dharmankur Sabha.

Donaldson, Margaret. 1992. *Human Minds: An Exploration.* London: Penguin Books.

Dua, K. 1983. "Political Notebook." *Indian Express* (New Delhi), 10 August.

Edwardes, Michael. 1967. *British India 1772–1947.* London: Sidgwick.

Encyclopedia of Buddhism. 1979. Vol. V: *Colombo: The Government of Ceylon.*

Faber, M. D. 1988. "Back to a Crossroad: Nietzsche, Freud, and the East." *New Ideas in Psychology* 6, no. 1.

Fernando, Nihal. 1993. "A Plea for Tolerance." *Sunday Observer,* 19 December.

Fields, Rick. 1992. *How the Swans Came to the Lake: A Narrative History of Buddhism in America.* Boston and London: Shambhala.

Finnegan, R. 1971. "The Kinship Ascription of Primitive Societies, Actuality or Myth." *International Journal of Comparative Sociology* 11 (Canada).

Fisher, Louis. 1950. *The Life of Mahatma Gandhi.* New York: Harper & Row.

Forman, Robert K. C. 1989. "Paramartha and Modern Constructivists on Mysticism: Epistemological Monomorphism vs. Duomorphism." *Philosophy East and West* 39, no. 4 (October), pp. 393–413.

Frank, Andre Gunder. 1976. "Anthropology—Ideology, Applied Anthropology—Politics." *Race and Class* (Institute of Race Relations, London) 17, no. 1 (Summer).

Friends for Peace in Sri Lanka. 1995. "Hong Kong Consultation—Eminent Persons Group with Sri Lankan Representatives." *Tamil Voice: Newsletter of the Ilankai Thamil Sangam* (London), 11–14 April.

Fromm, Erich. 1967. *Marx's Concept of Man.* New York: Frederik Ungar.

Geiger, Wilhelm. 1950. *Mahavamsa or the Great Chronicle of Ceylon.* Colombo: Information Department.

Ghosh, Partha. 1995. "Ethnic Conflict: An Indian Reading." *Sunday Times* (Colombo), 6 August. Reproduced from the *Economic and Political Weekly* of India.

Gjessing, Gutorm. 1968. "The Social Responsibility of the Social Scientist." *Current Anthropology* (Chicago) 9.

Glaser, Barney G., and Strauss, Anselm S. 1967. *The Discovery of Grounded Theory: Strategies for Qualitative Research.* Chicago: Aldine Publishing Co.

Gluckman, Max. 1958. *Analysis of a Social Situation in Modern Zululand.* Rhodes–Livingstone Institute Paper 28. Manchester: Manchester University Press.

Goddard, D. 1969. "Limits of British Anthropology." *New Left Review*, no. 58 (London).

Goleman, Daniel. 1980. *The Buddha on Meditation and Higher States of Consciousness.* Wheel Publication no. 189/90. Kandy: Buddhist Publication Society.

——. 1981. "Buddhist and Western Psychology: Some Commonalities and Differences." *Journal of Transpersonal Psychology* 13, no. 2.

——. 1988. *The Meditative Mind: The Varieties of Meditative Experience.* New York: G. P. Putnam's Sons.

——. 1996. "Anthropology Group Takes Activist Stand to Protect Cultures." *New York Times*, 19 March, Sec. C, Science Desk.

GombObey. *See* Gombrich and Obeyesekere 1988.

Gombrich, Richard. 1991. *Buddhist Precept and Practice: Traditional Buddhism in the Rural Highlands of Ceylon.* Delhi: Motilal Banarsidass.

Gombrich, Richard, and Obeyesekere, Gananath. 1988. *Buddhism Transformed: Religious Change in Sri Lanka.* Princeton, N.J.: Princeton University Press.

Goonatilake, Hema. 1974. "The Impact of Some Mahayana Concepts on Sinhalese Buddhism." Ph.D. thesis, University of London.

——. 1981. "Press Attention to Women's Rights, Emancipation, and Interests." *Economic Review* (January/February).

——. 1982. "Media Reactions to a Journalists' Workshop on Women and Development: A Case Study." Conference on Creative Women in Changing Societies, United Nations Institute for Training and Research (UNITAR), New York.

——. 1987. "Ethnic Perceptions and Attitudes among the Urban Poor in the City of Colombo." Proceedings of the Sri Lanka Association for the Advancement of Science, 43rd Annual Report, December.

Goonatilake, Hema, and Goonatilake, Susantha. 1993. "Review: Tambiah's *Buddhism Betrayed?*" *South Asia Research* 13, no. 2 (November).

Goonatilake, Susantha. 1971. "A Study of the Authority Structure of an Industrial Organization: A Transitional Setting." M.A. thesis, University of Exeter (U.K.).

——. 1972. "Environmental Influence on an Industrial Organisation in Ceylon." *Modern Ceylon Studies* 3, no. 1 (July).

——. 1973. "Organizations in Post Traditional Societies." Ph.D. thesis, University of Exeter (U.K.).

——. 1978. *Tourism in Sri Lanka: The Mapping of International Inequalities and Their Internal Structural Effects.* Working Papers no. 19. Montreal: Centre for Developing Area Studies, McGill University, January.

——. 1981. "The Formation of Sri Lankan Culture, Reinterpretation of Chronicle and Archeological Material." *Ancient Ceylon* 4 (May) (Department of Archeology, Colombo).

——. 1982. *Crippled Minds: An Exploration into Colonial Culture.* New Delhi: Vikas Publishers.

——. 1984. *Aborted Discovery: Science and Creativity in the Third World.* London: Zed Press.

——. 1985. "The Search for True Racial Identity." *Island* (Colombo), 3 February.

——. 1990. "The Science System in Sri Lanka." In *Science and Technology in the Indian Subcontinent,* ed. A. Rahman. London: Longmans.

——. 1991. "The Debate on 'Jathika Chintanaya': A Clash of Two Provincialities." Paper presented at the Annual Sessions of the Sri Lanka Association for the Advancement of Science, Section F, 1988. Also presented at Sri Lanka Studies Conference, April 1991, Amsterdam.

——. 1993. "The Social Science Construction of Sri Lankan Ethnicity." Paper presented at conference on the Anthropology of Ethnicity: a Critical Review," SISWO etc., Amsterdam, December.

——. 1997. "Not with a Ban, but a Whimper." *The Sunday Leader* (Colombo), 28 December.

——. 1998. *Toward a Global Science: Mining Civilizational Knowledge.* Bloomington: Indiana University Press.

Gough, K. 1968. "New Proposals for Anthropologists." *Current Anthropology* (Chicago) 9.

Graves, John Cowperthwaite. 1971. *The Conceptual Foundations of Contemporary Relativity Theory.* Cambridge, Mass.: MIT Press.

Guardian (London).

Gunaratne, Rohan. 1990. *War and Peace in Sri Lanka.* Kandy: Institute of Fundamental Studies.

——. 1993. *Indian Intervention in Sri Lanka.* Colombo: South Asian Network on Conflict Research.

Gunasekere, Prins. 1994. "Transgression of Ethics in Buddhism Betrayed." *The Sunday Observer* (Colombo), 16 January.

Gunatilleke, Godfrey. 1987. *Statement on the Accord.* Colombo: Center for Society and Religion.

Gunatilleke, M. H. 1978. *Masks and Mask Systems of Sri Lanka.* Colombo: Tamarind Books.

Gunawardene, Leslie. 1979. "'People of the Lion': The Sinhala Identity and Ideology in History and Historiography." *Sri Lanka Journal of the Humanities* 5.

Gunawardene, Victor. 1986. "Impact of Internal Ethnic Conflicts on the Region: Sri Lanka Case." *Marga Quarterly Journal* 8, no. 3.

Guruge, Ananda W. P., ed. 1965. *Return to Righteousness: A Collection of Speeches, Essays, and Letters of the Anagarika Dharmapala.* Colombo: The Government Press.

———, ed. 1984. *From the Living Fountains of Buddhism: Sri Lankan Support to Pioneering Western Orientalists.* Colombo: Sri Lanka Ministry of Cultural Affairs.

———. 1993. "From Tamraparni to Taprobane and from Ceylon to Sri Lanka." In *The Cultural Triangle of Sri Lanka.* Paris: UNESCO.

Halbfass, Wilhelm. 1988. *India and Europe: An Essay in Understanding.* Albany: State University of New York Press.

Hanna, Fred J. 1993. "The Transpersonal Consequences of Husserl's Phenomenological Method." *Humanistic Psychologist* 21 (Spring).

Harris, Richard L., and Kearney, Robert N. 1963. "A Comparative Analysis of the Administrative Systems of Canada and Ceylon." *Administrative Science Quarterly* 8.

Hellmann-Rajanayagam, Dagmar. 1988. "The Tamil Movement in Jaffna and in India: A Comparison." *Bulletin of Tamil Studies* (June).

———. 1990. "The Concept of a 'Tamil Homeland in Sri Lanka: Its Meaning and Development." *South Asia* 13, no. 2 (German Historical Institute, London).

Helsingin Sanomat (Helsinki). 1993. 6 February, main news page.

Hettige, S. T. 1984. *Wealth, Power, and Prestige: Emerging Patterns of Social Inequality in a Peasant Context.* Colombo: Ministry of Higher Education.

———. 1997. "Is There a Crisis in the Social Sciences?" In *Proceedings,* Part 11: *Sri Lanka Association for the Advancement of Science.* Colombo: SLAAS.

Hodge, M. C. 1981. "Buddhism, Magic, and Society in a Southern Sri Lankan Town." Ph.D. thesis, University of Manchester.

Holt, John Clifford. 1991. *Buddha in the Crown.* New York: Oxford University Press.

Hooker, J. R. 1963. "The Anthropologists' Frontier: The Last Phase of African Exploitation." *Journal of Modern African Studies* 1 (London).

Huber, Jack. 1967. *Through an Eastern Window.* Boston: Houghton Mifflin Company.

Huxley, Andrew, ed. 1996. *Thai Law, Buddhist Law: Essays on the Legal History of Thailand, Laos and Burma.* Bangkok: White Orchid Press.

Ilangasinghe, Mangala. 1996. "Ithihasaya ha Kuppameniyawa" *Irida Divayina,* 15 December.

———. 1997. *Professor Paranvithana Memorial Lecture: State Formation in Ancient Sinhala.* Colombo: Department of Archaeology and Department of Archives.

———. 1998. *Bauddha Maha Sammatha: Athithaye Sita Shri Lanka Vyawasthawa Kriyathmaka Wu Ayuru.* Bauddha Sanskrtha Lecture. Colombo: Ministry of Culture.

———. 1999. Review of Indrani Munasinghe's *Parani Lakdiva Kanthawa. Irida Divayina,* 7 February.

Inada, Kenneth K., and Jacobson, Nolan B., eds. 1984. *Buddhism and American Thinkers.* Albany: State University of New York Press.

Iriyagolla, Gamini. 1994. "Propagandemics: Or, Academics as Propagandists." *Island* (Colombo). Part I, 22 February, p. 111; Part II, 1 March, p. 7; Part III, 8 March, p. 7; Part IV, 16 March, p. 9; Part V, 24 March, p. 9.

Iriyagolla, I. M. 1965. "Foreword." In *Return to Righteousness: A Collection of Speeches, Essays, and Letters of the Anagarika Dharmapala*, ed. Ananda W. P. Guruge. Colombo: The Government Press.

Ismail, Qadri, and Jeganathan, Pradeep, eds. 1995. *Unmaking the Nation: The Politics of Identity and History in Modern Sri Lanka*. Colombo: SSA.

Jackson, Carl T. 1968. "The Meeting of East and West: The Case of Paul Carus." *Journal of the History of Ideas* 29, no. 1 (January–March).

Jacobson, Nolan Pliny. 1969. "The Possibility of Oriental Influence in Hume's Philosophy." *Philosophy East and West* 19, no. 1 (January).

———. 1988. *The Heart of Buddhist Philosophy*. Carbondale and Edwardsville: Southern Illinois University Press.

Jaggi, O. P. 1973. *Indian System of Medicine*. Vol. 4 of *History of Science and Technology in India*. Delhi: Atma Ram & Sons.

"Jayadeva." 1993. "Thamby's Book: Text or Context? Marginal Comments." *Island* (Colombo), 19 December.

Jayatilaka, Tissa. 1993. "Ban or Burn Tambiah?" *Island* (Colombo), 5 December.

Jayatilake, Dayan. 1989. "The Unfinished Wars." *Lanka Guardian* (Colombo) 12, no. 10 (15 September), p. 21.

Jayatillake, K. N. 1963. *Early Buddhist Theory of Knowledge*. London: Allen and Unwin.

———. 1980. *Buddhism and Science*. Kandy: Buddhist Publication Society.

Jayatilleka, Dayan (Chintaka). 1979. "Nationhood: Myths and Realities." *Lanka Guardian* (Colombo) 2, no. 2 (15 May).

———. 1982. "Dayan Jayatilleka (Chintaka) Replies to Jagath Senaratne: JVP and the National Question." *Lanka Guardian* (Colombo) 5, no. 12 (October).

Jayawardena, Kumari. 1979a. "Bhikkhus in Revolt." *Lanka Guardian* (Colombo) 2, no. 2 (15 May).

———. 1979b. "Buddhist Radicals and the Labour Movement." *Lanka Guardian* (Colombo) 2, no. 5 (1 July).

———. 1986. *Ethnic and Class Conflicts in Sri Lanka*. Colombo: Centre for Social Analysis.

———. 1987. "Class/Ethnic Consciousness." *Seminar* (New Delhi) (September), p. 337.

———. 1992. "Sinhala Buddhism and Daughters of the Soil." *Pravada* 5, no. 1 (May), pp. 24–26.

Jayawardena, Kumari, and de Alwis, Malathi, eds. 1996. *Embodied Violence: Communalizing Women's Sexuality in South Asia*. New Delhi: Kali for Women.

Jayawardena, Visakha Kumari. 1984. "Ethnic Consciousness in Sri Lanka: Continuity and Change." In Committee for Rational Development, *Sri Lanka, The Ethnic Conflict: Myths, Realities, and Perspectives*. New Delhi: Navrang.

———. 1986. *Ethnic and Class Conflicts in Sri Lanka: Some Aspects of Sinhala Buddhist Consciousness over the Past 100 Years*. Dehiwala, Sri Lanka: Centre for Social Analysis.

Jayaweera, Neville. 1990. *Sri Lanka: Towards a Multi-ethnic Democratic Society*. Oslo: PRIO.

Jeganathan, P. 1995. "Authorizing History, Ordering Land: The Conquest of Anu-radhapura." In *Unmaking the Nation,* ed. P. Jeganthan and Q. Ismauil. Colombo: SSA.

John, Ravi. 1995. Interview in *Sunday Leader* (Colombo), June.

Johnson, Paul. 1994. *The Masters Revealed: Madame Blavatsky and the Myth of the Great White Lodge.* Albany: State University of New York Press.

Jones, Delmos J. 1970. "Towards a Native Anthropology." *Human Organization* 29 (Boston), pp. 24–31.

Jothipala, Gonahene. 1985. *Vesak Niwaduwa ha Baudhdha Kodiya (Vesak Holiday and the Buddhist Flag).* Colombo: Samayawardana.

Juergensmeyer, Mark. 1993. *The New Cold War: Religious Nationalism Confronts the Secular State.* Berkeley: University of California Press.

JVP. 1986. *Lankawe Jathika Gataluwa Saha Janatha Vimukthi Peramune Visanduma (Sri Lanka's Ethnic Problem and the JVP's Solution).* Colombo: JVP Educational Unit.

Kabat-Zinn, Jon, Massion, Ann O., Kristeller, Jean, Petersen, Linda Gay, Fletcher, Kenneth E., Pbert, Lori, Lenderking, William R., and Santorelli, Saki F. 1992. "Effectiveness of a Meditation-Based Stress Reduction Program in the Treatment of Anxiety Disorders." *American Journal of Psychiatry* 149, no. 7 (July).

Kailasapathy K. 1984. "Cultural and Linguistic Consciousness of the Tamil Community." In Social Scientists' Association, *Ethnicity and Social Change in Sri Lanka,* pp. 110–113. Colombo: SSA.

——. 1987. "Tamil Consciousness." *Seminar* (New Delhi) (September), pp. 34–39.

Kannangara, A. P. 1983. "The Riots of 1915 in Sri Lanka: A Study in the Roots of Communal Violence." *Past and Present* 102, pp. 130–165.

Kapferer, Bruce. 1988. *Legends of People, Myths of State: Violence, Intolerance, and Political Culture in Sri Lanka and Australia.* Washington, D.C.: Smithsonian Institution Press.

——. 1989. "Nationalism and the Crisis of Violence in Sri Lanka." *Lanka Guardian* (Colombo) 12, no. 10 (15 September), pp. 6–7.

——. 1991. *A Celebration of Demons: Exorcism and the Aesthetics of Healing in Sri Lanka.* 2nd ed. Providence, R.I.: Berg; Washington, D.C.: Smithsonian Institution Press.

——. 1993. "Buddhism Betrayed?" *Tamil Times* (London), 15 December.

——. 1997. *The Feast of the Sorcerer: Practices of Consciousness and Power.* Chicago and London: University of Chicago Press.

Kariyawasam, Tissa. 1973. "Religious Activities and the Development of a Poetical Tradition in Sinhalese 1852–1906." Ph.D. thesis, University of London.

Knox, Robert. 1911. *An Historical Relation of the Island of Ceylon.* Glasgow: MacLehose. Reprinted in *Ceylon Historical Journal* (Maharagama) 6, no. 1–4 (1958).

Kotahena Riots. 1883. "Kotahena Riots: The Report of a Commission appointed by the Governor to Inquire into the Cause of the Recent Riots at Kotahena in Ceylon." *Sessional Papers,* no. 4, pp. 4–5. Colombo: Government of Ceylon.

Lach, Donald, F. 1977. *Asia in the Making of Europe.* Vol. 2. Chicago: University of Chicago Press.

Lanka Guardian (Colombo). 1996. 21 March, pp. 260–261.

La Porte, Robert. 1970. "Administrative, Political, and Social Constraints on Economic Development in Ceylon." *International Review of Administrative Science* 36, no. 2.

Leary, Virginia. 1981. *Ethnic Conflict and Violence in Sri Lanka: Report of a Mission to Sri Lanka on Behalf of the International Commission of Jurists.* July/August. Geneva: International Commission of Jurists.

Leclere, G. 1972. *Anthropologie et Colonialisme.* Paris: Fayard.

Lévi-Strauss, C. 1966. "Anthropology: Its Achievements and Future." *Current Anthropology* 7 (Chicago).

Lewis, I. M. 1971. *Ecstatic Religion: An Anthropological Study of Spirit Possession and Shamanism.* Harmondsworth: Penguin.

Loy, David. 1993. "Indra's Postmodern Net." *Philosophy East and West* 43, no. 3 (July).

Mabbett, Lan W. 1995. "Nagarjuna and Deconstruction." *Philosophy East and West* 45, no. 2 (April).

Mafege, A. 1971. "The Ideology of Tribalism." *Journal of Modern African Studies* 9 (London).

Magubane, B. 1971. "Critical Look at Indices Used in the Study of Social Change in Colonial Africa." *Current Anthropology* 12 (Chicago).

Malalgoda, Kitsiri. 1976. *Buddhism in Sinhalese Society 1750–1900: A Study of Religious Revival and Change.* Berkeley and Los Angeles: University of California Press.

Manekshaw, Field Marshal Sam. 1992. "Foreword." In Lieutenant General Depinder Singh, *The IPKF in Sri Lanka.* Delhi: Trishul Publications.

Manor, James. 1989. *The Expedient Utopian: Bandaranaike and Ceylon.* Cambridge: Cambridge University Press.

Maquet, J. J. 1964. "Objectivity in Anthropology." *Current Anthropology* 5 (Chicago).

Maslow, Abraham H. 1968. *Towards a Psychology of Being.* New York: Van Nostrand.

McGowan, William. 1992. *Only Man Is Vile.* New York: Farrar, Straus and Giroux.

McGregor, Douglas N. 1957. "The Human Side of the Enterprise." In *Adventures in Thought and Action.* Proceedings of the Fifth Anniversary Convention of the School of Industrial Management, MIT.

Mererk, Phramaha Prayoon. 1988. *Selflessness in Sartre's Existentialism and Early Buddhism.* Bangkok: Mahachulalongkorn Buddhist University.

Miller, Arthur I. 1987. *Imagery in Scientific Thought: Creating 20th Century Physics.* Cambridge, Mass.: MIT Press.

Mirando, A. H. 1985. *Buddhism in Sri Lanka in the 17th and 18th Centuries with Special Reference to Sinhalese Literary Sources.* The Ceylon Historical Journal Monograph Series, vol. 10. Dehiwala: Tisara Prakasakayo Ltd.

Mitchell, J. C. 1956. *The Kalela Dance.* Rhodes–Livingstone Institute Paper 27. Manchester: Manchester University Press.

Mode, Heinz. 1981. *2500 Jahre Reisen nach Ceylon, Sri Lanka Aus Legende, Marchen,*

historischer Uberlieferung und Bericht. Leipzig and Weimar: Gustav Kiepen-
heuer Verlag.

Moyers, Bill. 1993. *Healing and the Mind.* New York: Doubleday.

Muttukumaru, Anton. 1987. *The Military History of Ceylon: An Outline.* Delhi:
Navrang.

Naipaul, Shiva. 1987. *An Unfinished Journey.* New York: Viking.

Nakamura, Hajime. 1973. "Buddhism." In *Dictionary of the History of Ideas,* ed.
Phillip B. Wiener. New York: Charles Scribner.

Nakkawita, Wijitha. 1994. "Book Review." *Island* (Colombo), 25 January.

Nesiah, Devanesan. 1997. *Discrimination with Reason: The Policy of Reservations in
the United States, India, and Malaysia.* Delhi: Oxford University Press.

Obeyesekera, Gananath. 1963. "The Great Tradition and the Little in the Perspective of Sinhalese Buddhism." *Journal of Asian Studies* 22, no. 2, pp. 139–153.

———. 1967. *Land Tenure in Village Ceylon.* Cambridge: Cambridge University Press.

———. 1970a. "Religious Symbolism and Political Change in Ceylon." *Modern
Ceylon Studies* 1, no. 1, pp. 43–63.

———. 1970b. "The Idioms of Demonic Possession: A Case Study." *Social Science
and Medicine* 4, pp. 97–111.

———. 1973. "Ban Tambiah? Open Letter to Minister of Buddhist Affairs." *Sunday
Observer* (Colombo), 12 December.

———. 1975. "Psycho-cultural Exegesis of a Case of Spirit Possession from Sri
Lanka." *Contributions to Asian Studies* 8, pp. 41–89.

———. 1977. "The Theory and Practice of Psychological Medicine in the Ayurvedic Traditions." *Culture, Medicine and Psychiatry* 1, pp. 155–181.

———. 1981. *Medusa's Hair.* Chicago: University of Chicago Press.

———. 1984. *The Cult of the Goddess Pattini.* Chicago: University of Chicago Press.

———. 1988. *A Meditation on Conscience.* Social Scientists' Association of Sri Lanka,
Occasional Papers. Colombo: Navamaga.

———. 1994. *The Apotheosis of Captain Cook: European Mythmaking in the Pacific.*
Princeton, N.J.: Princeton University Press; Honolulu: Bishop Museum Press.

———. 1996. "No Sri Lankan 'Tribe.'" *New York Times,* 28 March, Sec. A, Editorial
Desk.

Olcott, H. S. 1984. "Letter to Rev. Piyaratana Tissa Terunnanse." In *From the Living
Fountains of Buddhism: Sri Lankan Support to Pioneering Western Orientalists,* ed.
Ananda W. P. Guruge. Colombo: Ministry of Cultural Affairs.

Olcott, Henry Steele. 1974. *Old Diary Leaves: The History of the Theosophical Society.* 2nd Series, 1878–1883. Adyar, Madras: The Theosophical Publishing
House.

Onwuachi, P. Chikwe, and Wolte, Alwin W. 1966. "The Place of Anthropology in
the Future of Africa." *Human Organization* 25, pp. 93–95.

Oppenheimer, J. Robert. 1954. *Science and the Common Understanding.* London: Oxford University Press.

Palanithural, G., and Mohanasundaram, K. 1993. *Dynamics of Tamil Nadu Politics
in Sri Lankan Ethnicity.* New Delhi: Northern Book Center.

Paluch, Andrezej K. 1980. "The Philosophical Background of the Classical Functionalism in Social Anthropology." *Republica Philosophica* 4, pp. 25–38.,

Pandey, Gyanendra. 1990. *The Construction of Communalism in Colonial North India.*
New Delhi: Oxford University Press.

Paranawithana, Senarat. 1967. *Sinhalayo.* Colombo: Lake House Investments Ltd.

Paranawithana, Senarat, Labrooy, W. J. F., Natesan, S., and Nicholas, C. W., eds.
History of Ceylon. Vol. 1. Colombo: Ceylon University Press.

Pathiravitana, S. 1993. "Doffs Academic Cloak." *Island* (Colombo), 12 September.

Peebles, J. M. 1955. "Introduction and Annotations." In John Kapper, *Buddhism
and Christianity: Being an Oral Debate Held at Panadura.* Colombo: P. K. W.
Siriwardhana.

Peiris, G. H. 1991. "An Appraisal of the Concept of a Traditional Tamil Homeland
in Sri Lanka." *Ethnic Studies Report* 9, no. 1 (January).

Perera, Jayantha. 1985. *New Dimensions of Social Stratification in Rural Sri Lanka.*
Colombo: Lake House Investments Ltd.

Perera, Jehan. 1987. "The Turning Point: Facing the Reality of the Indo-Lanka Accord." *Daily News* (Colombo), 26 August.

———. 1988. "The Envy of Asia: Shame! I Had to Hear This from a Foreigner."
Daily News (Colombo), 29 December.

———. 1993. "Buddhism Betrayed? A Question Posed, Not Answered." *Island* (Colombo), 28 November.

Perera, L. S. 1959. "The Sources of Ceylon History." In H. C. Ray, editor in chief,
History of Ceylon, pp. 46–77. Colombo: Ceylon University Press.

Perera, Mahendra, and Eysenck, Sybil B. G. 1984. "A Cross Cultural Study of Personality: Sri Lanka and England." *Journal of Cross-Cultural Psychology* 15, no.
3 (September).

Perera, Ranjith. 1994. "Jataka kathave nirupitha striya." *Pravada* 6 (Sinhala)
(February–March), pp. 22–28.

Perinbanayagam, R. F. 1989. "Anthropology: How Not to Track Sri Lankan Elephants." *Lanka Guardian* (Colombo) 12, no. 3 (1 June), pp. 23–24.

Perry, Edmund F. 1976. "Foreword." In Rahula Walpola, *The Heritage of The Bhikkhu: A Short History of the Bhikkhu in Educational, Cultural, Social, and Political
Life.* New York: Grove Press.

Pfaffenberger, Bryan. 1990. "The Political Construction of Defensive Nationalism:
The 1968 Temple-Entry Crisis in Northern Sri Lanka." *The Journal of Asian
Studies* 49, no. 1 (February). Quoted in H.L.D. Mahindapala, "Oppression of
Tamils by the Tamils," *Sunday Times* (Colombo), 8 September 1996.

Pieris, Kamalika. 1996 "Communal Representation and Ethnopolitics in Sri
Lanka." *Island* (Colombo), 30 December.

Piyasena, S., and Senadheera, R. Y. 1986. *India "We Tamils" and Sri Lanka.* Delhi:
Sri Satguru Publications.

Pravada (Sinhala edition) (Colombo).

Price, H. H. 1955. "The Present Relations between Eastern and Western Philosophy." *Hiberts Journal* (Los Angeles) 53 (April), p. 229.

PRIO Report. 1990. "Report of a Meeting Held to Discuss the Outcome of Neville Jayaweera's Fact-Finding Mission, Nobel Institute, Oslo, 11 June 1990." *Lanka Guardian* (Colombo), 1 December.

Prothero, Stephen. 1996. *The White Buddhist: The Asian Odyssey of Henry Steel Olcott.* Bloomington and Indianapolis: Indiana University Press.

Rahula, Walpola. 1978. *What the Buddha Taught.* London: Gordon Fraser.

Ranasinghe, A. J. 1996. "Taped Interviews." *Sunday Times* (Colombo), 29 September.

Riepe, Dale. 1967. "The Indian Influence in American Philosophy: Emerson to Moore." *Philosophy East and West* 17, no. 14 (January–October).

Roberts, Michael. *Exploring Confrontation: Sri Lanka Politics, Culture and History.* Amsterdam: Harwood Academic Publishers.

Rohanadheera, Mendis. 1983a. "Palamuvana Siyawase Sita Ena Sinhala Dravida Suhadattvaya." *Riviresa,* 18 December.

———. 1983b. "Sinhala Dravida Sambandhata Ha Virodatha." *Divayina,* 19 December.

Russell, Jane. 1982. *Communal Politics under the Donoughmore Constitution, 1931–1947.* Dehiwala, Sri Lanka: Tisara Prakasakayo Ltd.

Sahlins, Marshall. 1995. *How "Natives" Think: About Captain Cook, for Example.* Chicago: University of Chicago Press.

Sarachchandra, E. R. 1953. *The Sinhalese Folk Play and the Modern Stage.* Colombo: Ministry of Cultural Affairs.

Sardeshpande Lt. Gen. S. C. 1992. *Assignment Jaffna.* New Delhi: Lancer Publishers Pvt. Ltd.

Sarkar, N. K, and Tambiah, S. J., eds. 1957. *The Disintegrating Village: Report of a Socio-Economic Survey Conducted by the University of Ceylon.* Colombo: Ceylon University Press Board.

Schalk, Peter. 1988. "'Unity' and 'Sovereignty': Key Concepts of a Militant Buddhist Organization." *Temenos* 4, pp. 55–82.

———. 1993. "The Vallipuvam Buddha Image—Again." *Serendipity* 2, ed. Jayadeva Uyangoda (LacNet). Internet Journal.

Scott, David. 1995. "Dehistorising History." In *Unmaking the Nation,* ed. P. Jeganthan and Q. Ismauil. Colombo: SSA.

Seager, Richard Hughes. 1995. *The World's Parliament of Religions: The East-West Encounter, Chicago, 1893.* Bloomington and Indianapolis: Indiana University Press.

Sena. 1993. "Tambiah Is Sorry, Agrees to Make Amends." *Island* (Colombo), 15 December.

Seneviratne, H. L. 1994. "The Heritage and the Dawn: Rahula's Two Revolutionary Classics." *Pravada* (Colombo) 3, no. 2 (March/April).

Seneviratne, H. L., and Wickramaratne. 1980. "Bodhi puja: Collective Representation of Sri Lanka Youth." *American Ethnologist Digest* 4, pp. 734–743.

Singer, Marshall R. 1964. *The Emerging Elite.* Cambridge, Mass.: MIT Press.

Singh, Depinder. 1992. *The IPKF in Sri Lanka.* Delhi: Trishul Publications.

Sinha, Rajesh. 1998. "I Admire Sen but Be Wary of His Nobel." *Indian Express* (New Delhi), 29 December.

Siriwardena, Reggie. 1979. "Where Are the Radical Buddhists?" *Lanka Guardian* (Colombo) (September), p. 17.

Siriwardena, Reggie, and Coomaraswamy, Radhika. 1987. "A Common Front against Ethno-populism." *Lanka Guardian* (Colombo), 1 October.

Smart, N. 1964. *Doctrine and Argument in Indian Philosophy.* London: Harvester Press.

Smith, H. 1965. "Foreword." In *The Three Pillars of Zen,* ed. P. Kapleau. New York: Doubleday.

Soysa, Ranjit. 1993. "Uyangoda and the Buddhist Right." *Island* (Colombo), 9 December.

Spencer, Jonathan. 1990. *A Sinhala Village in a Time of Trouble.* New Delhi: Oxford University Press.

——. 1995. "Occidentalism in the East: The Uses of the West in the Politics and Anthropology of South Asia." In *Occidentalism, Images of the West,* ed. James G. Carrier. Oxford: Clarendon Press.

"Sri Lanka Rebels: Ominous Presence in Tamil Nadu." 1984. *India Today,* 31 March, pp. 52–57.

Stavenhagen, R. 1971. "Decolonizing Applied Social Sciences." *Human Organization* 30 (Boston).

"Steel Corp. Men Storm Ministry." 1970. *Observer* (Colombo), 29 June.

Stirrat, R. L. 1992. *Power and Religiosity in a Post-colonial Setting: Sinhalese Catholics in Contemporary Sri Lanka.* Cambridge: Cambridge University Press.

Suzuki, D. T., Fromm, Erich, and De Martino, Richard. 1960. *Zen Buddhism and Psychoanalysis.* New York: Grove Press.

Swamy, M. R. Narayan. 1994. *Tigers of Lanka: From Boys to Guerrillas.* New Delhi: Konark Publishers Pvt. Ltd.

Sweet, Michael J., and Johnson, Craig G. 1990. "Enhancing Empathy: The Interpersonal Implications of a Buddhist Meditation Technique." *Psychotherapy* 27, no. 1 (Spring), pp. 19–29.

Tambiah, S. J. 1955. "Ethnic Representation in Ceylon's Higher Administrative Services, 1870–1946." *University of Ceylon Review* 13, nos. 2 and 3 (April–July).

——. 1986. *Sri Lanka: Ethnic Fratricide and the Dismantling of Democracy.* Delhi: Oxford University Press.

——. 1990. *Magic, Science, Religion, and the Scope of Rationality.* Cambridge: Cambridge University Press.

——. 1992. *Buddhism Betrayed? Religion, Politics, and Violence in Sri Lanka.* Chicago and London: University of Chicago Press.

——. 1996. *Leveling Crowds: Ethnonationalist Conflicts and Collective Violence in South Asia.* Berkeley: University of California Press.

Tamil Voice: Newsletter of the Ilankai Thamil Sangam (London).

Taussig, Michael T. 1987. *Shamanism, Colonialism, and the Wild Man: A Study in Terror and Healing.* Chicago: University of Chicago Press.

Thondaman, S. 1983. Speech in Parliament, 4 August. Quoted in Gamini Iriyagolla, "Propagandemics: Or, Academics as Propagandists." *Island* (Colombo), 1 March 1994, p. 7.

Thornstrom, Carl-Gustaf. 1986. *Sri Lanka: Development of Scientific Research and SAREC's Support 1976–1986.* Stockholm: SAREC Documentation.

Tonkinson, Carole, ed. 1995. *Big Sky Mind: Buddhism and the Beat Generation.* London: Thorsons.

"Transgression of Ethics in Buddhism Betrayed?" 1994. *Sunday Observer* (Colombo), 16 January.

Turner, V. W. 1957. *Schism and Continuity in an African Society.* Manchester: Manchester University Press.

———. 1968a. *The Drums of Affliction: A Study of Religious Processes among the Ndembu of Zambia.* Oxford: Clarendon Press.

———. 1968b. *The Forest of Symbols: Aspects of Ndembu Ritual.* Ithaca, N.Y.: Cornell University Press.

UNIAD—United Nations Internal Audit Division. 1993. *Audit of the United Nations World Institute for Development Economics Research.* Helsinki, Finland: UNU/WIDER, Assignment no. G93/107, 29 March.

"Unions Want Some Officers Removed." 1970. *Daily News* (Colombo), 26 June.

Varela, Francisco F., Thompson, Evan, and Rosch, Eleanor. 1993. *The Embodied Mind: Cognitive Science and Human Experience.* Cambridge, Mass.: MIT Press.

Venkatachalam, M. S. 1987. *Genocide in Sri Lanka.* Delhi: Gian Publishing House.

Vitharana, Vinnie. 1997. "Book Review: A Comprehensive Study on Asoka" (review of *Asoka the Righteous: A Definitive Biography,* by Ananda W. P. Guruge). In *Asoka 2300, Jagajiyoti: Asoka Commemoration Volume,* ed. Hemendu Bikash Chowdhury. Calcutta: Bauddha Dharmankur Sabha.

Vittachi, V. P. 1995. *Sri Lanka: What Went Wrong—J. R. Jayawardene's Free and Righteous Society.* New Delhi: Navrang.

Walsh, Roger. 1988. "Two Asian Psychologies and Their Implications for Western Psychotherapists." *American Journal of Psychotherapy* 42, no. 4 (October).

———. 1992. "The Search for Synthesis: Transpersonal Psychology and the Meeting of East and West, Psychology and Religion, Personal and Transpersonal." *Journal of Humanistic Psychology* 32, no. 1 (Winter).

Washington, Peter. 1993. *Madame Blavatsky's Baboon: A History of the Mystics, Mediums, and Misfits Who Brought Spiritualism to America.* New York: Schocken Books.

Weerasinghe, S. G. M. 1995. *A History of the Cultural Relations between Sri Lanka and China: An Aspect of the Silk Route.* Colombo: The Central Cultural Fund.

Weerawardena, I. D. S. 1960. *Ceylon General Election 1956.* Colombo: M. D. Gunasena & Co.

Wickramasinghe, Nira. 1995. *Ethnic Politics in Colonial Sri Lanka 1927–1947.* New Delhi: Vikas Publishing House Pvt. Ltd.

Wijeweera, Rohana. 1986. *The National Question in Lanka and the Solution of the Janatha Vimukthi Peramuna.* Colombo: JVP.

Wilson, A. J. 1988. Statement quoted in *Tamil Voice: Newsletter of the Ilankai Thamil Sangam* (London), Winter 1994/1995.

Wilson, D. Kanagasabal. 1975. *The Christian Church in Sri Lanka.* With a Preface by the Anglican Bishop of Colombo. Colombo: National Christian Council.

Wilson, P. J. 1967. "Status Ambiguity and Spirit Possession." *Man* n.s. 2, pp. 366–378.

Wimalananda, T. 1970. *The Great Rebellion of 1818: The First War of Independence.* Colombo: M. D. Gunasena.

——. 1984. *Sri Wickrema, Brownrigg and Ehelepola.* Colombo: M. D. Gunasena.

Worsley, P. 1966. "The End of Anthropology." Paper presented to Sociology and Social Anthropology Working Group, 6th World Congress of Sociology, May.

Yoshino, M. Y. 1968. *Japan's Managerial System: Tradition and Innovation.* Cambridge, Mass.: MIT Press.

INDEX

■

SUSANTHA GOONATILAKE is presently attached to the Center for Studies of Social Change, New School for Social Research, New York, and the Vidyartha Centre, Colombo. He has taught at several universities and research institutes in Asia, Europe, and America. He has also worked at the United Nations and has been a senior consultant to all the UN organs dealing with knowledge and science issues. His numerous publications on knowledge systems include *Toward a Global Science: Mining Civilizational Knowledge* (Indiana University Press, 1998); *Merged Evolution: The Long Term Implications of Information Technology and Biotechnology; Technological Independence: The Asian Experience; Evolution of Information: Lineages in Genes, Culture, and Artefact; Aborted Discovery: Science and Creativity in the Third World; Crippled Minds: An Exploration into Colonial Culture;* and *Food as a Human Right.*